Advances in Petri Net Theory and Applications

edited by
Dr. Tauseef Aized

Advances in Petri Net Theory and Applications
Edited by Dr. Tauseef Aized

Republished by InTech
Janeza Trdine 9, 51000 Rijeka, Croatia

Publishing Process Manager Iva Lipovic

Technical Editor Teodora Smiljanic

Cover Designer InTech Design Team

Additional hard copies can be obtained from orders@intechopen.com

Advances in Petri Net Theory and Applications, Edited by Dr. Tauseef Aized
p. cm.
ISBN 978-953-307-108-4

For EU product safety concerns:
IN TECH d.o.o., Prolaz Marije Krucifikse Kozulić 3, 51000 Rijeka, Croatia,
info@intechopen.com or visit our website at intechopen.com.

Meet the editor

Dr. Tauseef Aized received his Ph.D. from Tokyo Institute of Technology. He held two research fellowships; first Endeavour Research Fellowship at Monash University and the second Commonwealth Fellowship at the University of Cambridge. He has a number of papers in reputed journals and conferences. His teaching and research interest include energy technology and policy, computer integrated manufacturing and operations management. Currently, he is a professor and chair of department of mechanical engineering, UET-KSK campus, Lahore-Pakistan.

Contents

Preface

Time-driven systems such as living organisms, ecological systems and world population have long been modeled and analyzed through differential equations. Man-made technological environments such as computer, transportation and telecommunication networks or manufacturing and logistics systems represent systems whose behaviors are governed by events occurring asynchronously over time. Events may be controlled or uncontrolled. Event-driven systems are of increasing importance in today's world because they are growing in number, size and sophistication. It is therefore imperative to have systematic design methodologies in order to achieve desirable performance and to avoid catastrophic failures. These systems may be asynchronous and sequential, exhibiting many characteristics: concurrency, conflict, mutual exclusion and non-determinism. These characteristics are difficult to describe using traditional control theory which deals with systems of continuous or synchronous discrete variables modelled by differential or difference equations. In addition, inappropriate control of the occurrence of events may lead to system deadlock, capacity overflows or may otherwise degrade system performance. These systems are typically referred to as discrete event dynamical systems (DEDS). In order to capture the properties of DEDS, several mechanisms have been proposed and developed for modelling such systems. These are state machines, Petri nets, communicating sequential processes and finitely recursive processes. In order to conduct performance analysis of these kinds of systems, methods such as perturbation analysis, queuing network theory and Markov processes have been formulated and applied. Petri net as a graphical tool provides a unified method for design of discrete event systems from hierarchical systems description to physical realizations.

This reading is a selection of articles authored by distinguished researchers and academics working in Petri net field and gives an in-depth treatment on selected topics. In order to fully comprehend the material presented, the readers are expected to have background knowledge in the field. This collection of articles attempts to give a state-of-the-art implementation of Petri net theory which may encourage the readers to apply Petri net in their own way.

July 31, 2010.

Editor

Dr. Tauseef Aized, Professor and Chair
Department of Mechanical, Mechatronics and Manufacturing Engineering, KSK Campus, University of Engineering and Technology, Lahore, Pakistan

1

Production Process Object Model Research Based on Petri Net Techniques

Chen You-ling Sun Ya-nan Yang Qing-qing Xie Shu-hong
Chongqing University
China

1. Introduction

A bottleneck in production process is a link which hindered business process to increase effective output greater or reduce inventory and cost [1]. Solve the bottleneck of the traditional method of production is usually through improved technology, increased scale of production [2], increasing capital investment, etc. to achieve. However, this method is usually the bottleneck occurs in quite a long time before they can be discovered and resolved, often resulting in wasted production capacity.

In recent years, with a variety of simulation techniques become more sophisticated, people started to recognize the use of simulation technology to address bottleneck in business results are quite remarkable [3]. Such as the use of SIMOGRAMS method to determine the production process bottleneck workshop and improve the bottleneck cell [4]; use Em-plant to build production line simulation model and optimize production line configuration and layout [5] [6];the use of WITNESS studied the production efficiency of the system issues to improve the initiative and creativity of workers [7].

To some extent the use of simulation technology can solve production bottleneck problem, but the simulation model building takes longer, is not strong universal and the need of trained professional model talent, so it is not conducive for the production process widely used in various sectors. Through research, the production process conduct the dynamic system model Petri net techniques [8], combined with simulation software, and put forward the production process object model (referred to as PPOM) method.

2. Production Process Object Model (PPOM)

2.1 PPOM thought

PPOM is a production process object model method, which combines object-oriented thought (Object Oriented, OO) and Petri net techniques, make each processing site in the production process, production cell or working procedure to a high degree of abstraction [9],then abstract entity place sub-module, combined with the actual situation of production, optimize the abstract entity place sub-module, establish an PPOM abstract model of production system and form an organic production system, build production capacity analysis objective function model, using simulation annealing algorithm to find out the minimum production cell and detect the bottleneck cell of the production system.

PPOM method not only can analyse the dynamic production capacity of the production process and working procedure,but also has the advantages of modular, object-oriented as well as visually and clear hierarchy, also suitable for model of various processing cells.in each cell, production capacity is estimated that production systems will help to predict the bottleneck in advance, and to improve the processing cell to make a timely manner in order to shorten the production cycle, increase productivity and efficiency of production systems.
As OO thought emphasizes the specific data and operations are encapsulated in black boxes, no need to consider the object's internal operations and state change, but only care about the message exchange through the interface between objects, therefore, putting forward the PPOM Theoretical Basis is feasible.

2.2 PPOM definition

Petri nets can be used to describe the system's complex event logic and sequential relationship graphically, but also can analyse the system based on mathematical methods of quantitative, so in the manufacturing system analysis, model and control, they are widely used [10]. As system complexity increases, the system PN model and analysis become very complicated, due to the lack of modular, reusability and other shortcomings, increases the reconstruction time of PN model.To this end, in the production process model, the introduction of PPOM thought, combined with high-level Petri net (OPN) techniques, putting forward Production process object modeling-Object-oriented Petri nets ($PPOM - OPN$) method.
Application of the concept of OPN, regard the production system as a series of objects and message transmisson between the objects, use CPNs (colored Petri net) describing the object, The CPNs model of the object obtained was called Object-oriented Petri nets (OPN); message transmission between objects was described by network diagram, which was built by transition and directed arc,also called Message Passing Relation nets(MPRN).

Definition 1.1 PPOM Definiton

Seven-tuple is expressed as

$$PPOM - OPN_i = \{SP_i, AT_i; IM_i, OM_i, I_i, O_i, C_i\} \quad (1.1)$$

Thereinto:

1. SP_i —State Place finite set
2. AT_i —Activity transition finite set
3. IM_i —input message place finite set
4. OM_i —output message place finite set
5. $C(SP_i)$ —state place color Collection
6. $C(AT_i)$ —Activity transition color collection
7. $C(IM_i)$ —input message place color collection
8. $C(OM_i)$ —output message place color collection
9. $I_i(P,T)$ —from place P to transition T input mapping function : $C(P)\times C(T)\to N$ (Non-negative integer), Corresponds to the color directed arc from P to T,here $P = SP_i \cup IM_i$, $T = AT_i$, $I(P,T)$ for the matrix.
10. $O_i(P,T)$ —from transition T to the place P output mapping function: $C(T)\times C(P)\to N$ (Non-negative integer), Corresponds to the color directed arc from T to P.here $P = SP_i \cup OM_i$, $T = AT_i$, $O(P,T)$ for the matrix.

$PPOM-OPN_i$ The internal state place and activity transition describes the dynamic properties of OPN object model, that the production process or working procedure bring changes in the internal state of the production cell, while the input message received from other objects (as the previous production cell) of message and through output message place gate on the activities of production cells to the next incoming process or procedure(that is the input message place).

Definition 1.2 Message Passing Relation nets among production cells

In the production process, message Passing Relation nets from message exporter Ob_i to message inporter Ob_j ($i \neq j$) are expressed as:

$$R_{ij} = \left\{OM_i, g_{ij}, IM_i, C(OM_i), C(IM_j), C(g_{ij}), I_{ij}, O_{ij}\right\} \tag{1.2}$$

Thereinto:

1. OM_i —Object Ob_i input message place finite set
2. IM_j —Object Ob_j output message place finite set
3. g_{ij} —from Ob_i to Ob_j message transmission gate finite set
4. $C(OM_i)$ — Ob_i output message place color collection
5. $C(IM_j)$ — Ob_j input message place color collection
6. $C(g_{ij})$ — g_{ij} color collection
7. $I_{ij}(OM_i, g_{ij})$ —from output message place OM_i to the gate g_{ij} input mapping function,it's $C(OM_i)\times C(g_{ij})\rightarrow N$ (Non-negative integer), corresponds to the color directed arc from OM_i to the g_{ij} .

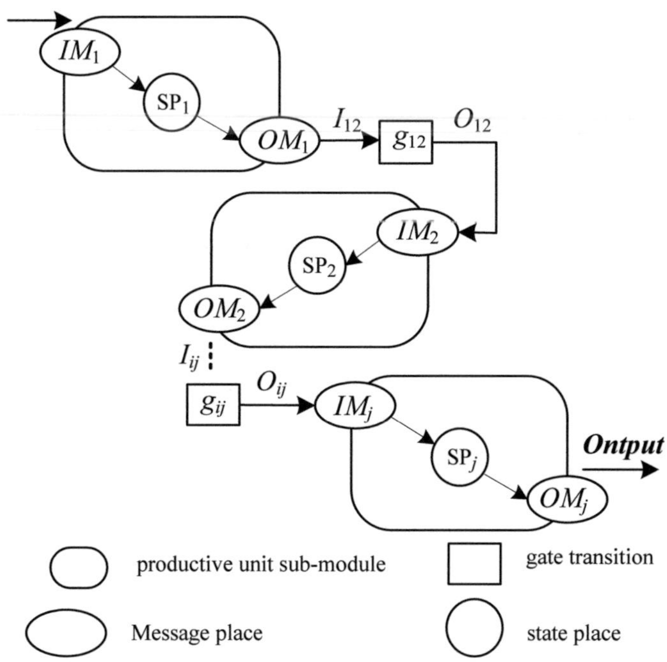

Fig. 1. Relation nets among production cells

8. $O_{ij}(IM_j, g_{ij})$ —The gate g_{ij} to the input message place IM_j output mapping function,it's $C(g_{ij}) \times C(IM_j) \rightarrow N$ (Non-negative integer), corresponds to the color directed arc from g_{ij} to OM_i .

Known by definition 1.2, the production sub-module are through input / output mapping functions and message transmission gate to fulfill message transmission and feedback. Message gate is a special transiton in OPN that express message transmission between different OPN "incident", as shown in Figure 1.

3. Bottleneck detection based on PPOM

3.1 Bottleneck detection based on PPOM

PPOM is a dynamic model method of production process, this method not only for the pre-estimation of the bottleneck before products into production, and is also suitable to explore the new bottleneck cell after bottleneck transfer occurred. PPOM bottleneck detection process is as follows:

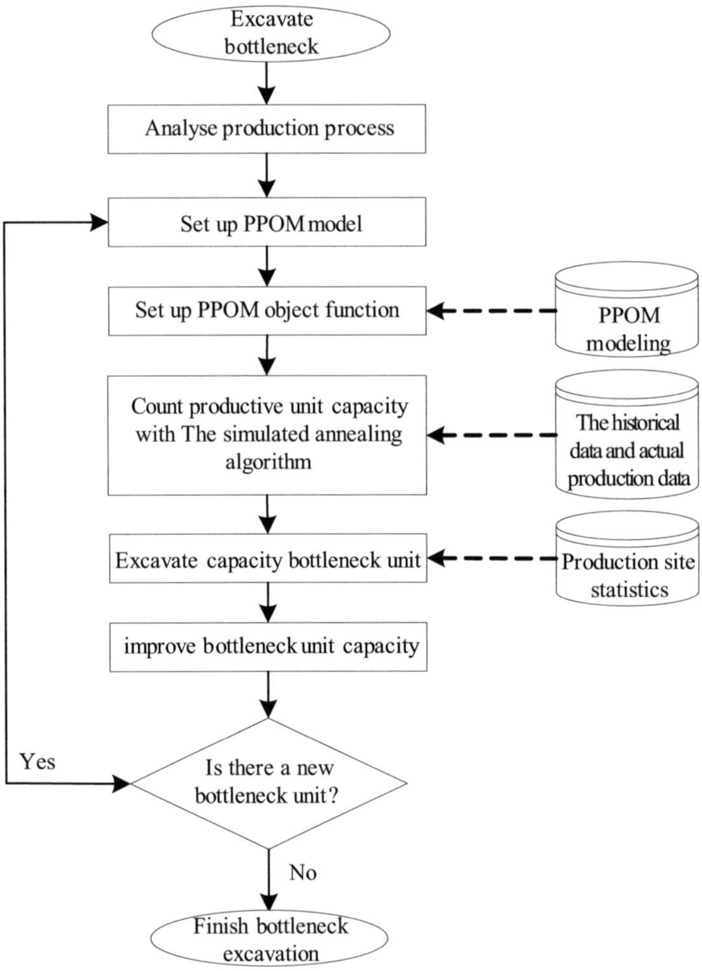

Fig. 2. Bottleneck detecting process based on PPOM

1. PPOM abstract model
2. PPOM objective function model
3. Use simulated annealing algorithm to calculate the production cell capacity
4. Find the minimum production capacity process cell
5. Detect bottleneck production capacity cell
6. Put forward improvement measures accordingly
7. Analyse whether appear new bottleneck in production cells, if it exists, back to Step 2 to re-cycle, otherwise end the bottleneck detection process, specifically shown in Figure 2.

3.2 Abstract model based on PPOM

3.2.1 Abstract model

The production process has the specific entitity object $PPOM-OPN$ on the level of OPN from its inherited class, reflecting the succession of OPN method, that is the object class has its own properties and methods. Therefore, in the build-time of $PPOM-OPN$, not only to examine entity object state place SP and activities transition AT as to establish common PN, but also know all input message place IM and output message place OM of entities.

Use PPOM method, abstract each processing cell in the production process to closed entity place Mi, IMi shows i production cell input message place, OMi shows i production cell output message place after operation, SPi shows i-production cell state place, that is intermediate processing status of production place Mi. Methods using PPOM abstract model shown in Figure 3.

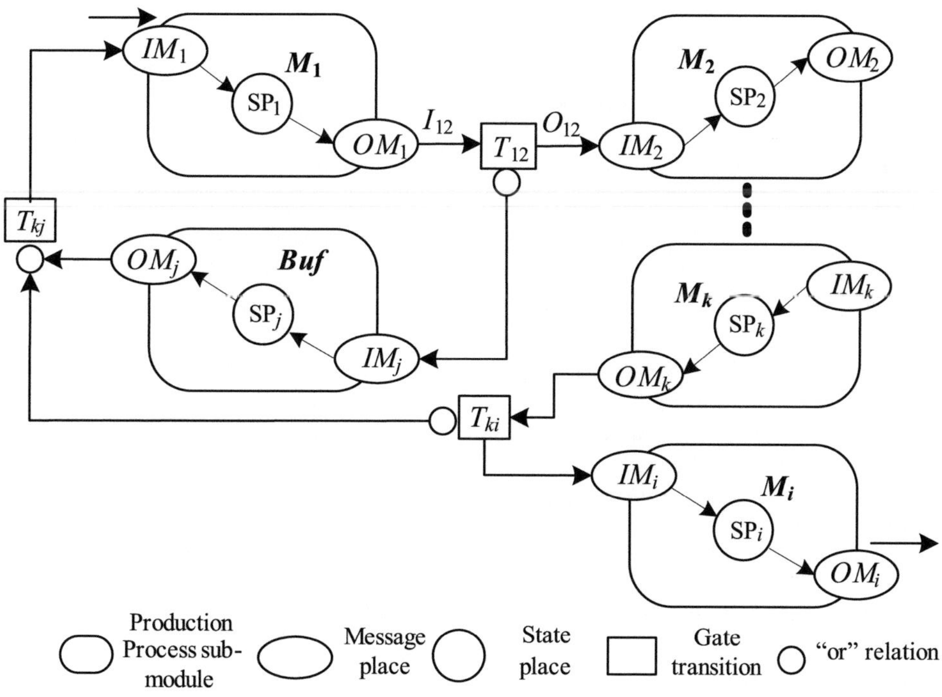

Fig. 3. Abstract model construction based on PPOM

Figure 3 shows the abstract model of the entire production process $PPOM-OPN$, the concrete operation of the various production cells are encapsulated in rounded rectangular frame, each production cell sub-module through input / output mapping functions and message transmission gate to fulfill message transition and feedback. Message gate is a special transiton in OPN that express message transmission between different OPN "incident".

3.2.2 Capacity analysis of abstract model

1. Deadly embrace analysis

Manufacturing system dynamics characteristics can be described by various objects OPN(Obi) of manufacturing system OPN and the relationship between objects (R_{ij}),the various sub-objects can inherit from its parent class property.Therefore,by constructing Object Communication Net(OCN) between object classes, the use of non-variable analysis can be carried out for deadly embrace detection. An analysis of the capability of each object class OCN, also mastered the situation of the whole production system. If an object class OCN exists deadly embrace , there may be message transmission between object classes result. For any sub-module object of abstract model, using the module objects to constructe the corresponding OCN (OCi). Construction of sub-module object class OCN steps:

1. Start from any output message place $om(om \in OM_i)$ of O_i, identify the connected relationship $R_{ij} = (OM_i, g_{ij}, IM_j)$ and defining input message place $im(im \in IM_j)$ corresponding to O_j. Meanwhile, with the state place $sp(sp \in SP_j)$ by using abstract objects $AO_{ij}(sp)$ instead of objects O_j,here sp is decided by input / output relationship $IM_j - AT_j - SP_j$.
2. Through stimulating transition $g(g \in g_{ij})$ immediately connects om and $AO_{ij}(sp)$ of O_i.
3. For the abstract object O_j,from it's definition input / output relationship $SP_j - AT_j - OM_j$ to find output message place $om(om \in OM_j)$;
4. If what 3) found of om is equal to the start output message place from O_i, then stop (that is the object OCN has been built). Otherwise, the next step;
5. According to the corresponding mutual connection relationship $R_{jj'}(OM_{j'}, g_{jj'}, IM_{j'})$ $j' = j, j = 1, 2, \cdots, I$,through stimulating transition g immediately to find input message place $im(im \in IM_{j'})$ Corresponding to O_j.meanwhile, with the state place $sp(sp \in SP_j)$ by using abstract object $A_{jj'}(sp)$ instead of object O_j,here sp was decided by input / output relationship $IM_j - AT_j - SP_j$.
6. Through connection gate transition $g(g \in g_{jj'})$ to connect om and $AO_{jj'}(sp)$ of O_j;
7. Use j' to place j, and back to (3).

In summary, if each activity transition and the gate of abstract sub-module object OCN is in the initial identification, through appropriate transition and the gate can be stimulated, it indicates there is no deadly embrace; similarly, if all the abstract sub-module objects can stimulate OCN, it indicates there is no deadly embrace abstract model.

2. Conflict Analysis

Abstracting model of the production system is highly abstract, and manufacturing system is the limited capacity of the resource allocation system, a resource may be object for a few services, but often only as a resource at the same time object for one service, which will lead to conflict occurred. In addition, some constraints of the system will lead to conflict. These conflicts can occur within OPN object (such as the number of simultaneous transitions at the same time only one can be stimulated), OPN may also occur in the mutual connection (as a time to the operation of two or more requests for the same resources). OPN on the abstract model for conflict analysis is intended to first identify all possible conflicts, and then offer all kinds of conflict most appropriate conflict resolution / decision-making programs to ensure the system agility, flexibility and reliability. In OPN, the conflict generally fall into two categories: input and output conflict [11].

1. input conflict: this kind of conflict happens when two or more transitions share the same input message place. (Figure 4(a) shows); or one transition has two or more input message places, and these input message places through "(OR)" logic to connect with the transition(Figure4(b)shows). In the manufacturing system, several processing tasks competing for the same resource will enter the conflict.

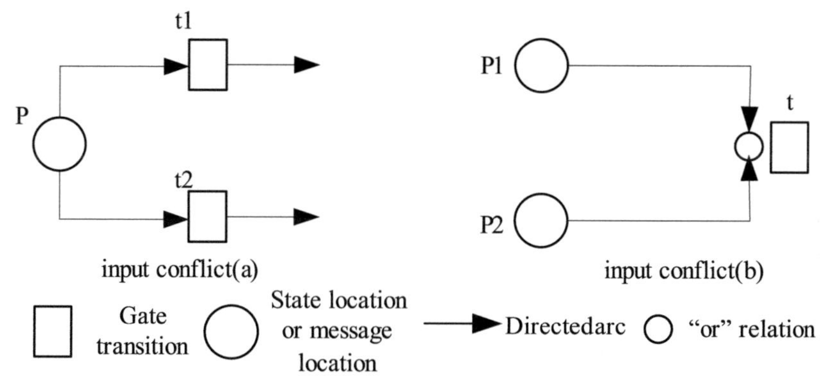

Fig. 4. A Petri net with input conflict

2. output conflict: this kind of conflict happens when one transition has two or more output message places,and the place through "(OR)" logic to connect with the transition(Figure 5 shows). In the manufacturing system, when the current processing is completed, there are several resources available to complete the next processing task, the output of conflict arises.

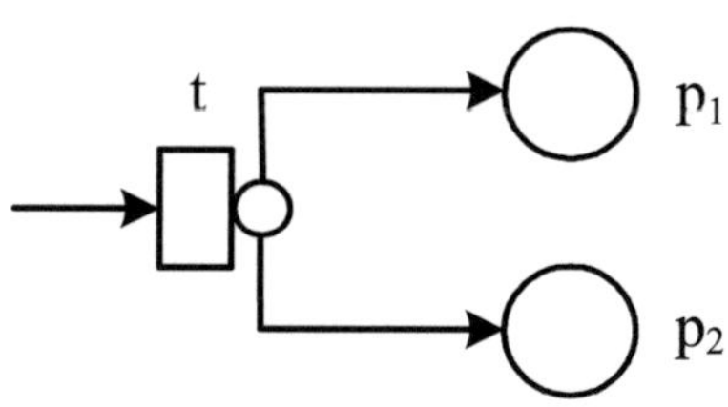

Fig. 5. A Petri net with output conflict

3. Conservation analysis

Conservation is another important feature of the model, as System resources are limited, if the model is not conservative, then the system exists overflow phenomenon, otherwise it will be security. According to the literature [14], when there is a P invariant for a non-negative integer vector x of $n \times 1$, so $x^T C = 0$ (C is the incidence matrix), then the Petri net is strictly binding. On the analysis of the actual situation, as long as the actual data system satisfies literature [14] required, then the Petri net is strictly binding, that is conservative and bounded, overflow phenomenon will not occur.

4. Production system objective function model based on PPOM

Owing to production system widely refers to the aspects of capacity, cost, stock and efficiency, etc, which covers a wide rage The following contents will only regard the capacity, which is mainly concerned by the companies, as the main study object, and build up the objective function model. According to the TOC theory, Bottleneck site or the capacity of bottleneck process decides the maximum capacity of production system. Detecting the bottleneck cell in time and improving its capacity are vital to capacity maximize and benefit maximize of the whole production capacity system.

4.1 Calculation of capacity

In the mass and single production enterprises, capacity is usually calculated in unit of the production cell or processing site. The equipment cells which constitutes the production cells have the nature of interchangeability, namely, any equipment in production cells can complete any same procedure assigned to this cell and meet its quality requirements. The calculation of production cell capacity is as follows [12]:

$$M = \frac{SF_e}{t} \tag{1.3}$$

$$t = \frac{1}{n}\sum_{i=1}^{n} t_i \cdot \theta_i \tag{1.4}$$

In the formula, M is the capacity of a production cell, Fe is the effective working time of one single equipment, S is the equipment number of a production cell, t is the average number of required equipments per hour of one single product, ti is the average number of required equipments per hour of No. I product in virtual factory, θ_i is the proportion of the output of No. I product in the planned total output, n is the variety number of products in virtual factory.
The effective working hours of production cell per day:

$$\varphi(\delta) = 8\,\delta \times (1 - \lambda) \tag{1.5}$$

Thereinto, λ is allowance rating (including allowance time like going to the WC, exercise during breaks and drinking,etc), δ is the frequency of the changing shifts of factory, in general, $\delta = \{1, 2, 3\}$, δ =1 means the factory takes the single shift producing mode. δ =2 means the factory takes the double-shift producing mode, δ =3 means the factory takes the three shifts producing mode.

$$F_e = (1 - ST - DT - PM - PC) \times \varphi(\delta) \tag{1.6}$$

In the formula (1.6), *ST* is the probability of Set up time occurs in the total working time per day, *DT* is the probability of Down time occurs in the total working time per day, PM is the probability of Preventive Maintenance time occurs in the total working time per day, *PC is* the probability of presupposed Protective capacity time occurs in the total working time per day.
From the formula (1.3) ~ (1.6) we can know:

$$M = \frac{S \times (1 - ST - DT - PM - PC) \times \varphi(\delta)}{\frac{1}{n}\sum_{i=1}^{n} t_i \cdot \theta_i} \tag{1.7}$$

In the actual production process, ST obeys the binomial distribution.
order $X = ST \sim B(n, p)$, then

$$f(x) = P(X) = C_n^x p^x q^{n-x} \tag{1.8}$$

thereinto $0 < p < 1,\ p + q = 1$, $x = 0, 1, 2, \cdots, n$
As machines break down randomly in processing cell, it obeys the normal distribution commonly. Order $Y = DT \sim N\left(\mu, \sigma^2\right)$, so

$$f(y) = \frac{1}{\sqrt{2\pi}\sigma} e^{-\frac{(y-\mu)^2}{2\sigma^2}} \quad , -\infty < y < +\infty \tag{1.9}$$

The routine preventive maintenance of enterprises includes week maintenance, mouth maintenance, season maintenance and year maintenance, get rid of producing anomaly, PM consistent with gamma distribution basically.order $Z = PM \sim Gamma(\beta, \alpha)$, then

$$f(z) = \begin{cases} \dfrac{\beta^{-\alpha} z^{\alpha-1} e^{-z/\beta}}{\Gamma(\alpha)} & z > 0 \\ 0 & others \end{cases} \tag{1.10}$$

thereinto, Γ is the gamma function, its expression is:

$$\Gamma(\alpha) = \int_0^\infty t^{\alpha-1} e^{-t}\, dt$$

For actual factory production, Protective Capacity PC corresponds to the Buffer builded up for Bottleneck process, order $f(q) = PC$, and then $f(q)$ obeys the condition functions as follows:

$$f(q) = \begin{cases} q & \text{if the production cell is bottleneck} \\ 0 & \text{others} \end{cases} \tag{1.11}$$

Synthesize formula(1.8)~(1.11), we can conclude the capacity calculation formula of production cell is:

$$M = \frac{S \times [1 - f(x) - f(y) - f(z) - f(q)] \times \varphi(\delta)}{\frac{1}{n}\sum_{i=1}^{n} t_i \cdot \theta_i} \tag{1.12}$$

4.2 The expanding capacity analysis function

According to the actual production situation of factory, the equipment number, Protective Capacity, daily effective working hours, average number of required equipments per hour of each virtual product $\sum_{i=1}^{n} t_i \cdot \theta_i$, in a period of time, can be simplified as constants .Then build up the PPOM objective function model of capacity combines with the capacity calculation formula (1.12),

$$F_k = \frac{S_k \times [1 - f(x) - f(y) - f(z) - f(q)] \times \varphi(\delta)}{\frac{1}{n}\sum_{i=1}^{n} t_i \cdot \theta_i} \tag{1.13}$$

$$S.T.\begin{cases} f(x) = Cn^x p^x q^{n-x}, & x = 0,1,2,\ldots,n \\ f(y) = \frac{1}{\sqrt{2\pi}\sigma} e^{-\frac{(y-\mu)^2}{2\sigma^2}}, & -\infty < y < +\infty \\ f(z) = \frac{\beta^{-\alpha} z^{\alpha-1} e^{-z/\beta}}{\Gamma(\alpha)}, & z > 0 \\ \varphi(\delta) = 8\delta \times (1-\lambda), & 0 < \lambda < 1 \\ \delta \in (1,2,3) & \\ k,i,\omega > 0, & 0 < \theta_i < 1 \end{cases}$$

4.3 Bottleneck detection cell based on PPOM

According to the capacity calculation objective function (1.13), combines with the historical data and actual situation of the factory, calculate the capacity of production cell 1:

$$f_1 = \frac{S_1 \times [1 - f_1(x) - f_1(y) - f_1(z) - f(q)] \times \varphi(\delta)}{\frac{1}{n}\sum_{i=1}^{n} t_i \cdot \theta_i}$$

Similarly, calculate the capacity of each production cell respectively:

$$f_2 = \frac{S_2 \times [1 - f_2(x) - f_2(y) - f_2(z) - f(q)] \times \varphi(\delta)}{\frac{1}{n}\sum_{i=1}^{n} t_i \cdot \theta_i}$$

$$\vdots$$

$$f_n = \frac{S_n \times [1 - f_n(x) - f_n(y) - f_n(z) - f(q)] \times \varphi(\delta)}{\frac{1}{n}\sum_{i=1}^{n} t_i \cdot \theta_i}$$

After that, using the simulated annealing algorithm and Matlab to write the programming code, making comparisons between f_1, f_2, $\cdots$, f_n respectively. According to TOC theory, define the minumum function of production cell as the bottleneck cell in the production process. This cell decides the maximum production capacity and actual production efficiency of factory. In the actual production process, we should meet the actual demand of bottleneck cell as far as possible and make efforts to improve its capacity.

5. The application of PPOM

5.1 The description of the power transformer production process in M company

M company was founded in August 1999,it was invested a total investment of 30 million U.S. dollars by A company ---- the top 500 enterprises in the world, as the third power transformers joint venture established in China. Its main business is to design, product, sale and maintain of 110KV/220KV medium and large power transformer. In 2008, M company's sales revenue had been reached more than 1.4 billion Yuan and the production capacity had been reached 12000MVA with more than 460 employees. The M company had also received the awards of The Top 100 Electric Company in China, and had been selected as the Top Ten Growth Competitiveness Enterprises of China's Electric Power Industrial. In 2009, as the company undertook parts of the national power grids' alteration and Wenchuang earthquake reconstruction projects, its production order number had jumped to 64 per year, the annual effective capacity requisition had reached to 15160 MVA.

Here we will take the most representative product 240MVA/220KV transformer of this company as the example to analyze. The production process of Power transformer starts from raw material, and through cells of Coil Winding, High Frequency Welding (HFW),

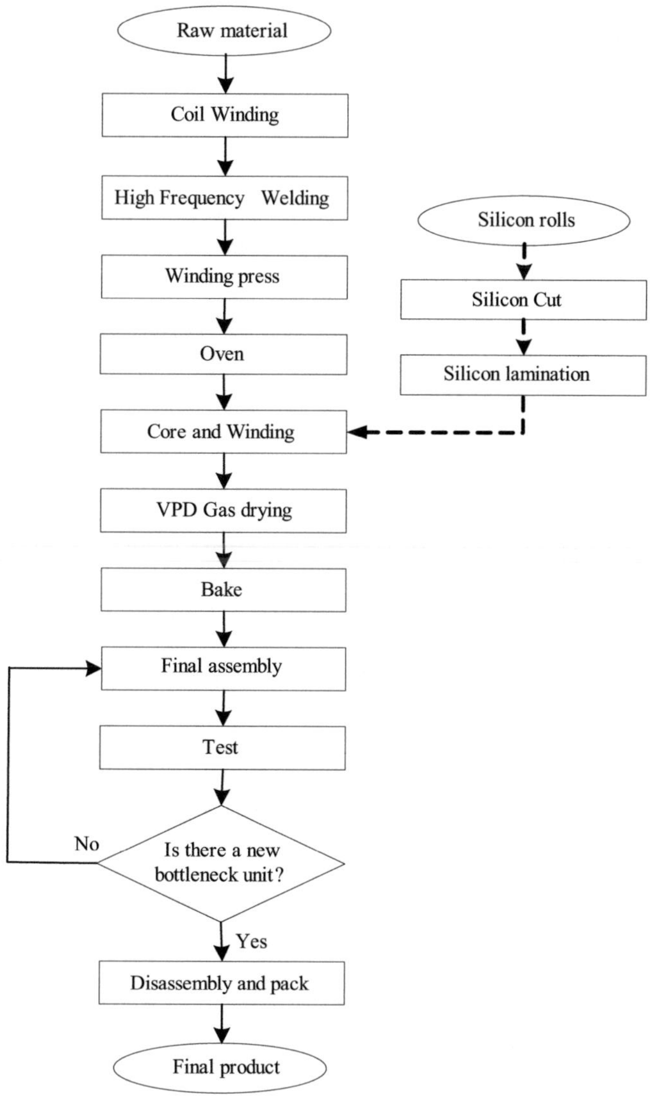

Fig. 6. Power Transformer production process of M company

Coil Oven, Iron Cut, Iron Lamination, Down-lead, Walkthrough, Core, Winding Assembly, Oven, Final Assembly, Test, Pack, etc. Then is the finally transformer. The production process of Power transformer in M company shown in Figure 6.

5.2 Power transformer production abstract model based on PPOM

5.2.1 Power transformer production abstract model

For the actual situation of M company power transformer production, use PPOM method, we can abstract raw material warehouse, coil winding cell, HFW cell, Winding press cell, Coil Oven cell, Winding assembly cell, Iron Cut cell, Iron Lamination cell, Down-lead Walkthrough cell, Core and Winding Assembly cell, Oven cell, Final Assembly cell, Test cell and knocked-down packing cell to 14 place sub-module $P_1 \sim P_{14}$,then optimize these 14 place sub-modules according to production process, and build M company power transformer production abstract model, as shown in figure 7.

The particularization for each place and transition in figure 7 are shown as table 1.

5.2.2 Power Transformer production abstract model capacity analysis

1. deadly embrace analysis

The occurrence of deadly embrace would lead to suspension of the entire power transformer production abstract model system running and seriously affect system capacity. Therefore,

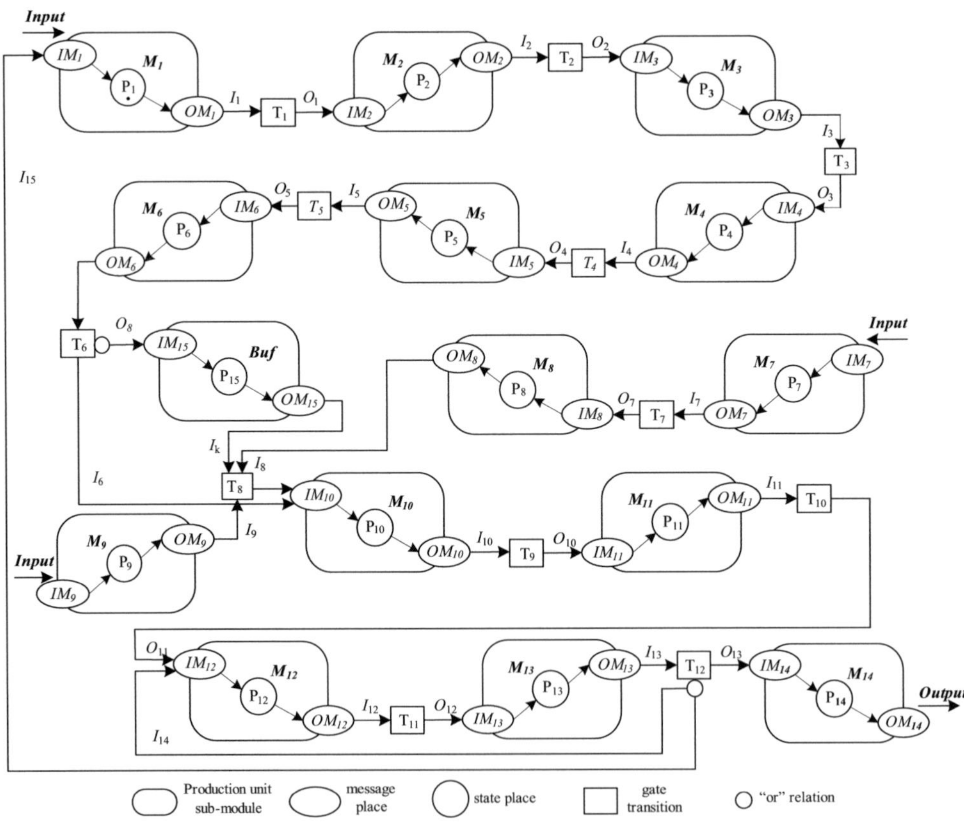

Fig. 7. Power Transformer production abstract model based on PPOM

Production cell	mean	place	mean	transition	mean
M1	Raw material storage	P1	Transformer material preparing	T1	Material has been prepared
M2	Coil Winding	P2	Vertical and Horizontal winding	T2	Coil winding finished
M3	HFW	P3	High winding HFW	T3	High winding HFW finished
M4	Winding press	P4	Winding press size adjustment	T4	Press finished and prepared to oven
M5	Coil Oven	P5	Coil to oven	T5	Coil oven finished and prepared to assembly
M6	Winding assembly	P6	Coil assembly	T6	Coil assembly finished,goes to Core and Winding Assembly or Buffer Core and Winding Assembly
M7	Iron Cut	P7	Georg cut	T7	Iron Cut finished
M8	Iron Lamination assembly	P8	Iron Lamination	T8	Lamination Finished and enter to Core and Winding Assembly worktable
M9	Down-lead Walkthrough	P9	Down-lead Walkthrough	T9	Core and Winding Assembly finished and prepared to VPD
M10	Core and Winding Assembly	P10	Core and Winding Assembly	T10	Out of oven and prepared to Final Assembly
M11	VDP Oven	P11	VDP Oven	T11	Final Assembly finished and prepared to test hall
M12	Final Assembly	P12	Final Assembly	T12	Transformer test finished,if it up to grade,goes direct to knocked-down packing;if not,back to transfomer final Assembly cell to re-assembly or roll to coil cell to re-coil
M13	Test	P13	Transformer capacity test		
M14	knocked-down packing	P14	knocked-down packing pre-rollout		
Buf	assembly buffer cell	P15	Assembly buffer		

Table 1. Meaning of places and transitions in Fig.7

after the power transformer production process $PPOM-T$ model is established, the system must determine whether there exists deadly embrace, and find out all possible deadly embrace situation, to avoid its occurrence before the excitation system controls. For convenience, OCN incidence matrix of the transformer production process $PPOM-T$ model and initial marking are listed in tabular form, as shown in Table 2.

Set the following stock preparation module T_1 transition of power transformer production raw materials as an example, use Invariant theory: $vC=0$, $im=im_0$ (v is p invariant, C is the incidence matrix)to do capacity analysis.

Incidence matrix between power Transformer production $PPOM-T$ model place and transitions is $C=[c_{ij}]_{15\times12}$, thereinto:

C	T_1	T_2	T_3	T_4	T_5	T_6	T_7	T_8	T_9	T_{10}	T_{11}	T_{12}	m_0
P_1	-1	0	0	0	0	0	0	0	0	0	0	-1	1
P_2	1	-1	0	0	0	0	0	0	0	0	0	0	0
P_3	0	1	-1	0	0	0	0	0	0	0	0	0	0
P_4	0	0	1	-1	0	0	0	0	0	0	0	0	0
P_5	0	0	0	1	-1	0	0	0	0	0	0	0	0
P_6	0	0	0	0	1	-1	0	0	0	0	0	0	0
P_7	0	0	0	0	0	0	-1	0	0	0	0	0	0
P_8	0	0	0	0	0	0	1	-1	0	0	0	0	0
P_9	0	0	0	0	0	0	0	-1	0	0	0	0	0
P_{10}	0	0	0	0	0	1	0	1	-1	0	0	0	0
P_{11}	0	0	0	0	0	0	0	0	1	-1	0	0	0
P_{12}	0	0	0	0	0	0	0	0	0	1	-1	-1	0
P_{13}	0	0	0	0	0	0	0	0	0	0	1	-1	0
P_{14}	-1	0	0	0	0	0	0	0	0	0	0	1	0
Buf	0	0	0	0	0	1	0	-1	0	0	0	0	1

Table 2. OCN matrix of transformer abstract model

$$c_{ij} = c_{ij}^{+} - c_{ij}^{-}, \quad i \in \{1,2,...,15\},\ j \in \{1,2,...,12\},$$

$$c_{ij}^{+} = \begin{cases} 1 & (t_j, p_i) \in F \quad i \in \{1,2,\cdots,15\}, j \in \{1,2,\cdots,12\} \\ 0 & others \end{cases}$$

$$c_{ij}^{-} = \begin{cases} 1 & (p_i, t_j) \in F \quad i \in \{1,2,\cdots,15\}, j \in \{1,2,\cdots,12\} \\ 0 & others \end{cases}$$

So, the incidence matrix C

$$C = \begin{bmatrix} -1 & 0 & 0 & 0 & 0 & 0 & 0 & 0 & 0 & 0 & 0 & -1 \\ 1 & -1 & 0 & 0 & 0 & 0 & 0 & 0 & 0 & 0 & 0 & 0 \\ 0 & 1 & -1 & 0 & 0 & 0 & 0 & 0 & 0 & 0 & 0 & 0 \\ 0 & 0 & 1 & -1 & 0 & 0 & 0 & 0 & 0 & 0 & 0 & 0 \\ 0 & 0 & 0 & 1 & -1 & 0 & 0 & 0 & 0 & 0 & 0 & 0 \\ 0 & 0 & 0 & 0 & 1 & -1 & 0 & 0 & 0 & 0 & 0 & 0 \\ 0 & 0 & 0 & 0 & 0 & 0 & -1 & 0 & 0 & 0 & 0 & 0 \\ 0 & 0 & 0 & 0 & 0 & 0 & 1 & -1 & 0 & 0 & 0 & 0 \\ 0 & 0 & 0 & 0 & 0 & 0 & 0 & -1 & -1 & 0 & 0 & 0 \\ 0 & 0 & 0 & 0 & 0 & 1 & 0 & 1 & -1 & 0 & 0 & 0 \\ 0 & 0 & 0 & 0 & 0 & 0 & 0 & 0 & 1 & -1 & 0 & 0 \\ 0 & 0 & 0 & 0 & 0 & 0 & 0 & 0 & 0 & 1 & -1 & -1 \\ 0 & 0 & 0 & 0 & 0 & 0 & 0 & 0 & 0 & 0 & 1 & -1 \\ -1 & 0 & 0 & 0 & 0 & 0 & 0 & 0 & 0 & 0 & 0 & 1 \\ 0 & 0 & 0 & 0 & 0 & 1 & 0 & -1 & 0 & 0 & 0 & 0 \end{bmatrix}$$

From Invariant theory,we can get OCN incidence matrix of power Transformer production abstract model is $rank(C) = 15$,from $x^T m = x^T m_0$ (x is the vector of $n \times 1$, m_0 is Initial state) gets,all the m can be reached by m_0.
From Petri net definition identification knows, $m(P_i)$ shows the number of tokens in P_i.so $m(P_1) = 1, m(P_1) + m(P_2) + \cdots m(P_{14}) + m(IM_1) - m(OM_2) + \cdots + m(IM_{14}) - m(OM_{14}) = 0(X)$, now T_1 can be stimulated.
Similarly, other transitions T_2, T_3 ..., T_{14} of Power Transformer production abstract model OCN in the initial identification m_0, through appropriate action all can be stimulated, thus shows the power transformer production abstract model exists no deadly embrace.

2. Conflict analysis

In the power transformer production abstract model petri net, the abstract model PPOM-T is a highly abstraction of transformer production system, while in the production process, between the production processing cells or working procedures, production capacity can be of different sizes, time differences, which leads to conflict. In addition, certain constraints of the system, such as materials needed for the transformer production, aid tools, staff and other resources may service for a few sets in the production of transformer, will lead to conflict.in the power transformer production PPOM-T model, transiton T_{12} exists output conflict, as shown in Figure 8.

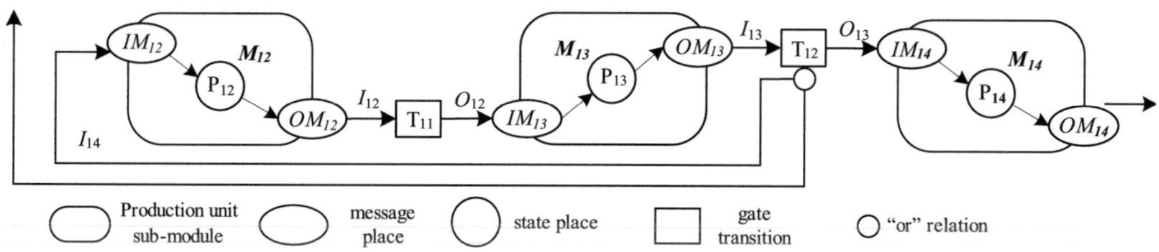

Fig. 8. A conflict model in T_{12}

As the power transformer production system is a complex system, when it encounter conflicts, the system should be based on characteristics of power transformers and the actual production and use appropriate conflict resolutiono in a timely manner.as Figure 8 mentioned above, transition T_{12} exists output conflict,we can adopt the follow-up working procedure minimum priority principle,give priority to follow-up working procedure minimum production cell M_{12},that is returned to transformer final assembly cell to re-assembly for those which can not meet test capacity requirements of components; and then consider the cell M1 (it has the most follow-up working procedures).

3. Conservation Tests

Conservation analysis is another important feature of the model, it shows whether the system exists overflow phenomenon and security. According to the literature [14], when there is a P invariant for a non-negative integer vector x of $n \times 1$, so $x^T C = 0$ (C is the incidence matrix), then the Petri net is strictly binding, that is conservative and bounded, overflow phenomenon will not occur.

$$
if\ x^T \cdot \begin{bmatrix}
-1 & 0 & 0 & 0 & 0 & 0 & 0 & 0 & 0 & 0 & 0 & -1 \\
1 & -1 & 0 & 0 & 0 & 0 & 0 & 0 & 0 & 0 & 0 & 0 \\
0 & 1 & -1 & 0 & 0 & 0 & 0 & 0 & 0 & 0 & 0 & 0 \\
0 & 0 & 1 & -1 & 0 & 0 & 0 & 0 & 0 & 0 & 0 & 0 \\
0 & 0 & 0 & 1 & -1 & 0 & 0 & 0 & 0 & 0 & 0 & 0 \\
0 & 0 & 0 & 0 & 1 & -1 & 0 & 0 & 0 & 0 & 0 & 0 \\
0 & 0 & 0 & 0 & 0 & 0 & -1 & 0 & 0 & 0 & 0 & 0 \\
0 & 0 & 0 & 0 & 0 & 0 & 1 & -1 & 0 & 0 & 0 & 0 \\
0 & 0 & 0 & 0 & 0 & 0 & 0 & -1 & -1 & 0 & 0 & 0 \\
0 & 0 & 0 & 0 & 0 & 1 & 0 & 1 & -1 & 0 & 0 & 0 \\
0 & 0 & 0 & 0 & 0 & 0 & 0 & 0 & 1 & -1 & 0 & 0 \\
0 & 0 & 0 & 0 & 0 & 0 & 0 & 0 & 0 & 1 & -1 & -1 \\
0 & 0 & 0 & 0 & 0 & 0 & 0 & 0 & 0 & 0 & 1 & -1 \\
-1 & 0 & 0 & 0 & 0 & 0 & 0 & 0 & 0 & 0 & 0 & 1 \\
0 & 0 & 0 & 0 & 0 & 1 & 0 & -1 & 0 & 0 & 0 & 0
\end{bmatrix} = 0,\ then
$$

Non-zero positive vector $x^T = \begin{bmatrix} 1 & 1 & 1 & 1 & 1 & 6 & 1 & 2 & 1 & 1 & 1 & 2 \end{bmatrix}$, so that $x^T C = 0$.

Therefore, this power transformer production abstract model exists $x^T = \begin{bmatrix} 1 & 1 & 1 & 1 & 1 & 6 & 1 & 2 & 1 & 1 & 1 & 2 \end{bmatrix}$, so that $x^T C = 0$. From this we know, the power transformer production process abstract model object OCN is conservation bounded, overflow will not occur, and the model has good performance.

5.3 The objective function model of the power transformer

According to M company's power transformer's actual production situation, combines with the capacity calculation formula (1.13), the objective function model of the power transformer can be built up as:

$$
F_{PPOM-Tk} = \frac{S_k \times [1 - f(x) - f(y) - f(z) - f(q)] \times \varphi(\delta)}{\frac{1}{n}\sum_{i=1}^{n} t_i \cdot \theta_i} \tag{1.14}
$$

$$
S.T. \begin{cases}
f(x) = C_n{}^x p^x q^{n-x}, & x \in \{0, 1, \cdots, n\} \\
f(y) = \dfrac{1}{\sqrt{2\pi}\sigma} e^{-\frac{(y-\mu)^2}{2\sigma^2}}, & -\infty < y < +\infty \\
f(z) = \dfrac{\beta^{-\alpha} z^{\alpha-1} e^{-z/\beta}}{\Gamma(\alpha)}, & z > 0 \\
f(q) = q, & 0 \le q < 1 \\
\varphi(\delta) = 8\,\delta \times (1 - \lambda), & \delta \in \{2\} \\
k, i, \omega > 0,\ \ 0 < \theta_i, \lambda < 1
\end{cases}
$$

Thereinto, S_k is the equipment number contained by the production cell, $f(x)$ is the distribution function of Set up time, $f(y)$ is the distribution function of Down time, $f(z)$ is the distribution function of Routine maintenance time , $\varphi(\delta)$ is the function of the daily effective working hours of production cell, λ is allowance rating (including allowance time like going to the WC, exercise during breaks and drinking,ect) , δ is the frequency of changing shifts of factory, t_i is the average number of required equipments per hour of No.i product in virtual factory, θ_i is the proportion of the output of No.i product in the planned total output, ω is the variety number of products.

5.4 Power transformer to detect the production process bottleneck cell

In the Period of time, the number of equipment per production process cell, protective capacity, the effective working hours per day and average number of required equipments per hour for virtual product $\sum_{i=1}^{n} t_i \cdot \theta_i$, Can be considered as constant to simplify handling.

oder
$$t_k = \frac{1}{n}\sum_{i=1}^{n} t_i \cdot \theta_i \tag{1.15}$$

$$\psi_k = f(x) + f(y) + f(z) + f(q) \tag{1.16}$$

And as $\varphi(\delta) = 8 \times 2 \times (1 - 15\%) = 13.6\ \text{h}$

Use the formula (1.15) (1.16) into formula (1.14) can make power transformer production capacity objective function model (1.14) simplified to:

$$F_k = \frac{13.6 S_k \times (1 - \psi_k)}{t_k} \tag{1.17}$$

$$S.T.\begin{cases} \psi_k = f(x) + f(y) + f(z) \\ t_k = \frac{1}{n}\sum_{i=1}^{n} t_i \cdot \theta_i \\ 0 < f(x), f(y), f(z) < 1, x, z, k, t, n > 0, y \in R \end{cases}$$

Then, using the simulated annealing algorithm in the production function to calculate the minimum producion capacity, that is the bottleneck of the production process cell.

1. Solution space: Solution space S is just counted once for each site,is a set of all permulations of $k \in \{1,2,\cdots,15\}$, the members of s denoted by $(s_1, s_2, \cdots, s_{15})$,and notes $s_{n+1}=s_1$, optional for the initial solution can be $(1,2,\cdots,15)$.
2. objective function: defining transformer capacity function as cost function

$$F(s_1, s_2, \cdots, s_{15})_k = \frac{13.6 S_k \times (1 - \psi_k)}{t_k} \tag{1.18}$$

3. difference cost function: set $(s_1, s_2, \cdots, s_{15})$ transformed to $(\eta_1, \eta_2, \cdots, \eta_{15})$,then the difference cost function is

$$\Delta F = F(\eta_1, \eta_2, \cdots, \eta_{15}) - F(s_1, s_2, \cdots, s_{15}) \tag{1.19}$$

Use Matlab Write code as follows:

```
begin
init-of-T; { T is Initial temperature}
 S={1, 2, …,15}; {S is Initial value}
 termination=false;
 while termination=false
  begin
   for i=1 to L do
     begin
       generate(S'form S); { from the current loop circuit S to generate new S'}
       Δt:=F(S'))-F(S);{ F (S) is capacity value for each site}
          if(Δt<0) or (exp (-Δt/T)>Random-of-[0,1])
       S=S';
     if the-halt-condition-is-TRUE THEN
     termination=true;
   End;
   T_lower;
  End;
End
```

After using the simulated annealing algorithm, it can quickly detect the minimum production process capacity, as winding assembly is the Z power transformer company's capacity bottleneck cell of production system.

5.5 The proposion of improvement measures

As the daily capacity of production cell of Winding assembly is:

$$F(s_6)=\frac{13.6S_6\times(1-\psi_6)}{t_6}=\frac{13.6\times4\times(1-13.8\%)}{229.67}=0.204\ (\text{unitage/day})$$

Take the product 240MVA and the annual working days as 250 days for Calculation, the annual production capacity cell of Winding assembly is

$$F_Y(s_6)=0.204\times250\times240=12250.48\ (\text{MVA/year})$$

Obviously, the calculation of the annual production capacity cell of Winding assembly $F_Y(s_6)$ is less than the M company's actual required annual production capacity of 15160 MVA. According to the actual situation of the enterprise, the Winding assembly cell takes the early, middle and late three shifts, thereby, the daily production capacity cell of Winding assembly can be calculate out:

$$F'(s_6)=\frac{S_6\times(1-\psi_6)\times8\times3\times(1-15\%)}{t_6}=\frac{4\times(1-13.8\%)\times20.4}{229.67}=0.306\ (\text{unitage /day})$$

The annual production capacity cell of Winding assembly is:

$$F_Y'(s_6)=0.306\times250\times240=18375.72\ (\text{MVA/year})$$

At this point, the annual production capacity cell of Winding assembly of 18375.72MVA was greater than the actual requirements of the 15160 MVA, the capacity requirements problem was resolved. At the same time, the capacity bottleneck might be transferred to other production cells, therefore, the changed actual data is needed to re-simulated annealing calculation (shown in Figure 7), and analyze the capacity of the possible new bottleneck cells, taking the improvement measures for these new bottleneck capacity cell and recycling until all production capacity cells have meet the actual requirements

5.6 The results of improvements

After the PPOM method had been implied in M company, we detect the bottleneck production capacity cell, proposed improvement measures in time and made the annual production capacity of Winding assembly cell increased $(76.5-57.8)\div 57.8=$ 32.47% than the original annual production capacity of 57.8 , besides, the production cycle time TPT was shortened correspondingly. Concrete results are shown in Table 3.

Items	Before improvement	After implied PPOM	Effects
Production cycle time TPT(h)	724.1	646.4	77.7
Annual production capacity	57.8	76.5	18.7
Increased production efficiency per year (million)	--	--	202.14

Table 3. Effect statistics

1. The average production cycle time of each power transformer reduced 77.7h;
2. The production capacity increased 32.47%;
3. The production efficiency increased 2.0214 million Yuan per year.

6. Conclusion

Each production system will has the minimum capacity bottleneck site, which restricted the production system to further enhance the capacity, it is important for production scheduling at the bottleneck core site. In this paper,combine with Petri net technology, OO method and agile manufacturing ideas, put forward agile production scheduling PPOM, described using capacity bottleneck core site as the scheduling core and to the other times (or re) production bottleneck site divergence PPOM production scheduling model method, and finally through empirical research methods to further validate correctness and feasibility of PPOM. The method extends the traditional capacity calculation function model and is closer to actual production, the enterprise production process model are of considerable practical value.

PPOM method of the production process for the manufacturing enterprise model provides a scientific basis and an operational new method,it is an exploratory study focuing on manufacturing production process model,for sub-modules internal computing methods of the PPOM abstract model and existing ERP system links and PPOM information system development, also need to produce in-depth exploration of the actual situation..

7. Acknowledgement

Foundation items: Project supported by Natural Science Foundation of Chongqing Municipality, China(No.2009BB3362), the Science & Technology Research of Chongqing Municipal Education Commission, Chain(No.KJ08A06), and the Chongqing University Innovative Talent Training Program During the 3rd Stage of 211 Project,China(No.S-09107).

8. References

[1] LI Bing; Bottleneck Analysis of Manufacturing Cell based on Simulation[J]; Modular Machine Tool & Automatic Manufacturing Technique;2009-01-029.

[2] XU Han-chuan; XU Xiao-fei; ZHAN De-chen; WANG Hong-yu; A heuristic procedure of master production scheduling for balanced and optimized utilization of bottleneck capacities[J];Journal of Harbin Institute of Technology;2009-01-019

[3] ZHANG Shao-yang~1; WANG Xuan-cang~2; Bottle-neck Identification of Resources in Highway Construction and Its Elimination Methods Based on Petri Nets[J]; Journal of Chang'an University(Natural Science Edition;2006, 26(1);38~42.

[4] Guo Fu; Zhang Guo-jun; Applications of SIMOGRAMS to Resolve the Bottleneck of the Production Line[J]; Industrial Engineering and Management; 2006(6); 107~113.

[5] JIA Chen-hui~1; ZHANG Hao~2; LU Jian-feng~1; Planning and Simulation of Virtual Production System[J]; Modular Machine Tool & Automatic Manufacturing Technique,2006(8): 94~97.

[6] Heinicke, Matthias U.; Hickman, Alan. Eliminate bottlenecks with integrated analysis tools in eM-Plant[J]. Winter Simulation Conference Proceedings, v 1, p 229-231, 2000

[7] SHI Guo-hong; ZHANG Hua; Simulation of human-oriented production systems based on cooperration[J]; Machinery Design & Manufacture,2005 (1): 88~90.

[8] JIA Guo-zhu; Optimized Method of Petri Net Modeling and Simulation for Production Systems[J];Journal of System Simulation , 2006, 18(2): 559~562.

[9] Zhang Yong-yang, Chen You-ling, Qin Cheng-hai, et al. Research on Production Process Model Simulation in Manufacturing Enterprise Based on Petri Nets[C]// Xia Guoping. Proceedings of the 38th International Conference on Computers and Industrial Engineering. Beijing: Publishing House of Electronics Industry, 2008: 1798-1802.

[10] Jiang Zhi-bin. Petri nets and its applications in manufacturing system modeling and control [M]. BeiJing: Mechanical industry press, 2004: 138-157.

[11] Wu Zhe-hui. Petri net introductory theory[M]. BeiJing: Mechanical industry press, 2004: 138-157.

[12] WANG Liya, CHEN Youling, MA Hanwu, et al. Production planning and control[M]. Beijing: Tsinghua University Press, 2007:135-139(in Chinese).

[13] Chen You-ling, ZHANG Yong-yang, QIN Cheng-hai, et al. Production process object model based on Petri nets[J]. Computer Integrated Manufacuring Systems, 2009, 15(6):1075-1080(in Chinese).

[14] Liu C M, Wu F C. Using Petri nets to solve FMS problems[J]. International Journal Computer Integrated Manufacturing, 1993, 6 (3):175-185.

2

Synthesis of Coloured Petri Nets from Natural-like Language Descriptions

Enrique Arjona[1], Graciela Bueno[1] and Ernesto López-Mellado[2]
[1]*Colegio de Postgraduados Campus Montecillo*
[2]*CINVESTAV-IPN Unidad Guadalajara*
México

1. Introduction

Coloured Petri nets (CPN) (Jensen, 1981) have been widely used for the modelling of tasks in flexible manufacturing systems at different levels of functioning (Aized et al., 2007; Da Silva et al., 2008; Diaz, 2009). Since their conception, there have been several attempts to take advantage of the formalism of CPN to adapt them as a universal, discrete-event modelling language by extending their original definition (Jensen, 1991; Yeung et al., 1999; MengChu, 2009). Despite these attempts, however, complex and large-scale models are very hard to build using CPN or their extensions.

In order to ease the modelling of complex systems using Petri nets, some synthesis methods have been proposed, both for ordinary Petri nets (Der Jeng & Di Cesare, 1990; Zhou et al., 1992; He et al., 2000; Badouel & Darondeau, 2004; Zhi-Jun et al., 2008; etc.) and for CPN (Micovsky et al., 1990; Baldassari & Bruno, 1991; Ezpeleta, 1993; Shang et al., 2004; Khadka, 2007; etc.). These methods can be classified into two groups.

The first group (Der Jeng & Di Cesare, 1990; Zhou et al., 1992; Ezpeleta, 1993; He et al., 2000; Badouel & Darondeau, 2004; Khadka, 2007) includes those methods that preserve the formal nature of Petri nets. In order to achieve this, the methods impose restrictions on the type of situations that can be modelled and do not include the indiscriminate use of shared resources and complex ordering and selecting criteria (AND's, OR's, NOT's, and their combinations). Therefore, the range of applicability of the methods is very limited. Der Jeng & Di Cesare (1990) review some representative methods, all of them are of low level and do not allow the modelling of shared resources or the modelling of ordering and selecting criteria. Zhou et al. (1992) present a method that allows the modelling of some particular types of shared resources but does not allow the modelling of ordering and selecting criteria. Ezpeleta (1993) includes a method for the synthesis of models expressed by a restricted class of CPN called simple sequential processes; in this method, ordering and selecting criteria are limited to the use of FIFO policies. The other methods included in this group use an interface to facilitate the modeling of the systems and a fixed catalogue of subnets for the synthesis of the corresponding Petri net; in none of these methods is allowed the modelling of ordering and selecting criteria. He et al. (2000) define manufacturing processes in an interface called IDEF3 (Integrated Definition 3) and transform the model obtained to a Petri net using a sequential cluster identification algorithm. Badouel & Darondeau (2004) establish relations that the system to model has with a predefined set of

paths and use a bijection to construct a Petri net of the system. Khadka (2007) uses a sequence chart to represent the system and transforms the chart to a CPN using a tool called LSCTOCPN (Live Sequence Charts to CPN).
The second group (Micovsky et al., 1990; Baldassari & Bruno, 1991; Shang et al., 2004; Zhi-Jun et al., 2008) comprises those methods that do not preserve the nature of Petri nets. They use Petri net extensions that include facilities of procedural nature that allow great flexibility with respect to the situations that can be modelled, but the models obtained cannot be formally analyzed because these models are hybrids composed of subnets and/or computer procedures. Micovsky et al. (1990) propose a method that uses modified CPN that are interpreted using a proprietary language called DOOR that is implemented in a TPL (typeless procedural language); the programs obtained are used as input of a simulator. Baldassari & Bruno (1991) present a method that obtains computer programs to the situations that can be modelled, but the models obtained cannot be formally analyzed because these models are hybrids composed of modified CPN subnets called PROT nets and computer object-oriented concepts. Shang et al. (2004) synthesize system behavioural specifications into a mixture of labeled Petri nets and CPN. Finally, Zhi-Jun et al. (2008) present a method to combine existing web service models and synthesize them into a mixture of control flow nets and Petri nets.
This chapter presents a method of synthesis of CPN for the formal specification of simple and complex tasks in flexible manufacturing systems. The method differs significantly from other published methods in that it preserves the formalism of CPN without imposing restrictions on the system modelled, and therefore it allows the modelling of shared resources and complex ordering and selecting criteria. The proposed method allows one to systematically obtain CPN models from declarative descriptions of a very high level of abstraction. These descriptions are activity models (ABAM) expressed in a natural-like language. The language is not extensive and it is easy to master. In the language, the stochastic occurrence of many events is implicitly embedded in exogenous and endogenous variable conditions, and material and resource flows can be easily modelled using a single flow statement. ABAM are built using the activity-based approach, a non formal modelling tool for discrete event systems, which has proven to be valuable for the modelling of complex systems and also to be user friendly, to such an extent that some event- and process-based simulation languages have input interfaces that use this approach.
The CPN generated can be structurally validated, analyzed, and used for control or simulation.
The remainder of the chapter is divided in 6 sections and an appendix. Section 2 is a brief account of similarities and differences between ABAM and CPN. Section 3 presents basic support modules for the CPN synthesis and the mathematical proofs of their validity. Section 4 discusses the main features of the natural-like language. Section 5 gives an outline of the proposed method to build CPN. Section 6 illustrates the synthesis method through an example of an automotive workshop, its complete specification in the natural-like language and the CPN synthesized. Section 7 discusses some conclusions. Finally, an appendix includes the formal grammar of the language.

2. ABAM and CPN

Formally, both ABAM and CPN can be defined as directed bipartite graphs (Jensen, 1981; Kreutzer, 1986) that include two kinds of nodes (ABAM have activities and waiting lines,

CPN have places and transitions), sets of objects associated to those nodes (admissible entities in the case of ABAM, colours in the case CPN), input and output functions, and time functions (these are included only in temporized models). Pictorially, nodes are represented with circles and rectangles and functions as directed arcs that have associated symbolic expressions (see figs. 1 and 4).

At first glance it may appear that by associating waiting lines to places and activities to transitions ABAM and CPN are equivalent, nevertheless there are fundamental differences between them. (1) The expressive power (level of abstraction) of CPN is lower than that of ABAM because the former does not allow all kinds of input and output functions. (2) Transitions in CPN may represent events or activities, depending on the interpretation of the model. (3) In CPN there is no explicit association of objects to colours. (4) When the CPN definition includes time, temporization can be carried out indistinctly in the places or in the transitions. (5) Input and output functions in CPN are always expressed in mathematical and not in declarative form (despite the fact that functions in a CPN can be temporarily stated in declarative form, they must be able to be expressed as linear functions).

3. Modules for CPN synthesis

As was stated before, CPN definition does not allow for direct specification of all kinds of input and output functions. To facilitate the building of CPN, for systems where complex situations arise, a bottom-up synthesis process is proposed. CPN models are built using a set of CPN predefined modules, each one of them representing a particular situation. Predefined modules can be embedded between them to represent two or more particular situations simultaneously.

To determine a partition of the situations that can arise when modelling discrete event systems with CPN, and thus define the necessary modules for the synthesis, we performed an analysis of the models that can be obtained using the activity-based approach. This does not impose any restrictions because if on the one hand we cannot assume that in general ABAM are CPN, the reverse is true. Complex situations in CPN arise when we try to associate ordering criteria to places and individual or multiple selecting criteria to input-output functions of transitions (for example, when we want to include in a CPN an input function that has priorities in the selection of colours, and the number of these is not fixed but variable).

In total, 13 CPN modules were defined for the synthesis process, and their validity was proved using induction. Two of the simplest modules are the CPN that correspond to a FIFO and a LIFO waiting lines. Their pictorial representations are given in figs. 1 and 2.

Figure 1 depicts a CPN module that simulates a FIFO ordering of entities in a place P that has a capacity of n. Transitions TIN and TOUT are used to store/remove entities in/from the place. Transition TMOVE is used to move entities in the place. The colour sets used in the module are:

$E = \{ \langle e,i \rangle ; i=1,\ldots,m \}$
$S = \{ \langle s,j \rangle ; j=1,\ldots,n \}$
$ES = E \times S$

Colour set E represents the entity types that can be admitted in the place, colour set S represents numbered spaces in the place, and colour set ES represents entities stored in numbered spaces. The colour sets associated to the place and the transitions are:

$C(P) = ES \cup S$
$C(TIN) = C(TOUT) = E$
$C(TMOVE) = ES - \{ <<e,i>,<s,1>> ; i=1,...,m \}$

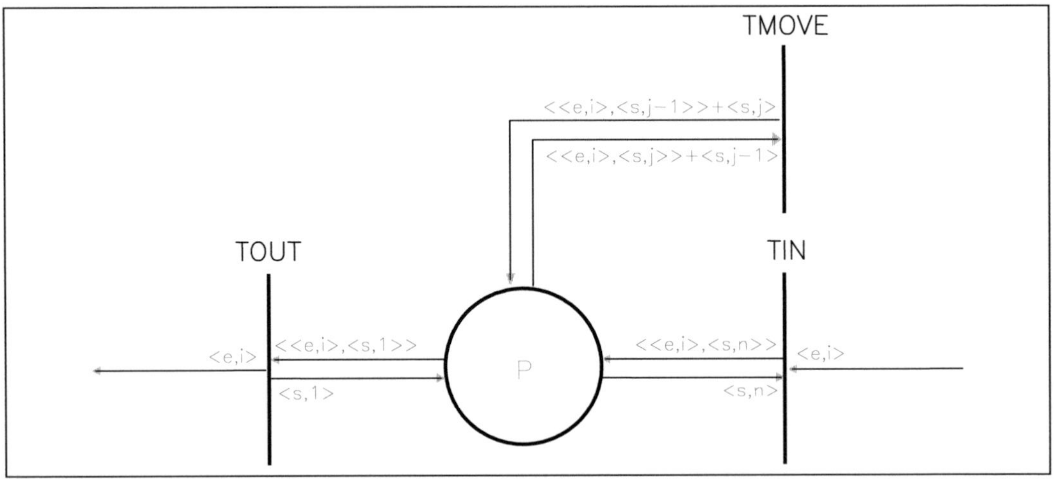

Fig. 1. A CPN module for FIFO ordering of entities in a place

The input/output functions of the transitions are given in Figure 1. Place P must be initialized with a set of n tokens (colour instances) taken from S and ES. All the elements of S that appear in these tokens must be different. That is, all the spaces of the place, occupied or unoccupied, must be included in the initialization. At any moment, the cardinality of the set of tokens in place P is equal to the maximum length of the waiting line.
The module execution is as follows: transition TIN stores an entity in the last position of the place (space n). Transition TMOVE moves an entity from its actual position to the previous one whenever possible. Transition TOUT removes the entity stored in the first position of the place.
A proof of the proper execution of the module using mathematical induction is the following: Assume that the place contains k ($k<n$) ordered entities according to a FIFO criterion, and that an entity arrives and is not properly ordered. This means that the entity was moved by transition TMOVE from the position n to a position p such that $p>k+1$ or $p<=k$. In the first case, transition TMOVE ceased firing in spite that the position p-1 was empty (by the induction hypothesis only the first k positions were occupied and $p-1>k$). In the second case, transition TMOVE moved the arriving entity to an occupied position (by the induction hypothesis first k positions were occupied and $p<=k$). Both cases lead to contradictions because transition TMOVE moves an entity if, and only if, the previous position is empty.
Figure 2 depicts a CPN module that simulates a LIFO ordering of entities in a place P that has a capacity of n. Transitions TIN and TOUT are used to store/remove entities in/from the place. Transition TMOVE is used to move entities in the place. The colour sets used in the module are:

$E = \{ <e,i> ; i=1,...,m \}$
$S = \{ <s,j> ; j=1,...,n \}$
$DS= \{ <s,n+1> \}$
$ES = E \times S$

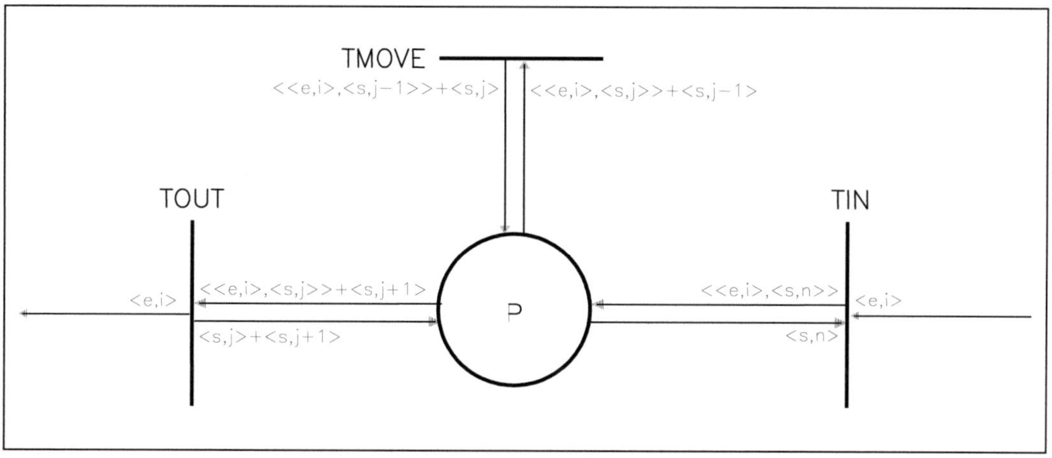

Fig. 2. A CPN module for LIFO ordering of entities in a place

Colour set E represents the entity types that can be admitted in the place, colour set S represents numbered spaces in the place, and colour set ES represents entities stored in numbered spaces. Colour set DS represents a dummy extra space used by transition TOUT when the place is full. The colour sets associated to the place and the transitions are:

$C(P) = ES \cup S \cup DS$
C(TIN) = C(TOUT) = E
C(TMOVE) = ES - { <<e,i>,<s,1>> ; i=1,...,m }

The input/output functions of the transitions are given in Figure 2. Place P must be initialized with a set of n+1 tokens. One token is taken from DS. The other n tokens are taken from S and ES. All the elements of S that appear in these n tokens must be different. That is, all the spaces of the place, including the dummy space, must be included in the initialization. At any moment, the cardinality of the set of tokens in place P is equal to the maximum length of the waiting line plus one.

The module execution is as follows: Transition TIN stores an entity in the last position of the place (space n). Transition TMOVE moves an entity from its actual position to the previous one whenever possible. Transition TOUT takes the entity stored in the last non-empty position of the place. This entity is easily recognized because the position next to it is always empty, even when the place is full. In this case, the empty position is the dummy space. Note that priority of transition TMOVE must be higher than the priority of transition TOUT. The proof of the proper execution of the module is similar to the proof given for the FIFO module.

The other modules deal with more complex situations, namely ascendant/descendent ordering criteria with respect to a given attribute, extraction of m items, contained from position i, of a n-position waiting line ($0 \le i \le n - m; m \le n; m$ predefined or variable), and accessing of a specific position of a FIFO/LIFO waiting line. In (Arjona & Bueno, 2007) are included two of the CPN modules for the modelling of complex selecting criteria (the selection of a constant and a variable number of entities from a set of places), mathematical proofs of their validity, and an example of their application to a real life simulation model of a sugarcane plantation.

4. Specification of models in a natural-like language

The specification of a model in the natural-like language consists of definition of entities, waiting lines, variables, and activities. Definition of entities and variables can include attributes, and definition of waiting lines can include ordering criteria. Activity definitions consist of the specification of starting and ending conditions, flows, and attribute modifications. Besides declarations, the language only uses two types of statements: the first one is for flow specifications and the second one for explicit state change specifications when events occur. These statements can model all individual and multiple flows mentioned in the preceding section.

Although the purpose of the natural-like language developed was to model flexible manufacturing systems, as a matter of fact, it is domain independent and was designed taking into consideration all kinds of possible material and resource flows in discrete event systems. This proved to be very useful for modelling very complex situations in real systems. In the appendix it is included the complete formal grammar of the language with an explanation of the symbols used to define it. In section 6 it is included an example of the language usage.

5. CPN synthesis from models specified in a natural-like language

The CPN modules and the natural-like language mentioned above have been utilized as the basis of a method for CPN synthesis. In this method, instead of using a bottom-up approach as before, a top-down technique is utilized. The CPN are synthesized by successive refinements of analysis of ABAM specified in the language.

The CPN synthesis process comprises six steps. The first five steps do not take into consideration complex situations in the input model and determine successively the place set, transition set, place set, transition colour set, and input and output functions. The sixth step performs refinements to the CPN already obtained in order to take into account complex situations.

Step 1. *Determination of the Place Set.* For the determination of the place set, entities and their attribute values in the input model are analyzed. There will be as many places as different states of the entities are actually used in the activities of the model. This avoids, to the extent possible, combinatorial explosion of the number of places and comprises a reduction process that unifies states, makes implicit some information (information that is not fundamental for the real-time execution of the model), and eliminates superfluous information (entities and attribute values that were defined but never used in the activities).

In the reduction process, entities and attributes are classified internally according to their use in the input model. Entities can be individual or multiple, depending on whether they represent a single resource of the system or a set of resources that have some logical or physical association. Attributes can be of constant or variable value. Attributes of constant value distinguish only members of the same family of resources and never represent the state of an entity. Attributes of variable value can be used to indicate contents, position, or physical characteristics. Attributes that indicate contents, independently of their values, can represent only two states of the entity to which they belong. Other attributes of variable value can represent as many states as values of the former are used in the activities. The number of places corresponding to an entity will be the product of the number of states that its attributes represent. When an entity has no attributes, it will be modelled with one place that represents its availability.

Step 2. *Determination of the Transition Set.* Transitions in a CPN correspond to state changes, and therefore there will be one transition in the transition set for each possible configuration of the system that allows the start of an activity. The number of input places of the transition will be the number of concurrent entities that the activity requires to start. The number of output places of the transition will be the number of entities that go out from the activity when it ends.

Step 3. *Determination of the Place Colour Set.* Because places represent a state of an entity, the colour set associated to a place will take into consideration only attributes of constant value, or of variable value that indicate contents and whose values are not uniquely represented by the state of the entity. The colour set consists of n-tuples with as many components as attributes of these types the entity has defined.

Step 4. *Determination of the Transition Colour Set.* The number of ways in which a transition can be fired depends on the different colours admissible in its input places. Therefore, the colour set associated to a transition will be the set of the n first natural numbers where n is the maximum of the cardinalities of the colour sets of its input places.

Step 5. *Determination of the Input and Output Functions.* Input (output) functions of a transition are the sum of individual functions associated to its input (output) places. The individual function of a place is the composition of two functions: the first one maps the set of colours of the place with the set of colours of the transition, and the second one determines which colours of the place are taken for each colour of the transition.

Step 6. *Refinements to Include Complex Situations.* In the last step of the synthesis process, complex situations in the input model are analyzed and the CPN already obtained is refined by introducing, one by one, the necessary modules. These refinements do not change the basic properties of the net, and its analysis can be done before this step is performed.

6. An example of CPN synthesis

Next, an example of the application of the synthesis process is included; it is taken from (Colom et al., 1990), where a CPN model is presented. The system considered is a puttying car body workshop designed and operated by a European automobile firm, whose layout is depicted in fig. 3.

The workshop has 12 working posts divided into two groups of 6. There is a conveying system that consists of roller tables where each table can contain one car body. Roller tables RT only convey. Roller tables TT in front of stations, in addition to conveying, rotate for loading and unloading. Roller tables ST, in addition to conveying, can also slide and allow distribution between groups of tables. A working post consists of three tables, one for loading (LT), one for processing (puttying) (PT), and one for unloading (UT). Loading and unloading tables in each workstation are integrated in a sliding bench that changes position for loading and unloading. At any moment a workstation can contain at most two car bodies. Car bodies in the conveying system have assigned the workstation number where they will be processed.

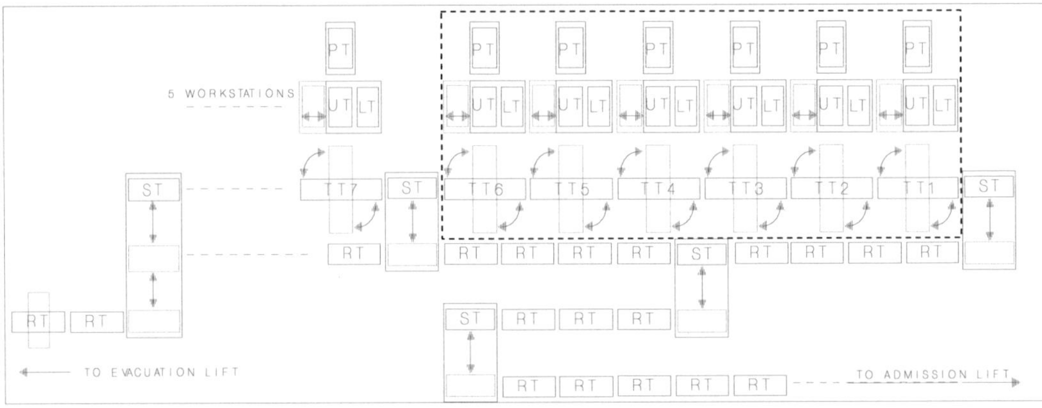

Fig. 3. Workshop layout

In this example, we consider only the section in the dashed rectangle. In general, the model will work as follows: car bodies arrive at the section on roller table number 1. Upon arrival, a pass with a number that corresponds to the workstation where it will be processed is assigned to the car body (in the complete model, passes are assigned elsewhere outside the section). Car bodies are moved from one roller table to the next until they arrive at the workstation to which they have been assigned. Upon arrival, they are transferred successively to the loading, processing, and unloading tables of the workstation, and again to the roller table in front of the workstation. After this, the car bodies will be moved from one roller table to the next until they arrive at roller table number 6, from where they leave the section.

An activity-based approach input model is depicted in fig. 4; it consists of three entities, three waiting lines, and seven activities. Entities considered are: passes (PASS AV), with one attribute that represents their number (its admissible values are integers from 1 to 6); roller tables (RT) with two attributes, the first represents its number (its admissible values are integers from 1 to 6) and the second the workstation number where the car body on the roller table will be or was processed and that we will call body destination (its admissible values are integers from -6 to 6, zero indicates that a roller table is free and a negative number that the body has already been processed); and workstations (WS) with four attributes, the first representing its number (its admissible values are integers from 1 to 6) and the others the states of its loading, processing, and unloading tables (its admissible values are integers 0 or 1). The bodies were not considered entities because the passes are sufficient to represent them. Also, the numbers of the passes were not considered in the attributes of the workstations because, as was stated above, pass numbers always coincide with the number of the workstations where the bodies are processed.

The waiting lines correspond to the inactive states of the entities and are: available passes, inactive roller tables, and workstation pool.

The activities are: body arrival (BA), body conveyance (BC), load from roller table (LFRT), load from loading table (LFLT), unload from processing table (UFPT), unload from unloading table (UFUT), and body leaving (BL). Following it is given the complete description of the model in the natural-like language.

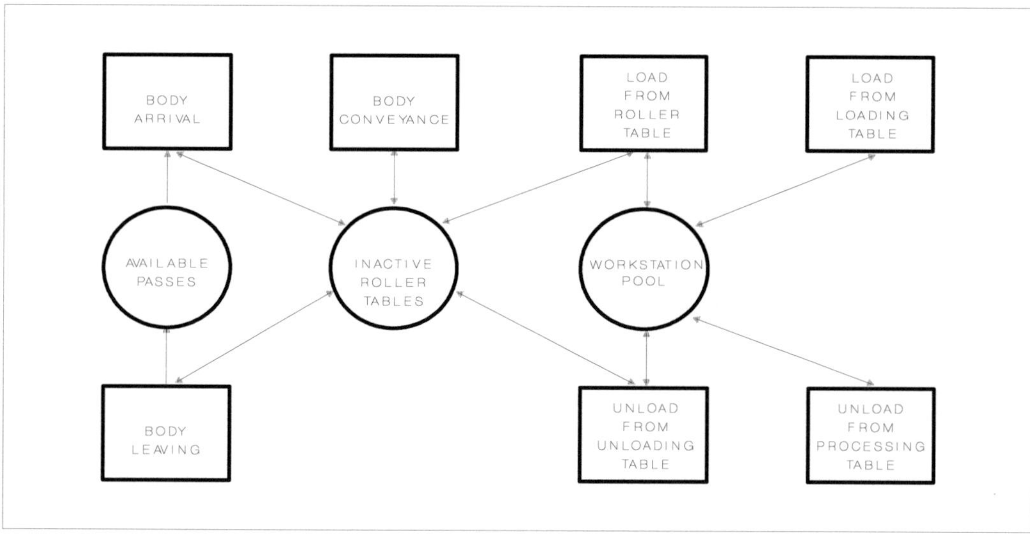

Fig. 4. Activity model of the workshop

MODEL NAME:
  AUTOMOTIVE_WORKSHOP.
ENTITIES:
  PASS WITH THE FOLLOWING ATTRIBUTES:
    NUMBER (ADMISSIBLE VALUES 1 TO 6).
  ROLLER_TABLE WITH THE FOLLOWING ATTRIBUTES:
    NUMBER (ADMISSIBLE VALUES 1 TO 6)
    BODY_DESTINATION (ADMISSIBLE VALUES -6 TO 6).
  WORKSTATION WITH THE FOLLOWING ATTRIBUTES:
    NUMBER (ADMISSIBLE VALUES 1 TO 6)
    STATE_OF_LOADING_TABLE (ADMISSIBLE VALUES 0 TO 1)
    STATE_OF_PROCESSING_TABLE (ADMISSIBLE VALUES 0 TO 1)
    STATE_OF_UNLOADING_TABLE (ADMISSIBLE VALUES 0 TO 1).
WAITING LINES:
  AVAILABLE_PASSES CONTAINS PASSES.
  INACTIVE_ROLLER_TABLES CONTAINS ROLLER TABLES.
  WORKSTATION_POOL CONTAINS WORKSTATIONS.
EXTERNAL VARIABLES:
  START_OF_BODY_CONVEYANCE.
  END_OF_BODY_CONVEYANCE.
  START_OF_LOAD_FROM_ROLLER_TABLE.
  END_OF_LOAD_FROM_ROLLER_TABLE.
  START_OF_LOAD_FROM_LOADING_TABLE.
  END_OF_LOAD_FROM_LOADING_TABLE
  START_OF_UNLOAD_FROM_PROCESSING_TABLE.
  END_OF_ UNLOAD_FROM_PROCESSING_TABLE.
  START_OF_UNLOAD_FROM_UNLOADING_TABLE.
  END_OF_UNLOAD_FROM_UNLOADING_TABLE.

```
  START_OF_BODY_LEAVING.
  END_OF_BODY_LEAVING.
ACTIVITY:
  BODY_ARRIVAL.
 ENTITY FLOWS:
  GET A PASS FROM AVAILABLE_PASSES.
  GET A ROLLER_TABLE WITH NUMBER=1 AND BODY_DESTINATION=0
   FROM INACTIVE_ROLLER_TABLES AND AT END OF ACTIVITY PUT BACK
   IN INACTIVE_ROLLER_TABLES.
 ATTRIBUTE MODIFICATIONS:
  BODY_DESTINATION OF ROLLER_TABLE := NUMBER OF PASS.
ACTIVITY:
  BODY_CONVEYANCE.
 ENDING_CONDITIONS:
  END_OF_BODY_CONVEYANCE=1.
 ENTITY FLOWS ( 1 OF THE FOLLOWING FLOWS):
  GET A ROLLER_TABLE WITH BODY_DESTINATION >=
   NUMBER OF ROLLER_TABLE FROM INACTIVE_ROLLER_TABLES AND
   AT END OF ACTIVITY PUT BACK IN INACTIVE_ROLLER_TABLES.
  GET A ROLLER_TABLE WITH BODY_DESTINATION < 0
   FROM INACTIVE_ROLLER_TABLES AND AT END OF ACTIVITY PUT BACK
   IN INACTIVE_ROLLER_TABLES.
 ENTITY FLOWS:
  GET A ROLLER_TABLE WITH NUMBER = NUMBER OF
   ROLLER_TABLE (#1) + 1 AND BODY_DESTINATION = 0
   FROM INACTIVE_ROLLER_TABLES AND AT END OF ACTIVITY
   PUT BACK IN INACTIVE_ROLLER_TABLES.
 ATTRIBUTE MODIFICATIONS:
  START_OF_BODY_CONVEYANCE := 1.
  BODY_DESTINATION OF ROLLER TABLE (#2) :=
   BODY_DESTINATION OF ROLLER TABLE (#1).
  BODY_DESTINATION OF ROLLER TABLE (#1) := 0.
ACTIVITY:
  LOAD_FROM_ROLLER_TABLE.
 ENDING_CONDITIONS:
  END_OF_LOAD_FROM_ROLLER_TABLE=1.
 ENTITY FLOWS (SELECTING BODY_DESTINATION OF ROLLER_TABLE IN
   INACTIVE_ROLLER_TABLES = NUMBER OF WORKSTATION IN
   WORKSTATION_POOL) :
  GET A ROLLER_TABLE FROM INACTIVE_ROLLER_TABLES AND
   AT END OF ACTIVITY PUT BACK IN INACTIVE_ROLLER_TABLES.
  GET A WORKSTATION WITH STATE_OF_LOADING_TABLE = 0 AND
   STATE_OF_LOADING_TABLE + STATE_OF_PROCESSING_TABLE +
   STATE_OF_UNLOADING_TABLE <= 1 FROM WORKSTATION_POOL AND AT
   END OF ACTIVITY PUT BACK IN WORKSTATION_POOL.
 ATTRIBUTE MODIFICATIONS:
```

```
  START_OF_LOAD_FROM_ROLLER_TABLE := 1.
  STATE_OF_LOADING_TABLE OF WORKSTATION := 1.
  BODY_DESTINATION OF ROLLER_TABLE := 0.
ACTIVITY:
  LOAD_FROM_LOADING_TABLE.
 ENDING_CONDITIONS:
  END_OF_LOAD_FROM_LOADING_TABLE=1.
 ENTITY FLOWS:
  GET A WORKSTATION WITH STATE_OF_PROCESSING_TABLE = 0
   AND STATE_OF_LOADING_TABLE = 1 FROM WORKSTATION_POOL
   AND AT END OF ACTIVITY PUT BACK IN WORKSTATION_POOL.
 ATTRIBUTE MODIFICATIONS:
   START_OF_LOAD_FROM_LOADING_TABLE := 1.
   STATE_OF_LOADING_TABLE OF WORKSTATION := 0.
   STATE_OF_PROCESSING_TABLE OF WORKSTATION := 1.
ACTIVITY:
  UNLOAD_FROM_PROCESSING_TABLE.
 ENDING_CONDITIONS:
  END_OF_UNLOAD_FROM_PROCESSING_TABLE=1.
 ENTITY FLOWS:
  GET A WORKSTATION WITH STATE_OF_PROCESSING_TABLE = 1
   AND STATE_OF_UNLOADING_TABLE = 0 FROM WORKSTATION_POOL
   AND AT END OF ACTIVITY PUT BACK IN WORKSTATION_POOL.
 ATTRIBUTE MODIFICATIONS:
  START_OF_UNLOAD_FROM_PROCESSING_TABLE := 1.
  STATE_OF_PROCESSING_TABLE OF WORKSTATION := 0.
  STATE_OF_UNLOADING_TABLE OF WORKSTATION := 1.
ACTIVITY:
  UNLOAD_FROM_UNLOADING_TABLE.
 ENDING_CONDITIONS:
  END_OF_UNLOAD_FROM_UNLOADING_TABLE=1.
 ENTITY FLOWS:
  GET A WORKSTATION WITH STATE_OF_UNLOADING_TABLE = 1
   FROM WORKSTATION_POOL AND AT END OF ACTIVITY
   PUT BACK IN WORKSTATION_POOL.
  GET A ROLLER_TABLE WITH NUMBER = NUMBER OF
   WORKSTATION AND BODY_DESTINATION = 0
   FROM INACTIVE_ROLLER_TABLES AND AT END OF ACTIVITY
   PUT  BACK IN INACTIVE_ROLLER_TABLES.
 ATTRIBUTE MODIFICATIONS:
   START_OF_UNLOAD_FROM_UNLOADING_TABLE := 1.
   STATE_OF_UNLOADING_TABLE OF WORKSTATION := 0.
   BODY_DESTINATION OF ROLLER_TABLE := - NUMBER OF WORKSTATION.
ACTIVITY:
 BODY_LEAVING.
 ENDING_CONDITIONS:
```

END_OF_BODY_LEAVING=1.
ENTITY FLOWS:
GET A ROLLER_TABLE WITH NUMBER=6 AND BODY_DESTINATION < 0
FROM INACTIVE_ROLLER_TABLES AND AT END OF ACTIVITY PUT BACK
IN INACTIVE_ROLLER_TABLES.
AT END OF ACTIVITY PUT A PASS IN AVAILABLE_PASSES.
ATTRIBUTE MODIFICATIONS:
END_OF_BODY_LEAVING :=1.
NUMBER OF PASS := - BODY_DESTINATION OF ROLLER_TABLE.
BODY_DESTINATION OF ROLLER_TABLE := 0.
END OF MODEL.

Figs. 5 to 8 depict the synthesis process of a CPN corresponding to the above model.
The result of step 1 is shown in fig. 5. The place set includes only one place for the passes because its only attribute is of constant value.

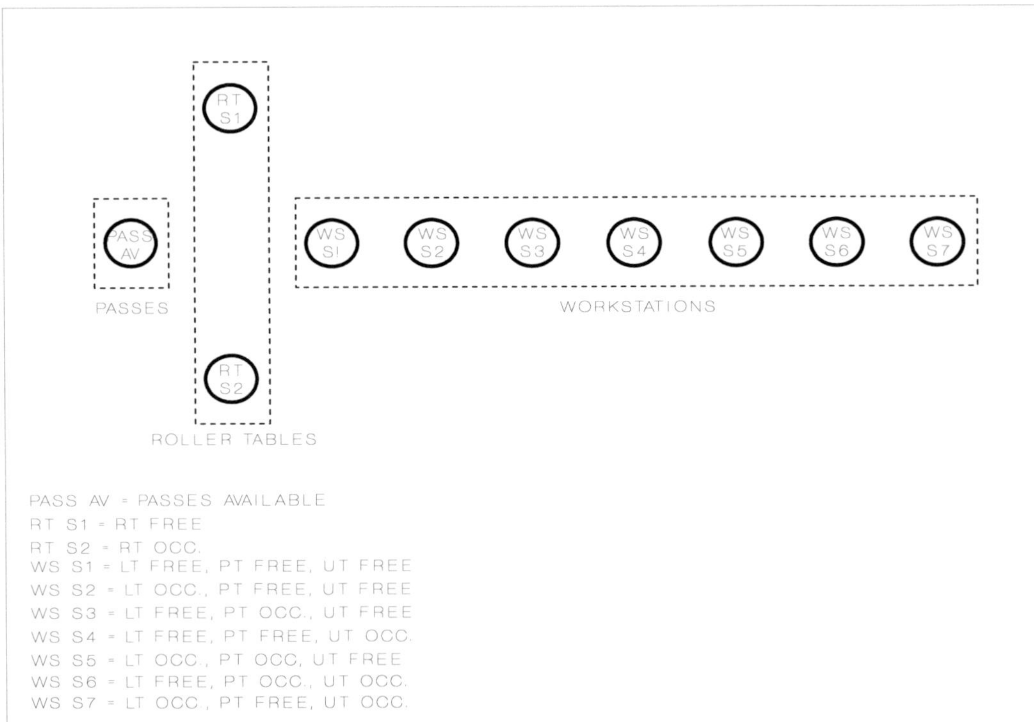

Fig. 5. Place set generated

Only two places were included for the roller tables because, in spite of the fact that the attribute corresponding to body destination can take 13 values, the roller table can only be in two states: free (RT S1) or occupied (RT S2). Workstations have seven different states (WS S1 to WS S7).
Fig. 6 depicts the transition sets corresponding to each one of the activities (step 2). There is one transition for each valid configuration of the system that allows the start of an activity. For example, activity LFRT is represented by the transitions LFRT1, LFRT2 and LFRT3.

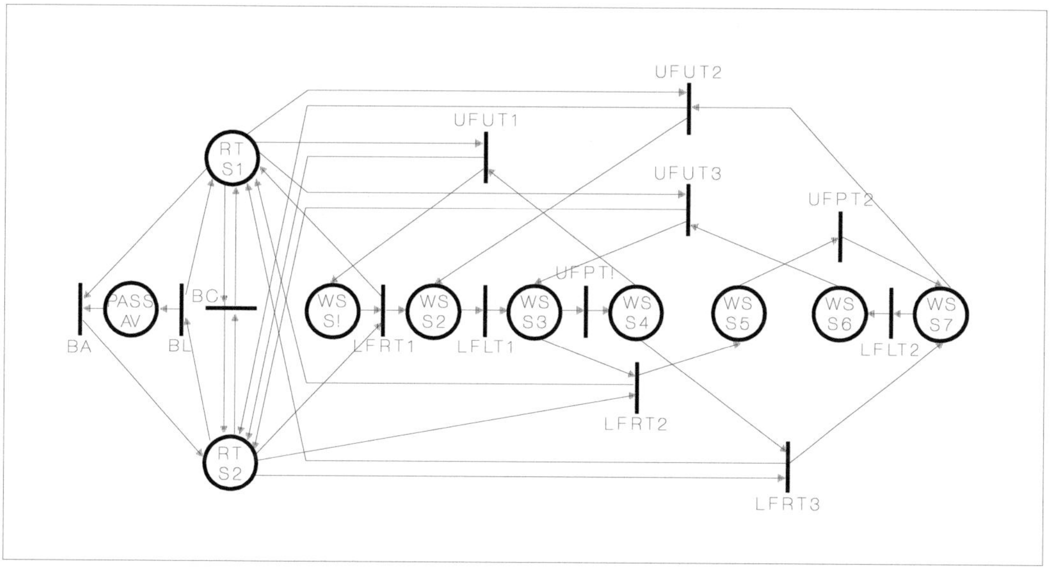

Fig. 6. Transition set generated by all activities

Fig. 7 summarizes the place and the transition colour sets (steps 3 and 4). First 10 colour sets correspond to places. All the places except one, the one corresponding to a roller table in an occupied state, have simple colours assigned because the values of the entity-variable attributes are uniquely determined by the states that the places represent. All the transitions have simple colours except transition BC that can fire in 36 different ways.

```
C(PASS AV)={<i>} i=1,…,6
C(RT S1)={<i>} i=1,…,6
C(RT S2)={<i,j>} i=1,…,6; j=1,…,6
C(WS S1)={<i>} i=1,…,6
C(WS S2)={<i>} i=1,…,6
C(WS S3)={<i>} i=1,…,6
C(WS S4)={<i>} i=1,…,6
C(WS S5)={<i>} i=1,…,6
C(WS S6)={<i>} i=1,…,6
C(WS S7)={<i>} i=1,…,6
C(BA)={<i>} i=1,…,6
C(BL)={<i>} i=1,…,6
C(BC)={<I,j>} i=1,…,6; j=1,…,6
C(LFRT1)={<i>} i=1,…,6
C(LFRT2)={<i>} i=1,…,6
C(LFRT3)={<i>} i=1,…,6
C(LFLT1)={<i>} i=1,…,6
C(LFLT2)={<i>} i=1,…,6
C(UFPT1)={<i>} i=1,…,6
C(UFPT2)={<i>} i=1,…,6
C(UFUT1)={<i>} i=1,…,6
C(UFUT2)={<i>} i=1,…,6
C(UFUT3)={<i>} i=1,…,6
```

Fig. 7. Associated colours sets to places and transitions

Fig. 8 depicts the input and output functions (step 5). Because many of the colour sets of the transitions coincide with the colour sets of their input places, many of the functions are identity functions. Identity functions are represented by dashed arcs.

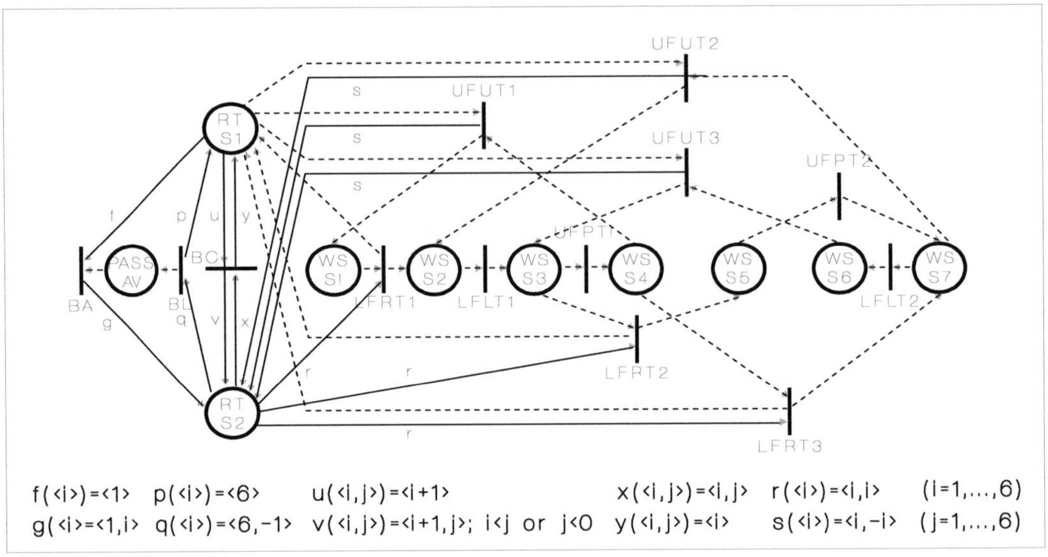

Fig. 8. Input-output functions generated

Function f takes from place RT SI the token that corresponds to roller table 1. Function g puts in place RT S2 a token that corresponds to roller table 1 occupied with a car body.
The body destination was taken by transition BA from place PASS AV (passes available). Functions *x* and u take from places RT S2 and RT SI, respectively, tokens corresponding to two consecutive roller tables, the first one occupied and the second one free. Functions y and v put tokens corresponding to those roller tables, but with the first one free and the second occupied, in places RT SI and RT S2, respectively. Function r, used in transitions corresponding to activity loading from roller table, takes from place RT S2 a token corresponding to a roller table whose number and body destination coincide. Function s, used in transitions corresponding to activity unloading from roller table, puts in place RT S2 a token corresponding to a roller table with a car body just processed, that is, the number of the roller table is the opposite of its body destination. In this example complex situations are not present in the input model, and therefore refinements (step 6) were not made to the net of fig. 8. This model is very close to that presented in (Colom et al., 1990), from where the real-life example is taken, but the functions of this model are simpler than those obtained by Colom.

7. Conclusion

A synthesis method for CPN was presented, a top-down technique in which the starting specifications of tasks are high-level expressed and predefined CPN modules are utilized. The method differs significantly from other methods published in that it preserves the formalism of CPN without imposing restrictions on the system modelled, and therefore it allows the modelling of shared resources and complex ordering and selecting criteria. The analysis of situations that can occur during the synthesis process is conducted using the philosophy of the activity-based approach for discrete-event systems. Input models of the synthesis process are specified in a natural-like language interface, which greatly facilitates

the expression of situations involving complex manipulations of items in waiting lines. These features also establish an advantage over other published methods.
The predefined modules, which deal with complex situations, are live and bounded; nevertheless the synthesized CPN model must be analyzed with existing mathematical methods for their validation and proof of properties; then it can be used for real-time control and simulation.

8. References

Aized, T., Takahashi, K. & Hagiwara I. (2007). Advanced multiple product flexible manufacturing system modelling using Coloured Petri Net. *Journal of Advanced Computational Intelligence and Intelligent Informatics*. Vol. 11, No. 6, pp. 715-723, ISSN: 1343-0130.

Arjona, E. & Bueno, G. (2007). Using simulation to integrate ordering and complex selecting criteria into Coloured Petri Net Models. *Agrociencia* Vol. 41, No. 8, pp. 883-901, ISSN: 1405-3195.

Badouel, E. & Darondeau, P. (2004). The synthesis of Petri nets from path-automatic specifications. *Information and Computation* Vol. 193, pp. 117-135, ISSN: 0890-5401.

Baldasari, M. & Bruno, G. (1991). PROTOB: an object oriented methodology for developing discrete event dynamic systems. *Computer Languages*, Vol. 16, No. 1, pp. 39-63, ISSN: 0096-0551.

Colom, J.M., Esparza, J., Martinez, J. & Silva, M. (1990). *DEMON: Design methods based on nets*, Esprit Basic Research Action 3148, University of Zaragoza, Spain, June 1990.

Da Silva, A., Montgomery, E. & Lima E. (2008). Flexible manufacturing systems modelling using high level Petri Nets. *Proceedings of ABCM Symposium Series in Mechatronics*, Vol. 3, pp. 405-413.

Der Jeng, M. *&* DiCesare, F. (1990). A review *of* synthesis techniques for Petri nets. *Proc. of the IEEE 2nd. International Conference on Computer Integrated Manufacturing*, pp. 348-355, Troy, NY, May 1990.

Diaz, M. (2009). Petri Nets: Fundamental Models, Verification and Applications, Wiley-ISTE, ISBN: 1848210795.

Ezpeleta, J. (1993). Análisis y síntesis de modelos libres de bloqueos para sistemas concurrentes, doctoral diss., University of Zaragoza, Spain.

He, D.W., Strege, B., Tolle, H. & Kusiak, A. (2000). Decomposition in automatic generation of Petri Nets for manufacturing system control and scheduling. *International Journal of Production Research*, Vol. 38, No. 6, pp. 1437-1457, ISSN: 0020-7543.

Jensen, K. (1981). Coloured Petri nets and the invariant method. *Theoretical Computer Science, Vol. 14*, pp. 317-336, ISSN: 0304-3975.

Jensen, K. (1991). Coloured Petri nets: A high level language for system design and analysis, In: *Lecture Notes in Computer Science, Advances in Petri nets 1990*, G. Rosenberg, Ed., pp. 342-416, Springer-Verlag, ISBN: 978-3-540-53863-9, Berlin.

Khadka, B. (2007). Transformation of live sequence charts to Colored Petri Nets, *masters project report*, University of Massachusetts Dartmouth, USA.

Kreutzer, *W. (1986). System Simulation Programming Styles and Languages*, Addison-Wesley, ISBN: 0-201-12914-0, Reading, MA, USA.

MengChu, Z. (2009). *System modeling and control with resource-oriented Petri Nets*, CRC Press, ISBN: 978-1-4398-0884-9, Boca Raton, FL, USA.

Micovsky, A., Sesera, L., Veishab, *M. &* Albert, M. (1990). TORA: A Petri net based tool for rapid prototyping of FMS control systems. *Computers in Industry, Vol. 15, No. 4,* pp. 279-292, ISSN: 0166-3615.

Shang, D., Burns, F., Koelmans, A., Yakovlev, A. & Xia, F. (2004). Asynchronous system synthesis based on direct mapping using VHDL and Petri nets. *IEE Proceedings Computers and Digital Techniques,* Vol. 151, No. 3, ISSN: 1751-8601.

Yeung, D.S., Shiu, S.C.K. & Tsang, E.C.C. (1999). Modelling flexible manufacturing systems using weighted Fuzzy Coloured Petri Nets. *Journal of Intelligent and Fuzzy Systems,* Vol. 7, No. 2, pp. 137-149, ISSN: 1064-1246.

Zhi-Jun, D., Jun-Li, W & Chang-Jun, J. (2008). An approach for synthesis Petri nets for modeling and verifying composite web service, *Journal of Information Science and Engineering,* Vol. 24, pp. 1309-1328, ISSN: 1016-23.

Zhou, M., DiCesare, F., & Desrochers, A. (1992). A hybrid methodology for synthesis of Petri net models for manufacturing systems. *IEEE Trans. on Robotics and Automation,* Vol. 8, No. 3, pp. 350-361, ISSN: 1042-296X.

Appendix. Formal Grammar of the Language

Before giving the grammar of the language, we will explain the logic behind it, describe the different ways in which its elements can be used, and give some general examples of its use. These examples complement the language features showed in the automotive workshop example given in section 6.

The language was designed analyzing all possible situations that can occur when modeling a real life system using the activity-approach paradigm. As was said before, besides of declarations, the language uses only two types of statements. The first one is used for entity (material and resource) flows and the second one for attribute (state) modifications. Interactive actions are modeled by explicit starting and ending conditions in the activities and these conditions can use both internal and external variables. Only one type of statement is used for entity flows because the number of different ways in which is possible to store, or retrieve, an entity in a waiting line (storage areas, buffers, and queues) is very small. Storing and retrieving depend heavily on the ordering criteria of the waiting lines involved and, excluding nonsense ordering criteria, a waiting line can be ordered in only a few ways. Only one type of statement is used for attribute modifications because the only modifications that attributes are susceptible to are assignments. Flows of entities from waiting lines to activities can be individual or multiple. Individual flows can be unconditional or conditioned to attribute values of entities or to entity positions in waiting lines when these have associated ordering criteria (overriding). Conditions on attribute values can be absolute, relative to attribute values of other entities that already are in the activity, or relative to values of the model variables. Multiple flows consist of a fixed or variable number of individual flows. Priorities can be given to the entities required for a particular activity (alternate flows). Flows of entities from activities to waiting lines can only be individual. Alternate storage waiting lines can be specified based on attribute values of the entities. Also, when the output waiting lines have associated ordering criteria, a position for the storage of an entity can be specified (overriding). Assignments can be conditional or unconditional. Values assigned are the result of the evaluation of expressions that may have as operands attribute names, constants, variable names, and intrinsic and extrinsic functions. One assign statement will affect all similar entities that satisfy the conditions of the statement (implicit repeat). There is an intrinsic function (#) for the counting of entities included in an activity and that meet specific attribute characteristics. This function is of particular importance when using multiple flows with a variable (unknown) number of individual flows.

Specification of a model consists of six parts or sections. In the first section is given the name of the model. In the second section are given the names of the entities and attributes and the admissible values of the attributes. In the third section are given the names of the waiting lines, and their ordering criteria and admissible entities. In sections four and five, are given the names of the internal and external variables of the system. In the sixth section, the activities that make up the system are described. All declarations and statements must end with a point. Declarations are used in all sections, and statements are used only in the sixth section that corresponds to activity descriptions. All the names should start with an alphabetic character and may be followed by a string of alphanumeric or underscore characters. Entities may have or not attributes. Variables are defined in a similar way as entities. Internal variables correspond to endogenous variables and external variables correspond to exogenous or interactive variables. Variables for which admissible values are not specified are assumed boolean whose default admissible values are zero and one. Waiting lines can have an ordering criterion or a length specified. When it is not specified an ordering criterion the waiting line is ordered FIFO. The names of entities allowed in waiting lines can be pluralized to improve readability. Activities can have multiplicity. Activity multiplicity must be evaluated to an integer number that indicates the maximum number of concurrent occurrences of the activity; default multiplicity is one. Starting and ending conditions are boolean expressions that use relational expressions of variables and constants. Ending conditions and activity durations are mutually exclusive. Activity durations can be obtained from random variates using external variables or intrinsic functions. A flow statement may consist of one or more individual entity flows. Each individual flow can be a generator, a transmitter or a consumer of entities. The number of individual flows in a flow statement can be constant or variable. Priorities can be specified between individual flows as well as alternate choices. Entities in a flow can be conditioned by means of their attribute values to a constant or to other entities attribute values, in an absolute or a relative way. In addition, it is possible to override ordering criteria of the waiting lines from where the entities are removed, and it is possible to specify alternate destination waiting lines for the storage of entities. The scope of a flow statement is used to select a subset of a set of individual flows. The cardinality of the subset can be fixed or variable within a range. The selecting option is used to define local relations among entities. Repetition factors condense model specifications when identical flows are used. Many of the words included in the flow statements are optional. Finally, attribute modifications can only consist of a conditional or an unconditional assignment.

Examples of valid entity definitions are the following:

```
ENTITIES:
  CAR WITH THE FOLLOWING ATTRIBUTES:
    MAKE (ADMISSIBLE VALUES FORD OR CHRYSLER)
    PASSENGER_CAPACITY (ADMISSIBLE VALUES 2 TO 5).
  ELEVATOR.
  CRANE.
```

Examples of valid variable definitions are the following:

INTERNAL VARIABLES:
PRODUCT_GENERATED.
EXTERNAL VARIABLES:
USER_ANSWER (ADMISSIBLE VALUES HIGH OR MEDIUM OR LOW).

Examples of valid waiting line definitions are the following:

WAITING LINES:
WAREHOUSE CONTAINS BOXES.
ASSEMBLY_LINE (FIFO) CONTAINS CAR_BODIES AND ITS MAXIMUN LENGHT IS 10.
WAITING_ROOM CONTAINS PATIENTS ON DESCENDING ORDER BY ILLNESS_CONDITION.

Examples of valid starting and ending conditions definitions of activities are:

ACTIVITY:
BEST_QUALITY_CONTROL.
STARTING CONDITIONS:
USER_ANSWER=HIGH.
ACTIVITY DURATION: 3.

ACTIVITY:
DIRECT_ASSEMBLY.
STARTING CONDITIONS:
INFRARED_SENSOR=1.AND.RECOGNITION_TO_BE_DONE=0.
ENDING CONDITIONS:
END_OF_ASSEMBLY=1.

Examples of valid flow statements are the following:

ENTITY FLOWS:
GET A WORKER WITH SKILL>2 FROM CREW.
GET A BIT WITH SIZE=1/2 FROM THE BIT_PALETTE AND AT END OF ACTIVITY PUT BACK IN THE BIT_PALETTE.
AT END OF ACTIVITY PUT A PASS IN AVAILABLE_PASSES.

ENTITY FLOWS (FROM 30 TO 150 OF THE FOLLOWING FLOWS):
(AT MOST 20 TIMES) GET A PASSENGER WITH CLASS=FIRST FROM PASSENGER_LIST AND AT END OF ACTIVITY PUT IN IMMIGRATION_LANE.
(AT MOST 130 TIMES) GET A PASSENGER WITH CLASS=SECOND.OR.CLASS=THIRD FROM PASSENGER_LIST AND AT END OF ACTIVITY PUT IN IMMIGRATION_LANE.

ENTITY FLOWS (SELECTING ASSEMBLY_STATE OF ASSEMBLY_SITE IN ASSEMBLY_TABLE = TYPE_OF_PART OF PART IN STORAGE_TABLE -1):
GET A PART FROM STORAGE_TABLE.
GET AN ASSEMBLY_SITE FROM ASSEMBLY_TABLE AND AT END OF ACTIVITY PUT BACK IN ASSEMBLY_TABLE.

Examples of valid attribute modifications are the following:

ATTRIBUTE MODIFICATIONS:
TOTAL_NUMBER_OF_JOBS := TOTAL_NUMBER_OF_JOBS +1.
JOBS_DONE OF WORKER := JOBS_DONE OF WORKER +1.
COLOR OF CAR := COLOR OF PAINT_ORDER.
IF ASSEMBLY_STATE OF ASSEMBLY_SITE = 4 THEN POSITION OF ROBOT1 := 3.

Now, we will give the definition of the language. A computer language is defined by its formal grammar. A formal grammar defines rules for building syntactically correct sentences in the language. Sentences are made up of strings of characters that are logically combined into grammar elements using grammar rules. Grammar rules are specified by means of productions that state how a grammar element can be composed from other grammar elements. Each production defines a grammar element and has two sides separated by the symbol "::=". The left hand side of the production is the grammar element defined (represented by a nonempty string of characters enclosed in triangular parenthesis) and the right hand side its definition. This definition consists of grammar elements, character strings (letter, digits, keywords, punctuation marks, operators, etc.), and auxiliary symbols with specific meanings (square brackets indicate optional items, three periods indicate that the preceding element can be repeated one or more times, and a vertical bar indicate a choice of items). For example, the productions:

<identifier> ::= <letter> [<letter> | <digit> | _] ...
<letter> ::= A | B | C | D | E | F | G | H | I | J | K | L | M | N | O | P | Q | R | S | T |
U | V | W | X | Y | Z
<digit> ::= 0 | 1 | 2 | 3 | 4 | 5 | 6 | 7 | 8 | 9
<global criterion of ordering> ::= FIFO | LIFO

state that the grammar element called "identifier" is built up using a letter that may be followed by one or more letters or digits or the underscore character, and that the grammar element called "global criterion of ordering" consists of one of the keywords FIFO or LIFO. Note that the grammar elements called "letter" and "digit" used in the first production need to be defined because words or phrases used to represent grammar elements do not have any real meaning until defined.
Following, it is given the formal grammar of the language.

<model>::=MODEL NAME:<model name><period>
<entities definition>
[<internal variables definition>]
[<external variables definition>]
<waiting lines definition>
<activity definition>...
END OF MODEL <period>
<model name> ::= <identifier>
<identifier> ::= <letter> [<letter> | <digit> | _] ...
<letter> ::= A | B | C | D | E | F | G | H | I | J | K | L | M | N | O | P | Q | R | S | T |
U | V | W | X | Y | Z
<digit> ::= 0 | 1 | 2 | 3 | 4 | 5 | 6 | 7 | 8 | 9

```
<period> ::= .
<entities definition> ::= ENTITIES: <entity> <period> [<entity> <period>]...
<entity> ::= <entity name> [WITH THE FOLLOWING ATTRIBUTES: <attributes>]
<entity name> ::= <identifier>
<attributes> ::= <name and admissible values of the attribute>
                 [<name and admissible values of the attribute>]...
<name and admissible values of the attribute> ::= <attribute name> [(<admissible values>)]
<attribute name> ::= <identifier>
<admissible values> ::= [ADMISSIBLE VALUES] <range of values> |
                        [ADMISSIBLE VALUES] <specific values>
<range of values> ::= <integer> TO <integer>
<integer> ::= [+|-] <string of digits>
<string of digits> ::= <digit> [<digit>]...
<specific values> ::= <integer or literal> [OR <integer or literal>]...
<integer or literal> ::= <integer> | <literal>
<literal> ::= <identifier>
<internal variables definition> ::= INTERNAL VARIABLES: <internal variable><period>
                                    [<internal variable> <period>]...
<internal variable> ::= <internal variable name> [(<admissible values>)]
<internal variable name> ::= <identifier>
<external variables definition> ::= EXTERNAL VARIABLES: <external variable> <period>
                                    [<external variable> <period>]...
<external variable> ::= <external variable name> [(<admissible values>)]
<external variable name> ::= <identifier>
<waiting lines definition>::= WAITING LINES: <waiting line> <period> [<waiting line>
                              <period>]...
<waiting line> ::= <waiting line name>
                   [(<global criterion of ordering>)]
                   CONTAINS <admissible entity> [AND <admissible entity>]...
                   [AND ITS MAXIMUM LENGTH IS <integer>]
<waiting line name> ::= <identifier>
<global criterion of ordering> ::= FIFO | LIFO
<admissible entity> ::= <pluralized entity name> [<local criterion of ordering> BY
                        <attribute name>]
<pluralized entity name> ::= <entity name> [S | ES]
<local criterion of ordering> ::= ON ASCENDING ORDER | ON DESCENDING ORDER
<activity definition> ::= ACTIVITY: <activity name> <period>
                          [MULTIPLICITY: <expression of variables> <period>]
                          [STARTING CONDITIONS: <condition of variables> <period>]
                          [ENDING CONDITIONS: <condition of variables> <period>]
                          <flow statement> <period> [<flow statement> <period>]...
                          [<attribute modifications>]
                          [ACTIVITY DURATION: <expression of variables> <period>]
<activity name> ::= <identifier>
<condition of variables> ::= <boolean term of variables>
                             [.AND.<boolean term of variables>]
```

```
<boolean term of variables> ::= <boolean factor of variables>
                                [.OR.<boolean factor of variables>]
<boolean factor of variables> ::= <relation of variables> | (<condition of variables>)
<relation of variables> ::= <expression of variables> <relational operator>
                            <expression of variables>
<expression of variables> ::= <term of variables>
                              [+<term of variables> | -<term of variables>]
<term of  variables> ::= <factor of variables>
                         [*<factor of variables> | /<factor of variables>]
<factor of variables> ::= <atom of variables> | <factor of variables> @ <atom of variables>
<atom of variables> ::= <constant> |
                        <internal variable name> |
                        <external variable name> |
                        <function of variables> |
                        (<expression of variables>)
<relational operator> ::= > | < | = | <> | >= | <=
<constant> ::= <integer number> | [+|-].<string of digits> |
               <integer number>.<string of digits> | <literal>
<function of variables> ::= <function name> (<expression of variables>)
<function name> ::= <identifier>
<flow statement> ::= ENTITY FLOWS
                     [(<scope and select condition>)]:
                     <flow specification>...
<scope and select condition> ::= <scope> |<scope> <select condition> | <select condition>
<scope> ::= [ONLY] <expression> OF THE FOLLOWING FLOWS |
            FROM <expression> TO <expression> OF THE FOLLOWING FLOWS
<select condition> ::= SELECTING <relation of entities>
                       [AND <relation of entities>]...
<relation of entities> ::= <expression of entities> <relational operator>
                           <expression of entities>
<expression of entities> ::= <term of entities> [+<term of entities> |-<term of entities>]
<term of entities> ::= <factor of entities> [*<factor of entities> | /<factor of entities>]
<factor of entities> ::= <atom of entities> | <factor of entities> @ <atom of entities>
<atom of entities> ::= <constant> |  <attribute name> OF <entity name>
                       IN <waiting line name>
<flow specification> ::= [<repetition factor>] [IF <condition>] <flow>
<repetition factor> ::= ([AT MOST] <expression> TIMES)
<condition> ::= <boolean term> [.AND. <boolean term>]
<boolean term> ::= <boolean factor> [.OR. <boolean factor>]
<boolean factor> ::= <relation> | (<condition>)
<relation> ::= <expression> <relational operator> <expression>
<expression> ::= <term> [+<term> | -<term>]
<term> ::= <factor> [*<factor> | /<factor>]
<factor> ::= <atom> | <factor> @ <atom>
<atom> ::= <constant> |
           <internal variable name> |
```

```
                <external variable name> |
                <number of entities> |
                <entity attribute> |
                <function> |
                (<expression>)
<number of entities> ::= # <pluralized entity name> [WITH <entity condition>]
<entity condition> ::= <expression of attributes> <relational operator> <expression> [AND
                       <expression of attributes> <relational operator> <expression>]... |
                       (<entity condition>)
<expression of attributes> ::= <term of attributes> [+<term of attributes> |
                               -<term of attributes>]
<term of attributes> ::= <factor of attributes>
                         [*<factor of attributes> | /<factor of attributes>]
<factor of attributes> ::= <atom of attributes> | <factor of attributes> @ <atom of attributes>
<atom of attributes> ::= <constant> | <attribute name>
<entity attribute> ::= <attribute name> OF <entity name> [(# <string of digits>)]
<function> ::= <function name> (<expression>)
<flow> ::= <consumption flow> | <transmission flow> | <generation flow>
<consumption flow> ::= <input flow> <period>
<input flow> ::= GET [A | AN] <entity name>[WITH <entity condition>]
                 FROM [THE] [<position> OF THE] <name of waiting line>
<position> ::= FRONT | END
<transmission flow> ::= <input flow> AND [AT END OF <identifier>]
                        PUT [BACK] <output flow> [,<output flow>]... <period>
<output flow> ::= IN [<position> OF ] <name of waiting line> [IF <condition>]
<generation flow> ::= [AT END OF <identifier>] PUT [A | AN]
                      <entity name> <output flow>
<attribute modification> ::= ATTRIBUTE MODIFICATIONS:
                             <modification statement> <period>
                             [<modification statement> <period>]...
<modification statement> ::= [IF <condition> THEN]
                             <left side of assignment> := <expression>
<left side of assignment> ::= <internal variable name> | <external variable name> |
                              <entity attribute>
```

End of the formal grammar definition.

3

Petri Net as a Manufacturing System Scheduling Tool

Dr. Tauseef Aized, Professor and Chair
Department of Mechanical, Mechatronics and Manufacturing Engineering, KSK Campus, University of Engineering and Technology, Lahore, Pakistan

1. Introduction

Scheduling problems arise when different types of jobs are processed by shared resources according to their technological precedence conditions. There is a need to determine the optimal input sequence of jobs and resource usage for a given job mix. Production scheduling problems are very complex and have been proved to be NP-hard problems. Different approaches to production planning and scheduling have been adopted which are as follows:

1. **Heuristic dispatching rules.** Good rules are obtained based on experience. These rules work but often not at the optimum level. They are also developed based on the system simulation models. But simulation models are often too specific to particular situations and hence the results cannot be very well generalized.
2. **Mathematical programming methods:** These have been extensively studied and can produce good results for specific systems. The mathematical models have to ignore many practical conditions in order to solve these models efficiently. These practical conditions such as material handling capacity, complex resource sharing and routing, and sophisticated discrete-event dynamics are very difficult to be mathematically and concisely described. The optimality will not hold if any parameters or structures change during an operational stage.
3. **Computational intelligence based approaches**: These include knowledge based systems, neural networks, and genetic algorithms. Knowledge-based systems have difficulty in acquiring the efficient rules and knowledge and the results cannot be guaranteed the best.
4. **Other methods:** Other approaches such as algebraic models and control theoretic methods are difficult to offer efficient solution methodologies. The methods based on CPM/PERT and queuing networks provide efficient solution methodologies but cannot describe shared resources, synchronization, and lot sizes easily.

Time-driven systems such as living organisms, ecological systems and world population have long been modeled and analyzed through difference/ differential equations. Since such equations have become a universal modeling framework for time-driven systems, analytical and numerical techniques have been developed to solve the equations in order to understand, control and optimize system behavior. Man-made technological environments such as computer, transportation and telecommunication networks or manufacturing and logistics systems represent systems whose behavior is governed by events occurring asynchronously over time. Events may be controlled (e.g.; release of a new job in a manufacturing facility) or uncontrolled (e. g; arrival of a customer request at the same manufacturing facility). Such systems are usually encountered whenever a set of tasks is to be performed by a set of resources requiring coordination of events, resource contention management and performance monitoring and optimization. Event-driven systems are of increasing importance in today's world because they are growing in number, size and sophistication. It is therefore imperative to have systematic design methodologies in order to achieve desirable performance and to avoid catastrophic failures. These systems may be asynchronous and sequential, exhibiting many characteristics: concurrency, conflict, mutual exclusion and non-determinism. These characteristics are difficult to describe using traditional control theory which deals with systems of continuous or synchronous discrete variables modeled by differential or difference equations. In addition, inappropriate control of the occurrence of events may lead to system deadlock, capacity overflows or may otherwise degrade system performance. These systems typically referred to as *discrete event dynamical systems (DEDS).*The following are the characteristics embedded in DEDS.

- ***Event-driven*:** A discrete event system is characterized by a discrete state space where changes in state are triggered by event occurrences. Precedence is a key relation between events, that is, any event may be dependent on the occurrence of other events.
- ***Asynchronous*:** The asynchronous characteristic of discrete event systems is one of the most important properties by which they differ from traditional systems described by differential or difference equations. In time discretization of sampled systems, each change or step is synchronized by a global clock. In continuous systems, parameters vary continuously with time. However, in discrete event systems the events often occur asynchronously.
- ***Sequential Relation*:** Given a set of events, there may exist some sequential relationships among them. There is a sequential relation between two events if one event can occur only after the occurrence of the other.
- ***Concurrency*:** It means that there are no sequential relationships among the concerned events. For instance, two events are concurrent if either event may occur before the other.
- ***Conflict*:** It may occur when two or more processes require a common resource at the same time.
- ***Mutual exclusion:*** when conflict occurs, the events become mutually exclusive in the sense that they can not occur at the same time, whereas after one is complete, the other can occur.
- **Non-determinism:** Two kinds of non-determinism may occur. The first kind results from uncertain events' occurrence. For instance, if there is a conflict between two events, either of two events can occur randomly. The second kind of non-determinism results from small changes in process parameters, e.g.; processing time of an operation differ from time to time due to randomness , hence it can not be predicted accurately when an event will occur.
- ***System deadlock:*** A state may reach when none of the processes can continue. This can happen with the sharing of two resources between two processes and is usually the result of system design.

In order to capture the above properties, several mechanisms have been proposed and developed for modeling such systems. These are state machines, Petri nets, communicating sequential processes and finitely recursive processes. In order to conduct performance analysis of these kinds of systems, methods such as perturbation analysis, queuing network theory and Markov processes have been formulated and applied .An event-driven system can be abstracted as a state machine in which the states change when events occur. The finite state machine or automaton models results when the total number of states in a system is finite. However, when they are used to model discrete event system in a straight forward manner, the exponential increase in the number of states makes it very difficult to implement discrete event systems. Graphical representation is almost impossible and thus graphical visualization can not be easily realized .Some other models have also been developed for modeling and control of discrete event systems, e.g., supervisory control theory and finitely recursive processes. In supervisory control, the theory is elegant and is independent of the models used for applications. In most applications, each discrete event process is assumed to be modeled by an automaton or a state machine and its behavior is completely described by the language generated by the automaton. Many interesting theoretical results have been reported on controllability, observability and modular synthesis. However, the applicability to real-world distributed systems may be limited by the use of state machine representation. This approach encounters the state space explosion problem. Therefore, when a state machine is used to describe a complicated system, the design problem can easily become unmanageable. In addition, specifying the desirable language for a system is not easy. Finitely recursive processes (FRP) are mainly based on Hoare's communicating sequential processes. In the FRP formulation, given a set of events, a process is defined as a triple which consists of three components: a set of traces which the process can execute, an event function and a termination function. One of the important feature is that each process can be described as a set of recursive equations which implies that the description of a system can be implemented using equation forms. However, many problems remain open, e.g., the use of such equations to design supervisory controllers for real world systems.

2. Petri net as a DEDS modelling and scheduling mechanism

Petri net, as a graphical tool, provide a unified method for design of discrete event systems from hierarchical systems description to physical realizations. Compared with other models discussed above, they have the following advantages.

- Ease of modeling discrete event system characteristics: concurrency, asynchronous and synchronous features, conflicts, mutual exclusion, precedence relation, non-determinism and system deadlock,
- Ability to generate supervisory control code directly from the graphical Petri net representation,
- Ability to check the system for undesirable properties such as deadlock and instability,
- Performance analysis without simulation is possible for many systems. Production rates, resource utilization, reliability and performability can be evaluated.
- Discrete event simulation that can be driven from the model.
- Status information that allow for real-time monitoring
- Usefulness of scheduling because the Petri net model contains the system precedence relations as well as constraints on discrete event performance.

As a single representation tool, Petri net can aid in modelling, analysis, validation, verification, simulation, scheduling and performance evaluation at design stage. Once the system shows desirable behaviour, the net can be converted into control and monitor operations at run time. Therefore, Petri nets can be regarded as a powerful mathematical and graphical tool for design of various discrete events systems.

3. Petri net as a manufacturing system modelling mechanism

Modern manufacturing systems are highly parallel and distributed. They need to be analyzed from qualitative and quantitative points of view. Qualitative analysis looks for properties like the absence of deadlocks, the absence of overflows, or the presence of certain mutual exclusions in the use of shared resources. Its ultimate goal is to prove the correctness of the modeled system. Quantitative analysis looks for performance properties like throughput, responsiveness properties e.g., average completion times or utilization properties like utilization rates. Petri nets allow the construction of models amenable both for correctness and efficiency analysis. It can be considered as a graph theoretic tool especially suited to model and analyze Discrete Event Dynamical Systems (DEDS) which exhibit parallel evolutions and whose behavior are characterized by synchronization and sharing phenomena. Their suitability for modeling this type of system has led to their application in a wide range of fields. Examples of such DEDS are communication networks, computer systems and manufacturing systems. Petri nets have proven to be very useful in modeling, simulation and control of manufacturing systems. They provide very useful models for the following reasons:

- Petri nets capture the precedence relations and structural interactions of stochastic, concurrent and asynchronous events. In addition, their graphical nature helps to visualize such complex systems.
- Conflicts and buffer sizes can be modeled easily and efficiently.
- Deadlock in a system can be detected.
- Petri net models represent a hierarchical modeling tool with a well-developed mathematical and practical foundation.
- Various extensions of Petri nets allow for both qualitative and quantitative analyses of resource utilization, effect of failures and throughput rate.
- Petri net models give a structured framework for carrying out a systematic analysis of complex systems.
- Petri net models can also be used to implement real-time control for a flexible manufacturing system.

In this chapter, Petri net method is applied to model a semi-conductor manufacturing system, which is typically called multiple cluster tool system.

4. Multiple cluster tool system description

In a simple cluster tool, a material lot is loaded into a load-lock, pumped down to vacuum, and routed through a sequence of one or more modules in the cluster. After a wafer is completed, it is returned to the load-lock and after the completion of a lot, it is vented to atmosphere. In case loading/unloading time constitutes a significant component of total processing time, an improvement can be achieved by doubling the load-locks known as double load-lock cluster tool which can have throughput twice that of a single load-lock tool if material processing time is comparable with the sum of loading and unloading time. If the processing time is significantly greater than the loading/ unloading time, then the performance advantage of a double load-lock tool is rather insignificant. Processing chambers normally consist of two or more processing modules. For instance, chemical vapour deposition (CVD) cluster tools usually have six or eight modules which are process modules with an aligner and a cooler module. Also, one or more of the process modules may behave as bottleneck with the maximum service demand because of longest processing time. An obvious approach for improving throughput of such a system is to duplicate the critical chamber and use both chambers alternatively to increase the throughput of the tool. A Cluster tool may be a single/ double or a multiple -blade tool. A single blade tool is one in which a robotic transporter can carry only one wafer at a time whereas a double blade cluster tool can carry two wafers at the same time. For cluster tools with many chambers, it may be beneficial to use several robots, each of which services a group of chambers. A cluster tool is operated by control software called a cluster tool controller which manages the job data, communicates with the process modules and wafer handling robots and coordinates their activities.

The considered multiple cluster tool system in this paper has four cluster tools. Each cluster has four processing modules for material processing and two load-locks one of which is for incoming material and the other is for outgoing material. Each cluster tool has a double-blade tool. The angle between two arms of the robotic transporter, that is, double blade-tool is always 180 degrees. The material between successive cluster tools is transported using automated guided vehicles as shown in Figure 1.

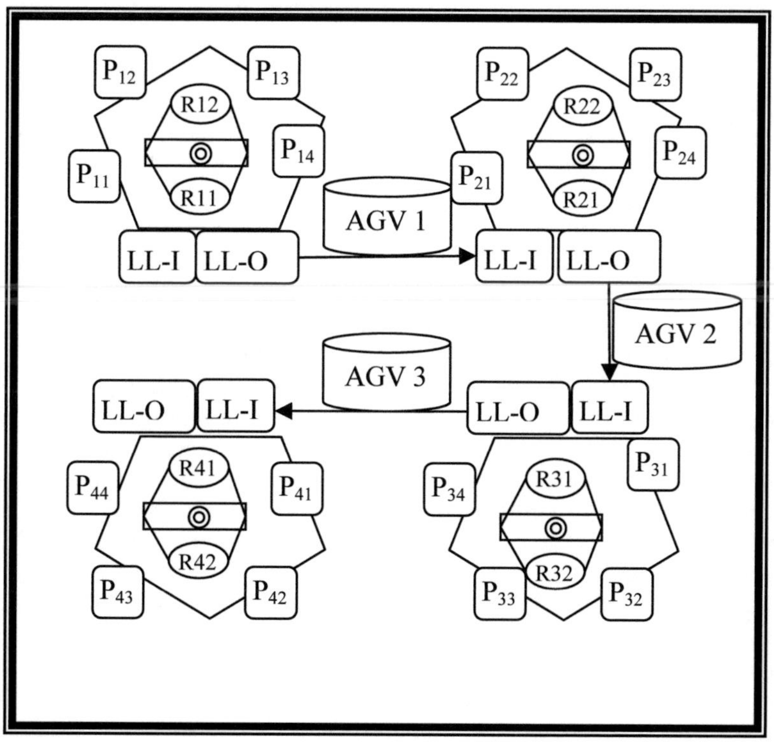

Fig. 1. The multiple cluster tool system.

Legend: P_{ij} – processing module 'j' of ith cluster tool, R_{ik}- robot arm 'k' for i^{th} cluster tool, LL-I --load-lock for incoming material, LL-O -- load-lock for outgoing material, AGV-automated guided vehicle

5. Coloured Petri net

A semi-conductor manufacturing system is a discrete event dynamical (DEDS) system, which is asynchronous, parallel, and event driven in its nature. A DEDS can be characterized by events and conditions, which can be described by Petri net method easily. In a semi-conductor manufacturing system, events are occurring in a parallel way that can be modelled compactly by coloured Petri net method. A Petri net consists of places, transitions and directed arcs represented by circles, rectangular bars and arrows, respectively. Arcs run between places and transitions. Places may contain any number of tokens. A distribution of tokens over the places of a net is called a marking. Transitions act on input tokens by a process known as firing. A transition can fire if it is enabled, i.e., there are tokens in every input place. When a transition fires, it consumes the tokens from its input places, perform some processing task and places a specified number of tokens into each of its output places. The conditions of a DEDS are described by places, events are described by transitions, relations between events and conditions are described by arcs and holding of conditions are described by tokens in places. The occurrences of events are described by firing of transitions which remove tokens from input places and add tokens to output places and the behaviour of a system is described by firing of transitions and movements of tokens. Places, transitions and tokens must be assigned a meaning for proper interpretation of a model. In manufacturing systems, normally places represent resources like machines, materials etc. and the existence of one or more tokens in a place represents the availability of a particular resource, while no token indicates that the resource is unavailable. A transition firing represents an activity or process execution, for instance, a machining process. Places and transitions together represent conditions and precedence relationships in a system's operation.
Sorensen and Janssens (2004) presented a Petri net model of a continuous flow transfer line with unreliable machines. This study proposed a Petri net in which a place represents the state of a machine or of a buffer. For each machine, four places are added indicating that the machine is up, down, blocked or starved. The proposed scheme is not suitable for practical manufacturing systems which have a great many conditions and events and modelling through Sorensen and Janssens (2004) method will generate a too complex and intractable models. Gharbi and Loualalen (2006) provided a detailed analysis of finite-source retrial systems with multiple servers subject to random breakdowns and repairs using generalized stochastic Petri net models. Cao et al. (2007) presented a queuing generalized stochastic coloured timed Petri net (QGSCTPN) based approach for modelling of semiconductor wafer fabrication. In the proposed QGSCTPN, Cao et al. (2007) introduced two kinds of places and five kinds of transitions and presented a small minfab model re-entrant line with three machine groups. The study emphasized to further explore methods to model large semiconductor manufacturing systems with practical constraints like random failures. Zhou and Venkatesh (1999) presented augmented timed Petri net for modelling and analysing manufacturing systems with breakdowns with the help of deactivation places, transitions and arcs but resource breakdowns can be handled compactly and more effectively through non-hierarchical and hierarchical coloured Petri net , defined in (Jensen, 1992), and is explained in the following paragraph. Additionally, in contrast to the papers mentioned where resource breakdowns have been modelled either before or after a processing activity, this study proposes a modelling approach which can model not only before or after a processing operation but also a resource breakdown activity can take place when a resource is carrying out its operation. This approach is more practical as resources are subject to breakdowns while they are performing their operations.

In this study, the random failures of all material processing modules are modelled in the same way and is elaborated by an example shown in Figure 2. This modelling feature is carried out through a transition 'Processing1'. There is a code segment attached to this transition which is executed each time the transition occurs (fires). This code is used to declare two *values*, that is, value *exec time* (execution time) and value *time break* (time until breakdown) as exponential distribution functions. As this code is executed, the exponential functions generate values for execution time and time until breakdown based on mean execution or processing time of the module. These two values are compared in such a way that if execution time is less than time until breakdown then the result is success; otherwise it is failure. The success means the operation has been executed successfully and the failure means that the module has been breakdown during execution. The arc variables correspond to the relevant places in Figure 2. The scheduled maintenance is modelled in such a way that process modules are allowed to perform a fix number of processing operations after which the modules become unavailable and are repaired/ maintained and then again modules can perform processing operations for a specific number of times. This process-repair-process cycle repeats itself indefinitely. Figure 3 shows the snapshot of the CPN model taken from CPN Tools whereas Table 1 describes places and transitions used in the model.

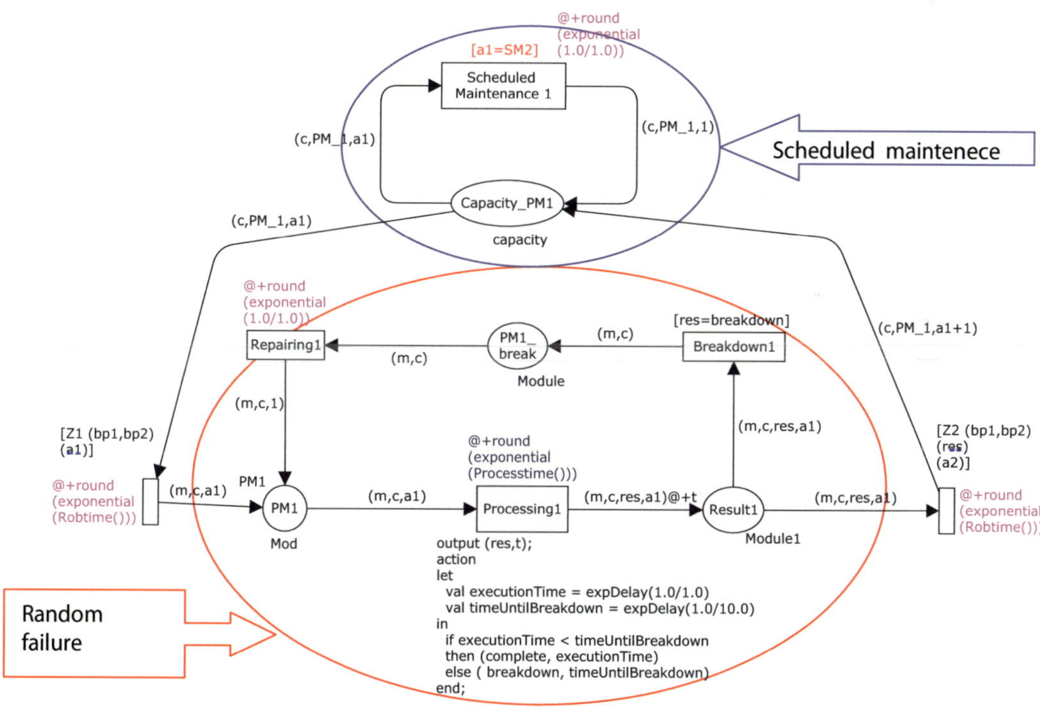

Fig. 2. The random failure and scheduled maintenance using CPN Tools.

6. Model development

The model is developed using CPN Tools which is a CPN-based program developed on the basis of CPN ML language. The CPN ML language is derived from Standard ML which is a general purpose functional language. All material loading/unloading, processing, repair

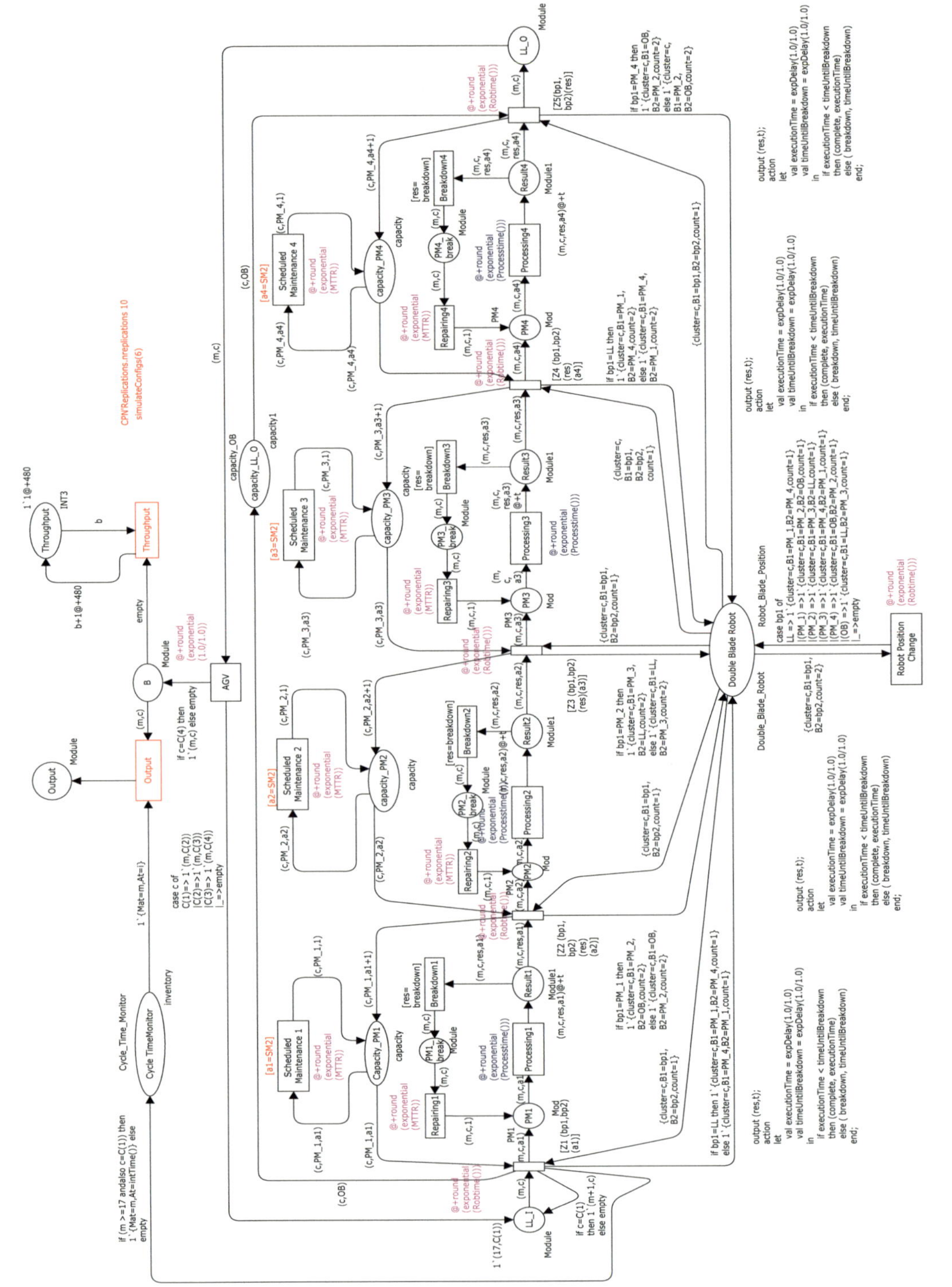

Fig. 3. The multiple cluster tool system model developed using CPN Tools.

Places	Description	Transitions	Description
LL_I	Load-lock for incoming material	Processing 1,2,3,4	Processing activity in progress at module 1,2,3,4
LL_O	Load-lock for outgoing material	Breakdown1,2,3,4	Process modules breakdowns
PM1,2,3,4	Processing modules 1,2,3 and 4	Repairing1,2,3,4	Process module 1,2,3,4 under repair
Result1,2,3,4	Result of processing modules 1,2,3,4 respectively (Material processing successful or module breakdown during processing)	Scheduled Maintenance1,2,3,4	Process module 1,2,3,4 under scheduled maintenance
PM1,2,3,4_Break	Processing module 1,2,3,4 in breakdown condition	AGV	Material transportation between successive cluster tools
Capacity_PM1,2,3,4	Capacity specification for Processing module 1,2,3,4	Robot Position Change	Change of position of double blade robot tool
Capacity_LL_O	Capacity specification for load-lock for outgoing material		
Blade_Position_Robot	Orientation specification of double blade tool		
Cycle Time Monitor	Monitoring cycle time		

Table1. Places and transitions description

and transportation operations have been modelled using exponential distribution functions. The following simulation assumptions have been used in developing the model:

- The raw material is always available.
- All material handling robot times are the same.
- All module processing times are the same.
- All module repair times are the same.
- The automated guided vehicles for material transportation between clusters are always available.

These assumptions can be easily relaxed in coloured Petri net modelling, if required. Before collecting the resulting data, it is important to detect the warm-up period to access the steady state behaviour of the system. This study uses four stage SPC approach (Robinson, 2002) to find out the steady state results. The warning Limit (WL) and action Limit (AL) are calculated as under:

$$WL = \hat{\mu} \pm 1.96\hat{\sigma} / \sqrt{n}\ , \ AL = \hat{\mu} \pm 3.09\hat{\sigma} / \sqrt{n}$$

Where $\hat{\mu}$ is mean value, $\hat{\sigma}$ is standard deviation and n is number of replications. As the input factors vary for individual simulation runs in this study, hence the warm-up period is also varying depending on the particular input factor settings. In general, ten independent replications have been carried out for each input factor settings and the warm-up period has been determined. This period has been excluded while collecting data from the simulation runs and the length of the steady state period has been determined according to the recommendations given in (Robinson, 2002) and hence simulation results are repeatable.

7. Results and discussion

There are three process execution input factors in this model, which are mean material handling robot loading/unloading time, MLT (minutes), mean module processing time, MPT (minutes) and mean time to repair related to processing module, MTTR (minutes) and two input factors represent resource breakdowns which are scheduled maintenance, SM (number of jobs) and mean time to failure, MTF (minutes). The impact of these factors on throughput (mean number of products per day) and cycle Time (mean number of minutes) is studied. The simulation results are given in Table 2.

In order to avoid the effects of different values, the same values are considered for respective ten levels of input factors. The throughput is decreasing as mean loading/ unloading time (MLT) is increasing because an increase in MLT requires materials to stay in the system for a longer time which causes an increase in cycle time and a corresponding decrease in throughput. The throughput is also decreasing with an increase of mean processing time (MPT) because more processing time means an increase in cycle time which causes a decrease in throughput. Mean loading/ unloading time has more adverse effect than mean processing time because for each module processing operation, there is one loading and another unloading operation. But this only holds true if the values of both MLT and MPT are the same. In an event where MPT is far more than MLT, it can impact throughput more adversely than MLT. Figures 4 and 5 show the impact of MLT and MPT on throughput and cycle time respectively.

SM and MTF are the measures of scheduled maintenance and random failures respectively. The scheduled maintenance is modelled in such a way that each processing module is down after a specific number of processing operations and is repaired after which it is again up for further processing. Figures 6 and 7 show an increase in throughput with a corresponding decrease in cycle time when the value of SM increases because an increase in SM value indicates that the processing module is capable of more operations before it needs to be repaired. MTF which represents random failure of modules during process execution has a more significant impact on throughput and cycle time. MTF is the mean time computed from the moment when a module starts process execution to the moment when that module breaks down provided the process execution is in progress. Hence MTF is computed each time when a module starts execution of a process and it is compared with process execution time to decide a success or failure of a process. If a module is processing a material/part and it breaks down during process execution, the material/part has to be unloaded from the resource and has to be reloaded on it after repair. This causes time wastage and increases cycle time and hence causes a decrease in throughput. Thus the values of MTF must be kept higher than mean values of process executions like MLT and MPT in order to achieve higher throughput and lower cycle time. At value 1, the values of MTF and process execution times are equal and hence throughput is lower due to a greater probability of resource breakdown during process execution. As the value of MTF increases up to value 2, there is a significant gain in throughput and decrease in cycle time because of a lower probability of resource

		Throughput			Cycle Time		
		Mean	95% CI	St.Dev	Mean	95% CI	St Dev
Robot loading/unloading time (MLT)	1	28.05	0.11	0.15	837.18	195.78	273.71
	2	20.87	0.08	0.11	1027.28	113.47	158.63
	3	15.67	0.06	0.09	1208.48	153.98	215.26
	4	12.28	0.05	0.06	1570.60	997.06	175.30
	5	10.01	0.05	0.07	1614.59	169.19	236.53
	6	8.39	0.05	0.07	1641.79	149.16	208.53
	7	7.20	0.05	0.08	2011.48	179.98	251.61
	8	6.30	0.02	0.03	2227.57	166.52	232.79
	9	5.59	0.04	0.06	2256.77	117.27	163.95
	10	5.00	0.03	0.05	2276.05	193.72	270.82
Module processing time (MPT)	1	28.09	28.09	0.16	831.39	94.86	132.62
	2	21.32	0.09	0.13	893.37	174.07	243.35
	3	16.96	0.07	0.10	948.82	173.09	241.98
	4	13.94	0.08	0.11	997.06	242.91	339.58
	5	11.87	0.06	0.09	1290.65	222.99	311.74
	6	10.26	0.09	0.13	1497.57	298.12	416.78
	7	9.04	0.09	0.13	1571.07	270.30	377.88
	8	8.12	0.06	0.08	2059.10	379.50	530.54
	9	7.31	0.07	0.10	2109.55	339.60	474.75
	10	6.73	0.08	0.11	2199.64	237.52	332.05
Mean time to repair (MTTR)	1	27.92	0.08	0.11	873.00	111.12	155.34
	2	20.68	0.13	0.18	1019.70	141.58	197.92
	3	16.07	0.11	0.15	1240.12	252.58	353.11
	4	13.17	0.05	0.07	1277.15	158.13	221.07
	5	11.09	0.08	0.11	1473.04	228.37	319.26
	6	9.52	0.08	0.11	1726.99	262.69	367.23
	7	8.37	0.05	0.07	1818.93	146.24	204.44
	8	7.46	0.07	0.10	1957.89	305.50	427.09
	9	6.74	0.06	0.08	2089.78	239.70	335.10
	10	6.12	0.05	0.07	2265.71	393.50	550.11
Scheduled maintenance (SM)	1	28.081	0.11	0.15	802.21	155.72	217.69
	2	29.373	0.08	0.12	761.51	132.57	185.33
	3	30.109	0.14	0.20	701.59	69.79	97.57
	4	30.95	0.12	0.16	663.18	190.21	265.91
	5	31.82	0.14	0.19	619.23	131.63	184.02
	6	33.04	0.20	0.28	576.98	144.21	201.61
	7	33.56	0.14	0.19	524.36	142.07	198.62
	8	34.06	0.10	0.14	490.37	137.48	192.19
	9	34.26	0.15	0.20	466.82	144.05	201.38
	10	34.59	0.09	0.13	449.38	142.16	198.73
Mean time to failure (MTF)	1	28.09	0.12	0.17	811.88	124.32	173.80
	2	36.24	0.10	0.14	583.03	83.10	116.18
	3	39.06	0.12	0.17	513.19	78.09	109.17
	4	40.24	0.10	0.15	460.94	85.71	119.82
	5	40.99	0.13	0.18	416.65	55.59	77.71
	6	41.47	0.09	0.13	380.64	84.47	118.09
	7	41.82	0.06	0.09	343.11	79.31	110.88
	8	41.96	0.07	0.10	319.81	84.10	117.57
	9	42.20	0.11	0.16	309.41	84.56	118.22
	10	42.34	0.16	0.22	298.08	40.01	55.94

Table 2. The simulation results (CI: Confidence interval)

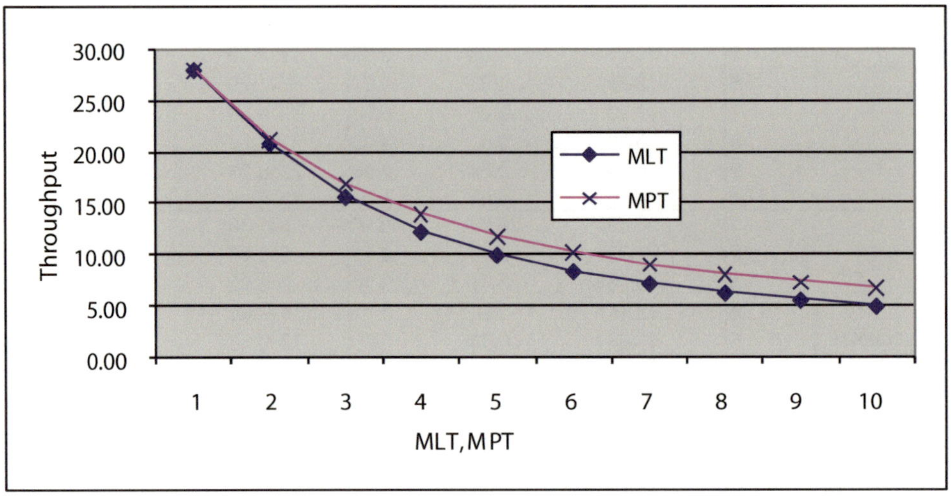

Fig. 4. The impact of robot loading/ unloading time and module processing time on throughput.

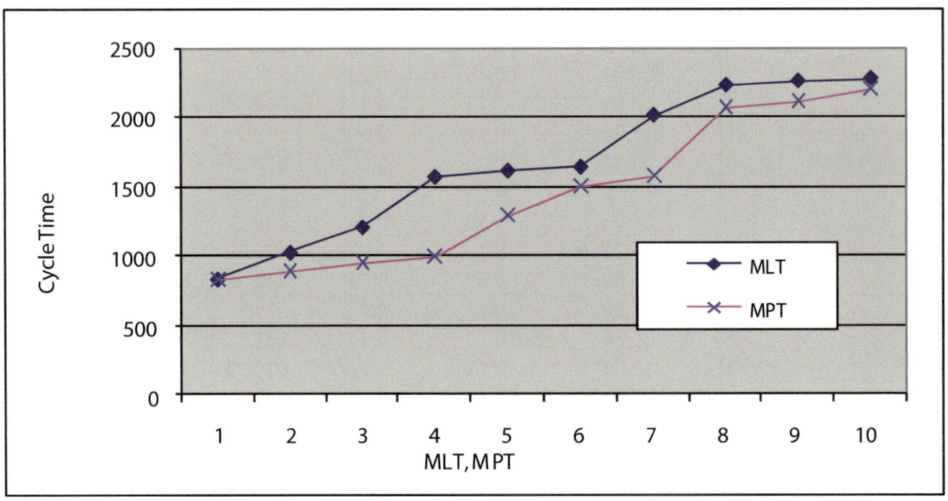

Fig. 5. The impact of robot loading/ unloading time and module processing time on Cycle time.

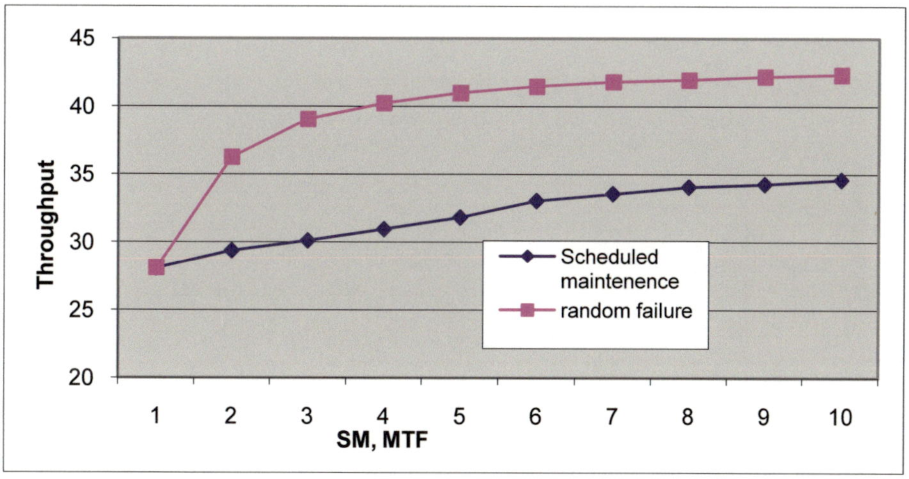

Fig. 6. The impact of scheduled maintenance and random failures on throughput.

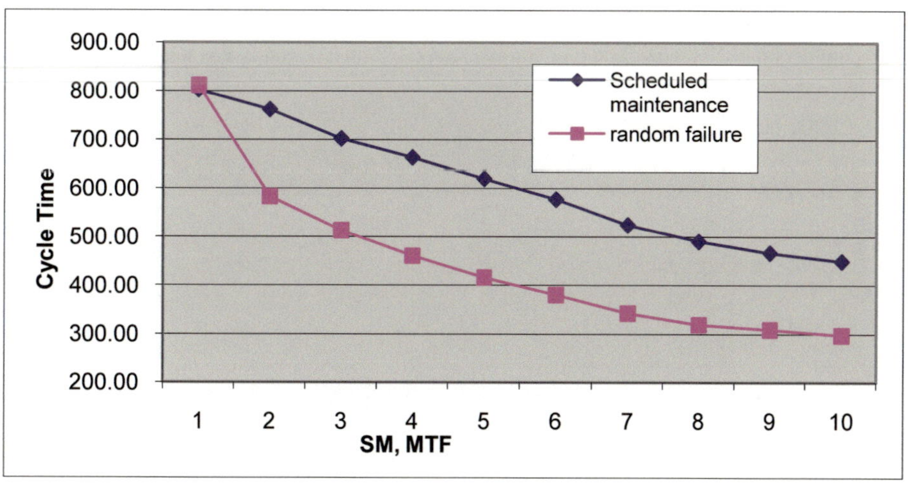

Fig. 7. The impact of scheduled maintenance/ random breakdowns on Cycle Time.

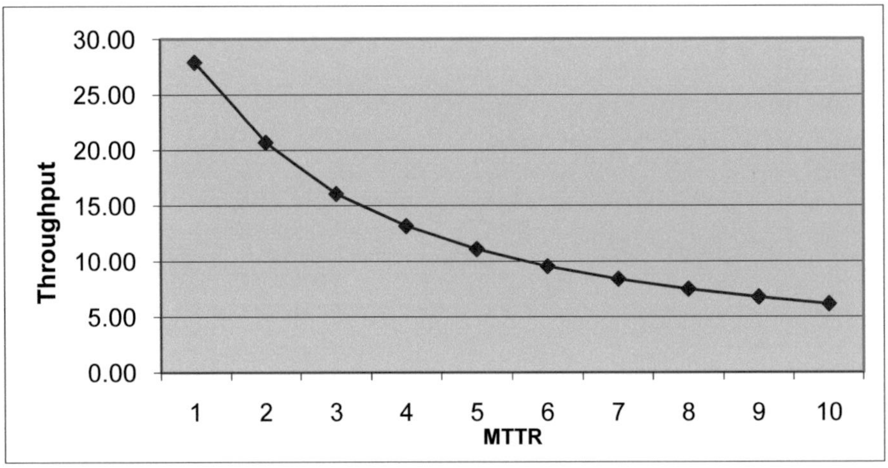

Fig. 8. The impact processing module mean time to repair on throughput.

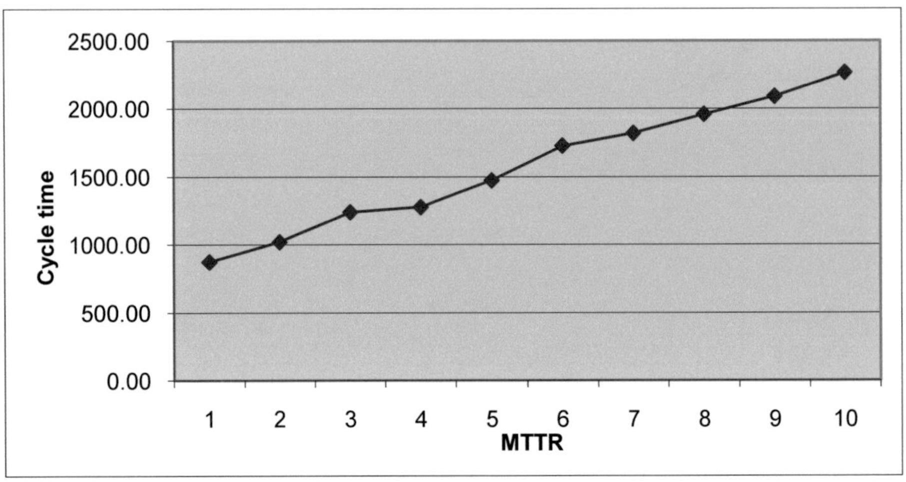

Fig. 9. The impact processing module mean time to repair on Cycle time.

breakdown during execution. This trend continues as MTF approaches higher values but the rate of increase in throughput and decrease in cycle time is reduced because after a certain value, value '7' in Figures 6 and 7, the probability of resource breakdown during execution is quite low. A resource with very high value of MTF, for instance 10, compared with its execution time means that it is highly reliable for the process. Such a resource is usually costly for the process and cannot contribute significantly, for instance compared with 7, 8 and 9 towards throughput and cycle time as is shown in Figures 6 and 7.

Figures 8 and 9 show the impact of processing module mean time to repair (MTTR) on throughput and cycle time. An increase in MTTR means more time is required to repair the processing module which decreases the working time to down time ratio of processing modules. The decrease in working to down times of processing modules forces the materials to stay a longer time in the system; thus increasing cycle time which deteriorates throughput of the system. In order to achieve higher throughput and lower cycle time values, the repair time of processing modules must be kept as low as possible.

8. Conclusion

Multiple cluster tool systems have emerged as an important semiconductor manufacturing system technology with the benefits of higher yield, shorter cycle time and tighter process control. This study has described a modelling technique using coloured Petri net to capture random failures of multiple cluster tool system and has shown that random failure is an important system limitation as far as throughput and cycle time are concerned. The random failures of cluster tools may be avoided by achieving a higher value of mean time between failures of process modules compared with process execution times. This multiple cluster tool system problem under discussion can be extended to incorporate the random failure modelling of internal robotic arms and AGV based transporters between clusters.

9. Acknowledgement

This chapter is partially based on the following publications.

1. Tauseef Aized "CPN and DoE based modeling and performance maximization of multiple product flexible manufacturing system with resource breakdowns". published by LAMBERT Academic Publishing, Germany,2010, ISBN: 978-3-8383-3888-0
2. Tauseef Aized "Modeling and analysis of multiple cluster tools system with random failures using colored Petri net" accepted, International Journal of Advanced Manufacturing Technology published by Springer ISSN: 0268-3768 (print version), ISSN: 1433-3015 (electronic version).
3. MengChu Zhou and Kurapati Venkatesh, "Modeling, Simulation and Control of Flexible manufacturing system: A Petri net approach". Published by World Scientific, 1999.

10. References

Sorensen, K. and Janssens, G.K. (2004). A Petri net model of a continuous flow transfer line with unreliable machines. European Journal of operational research, 152, pp. 248-262.

Gharbi, N., Loualalen, M. (2006). GSPN analysis of retrial systems with servers breakdowns and repairs. Applied mathematics and computation, 174, pp. 1151-1168.

Cao, Z.C., Qaio, F., Wu, Q. (2007). Queuing generalized stochastic colored timed Petri nets-based approach to modelling for semiconductor wafer fabrication. IEEE International Conf. on Control and Automation, Guangzhou. China, pp. 2834-2838.

MengChu Zhou and Kurapati Venkatesh. (1999). Modeling, simulation and control of flexible manufacturing systems. World Scientific Press.

Robinson, S. (2002). A statistical process control approach for estimating the warm-up period. Proceedings of 2002 winter simulation conference, pp. 439-445.

Jensen, K. (1992). Coloured Petri Nets: Basic Concepts, Analysis Methods and Practical Use, Vol. 1, Springer-Verlag.

4

Petri Net Model Based Implementation of Hierarchical and Distributed Control for Discrete Event Robotic Manufacturing Cells

Gen'ichi Yasuda
Nagasaki Institute of Applied Science
Japan

1. Introduction

Manufacturing systems, where the materials which are handled are mainly composed of discrete entities, for example parts that are machined and/or assembled, are called discrete manufacturing systems. The rapid development of industrial techniques makes the manufacturing systems larger and more complex, in which system control is divided into a hierarchy of control levels: planning, scheduling, coordination and local control (Silva, 1990). At the upper level, the global system is considered and its representation is strongly aggregated. Each low level is a disaggregation of the upper one; the portion of the system considered is smaller, but more details are taken into account. The time horizon of the low level is shorter, and real-time constraints are progressively hard. At the coordination level (shop, cell), the function is to update the state representation of the workshop in real-time, to supervise it, and make real-time decisions. The decision making system has to schedule and synchronize the machine utilizations to decide at each instant what has to be done and on which machine.

Frequently, a flexible manufacturing system is structured into manufacturing cells. A cell is an elementary manufacturing system consisting of flexible machine tools (or assembly devices), some local storage facilities for tools and parts and some handling devices such as robots in order to transfer parts and tools between the cell and the global transport system. Elementary manufacturing cells are called workstations. In a manufacturing cell, some devices operate concurrently and cooperatively or interfere to each other. Conventional representation methods such as time chart and state transition graph can not cope with the system like this. So a powerful method which can represent a discrete event system including nondeterministic parallel and concurrent action is desired.

As computer technology has been continuing to be upgraded to higher level year by year, the control system architecture has changed from centralized processing to distributed processing in order to reduce the development cost and to improve reliability. In developing distributed processing systems, major difficulties are that adequate expression methods and analyzing techniques for control mechanisms have not sufficiently been established. In the field of manufacturing systems that are typical examples of the event driven system, demands for the automatic control has diversified and the control logic has become extremely complicated. To deal with the complexity, a new methodology on control system design based on the discrete event driven system is necessary.

For the flexibility and expandability of the event driven system software, a programming paradigm based on a network model is considered to be useful, because the network model can describe the execution order of sequential/parallel processes or works directly without ambiguity. For this class of problems, Petri nets have intrinsic favorable qualities and it is very easy to model sequences, choices between alternatives, rendezvous and concurrent activities by means of Petri nets (Thuriot et al., 1983). Moreover, the formalism allowing a validation of the main properties of the Petri net control structure (liveness, boundedness, etc.) guarantees that the control system will not fall in a deadlocked situation. Petri net based programming technique makes it possible to realize systematic and high-level description of system specification (Gentina & Corbeel, 1987), (Jockovic et al., 1990), (Wang & Saridis, 1990). Furthermore, a real-time implementation of the Petri net specification by a software called the token game player can avoid implementation errors, because the specification is directly executed by the token game player and the implementation of these control sequences preserves the properties of the model.

The Petri net has been applied to a variety of system developments such as real-time systems, manufacturing systems, communication systems, and so on, as an effective tool for describing control specifications and realizing the control system in a uniform manner. However, there are some problems to be solved as follows.

1. Although the description capability of the Petri net is very high, in case of flexible manufacturing systems the network model becomes very complicated and it lacks for the readability and comprehensibility.
2. Although the specification analysis stage has been supported, the support for the control software coding stage is insufficient. The flexibility and expandability are not satisfactory in order to deal with the specification change of the control system.

This paper discusses problems of the system realization by using Petri nets and proposes a design method for hierarchical and distributed manufacturing control systems. The Petri net model can be used from the conceptual, the global design of the system to the detailed design of its partial systems so that the modeling, simulation and control of large and complex discrete event manufacturing systems can be consistently realized by Petri nets. The complex control system can be easily designed and realized by using the global Petri net as an upper controller which controls lower controllers designed by detailed Petri nets. The cooperation of each controller is implemented so that the aggregated behavior of the distributed system is the same as that of the original system and the task specification is completely satisfied. At this point of view, this paper shows the efficiency of the proposed hierarchical and distributed control method by the simulation experiments of cooperative transferring tasks with mechanical arm robots.

2. Manufacturing systems and Petri nets

At each level of discrete manufacturing system control, any modeling has to be based on the concepts of events and states (Fogel & Sebestyenova, 1992), (Holt & Rodd, 1994), (Kasturia & Dicesare, 1988), (Rogers & Williams, 1988). An event corresponds to a state change. When using Petri nets, events are associated with transitions. Activities are associated to the firing of transitions and to the marking of places which represents the state of the system. In addition to its graphic representation differentiating events and states, Petri nets allows the modeling of true parallelism and the possibility of progressive modeling by using stepwise refinements or modular composition. Libraries of well-tested subnets allow components reusability leading to significant reductions in the modeling effort. The possibility of progressive modeling is absolutely necessary for flexible manufacturing systems because they are usually large and complex systems. The refinement mechanism allows the building of hierarchically structured net models which leads to the implementation of hierarchical and distributed control.

Formally, a Petri net has two types of nodes, called places and transitions. A place is represented by a circle and a transition by a bar. The places and transitions are connected by arcs. The number of places and transitions are finite and not zero. An arc is connected directly from one place to a transition or a transition to a place. In other words a Petri net is a bipartite graph, i.e. places and transitions alternate on a path made up of consecutive arcs.

An ordinary Petri net (Murata, 1989) is represented by the 5-tuple $G = \{P,T,I,O,M_o\}$ such that:

$P = \{p_1, p_2, ..., p_n\}$ is a finite, not empty, set of places;

$T = \{t_1, t_2, ..., t_m\}$ is a finite, not empty, set of transitions;

$P \cap T = \phi$, i.e. the sets P and T are disjointed;

$I : P \times T \rightarrow \{1,2,3,\cdots\}$ is the input weight function;

$O : P \times T \rightarrow \{1,2,3,\cdots\}$ is the output weight function;

$M_o : P \rightarrow \{0,1,2,3,\cdots\}$ is the initial marking;

The pre-incidence matrix of a Petri net is $C^- = [c_{ij}^-]$ where $c_{ij}^- = I(p_i, t_j)$; the post-incidence matrix is $C^+ = [c_{ij}^+]$ where $c_{ij}^+ = O(p_i, t_j)$, then the incidence matrix of the Petri net $C = C^+ - C^-$.

Each place contains some (positive or zero) marks or tokens. The number of tokens in each place is defined by the marked vector or marking $M = (m_1, m_2, ..., m_n)^T$. The number of tokens in one place p_i is called $M(p_i)$. The marking at a certain moment defines the state of the Petri net, or the state of the system described by the Petri net. The evolution of the state therefore corresponds to an evolution of the marking, caused by the firing of transitions.

In an ordinary Petri net, where the current marking is M_k, a transition t_j is enabled if $\forall p_i \in P, M_k(p_i) \geq I(p_i, t_j)$. An enabled transition can be fired reaching a new marking M_{k+1} which can be computed as $M_{k+1} = M_k + C \cdot V$; this equation is called state equation of the Petri net, where $V = (v_1, v_2, ..., v_m)^T$ is the transition vector such that v_j=1 if transition t_j fires and 0 if not. When a transition is enabled, this does not imply that it will be immediately fired; this only remains a possibility. The firing of a transition is indivisible; the firing of a transition has duration of zero.

The firing of an enabled transition will change the token distribution (marking) in a net according to the transition firability rule. A sequence of firings will result in a sequence of markings. A marking M_n is said to be reachable from a marking M_0 if there exists a sequence of firings that transforms M_0 to M_n. The set of all possible markings reachable from M_0 is denoted $R(M_0)$. A Petri net is said to be k-bounded or simply bounded if the number of tokens in each place does not exceed a finite number k for any marking reachable from M_0, i.e., $M(p_i) \leq k$ for every place p_i and every marking $M \in R(M_0)$. A Petri net is said to be safe if it is 1-bounded. Bumping occurs when despite the holding of a condition, the preceding event occurs. This can result in the multiple holding of that condition. From the viewpoint of discrete event process control, bumping phenomena should be excluded.

The Petri net was modified so that the system is safe. The weight of the input and output weight functions I,O is 1 if the arc exists and 0 if not. Because the modified Petri net is safe, for each place p_i, $m_i = 0$ or 1, and a transition t_j is enabled if the two following conditions are met:

1. For each place p_k, such that $I(p_k,t_j)=1$, $m_k=1$
2. For each place p_l such that $O(p_l,t_j)=1$, $m_l=0$

Besides the guarantee of safeness, considering not only the modeling of the systems but also the actual manufacturing system control, the additional capability of input/output signals from/to the machines are required (Hasegawa et al., 1984). So gate arcs are classified as permissive or inhibitive, and internal or external. An external gate connects a transition with a signal source, and depending on the signal, it either permits or inhibits the occurrence of the event which corresponds to the connected transition. An internal signal arc sends the signal from a place to a machine. Thus a transition is enabled if and only if it satisfies all the following conditions:

1. It does not have any output place filled with a token.
2. It does not have any empty input place.
3. It does not have any internal permissive arc signaling 0.
4. It does not have any internal inhibitive arc signaling 1.

An enabled transition may fire when it does not have any external permissive arc signaling 0 nor any external inhibitive arc signaling 1.

When an enabled transition t_j fires, the marking M is changed to M', where

1. For each place p_k, such that $I(p_k,t_j)=1$, $m'_k=0$
2. For each place p_l such that $O(p_l,t_j)=1$, $m'_l=1$

To summarize it, the firing of a transition removes a token from each input place and put a token in each output place connected to it. As a natural requirement, in any initial marking, there must not exist more than one token in a place. According to these rules, the number of tokens in a place never exceeds one. Thus, the Petri net is essentially a safe graph; the system is free from the bumping phenomenon. The assignment of token into the places of a Petri net is called marking and it represents the system state.

If a place has two or more input transitions or output transitions, these transitions may be in conflict for firing. When two or more transitions are firable only one transition should fire using some arbitration rule. By the representation of the activity contents and control strategies in detail, features of discrete event manufacturing systems such as ordering, parallelism, asynchronism, concurrency and conflict can be concretely described through the extended Petri net.

The extended Petri net is a tool for the study of condition-event systems and used to model discrete event manufacturing systems through its graphical representation. Analysis of the net reveals important information about the structure and the dynamic behavior of a modeled manufacturing system. This information can then be used to evaluate the manufacturing system and suggest improvements or changes. The flow chart of simulation to check the dynamic behavior of the system quantitatively is shown in Fig. 1.

Implementation methods to do the real-time control are classified into two kinds (hardware and software). Hardware implementation realizes the places and transitions by hardware in a modular form, which are mutually connected in the same way as the Petri net model.

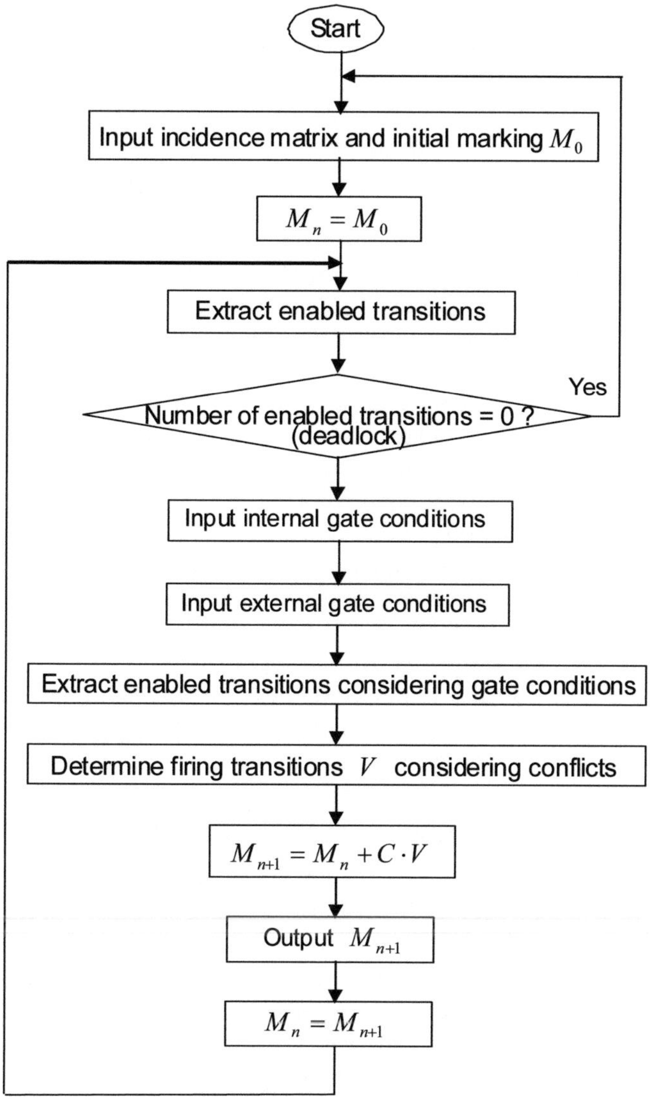

Fig. 1. Flow chart of extended Petri net simulator

Signals from controlled objects (machines and external sensors) are connected to the transitions as external gate conditions. When a token exists in a place, the control information assigned to the place is transmitted to the machine. The simulation is performed by monitoring the marking. Hardware implementation by decomposing the net model into several state transition diagrams, which are easily realized using conventional sequential controllers, and combining them with interlock signals, can be effective in many industrial applications.

On the other hand software implementation is performed by developing control software based on the logical structure of the Petri net model (Taubner, 1988). Simulation is performed by program called a token game player with graphic display, and real-time control is performed through the computer interface. Centralized schemes can be sequentially or concurrently implemented (Silva, 1990). Practically centralized sequential schemes are employed at the local control level frequently in special purpose real-time computers named Programmable Logic Controller (PLC) (Atabakhche et al., 1986) by means of converting the Petri net directly into a Boolean equation. Centralized concurrent implementations are basically composed of many specific tasks (possibly one per transition) and a coordinator. The coordinator plays the token game on the net model, initiating the execution of the tasks attached to the fired transitions. When a task ends its activity, it informs the coordinator to proceed with the next activations. The coordinator is an active task with a high priority that acts as the kernel of the application multitasking level. It provides indirect synchronization between the activities of specific tasks associated with the firing of transitions. The simplicity and easy modification of the synchronization/communication scheme are among the advantages of centralized implementation. The basic problems with this kind of solution are relatively inefficient execution (memory occupation and execution time) and weakness for safety. Decentralized implementation schemes are usually built by decomposing the net into a set of sequential processes and the required primitives concerning synchronization/communication between these processes are directly inserted, where required, in the body of the sequential processes (Georgeff, 1983), (Yasuda, 1999). The classical synchronization/communication mechanisms are based on synchronous rendezvous between tasks and asynchronous message passing implemented by means of buffers or mailboxes. In decentralized implementations, synchronization and communication between sequential processes are direct; there is no intermediate active element. In this paper, a hierarchical and distributed implementation is proposed, where a system controller with the global Petri net model coordinates several local controllers with detailed Petri net models.

3. Specification of manufacturing tasks using Petri nets

A Petri net model based consistent method for specification and implementation of hierarchical and distributed control of robotic manufacturing systems is proposed. A specification procedure for discrete event manufacturing systems based on Petri nets is as follows. First, the conceptual level activities of the manufacturing system are defined through a Petri net model considering the task specification corresponding to the aggregate manufacturing process. To deal with the problems related to the description of discrete event manufacturing systems using Petri nets, the system specification can be decomposed into two aspects: manufacturing sequence and resource allocation. A Petri net is associated to each aspect, and these two nets are strongly synchronized with the mechanism similar to transitions merging between the nets.

First, activities of manufacturing sequence must be executed to reach a given goal. For example a part is carried from a machine to another machine because the next operation has been scheduled on the machine. This activity modifies the physical state of the part according to the scheduled fabrication. In the Petri net specification, the location of the token shows the fabrication step of the part. An evolution of the process can be represented by distinct activities (starting event, effects and finishing event). Second, with respect to resource allocation, to execute the required activity, the process must be in a special state. For example, before executing a machining activity, on a given part, a machine must be free, and the required tool must be available, etc. These constraints depend on the layout and rules of operation of the process. They must be respected whatever the manufacturing sequence. In the Petri net specification, the location of the tokens models the state of the resources. The general representation of conceptual Petri net model by the above procedure is shown in Fig. 2, where the activity of each equipment as well as each subtask composing the task specification is represented as a place of the Petri net.

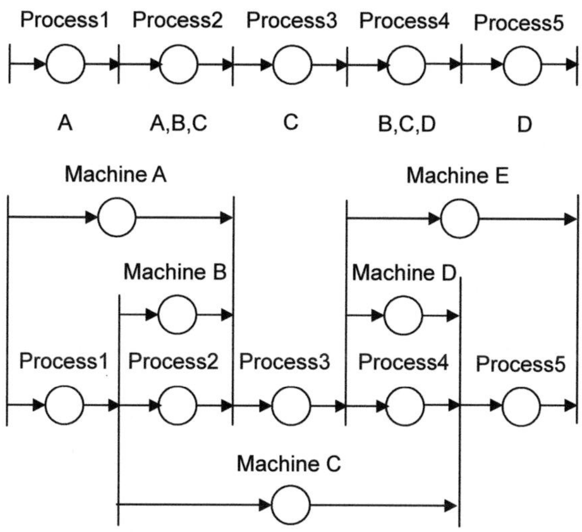

Fig. 2. General representation of conceptual Petri net model

4. Hierarchical representation of Petri nets

The detailed Petri nets are deduced to represent the control activities of associated machines. The macro representation of the manufacturing process is effectively used for achieving a top-down interpretation down to the concrete lower level activities using Petri nets. This procedure is repeated up to an appropriate level corresponding to the control level of the equipment responsible for the activity execution. At each step of detailed representation, a place of the Petri net are substituted by a subnet in a manner which maintains the structural properties such as liveness.

Petri nets for machine activity control are the loop structures because they eventually return to each home position. As required control strategies between equipment, the following two are frequently used: cooperative control and selective control. In cooperative control as shown in Fig. 3, transitions t1 and t2 indicate that two machines 1 and 2 should be controlled to start their actions synchronously. In selective control as shown in Fig. 4, where transitions t1and t2 are in conflict, one of two manufacturing processes is selected by an arbiter program which is substantially executed in the "Test" place.

For an example system of transferring task (Perez & Koutsourelis, 1987) by two robots (work transfer from the robot R1 to the robot R2), the conceptual Petri net model is shown in Fig. 5. Then Fig. 6 shows the detailed Petri net model, where places of work reception and work placement in the conceptual model are made detailed. The "Hand over" operation is accomplished through cooperative synchronized actions by two robots. The procedure of machine activity control is as follows. When a workpiece comes up to the initial position, which is represented as an external gate signal, the robot R1 takes the object, transfers it to the working space of the robot R2, and there waits for the robot R2 to taking the object. When the robot R1 stops, the robot R2 grasps it, then the robot R1 opens the hand. Then the robot R2 transfers it to the buffer and there releases it, and finally returns to the initial position.

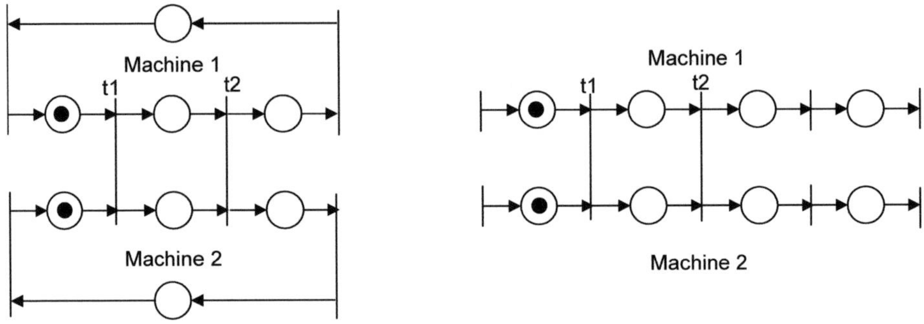

(a) Loop structure (b) Parallel structure

Fig. 3. Example representation of cooperative control between two machines

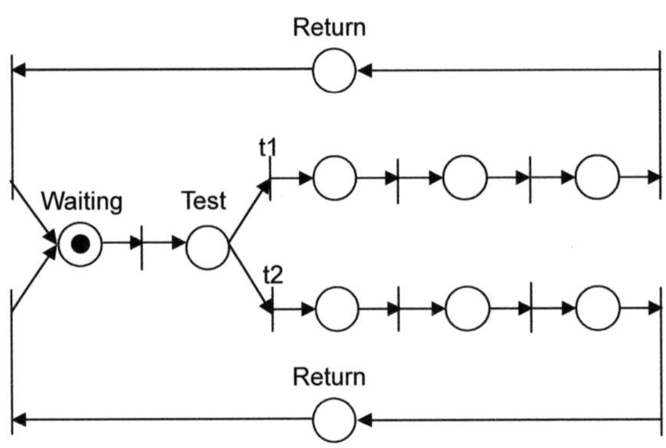

Fig. 4. Example representation of selective control between two manufacturing processes

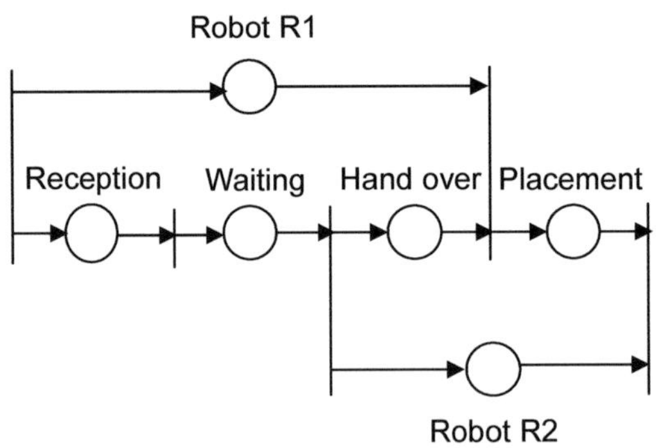

Fig. 5. Conceptual Petri net model of work transfer task by two robots

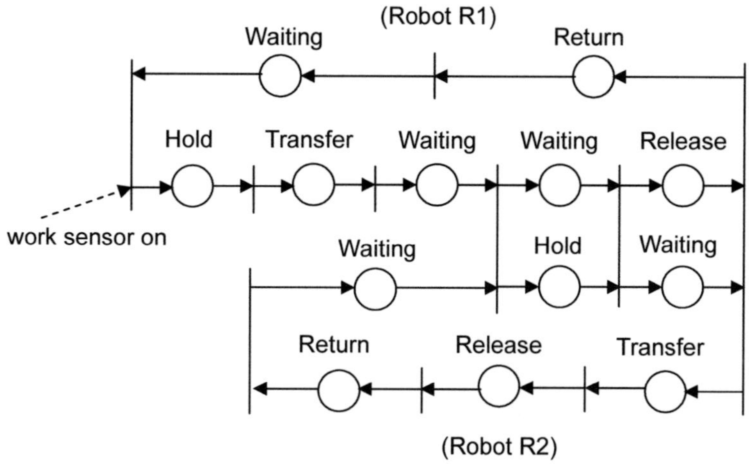

Fig. 6. Detailed Petri net model of work transfer task by two robots

The more detailed Petri net model at the actuator level of "Hold" and "Transfer" action, which is composed of opening, grasping and movement of each motor axis to the specified position, is shown in Fig. 7. In this figure, the "Dummy" place represents that its input and output transitions are start and end of unit action, respectively. This means that macro representation of a Petri net model can be achieved by replacing a detailed net with a dummy place.

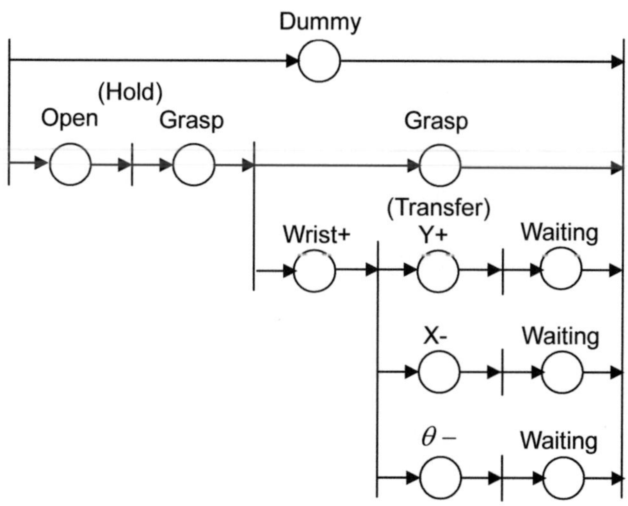

Fig. 7. Detailed Petri net model of "Hold" and "Transfer" action

The basic procedure of coordination by the communication between the coordinator and the local controllers is explained in detail as follows. As shown in Fig. 8, when a place in a Petri net model represents an "action", then the coordinator sends a "start" command with the parameter pointing to the detailed Petri net. The local controllers receive the command and the corresponding local controller executes the detailed subnet. When the execution is finished, the local controller returns the "end" signal to the coordinator. When a place represents the "waiting" state, then the coordinator sends a "ready" command with the parameter pointing to the next detailed Petri net. The local controller receives the command and executes the corresponding initialization. When the execution is finished, the local controller returns the "ack" signal to the coordinator.

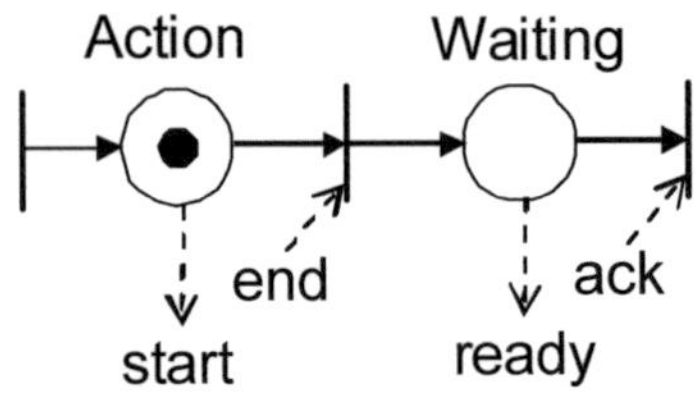

Fig. 8. Communication control between coordinator and local controllers

For the actual control, the operations of each machine are broken down into a series of unit motions, which is also represented by mutual connection between places and transitions. A place means a concrete unit motion of a machine. From these places, output signal arcs are connected to the machines, and external gate arcs from the machines are connected to the transitions of the Petri net when needed, for example, to synchronize and coordinate operations. When a token enters a place that represents a unit motion, the machine defined by the machine code is informed to execute a determined motion with a determined data; these are defined as the place parameters.

5. Implementation of hierarchical and distributed control

Transferring task by four robots (work transfer from the robot R1 to the robot R2, then transfer from the robot R2 to the robot R3 or R4 according to the type of workpiece) has been modeled and implemented as an experimental system. The configuration of the system contains four robots, one incoming and two outgoing conveyors, and a set of sensors. The sensor's set consists of touch sensors on robots, which indicate whether a robot has or has not grasped a workpiece, and limit switch sensors for robot arm positioning. The layout of the experimental system is shown in Fig. 9.

The cell works in the following way: Workpieces come on the incoming conveyor CV1 up to the take up position 1-1. The robot R1 waits in front of the conveyor CV1 in position 1-2 which is defined by the limit switch for positioning the arm, and on conveyor stopping the robot R1 approaches in position 1-1, grips the workpiece with an energized magnetic hand and a touch sensor and returns to position 1-2. Then the robot R1 turns to position 1-3, goes into the working space of the robot R2 and there waits for the robot R2 to taking the workpiece. When the robot R2 comes to position 2-1, the robot R1 hands over the workpiece to the robot R2 by deenergizing the hand. The robot R1 detects it with the touch sensor. The robot R2 tests the workpiece with the touch sensor, transfers it to the robot R3 or R4 according to the result. Then, the robot R2 hands over the workpiece to the robot R3 or R4 in position 2-2 or 2-3, while the robot R3 or R4 takes it in position 3-1 or 4-1 by energizing the hand. Finally, the robot R3 or R4 carries the workpiece over to position 3-2 or 4-2 and there leaves it, while the robot R2 returns to position 2-1. The conceptual Petri net model and the detailed model are shown in Fig. 10 and Fig. 11, respectively.

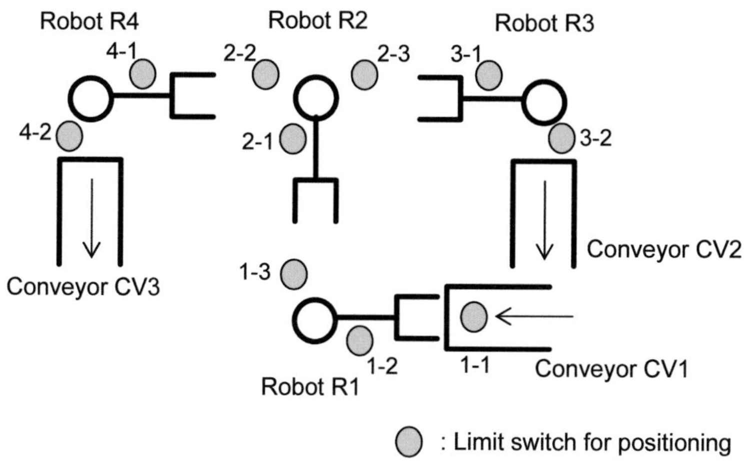

Fig. 9. Layout for work transfer task by four robots

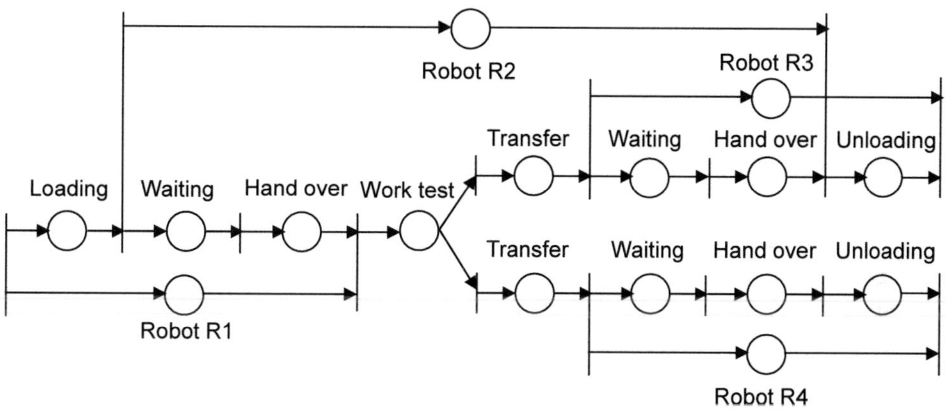

Fig. 10. Conceptual Petri net model of work transfer task by four robots

It is natural to implement a hierarchical and distributed control system, where one controller is allocated to each control layer or block. For the manufacturing system, an example structure of hierarchical and distributed control is composed of one system controller and several local controllers as shown in Fig. 12. The detailed Petri net is decomposed into subnets, which are executed by each local controller. The system controller is composed of the Petri net based controller and the coordinator. The conceptual Petri net model is allocated to the Petri net based controller in the system controller for management of the overall system. The coordinator monitors the overall system using external sensors and coordinates the local controllers by sending the commands and receiving the status. The detailed Petri net models are allocated to the Petri net based controllers in the local controllers. Each local controller directly monitors and controls the sensors and actuators of its machine. In the example system, one local controller is assigned to each robot and conveyor.

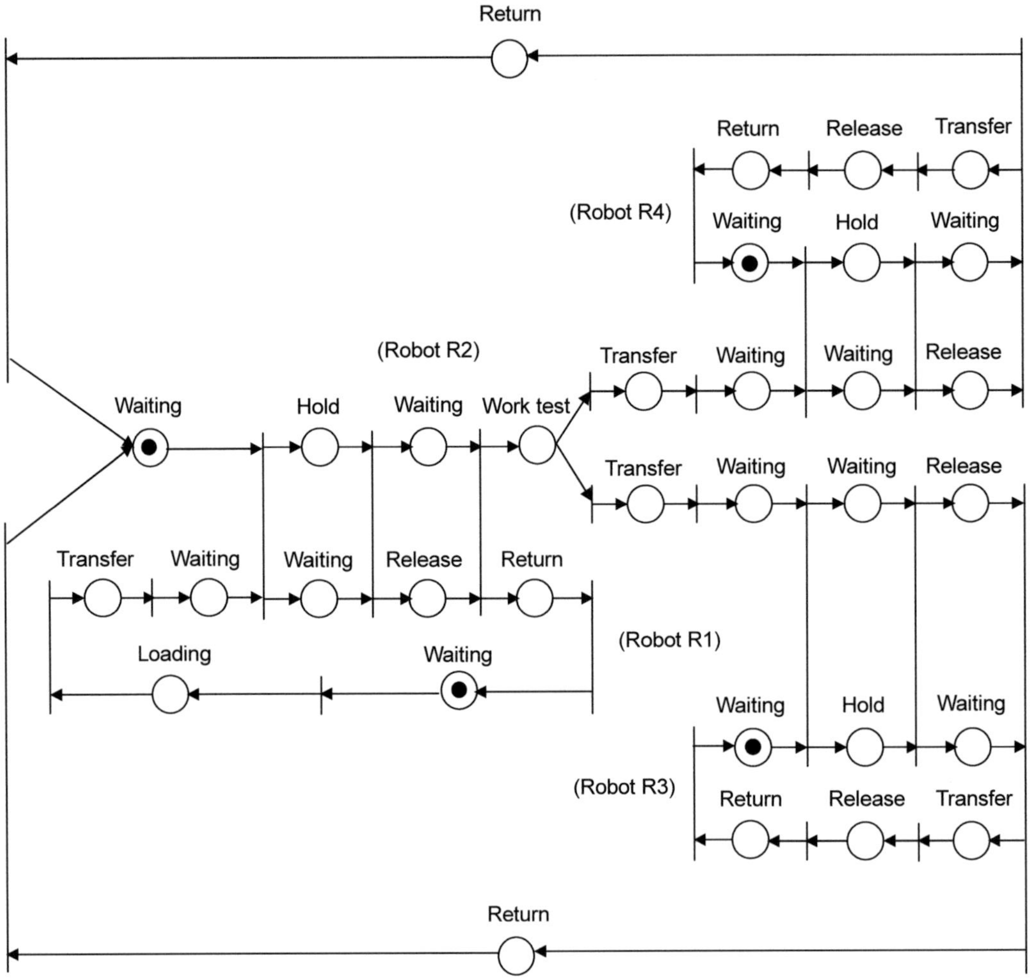

Fig. 11. Detailed Petri net model of work transfer task by four robots

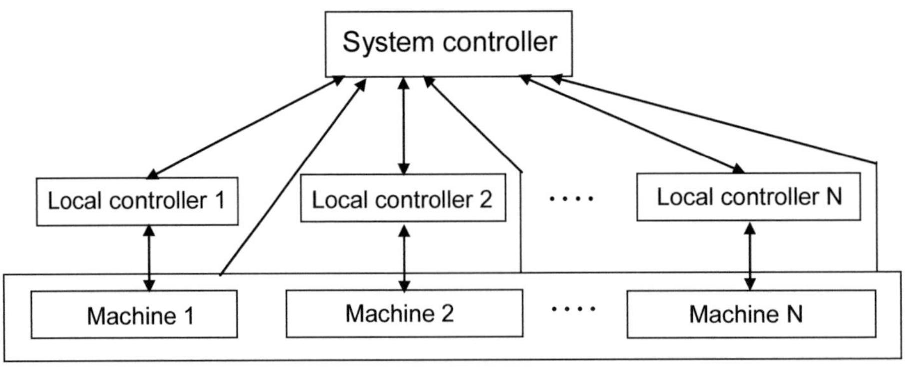

Fig. 12. Hierarchical and distributed control structure composed of system controller and local controllers

In the decomposition procedure, a transition may be divided and distributed into different local controllers as shown in Fig. 13. The local controllers should be coordinated so that these transitions fire simultaneously. Decomposed transitions are called global transitions, and other transitions are called local transitions.

As another example, loading a workpiece necessitates the cooperative or synchronized activities between the conveyor and the robot as shown in Fig. 14. First, "Carry in" operation to carry a workpiece is performed by the conveyor. At the end of the operation, when the robot is free, the "loading" operation is started. The conveyor starts waiting, the robot starts moving to grasp the workpiece. After holding the workpiece, the robot starts transferring it to another position and the conveyor is free. To exploit the above results, a coordinator program for simultaneous firing of decomposed transitions has been introduced so that the aggregate behavior of decomposed subnets is the same as that of the original Petri net.

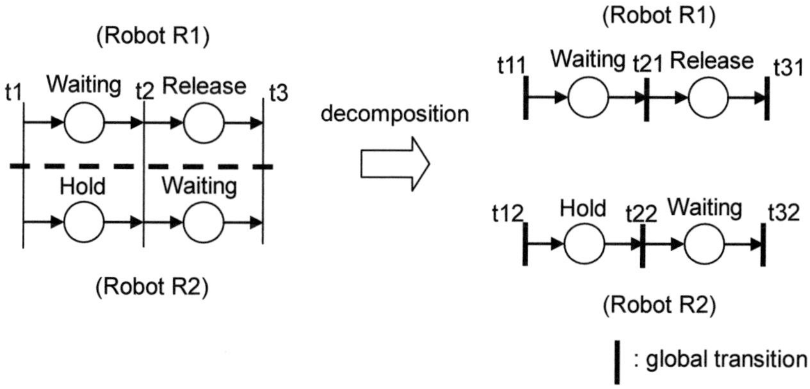

Fig. 13. Decomposition of transitions in "Hand over" operation

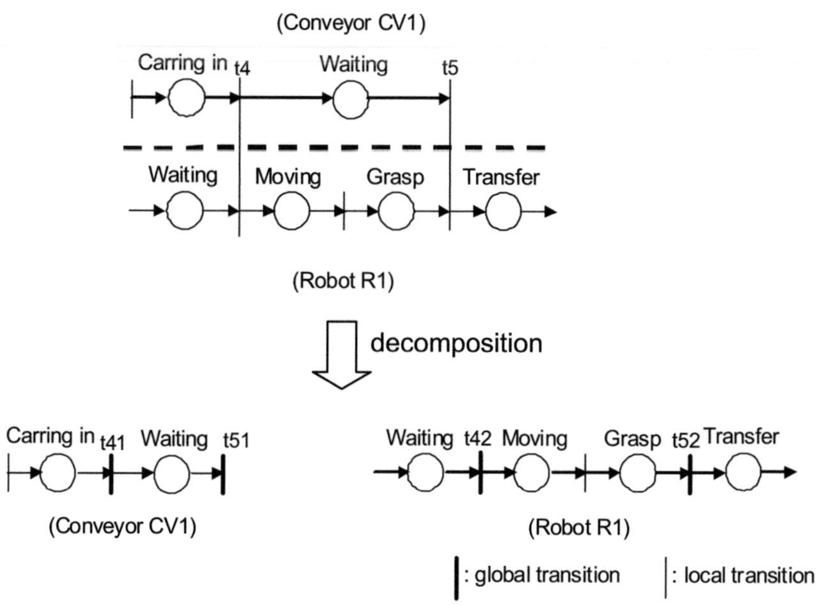

Fig. 14. Decomposition of transitions in the "Loading" operation

When some of the transitions in conflict are firable at the same time, only one of them must fire while the others become disabled. The choice for firing is done arbitrarily using an arbiter program. If arbitration of the transitions is performed independently in separate subnets, the results may be inconsistent with the original rule of arbitration. Therefore the transitions should be arbitrated together as a group by the system controller. On the other hand, arbitration of local transitions in conflict is performed by local controllers. When a robot can do several subtasks in cooperation with conveyors and machining tools in a flexible manufacturing system, transitions connected to the machine activities are found to be in conflict, in which the input place of the transitions represents the activity of the robot. In the decomposition of the detailed Petri net, these transitions also are decomposed and assigned to different machines. The global transitions should be arbitrated together as a group by the coordinator. Based on the decision of arbitration, the local controllers determine the firing transitions.

The overall control structure of an example robotic manufacturing system was implemented on a local area network of microcomputers. Each Petri net based local controller is implemented on a dedicated microcomputer (Renesas H8/3069) under the real-time OS ITRON 4.0. The local controller in charge of robot control executes robot motion control through the transmission of command and the reception of status report with serial interface to the real robot controller. The upper level coordinator is implemented on another microcomputer. Communications among the controllers are performed using TCP/IP protocol. The coordinator sends the commands based on the conceptual, global Petri net model and coordinates the global transitions, which are accessed by the system and local controllers as a shared file, such that decomposed transitions fire simultaneously.

In the simulation experiments, the names of global transitions and their conflict relations are loaded into the upper level controller. The connection structure of a decomposed Petri net model and conflict relations among local transitions are loaded into the Petri net based local controller. In the connection structure, a transition of a Petri net model is defined using the names of its input places and output places; for example, t1-1=b1-1, -b1-11, where the transition no.1 (t1-1) of controller no.1 is connected to the input place no.1 and the output place no.11. Using the names of transitions in the controllers, global transitions are defined; for example, in Fig. 13, global transitions are G1: t1-11, t2-12, G2: t1-21, t2-22, G3: t1-31, t2-32, and in Fig. 14, global transitions are G4: t5-41, t1-42, G5: t5-51, t1-52.

By executing the coordinator and Petri net based controllers algorithms based on loaded information, simulation experiments have been performed. The Petri net simulator initiates the execution of the unit actions attached to the fired transitions through the serial interface to the robots or other external machines. When the action ends its activity, it informs the simulator to proceed with the next activations by the external permissive gate arc. Experimental results show that the decomposed transitions fire at the same time as the original transition of the detailed Petri net of the whole system task. Firing transitions and marking of tokens can be directly observed on the display at each time sequence using the simulator (Yasuda, 2009).

6. Conclusions

A methodology to construct hierarchical and distributed control systems has been proposed. By introduction of the coordinator, the Petri net based controllers are arranged according to the hierarchical and distributed nature of the manufacturing system. The coordination

mechanism between the upper level and the lower level controllers is based on firability test of global transitions, and its software can be easily implemented using the token game player.
An example robotic work cell containing four industrial robot arms was constructed and system control experiments including synchronization control and selective task control were successfully performed. The Petri net model in each Petri net based local controller is not so large and easily manageable. The local controller provides a common interface for programming robots and other intelligent machines made by different manufacturers, and can be implemented using conventional programmable logic controllers (PLC). The control method can be expanded to large and complex, discrete event manufacturing systems. Thus, modeling, simulation and control of large and complex manufacturing systems can be performed consistently using Petri nets. The proposed methodology is now being adapted to advanced multiple robot applications such as exploration robots, rescue robots and home assist robots, besides industrial applications.

7. References

Atabakhche, H.; Barbalho, D. S., Valette, R. & Courvoisier, M. (1986). From Petri net based PLCs to knowledge based control, *Proceedings of IEEE International Conference on Industrial Electronics, Control and Instrumentation (IECON'86)*, 817-822

Fogel, J. & Sebestyenova, J. (1992). An object oriented conception of a real-time control of FMS, *Proceedings of IFAC Workshop on Algorithms and Architectures for Real-Time Control*, 351-356

Gentina, J. C. & Corbeel, D. (1987). Coloured adaptive structured Petri net : A tool for the automatic synthesis of hierarchical control of flexible manufacturing systems (F.M.S.), *Proceedings of 1987 IEEE International Conference on Robotics and Automation*, 1166-1173

Georgeff, M. (1983). Communication and interaction in multi-agent planning, *Proceedings of International Conference of AAAI-83*, 125-129

Hasegawa, K.; Takahashi, K., Masuda, R., & Ohno, H. (1984). Proposal of Mark Flow Graph for discrete system control. *Transactions of SICE*, Vol. 20, No. 2, 122-129

Holt, J. D. & Rodd, M. D. (1994). An architecture for real-time distributed AI-based control systems, *Proceedings of IFAC Distributed Computer Control Systems 1994*, 47-52

Jockovic, M.; Vukobratovic, M. & Ognjanovic, Z. (1990). An approach to the modeling of the highest control level of flexible manufacturing cell. *Robotica*, Vol. 8, 125-130

Kasturia, E. & Dicesare, F. (1988). Real time control of multilevel manufacturing systems using colored Petri nets, *Proceedings of 1988 IEEE International Conference on Robotics and Automation*, 1114-1119

Murata, T. (1989). Petri Nets: Properties, analysis and applications. *Proceedings of the IEEE*, Vol.77, No.4, 541-580

Perez, R. A. & Koutsourelis, D. I. (1987). A command language for multiple robot arm coordination. *IEEE Transactions on Education*, Vol. E-30, No. 2, 109-112

Rogers, P. & Williams, D. (1988). A knowledge-based system linking to real-time control for manufacturing cells, *Proceedings of 1988 IEEE International Conference on Robotics and Automation*, 1291-1293

Silva, M. (1990). Petri nets and flexible manufacturing, In: *Advances in Petri Nets 1989*, Lecture Notes in Computer Science, Vol. 424, Rozenberg, G., (Ed.), 374-417, Springer-Verlag, Berlin

Taubner, D. (1988). On the implementation of Petri nets, In: *Advances in Petri Nets 1988*, Lecture Notes in Computer Science, Vol. 340, Rozenberg, G., (Ed.), 418-439, Springer-Verlag, Berlin

Thuriot, E.; Valette, R., & Courvoisier, M. (1983). Implementation of a centralized synchronization concept for production systems, *Proceedings of IEEE Real-time Systems Symposium*, 163-171

Yasuda, G. (1999). An object-oriented multitasking control environment for multirobot system programming and execution with 3D graphic simulation. *International Journal of Production Economics*, Vol. 60/61, 241-250

Yasuda, G. (2009). Implementation of distributed cooperative control for industrial robot systems using Petri nets, *Preprints of the 9th IFAC Symposium on Robot Control (SYROCO '09)*, 433-438

Wang, F. & Saridis, G. N. (1990). A coordination theory for intelligent machines, *Proceedings of 11th IFAC World Congress*, 235-240

5

Intelligent Production Systems Reconfiguration by Means of Petri Nets and the Supervisory Control Theory

Zapata M. Germán[1], Chacón R. Edgar[2] and Palacio B. Juan[3]
[1]*Universidad Nacional de Colombia, sede Medellín*
[2]*Universidad de Los Andes, Mérida*
[3]*Universidad Nacional de Colombia, sede Medellín*
[1,3]*Colombia*
[2]*Venezuela*

1. Introduction

The current trend in industrial production processes is to have agile and flexible systems that respond quickly to the permanent changes and disturbances in the production environment. This trend has created an important volume of research and papers aimed at having production control, supervision and programming systems that respond to these demands. Most of the proposals are grouped inside what has been labeled as Intelligent Manufacturing Systems (IMS). Among them are virtual, fractal, bionic, holonic manufacturing. These proposals initially appeared for discrete manufacturing processes. However, continuous production processes such as oil and gas, chemical plants, and power generation, also face demands for flexibility and rapid response. Therefore the IMS proposals can be applied to these types of processes.

Holonic Production Systems (HPS) is one of the proposals that has advanced the most. It already shows evidence of its application in industrial systems.

In general terms, a HPS is formed by autonomous entities that cooperate proactively to reach a common goal. These entities are labeled holons and, through aggregation relationships, they can form groups to form the so called holarchies. The grouping of various holons or holarchies with the objective of carrying out a productive process is called a Holonic Production Unit (HPU).

The principal attributes of holons are: autonomy, cooperation, proactiveness, and reactivity. Other key characteristics are the distribution of intelligence and self-similarity to build complex structures from simpler systems.

In order to achieve agility and flexibility, HPSs need distributed coordination and supervision functions. These functions enable them to dynamically reconfigure the production structure and the control laws to accommodate to the new operative conditions.

Reconfiguration can only be faced if the production system has flexibility with regards to the allocation of manufacturing operations and of control architectures, which enable using different control policies for different types of services, or adapting control strategies to achieve new requirements.

The selection of a new configuration is basically a problem of state reachability in discrete dynamics systems. Therefore, Petri nets and the supervisory control theory have been deemed appropriate to find solutions that perform well in real time. Due to the demands for temporary performance, reconfiguration has been considered a function of real time in control architecture.

The work that is presented is inspired in the holonic paradigm, and supported by Petri nets and the supervisory control theory, to define, in real time, a new configuration for the production structure that adjusts to new requirements or disturbances.

For the holonic paradigm perspective, each production resource is seen as a HPU, with skills, availability and capacities. The HPU makes offers and negotiates its objectives or missions. Each holon, for a determined operation condition, offers its services based on its current capacities and state and, in this manner, a highly reconfigurable system is formed. Petri Nets (PN) are a mathematical and graphic tool with the ability to capture precedence relationships and structural relationships, to model blocking, sequences, concurrent processes, conflicts and restrictions.

Products manufactured by an HPU can also be modeled through PN, because of the ease to represent precedence relationships. A global HPU model is established through PN composition operations, composing the resources with the products. The initial marking of this global PN is generated from the state of the resources in real time which, in order to conduct a production mission, presents offers based on current operative conditions.

Once the initial marking for the resources state is established, the PN is executed and the complete state space of the possible HPU behavior is generated. The states space, or reachability tree, is an finite automata and the trajectories between states define the possible configurations to reach the objective. The configuration selected must be feasible and controllable and must also guarantee that there neither blocking nor forbidden states in the system. Besides, the selected trajectory must lead to a satisfactory termination of the product. The supervisory control theory (SCT) is suitable to solve this type of problems which are present in DES – Discrete Event Systems.

By guaranteeing properties as boundedness, a finite states space and the obtaining of a solution in finite time are assured.

Once a configuration to reach an objective, based on the capacities and the state of resources is selected, the holarchies are formed.

Generated for each holarchy, in a recursive manner, is a PN model of its behavior, following the same construction structure explained for the HPU. When a disturbance occurs, the holarchy tries to solve it internally by adjusting its production structure and following the proposed analysis technique. If the holarchy is incapable of achieving its mission for the new operative condition, it requests cooperation from the rest of the HPU. The new mission redistribution is carried out by following the same analysis technique, generating a global PN model formed by holarchies, and a marking for the current condition.

In this manner, a proposal for determining a new configuration, which shows the advantages of using the recursivity of the holonic paradigm and the description and analysis power of Petri nets, has been developed. Real time performance is noticeably improved as the reachability tree is considerably reduced.

This chapter is structured as follows. The first part presents related works highlighting research made from the holonic paradigm or making use of PN and SCT. Theoretical concepts are presented in the second part. The third part presents the construction of the HPU's global model and the obtaining of the reachability tree from the marking determined by resources states, and continuing with the definition of the holarchies. Once the holarchies are established, it is shown how the HPU responds to disturbances and how it reconfigures itself to cover the fault conditions. Finally, an application and implementation example is presented through CPNTools.

2. Previous works

It was only in 1989 that the concept of Holon proposed by Koestler in 1968 (Koestler, 1968), was applied to manufacturing concepts. Suda, in his work, proposes a "plug and play" proposal to design and operate manufacturing systems that combined optimum global performance with robustness to face disturbances. This gave birth to what is labeled Holonic Manufacturing Systems (HMS) (Suda, 1989). As a concept, HMS represents a methodology, tools and norms to design manufacturing control systems that are flexible and reconfigurable. A work that will always be a fixed reference, as it is a forerunning proposal, is the work presented by Jo Wyns in (Wyns, 1999), labeled PROSA: Product - Resource - Order – Staff Architecture. Concerning the control system's flexibility, PROSA, through the formation of temporary holarchies, establishes that mixed scenarios that combine hierarchies with heterarchies are the most optimal. Recently, PROSA began to add auto-organization capacities taken from biological systems and labeled its architecture PROSA + ANTS (Leitao et al., 2009).

ADACOR architecture (Adaptive Holonic Control Architecture) (Leitao, 2004), presents the holonic approach to introduce dynamic adaptation and agility to face disturbances. This architecture is based in a group of autonomous, intelligent and cooperative entities to represent Factory components. In this approach it is important to highlight the modeling of holon dynamics through Petri Nets.

Other architectures that can be highlighted include: Holobloc Fischer John (n.d.), Metamorph (Maturana et al., n.d.), Holonic Control Device (Brennan et al., 2003), Interrap (*Holonic Manufacturing Systems*, 2008), Holonic Component Based Architecture (Chirn & McFarlane, n.d.), HoMuCS (Langer, 1999), MaSHReC (El Kebbe, 2002) and HOMASCOW (Adam et al., n.d.).

The largest volume of research is centered around discrete manufacturing systems. In reality, there have only been a few works in which the holonic approach was applied in the industry of continuous processes. Nevertheless, these industries are also subject to the demands of today´s markets. Mass production personalization trends, rapid response times, shorter product life cycles, and the efficient use of energy and resources, force the process industry to consider aspects as flexibility, agility reconfigurability, decentralization and integration.

The works of (Chokshi & McFarlane, 2008b), can be cited as references of the holonic approach in continuous processes (Chokshi & McFarlane, n.d.) (McFarlane, 1995) (Agre et al., 1994) (Chacón & Colmenares, 2005). They mention that the principal works are conducted by groups aimed at automating the chemical industries, specially concerning for planning and production scheduling.

A group from Universidad de los Andes de Venezuela has proposed the concept of Holonic Production Unit- HPU for its acronym in Spanish - in which holonic principles are brought into continuous processes. Some of the works related are found in (Chacón et al., 2008) (Chacón & Colmenares, 2005) (Lobo, 2003) (Peréz, n.d.) (Durán, 2006) (Chacón & Colmenares, 2005) (Chacón et al., 2003).

The techniques of Discrete Even Systems (DES) have been used in some works related to holonic or similar systems - as multi-agent systems or distributed systems - to model dynamics, to model production control functions and to test/prove performance properties.
In (Caramihai, n.d.) a unified theory base is presented, based on the theory of DES, to model interactions between agents by composing Petri Nets (PNs). This method uses the Supervisory Control Theory (SCT) of DES through PNs, in the sense that all interactions among agents are obtained by analyzing the states space generated by the execution of the PN, and through the specification of undesired states such as blockings. A supervisory model eliminates the interactions that lead to those states.
For Celaya, the development of theoretical bases to guarantee the properties of a Multi-agent system (MAS) is critical. These systems can be considered as DES and use PNs to model interactions and to guarantee that the structural properties of these interactions are met. Blockings of the MAS are avoided, evaluating the properties of liveness and boundedness (Celaya et al., 2009).
According to Balasubramanian, control of holonic systems in real time requires responses that are radically different. These must adapt automatically and reconfigure according to the constantly changing requirements of the production system. It presents the architecture for dynamically reconfigurable systems based on IEC 61499 and in a structure of control levels driven by events. (Balasubramanian et al., n.d.)
A work by Hsieh (Hsieh, 2006) establishes a fusion of PNs with Contract Net, because of the difficulty of this protocol to avoid undesired states, such as blockings in the HMS. The modeling and analysis capacities of PNs with Contract Net are combined for the distribution of tasks among holons and the so-called collaborative Petri Nets are proposed. The complete process of production orders is proposed as a problem of supervisory control as different orders must compete for limited resources. These generate conflict situations that need to be solved through the coordination of PNs. The condition of liveness (non blocking) must be guaranteed in order to facilitate the feasibility of agreements.
The problem of configurations for scheduling and rescheduling has been deeply explored in (Ramos, n.d.), (Sousa & Ramos, 1998), (Bongaerts, 1998) and (Cheng et al., 2004). In (McFarlane, 1995), a Holon Configuration, which acts to reconfigure the system when required, is proposed.
A review of the works concerning distributed planning and scheduling of reconfigurable holons can be consulted at (Mcfarlane & Bussman, 2000), (Chokshi & McFarlane, 2008a) and (Chokshi & McFarlane, 2008b). These propose a distributed architecture, based on the holonic paradigm, for the reconfigurable control of operations in continuous processes. This approach distributes the functionalities of planning, scheduling, coordination and control.
PNs have gained the spotlight as a solution for the problem of scheduling and rescheduling in discrete and in continuous and batch processes (Tuncel & Bayhan, 2007), (http://research.curtin.edu.au/, 2010), (Fu-Shiung, n.d.), (Ghaeli et al., 2005), (Tittus & Akesson, 1999), (Tittus & Lennartson, 1997), (Zhou, 1995) and (Tittus et al., n.d.).
According to (Tuncel & Bayhan, 2007), PN based methods directly describe the current dynamic behavior and the control system's logic. The most significant advantage of using PNs, is their ability to capture precedence and structural relationships, and to model blockings, conflicts, buffer sizes and multi-resource restrictions. Concurrent and asynchronous activities, shared resources, route flexibility, limited buffers and complex restrictions in the process sequences can be, specifically and concisely, modeled through PNs.

Furthermore, according to (Music & D., 1998), synthesis methods based on PNs exploit the nets' structures avoiding the need to explore all the states spaces.
The characteristics of PN models have lead many authors to propose reconfiguration as a problem of supervisory control (Ramadge & Wonham, 1989), (Akesson, 2002), (Pétin et al., 2007) and (Tittus & Akesson, 1999). From this theory, a feasible combination of the resources in the time to reach an objective must be found. Therefore, a minimal restrictive supervisor that makes the system synchronize the optimal use of the resources by the products is synthesized. This guarantees behavior specifications and the reachability of the objective, preventing the system from going into blocked states or into forbidden states. Solutions based on this approach, that elaborate a model composed by products and resources through PNs and develop a synthesis from the supervisory control theory through an analysis of the reachability tree, can be found in (Tittus & Akesson, 1999), (Lennartson, Tittus & Fabian, n.d.), (Akesson, 2002), (Pétin et al., 2007), (Falkman et al., 2009), (Music & D., 1998), (Reveliotis, 1999) and (Lennartson, Fabian & Falkman, n.d.) . This last paper established that the supervisor must guarantee that the system remains alive (enabled to reach states where all products are produced) and safe (it never reaches undesired states).
Production scheduling based on Petri Nets and in the theory of supervisory control, along with the holonic concept of the formation of holarchies, can be appropriate for the rescheduling of continuous production systems with high demands for re-configurability.

3. Theoretical bases

3.1 Holonic Production Systems (HPS)

An HPS is understood as a system composed by individual autonomous units that cooperate proactively through temporary reconfigurable hierarchies to obtain a global goal. Each autonomous component is called a *Holon* and a group of holons is called a *Holarchy*. The aggregation of holons and holarchies, through properties of auto similarity, enables the construction of very complex systems as shown in 1. The added holons are defined as a set of grouped holons, forming a major holon with its own identity and a structure that is similar to the holons that form it.

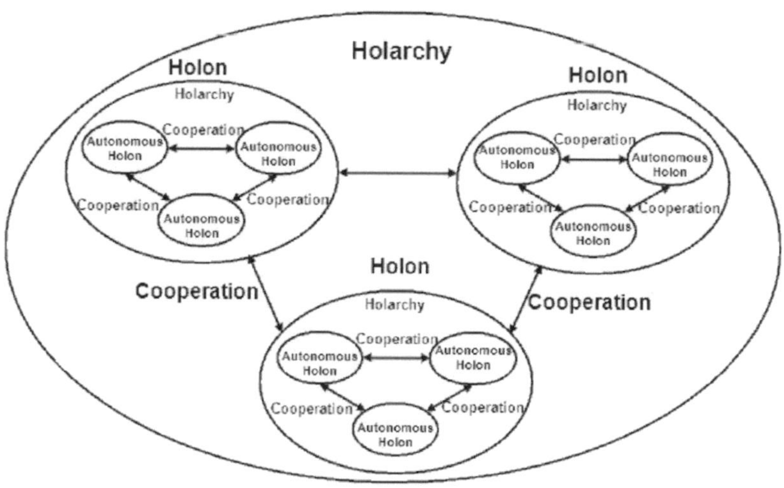

Fig. 1. Holarchy

The Consortium HMS defines a holon as: "a constitutive, autonomous and cooperative component of a manufacturing system whose purpose is to transport, transform, store, and/or validate information or physical objects"(HMS, 2004).

The principal attributes of a holon are: decentralization for taking decisions, autonomy, cooperation, and capacity to auto-organize. These enable a dynamic evolution and the reconfiguration of the organizational control structure, which in turn combine global optimization of production and agile reaction, to face unpredictable disturbances. Holons are also systems with objective oriented behaviors. HMS Consortium defined the following basic attributes:

Autonomy: The capability of an entity to create, control, and supervise the execution of its own behavior plans and/or strategies.

Cooperation: a set of entities that develop mutually acceptable plans and strategies and execute them in order to achieve common goals or objectives.

Proactiviness: the capability to anticipate changes in its plans and objectives.

Reactivity: the capability to react to stimuli in the environment.

In order to bring holonic attributes and characteristics into continuous production systems had been presented the Holonic Production Unit proposal (HPU).

Presented in this proposal, from an integrated vision of the productive process, is the conception of the production unit as a holon. Representation techniques must enable the understanding of relationships among them, for each one of the different components: graphic representations, capability attributes, availability, reliability and evolution of dynamics.

The HPU is conceived as the composition of a set of elemental units or resources that are organized and configured in a manner that enables performing the transformation processes in the value chain. The objective is to obtain the demanded products. The HPU takes its own decisions with regards to achieving its objective, but is obliged to inform its state in the compliance of a goal, or if such goal cannot be accomplished due to a fault or to errors in its behavior.

The HPU is formed by the following components:

- Mission, which describes the objective of production.
- Resources, which describe the necessary components for obtaining the products, which in turn can also be another HPU being consequent with the paradigm´s recursiveness.
- Engineering, which describes the necessary knowledge to obtain the products.

The relationship among these components is shown in Figure 2. Figure 3 shows the class diagram of the HPU proposal (Chacón et al., 2008).

Highlighted in this proposal are a component of Control and Supervision that measures, modifies, controls and supervises the production process; and the relationships that exist between the Configuration and the Production Method, and between the Process and the Resources.

The behavior of the HPU is presented in (Chacón & Colmenares, 2005) from the Supervisory Control Theory (SCT), describing its dynamics as a Discrete Event System (DES). The global behavior of the HPU is the result of coupling the behavior of the control system (supervisor) and the behavior of the process and the resources. Each component of a HPU is model through a Petri Net (PN).

In this manner, the behavior of a HPU focused in reaching a production goal, can be formulated as a supervisory control problem. In such, an entity (supervisor) restricts the behavior of a system so it achieves the desired states and does not go into forbidden states.

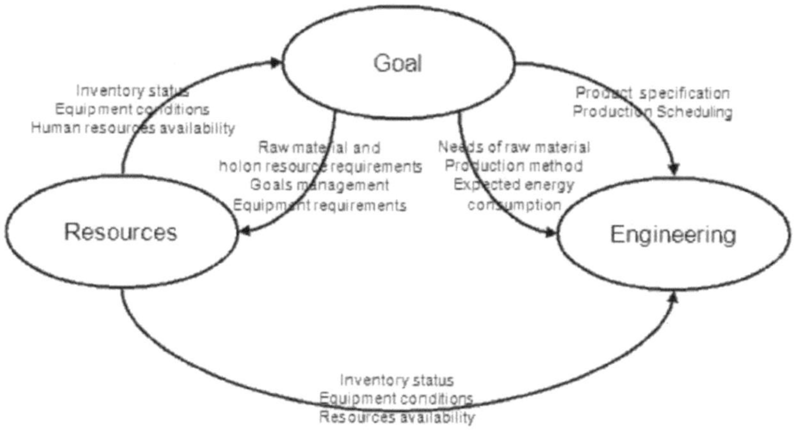

Fig. 2. HPU Components

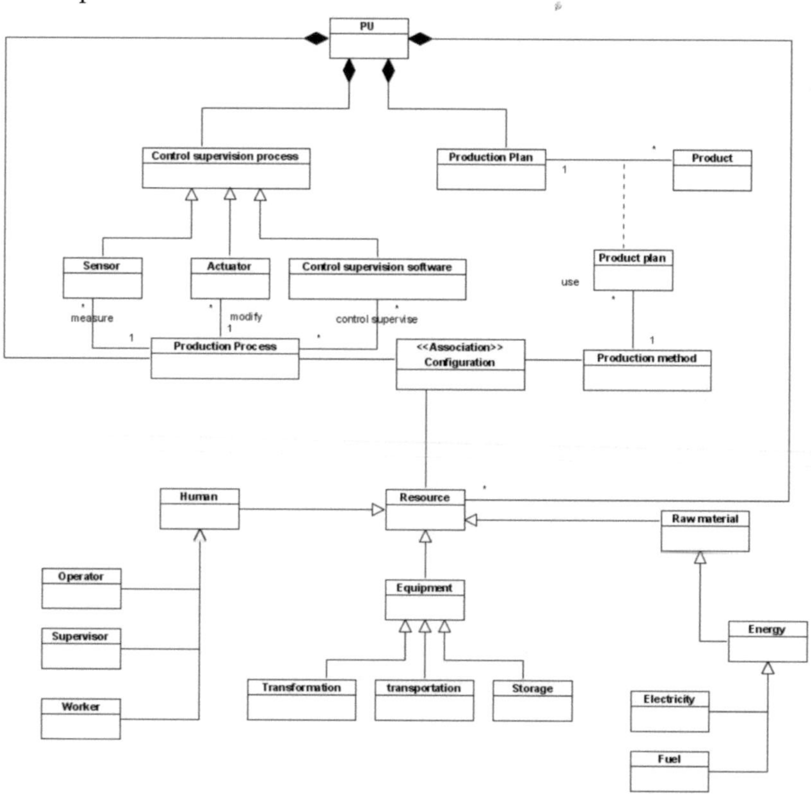

Fig. 3. Holonic Production Unit (From (Chacón et al., 2008))

3.2 Automata and languages

A Discrete Event System (DES) is defined as a dynamic system with a states spaces that is finite and numerable and that evolves because of the occurrence of spontaneous events. The decisions to "select" a configuration of the production resources to obtain a product in a continuous process, is classified in the DES category.

To specify a DES model, it is necessary to specify the set of states, the set of events and the structure of the system's transition. Formally, a DES is represented through an Automata $G = (Q,\Sigma, \delta, q_0,Q_m)$, where Q is the finite set of states; Σ is the finite set of events formed by two sub-sets: Σ_{nc} of non-controllable events and Σ_c of controllable events; a transition function $\delta: \Sigma \times Q \rightarrow Q$ that establishes the dynamic of the system; an initial state $q_0 \in Q$; and a set $Q_m \in Q$ of final or marked states. In addition, a set of co-reachable states Q_{co}, is described as the set formed by q states for which there is at least one path to take them from q to a marked state.

The behavior of a DES is characterized by a sequence of events produced during its operation. An event is called a string and is formed through the concatenation of events. Kleene closure is a set defined as the set of all strings formed through the concatenation of the elements of the set in any combination, including the identity element for the concatenation operator denoted ϵ and called the silent event. Kleene closure of the set of events is denoted by Σ^*.

A prefix of a string s is a sequence of events, which is also an initial sequence of s. This is $s \in\Sigma^*$, u is a prefix of s if $uw = s$ for some $w \in \Sigma^*$.

The set that includes all the prefixes of all its elements is said to be a prefix-closed. It is clear that Σ^* is a prefix-closed. The prefix closure of a set A is defined, and $\overline{A}$ is denoted as the set that contains all the prefixes of the elements of A.

A language is a set of strings (or words) formed by the concatenation of events. The language generated by automata G, denoted by $L(G)$, is the set of strings $L(G) = \{s \mid s \in \Sigma^*, \delta(s, q_0) \textit{ is defined}\}$

The marked language, denoted by $L_m(G)$,is a subset of $L(G)$ formed by all strings that lead to marked states. Formally: $L_m(G) = \{s \mid s \in \Sigma^*, \delta(s, q_0) \textit{ is defined}, \delta(s, q_0) \in Q_m\}$

3.3 Supervisory control theory

The results of the theory of automata and languages were used by Ramadge and Wonham (Ramadge & Wonham, 1989) to propose a theory for DES control called Supervisory Control Theory (SCT). In this theory, a supervisor controls the behavior of an automata representing the plant - enabling and disabling events - affecting the actual sequence and a trajectory to reach the desired states and avoid the forbidden ones.

To synthesize a supervisor, one departs from a language k called Specification which expresses the plant's desired behavior. The supervisor must guarantee that all marked states are reached from any reachable state. This property is called nonblocking and is defined by expressing that an automata is reachable and nonblocking if it is capable of reaching a marked state from any reachable state. It is formally described as: $\overline{L_m(G)} = L(G)$.

Furthermore, controllable specifications with regards to the plant must be guaranteed. Therefore, to verify this property, the following must apply: $\overline{k}\, \Sigma_{nc} \cap L(G) \subseteq \overline{k}$.

The nonblocking property is fundamental for the reconfiguration of a production system as, when a disturbance occurs and the failed system abandons a marked state, the control system must be able to bring it from the new state to another state $q \in Q_m$.

Along these lines, algorithms for synthesis of the DES supervisor are used in this work to establish a trajectory that leads the system to satisfactory termination states of the product when a disturbance occurs.

In synthesis, from a global behavior of the system, the forbidden states are removed through a purge function, the states that led to blockings are suppressed, and controllability is verified. It is expressed in the following algorithm where A is an automata, M_A is the set of marked states of A, X_A is the set of forbidden states of A, Q_x is the set of blockable states plus the previous forbidden states.

purge(S_0);
$i = 1$;
repeat
    $Q_{CO} = M_A$; $Q_A = X$; $Q = \emptyset$;
    repeat
        $Q = 0 \ \forall\ Q \in [Q_A \backslash (Q_{co} \cup Q_x)]$
        IF $[Q_A \backslash (Q_{co} \cup Q_x)] = \emptyset$ **THEN**
        END
        ELSE
            $\exists \sigma \in \Sigma_A / \{[\delta(q,\sigma) \in Q_x]$ or $[\forall \delta(q,\sigma)$ not defined$]\}$
            $Q_x = Q_x \cup \{q\}$;
            $Q_{co} = Q_{co} \cup Q$;
        END IF
    UNTIL $Q = \emptyset$;
    $Q_{si} = Q_{co} \backslash Q_x$;
    REPEAT
        $X_A = Q_A \backslash Q_{co}$;
        $Q_x = X_A$; $Q = \emptyset$;
        $\forall q \in Q_A \backslash Q_x$ **IF** $\exists \sigma \in \Sigma_{nc} / \delta(q,\sigma) \in Q_x$ **THEN**
            $Q = Q \cup \{q\}$;
            $Q_x = Q_x \cup Q$;
    UNTIL $Q = \emptyset$;
    $X_A = Q_x$;
    $Q_{si+1} = Q_{co} \backslash X_A$;
    $i = i + 1$;
UNTIL $Q_{si} - Q_{si+1}$;
$Q_s = Q_{si}$ //those are states of Supervisor

3.4 Petri nets as language generators

Petri Nets relate to the theory of supervisory control theory through automata and languages. The most appropriate PNs for language generation are the ones called labeled PN. Through attaining all the states spaces of the PN labeled, called reachability tree or graph, the net's automata and the languages generated and marked are obtained.

A Petri net can be presented through a tuple of the form $R = \langle P,T,A,B \rangle$, where P is the set of states of the system, T is the transitions set, A is the input incidence matrix, that represent arcs from a p_i to a transition t_j with weight $a(p_i, t_j) \in \mathbb{N}$, B output incidence matrix, that represents arcs from t_j to p_i with weight $b(p_i, t_j)$.

A labeled PN is a tuple $N = \langle P,T, F, l \rangle$, where P and T have the same meaning as in the previous case, $F \subseteq (P \times T) \cup (T \times P)$ is the set or arcs and l is a label that assigns to each transition an event $l : T \rightarrow 2^{\Sigma} \cup \epsilon$.

A marking vector is $M : P \rightarrow \mathbb{N} \cup \{0\}$ which assigns to each place a non-negative number of tokens. The net (N,M_0) is a net marked con initial marking M_0. Notation $M_0[\sigma\rangle M$ is used to express that the trigger of σ in the marking M_0 leads to M.
To convert a PN to an automata, it is used the procedure that is shown bellow
Formally, the equivalent automata of a net (N,M_0) can be expressed as $G = (Q,\Sigma, \delta, q_0,Q_m)$, with $Q= R(N,M_0)$, meaning all reachable states in the Petri net N from M_0; $\Sigma=U_{t\in T}l(t)\backslash\{\epsilon\}$, δ so that $M' \in \delta(M,\sigma)$ iff $M[t\rangle M'$ and $\sigma \in l(t)$, $q_0 = M_0$, obtaining thereby the reachability graph of (N,M_0) expressed as automata.
Now, the link between Petri nets and languages it is given by marked or closed language $(L_m(G))$and generated lenguage $(L(G))$.

$$L_m(G) = \{l(\sigma) \in \Sigma^* \mid \sigma \in T^*, M_0[\sigma\rangle M \in Q_m\} \text{ and } L(G) = \{l(\sigma) \in \Sigma^* \mid \sigma \in T^*, \exists M' \ni M_0[\sigma\rangle M'\}$$

Both lenguages can be found since the state space and that is way how PN, automata and lenguages have relation. It is had the PN behavior such an automata so it is posible to use Supervisory control theory (SCT) to restrict the system. In order to have finite and non blockeable graph, PN have to satisfy boundedness and liveness properties. However, by the re-scheduling characteristic of this proposal, PN have to be safe. The Net (N,M_0) is:

- Bounded, if there exist a non negative integer k such that $M(p) \leq k$ for every place p and for every marking $M \times R(N,M_0)$.
- Safe, if $M(p) \leq 1$ for every place p and for every marking $M \times R(N,M_0)$.
- Live, if for every marking $M \times R(N,M_0)$ there exist a firing sequence containing all transitions.

3.5 Composition through fusion places

The idea with composition methods is that from modular models, represented by automatas or PNs, a global model is determined without change the system´s dynamic evolution and, in this manner, the reachability tree of the whole system is obtained.
The fusion places has been proposed by Silva (n.d.) as a simplification method and by Jensen (2003) as a method for the hierarchical PNs.
In Jensen's proposal the idea with fusion is that places that undergo fusion represent the same place, even if they are represented as individual places. For instance, in figure 4(a) there are two modular models in which places labeled as **A** belong to the same fusion set, meaning that they are the same place and the model of figure 4(b) can be composed from them.

4. Description of the reconfiguration proposal

The proposal for the reconfiguration of continuous production systems uses models obtained through Petri Nets (PN), that combine holonic production resources with the products that they are in capacity to produce. The products are divided into operations and if a holon resource (HR) is able to perform an operation, then such holon is said to have the *skill* for this operation. A global PN of the Holon Production Unit (HPU) is built through models of the products and the HRs. When the HPU receives a mission, expressed as a production order, a negotiation process with the holon resources that form it is launched. If an HR has the skills to perform the operation for which the proposal is sent, it sends an offer that includes its availability, capacity and the cost of the operation. This enables determining the initial marking of the PN.

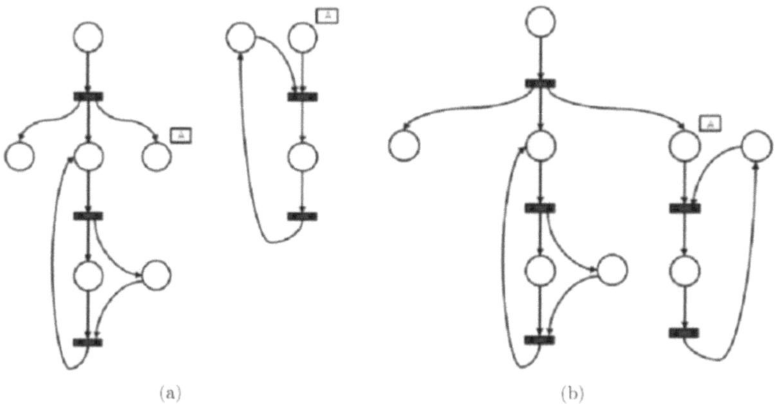

Fig. 4. Fusion Places

Established in the first phase of the negotiation is the existence of configurations in the HPU to develop the product, and the feasibility of the mission from the perspective of configuration. Configurations are obtained from a reachability tree of the PN, applying the supervisor synthesis algorithm that leads to satisfactory terminations of the product. If there are several possible configurations, the criteria of optimization are used to select the definite configuration of the HPU for the mission under negotiation. This phase of the negotiation is conducted out of line and it enables forming the holarchies that will be responsible for the production objective. A PN is generated for each holarchy following the same construction principles applied for the HPU. This evidences the recursivity of the holonic paradigm.
Once production is launched and disturbances appear response mechanisms are launched based on the attributes of autonomy and cooperation between holarchies. PN models are executed in each one of the cooperation levels in order to determine the new configuration that enables continuing with mission compliance despite the failure situation.

4.1 PN model construction

4.1.1 Product model

Construction of the global PN is based on the product´s model. There will be a model for each product made by the HPU, and each product will be specified independently of any production system. The required operational sequences required to obtain the product, are obtained in the model. P-Graphs proposed by Fiedler (Chokshi & McFarlane, 2008b), which are bigraphs used to model net structures, are used for the representation of products in continuous production processes. The graph´s vertices represent operations and raw material, and the connections represent material flow (see Figure 5).
The product's discrete dynamic is considered to determine a configuration. Its continuous dynamic is not used for this. This means that to obtain a product, the availability of raw material, and of the process node that performs the operation, are necessary. The model does not consider flows of mass and energy, but only the necessary conditions to produce them. Process nodes represent transformation operations as "heat", "cool", "mix", "separate", "pressurize" and these operations indicate the skills demanded from the resources that must perform them.
Product representation through a PN is made following the structure of figure 6, which shows the raw material, the operation required (resource skill) and the product obtained.

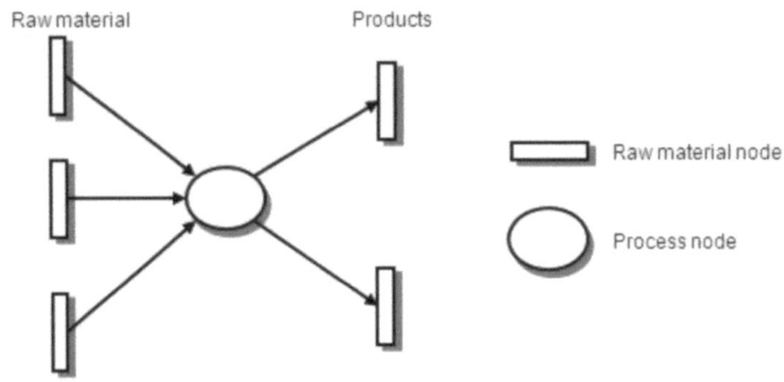

Fig. 5. Process graphs (P-graphs)

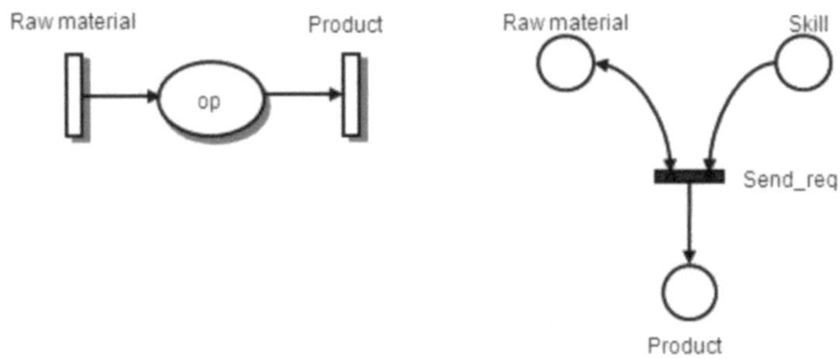

Fig. 6. PN product model

Example: the production line shown in Figure 7 enables obtaining a product with a model represented in Figure 8. The PN model of the discrete dynamic of the product is shown in Figure 9.

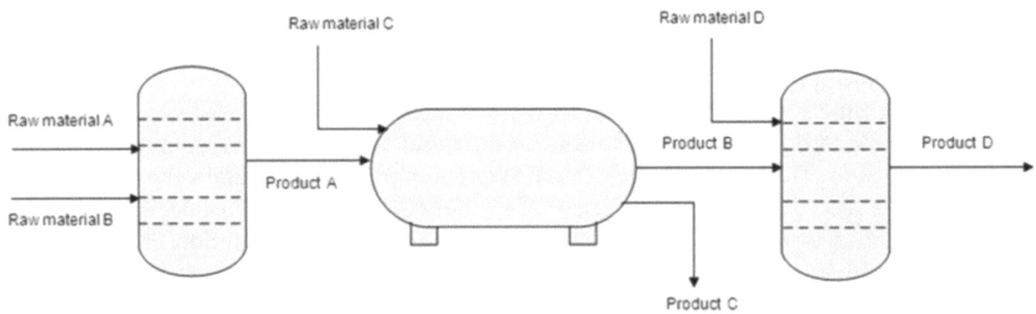

Fig. 7. Production line

4.1.2 Model of a Holon Resource

It is necessary to know the availability and skills of the HR to determine its configuration. Availability enables establishing the initial marking of the PN, and skills enable the link with the product's model.

Determined from the Petri Net of the HR the availability of resource (if it is on operation, or if it presents a failure or if it is on maintenance). Figure 10 shows the model and Table 1 presents the states and the events.

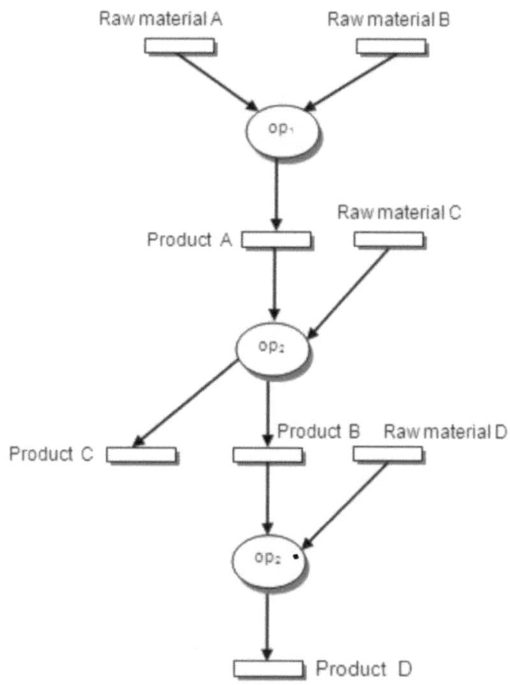

Fig. 8. P-graph of the production line

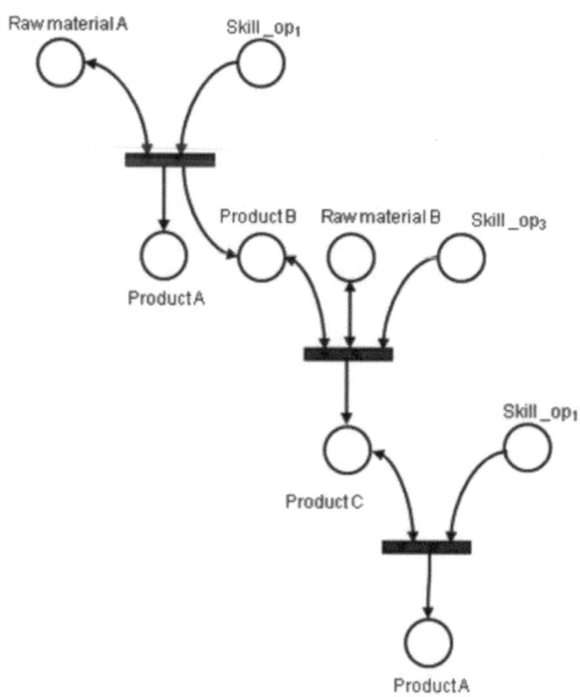

Fig. 9. PN of the production line

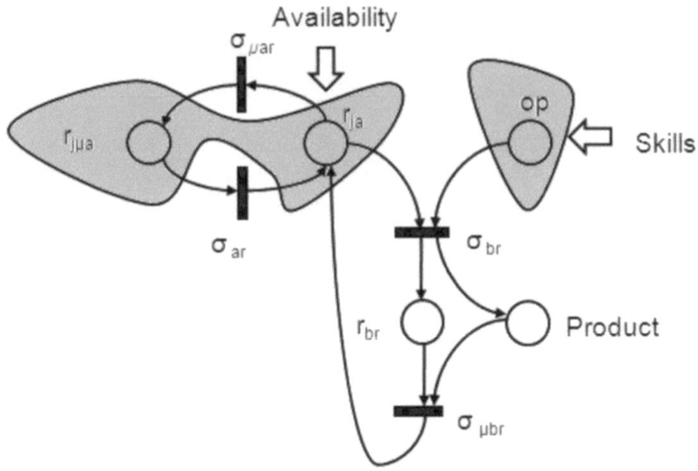

Fig. 10. PN Resource Model

States	Description
r_{ja}	resource *j* available
r_{jua}	resource *j* unavailable
op	skills
r_{jb}	resource *j* booked
Events	**Description**
σ_{nar}	non-availability
σ_{ar}	availability
σ_{br}	booked
σ_{ubr}	unbooked

Table 1. Resource model States and events description

4.1.3 Connections Model

Connections guarantee the flow of a product between resources and their availability, or lack of, affects the definition of the configuration. Connection models are obtained based on the operational and physical restrictions imposed by the process. Each resource has input and output ports. The PN for the connections is shown in Figure 11.

- **Asynchronous Junction (Multi-product):** enables the distribution, simultaneous or individual, of a product to two destinations. See figure 12
- **Synchronous Junction (Separation):** enables material flow only to one destination at a time. See figure 13
- **Asynchronous Union (Multi-feeding):** receives material flow from two sources, simultaneously or individually. See figure 14
- **Synchronous Union (Mix):** receives material flow from just one source at a time. See figure 15

Taken into account to connect resources is that an upstream resource enables the output port, and that connection is an additional condition to enable a downstream resource. The PN showing two resources connected is given in Figure 16.

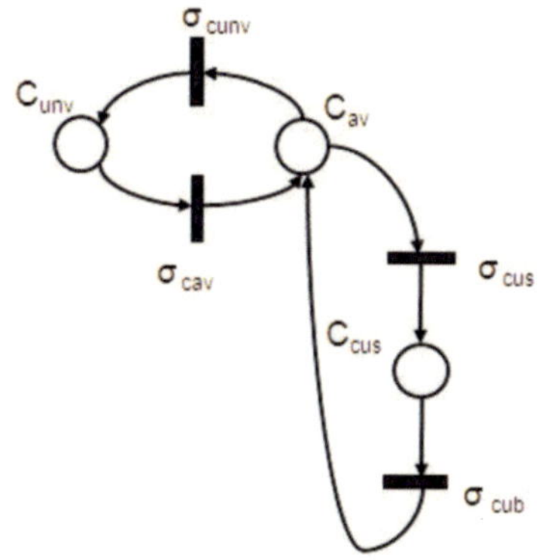

States	Description
C_{av}	Connection available.
C_{un}	Connection unvailable.
C_{cus}	Connection used.
Events	**Description**
σ_{cav}	Available.
σ_{cus}	Used.
σ_{cun}	Unbooked.

Fig. 11. Connections model

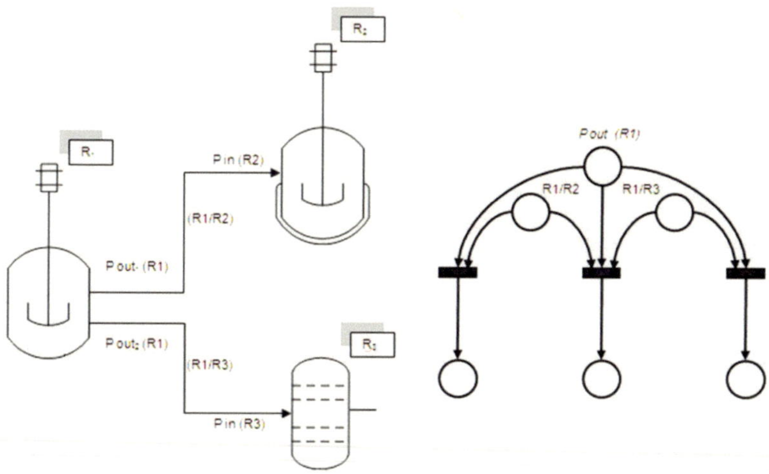

Fig. 12. Asynchronous Junction

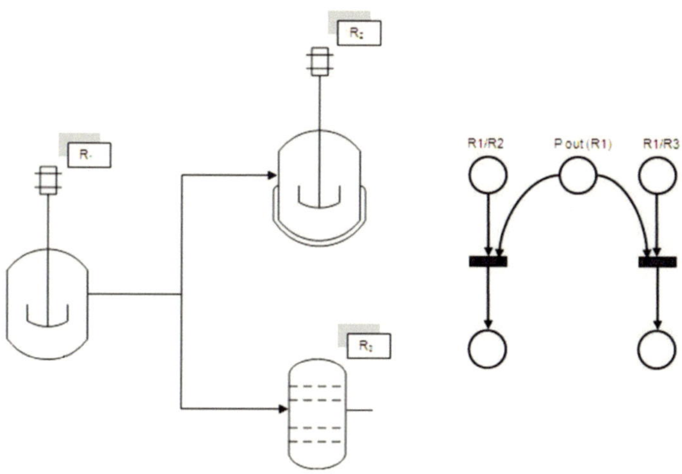

Fig. 13. Synchronous Junction

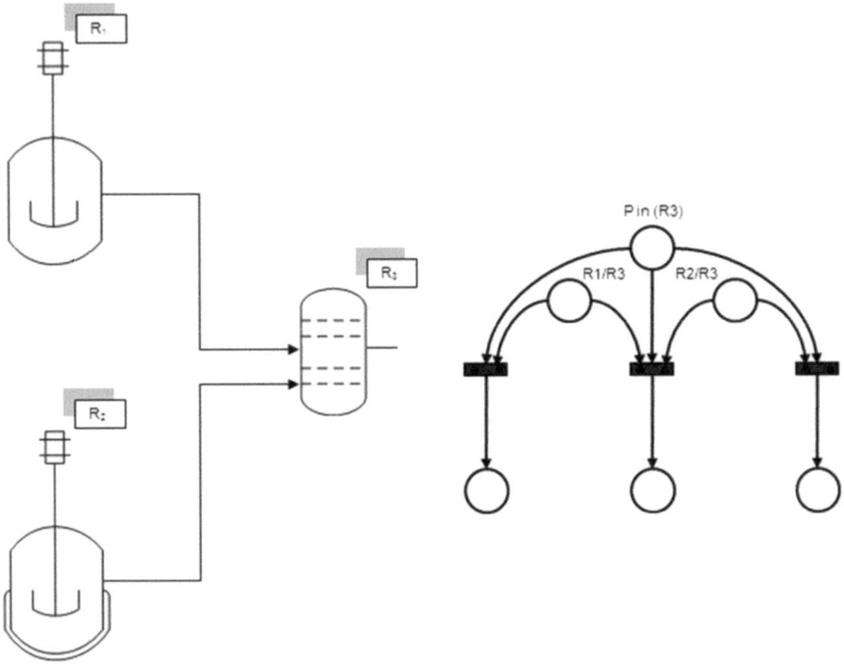

Fig. 14. Asynchronous Union

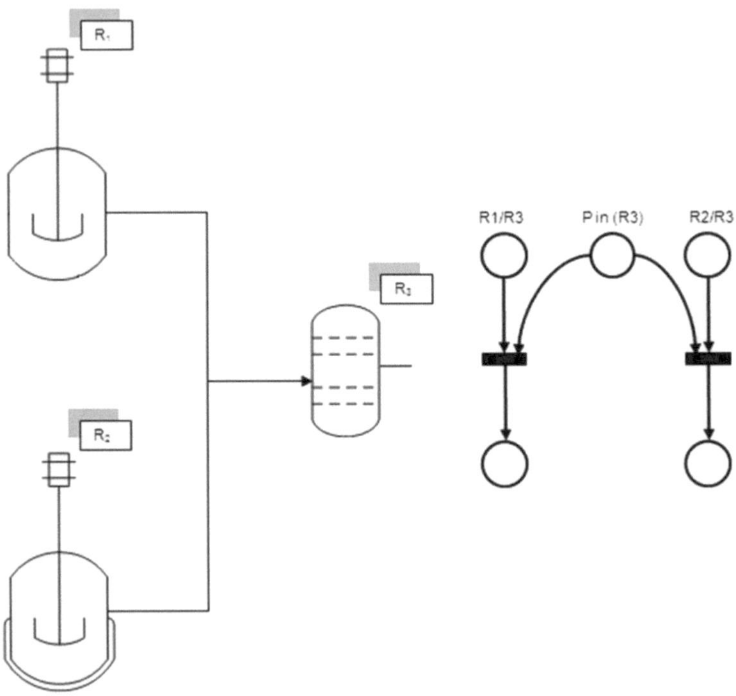

Fig. 15. Synchronous Union

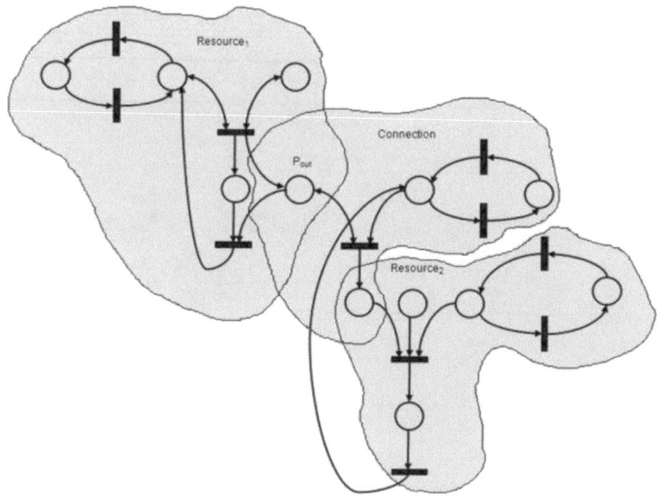

Fig. 16. Two connected resources

4.1.4 Service resources

Its function is to provide services to the HPU such as water, gas, steam and fuel. They have a unique skill and do not negotiate their capacity, thus the model used by them is equivalent to the one used be the connections.

4.1.5 Global model

The Petri Net model of the HPU is obtained through the composition of the models of the product, the resources and the connections. For the composition of the Product with the Resource the following construction is made: at the output of the transition *"send_req"* the "skill" places are created (see Figure 17). These are fusion places used by the product to call upon the HRs that have the skill to execute the operation. The product's "skill" places are fused with the "skill" places of the corresponding HRs, obtaining the model in Figure 18. The transition *"send_req"* is labeled as a silent event so it does not affect the generated and marked languages of the model, and the place "product" is activated when the resource goes into operation. This indicates the presence of a product.

Example: A continuous production plant as the one shown in Figure 19 is present. Table 2 shows resource skills. Figure 21 shows one of the products and its model in PN starting from figure 20. The structure of the connections is of asynchronous bifurcation/ asynchronous union. The plant's complete model is shown in Figure 22.

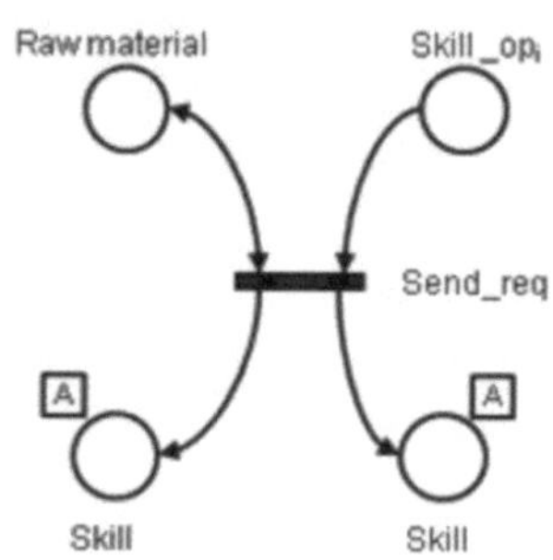

Fig. 17. Global model construction

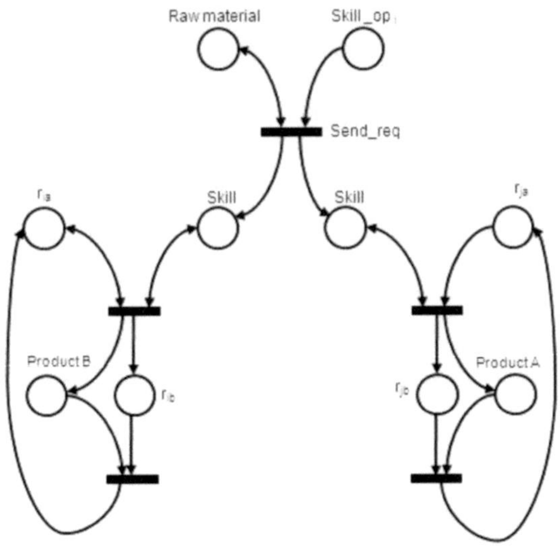

Fig. 18. Product - Resource composition

Holon	Skill
HR_1	op_1
HR_2	op_1
HR_3	op_2
HR_4	op_2
R_1	op_3
R_2	op_3

Table 2. Holon's skills

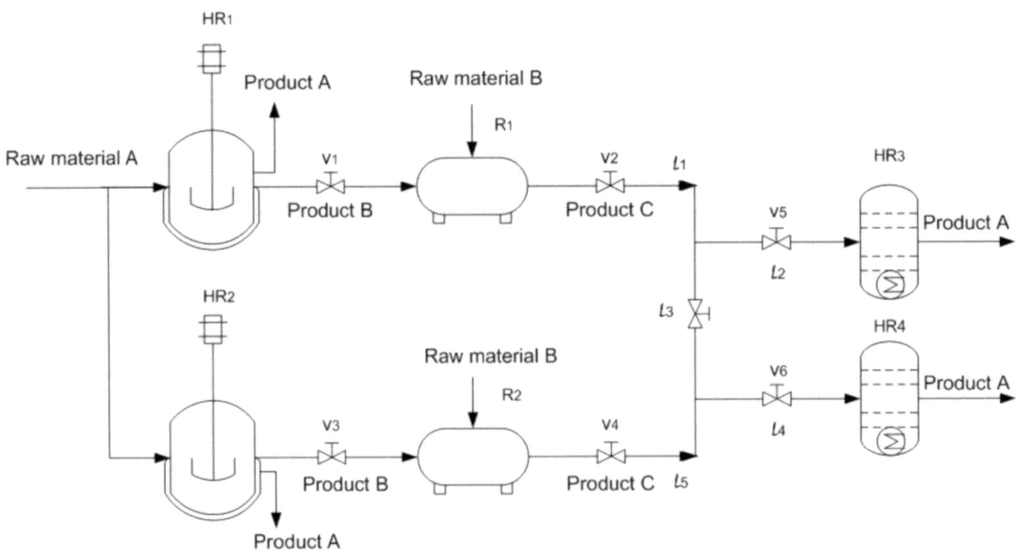

Fig. 19. Continuous Production plant

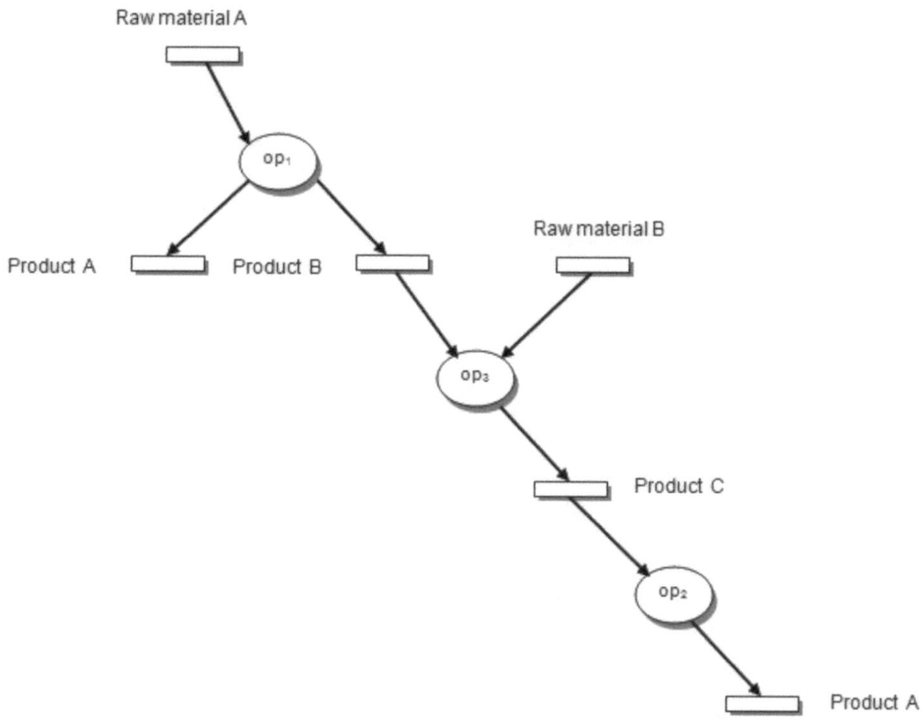

Fig. 20. P-Graph for a product of continuous plant

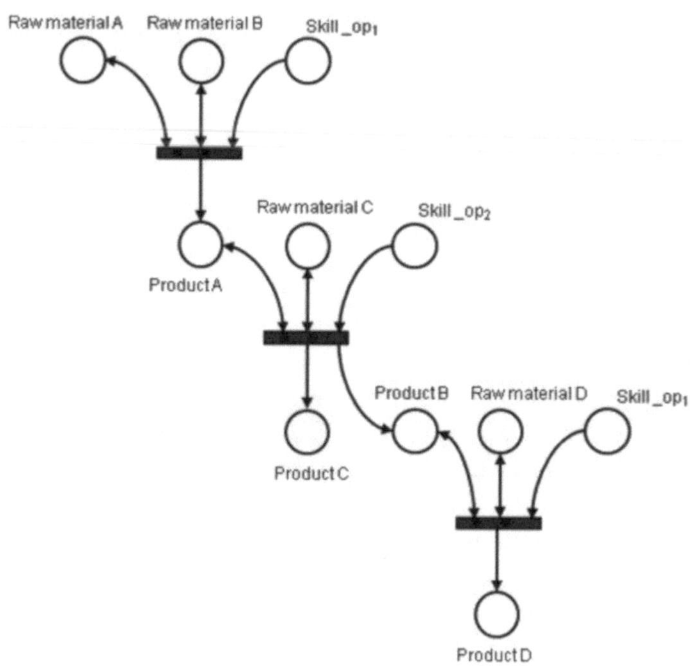

Fig. 21. PN product model for the example

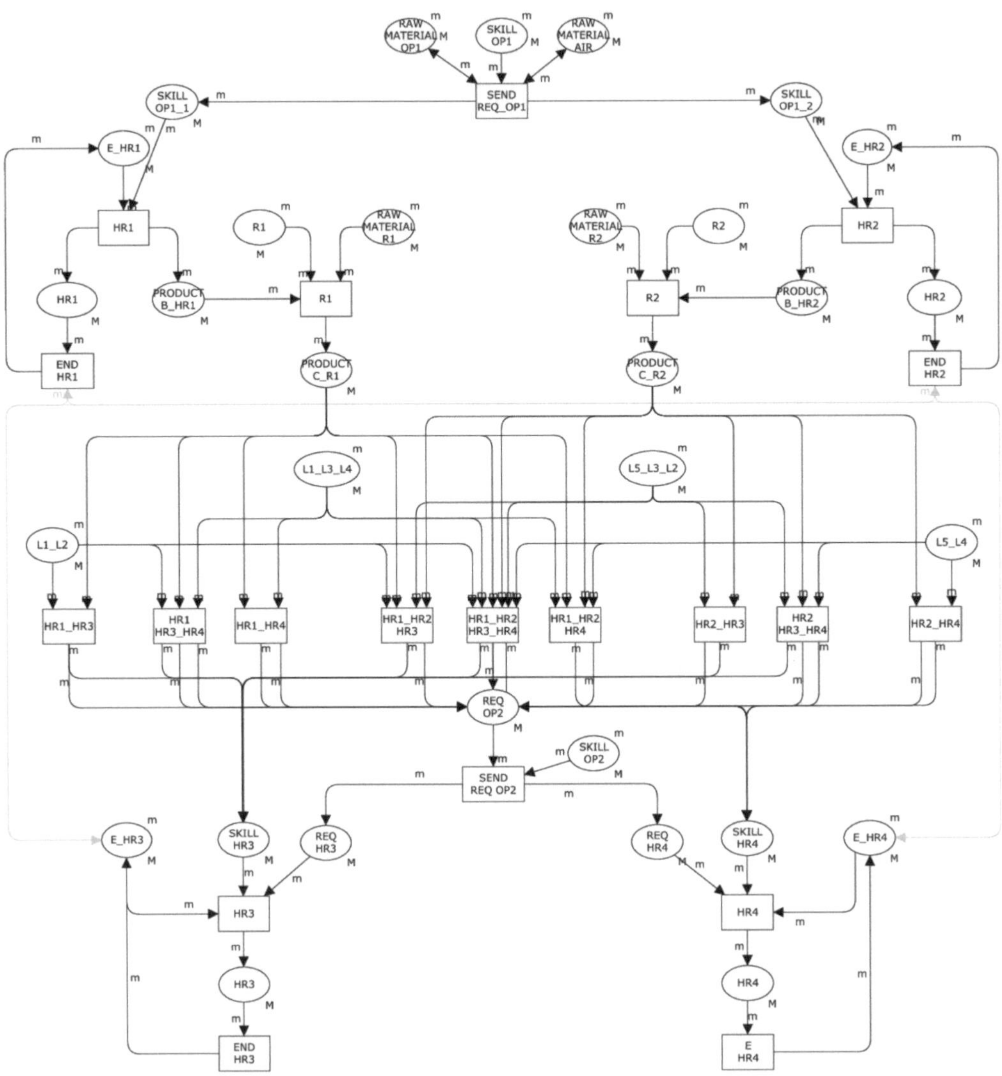

Fig. 22. Global PN model

The model obtained must comply with the properties of boundedness, safeness and liveness. This model was analyzed and simulated in CPNTools (Jensen, 2003) and the properties analysis gives a report where says that these properties are achieved.

4.2 Determination of configurations

When the negotiation process of a mission is launched, each holon sends a proposal that includes its availability, capacity and the cost of the operation. With the state (available / unavailable) the initial marking M_0 is determined. The PN is executed obtaining a reachability tree. The tree's arcs represent labeled events that enable determining the configurations through an operation of concatenation of the events.

For the example shown in Figure 19, if the following initial resource state is present ("1" for available).

$HR_1 = 1$ $HR_2 = 1$ $HR_3 = 1$
$HR_4 = 0$ $R_1 = 1$ $R_2 = 1$

Connection stretch $l_3 = 0$, which leads to the following state of the connections:

$HR_1 \rightarrow HR_4 = 0$
$HR_2 \rightarrow HR_3 = 0$

All other connections are available. The initial marking for this operative condition with a token in all states that represents an available resource and zero in the other one resources. Shown in the figure 23 are all the possible configurations of the HPU. The capacity of the configuration is shown in the units of the output variable or product of the HPU. Once the PN is obtained, the reachability tree of Figure 24 is found by means of CPNTools.

NUMBER	HPU	R	CONFIGURATION CAPABILITY (Product Units)
1	HR1		100
2	HR2		100
3	HR1 + HR2		200
4	HR1 + HR3	1	150
5	HR1 + HR4	1	150
6	HR1 + HR3 + HR4	1	150
7	HR2+ HR3 + HR4	2	150
8	HR2+ HR3	2	150
9	HR2 + HR3	2	150
10	HR1 + HR2 + HR3	1	250
11	HR1+ HR2+ HR3	2	250
12	HR1 + HR2 + HR3	1 + 2	300
13	HR1 + HR2 + HR4	1	250
14	HR1 + HR2 + HR4	2	250
15	HR1 + HR2 + HR3	1 + 2	300
16	HR1 + HR2 + HR3 + HR4	1	250
17	HR1 + HR2 + HR3 + HR4	2	250
18	HR1 + HR2 + HR3 + HR4	1 + 2	300

Fig. 23. Configurations

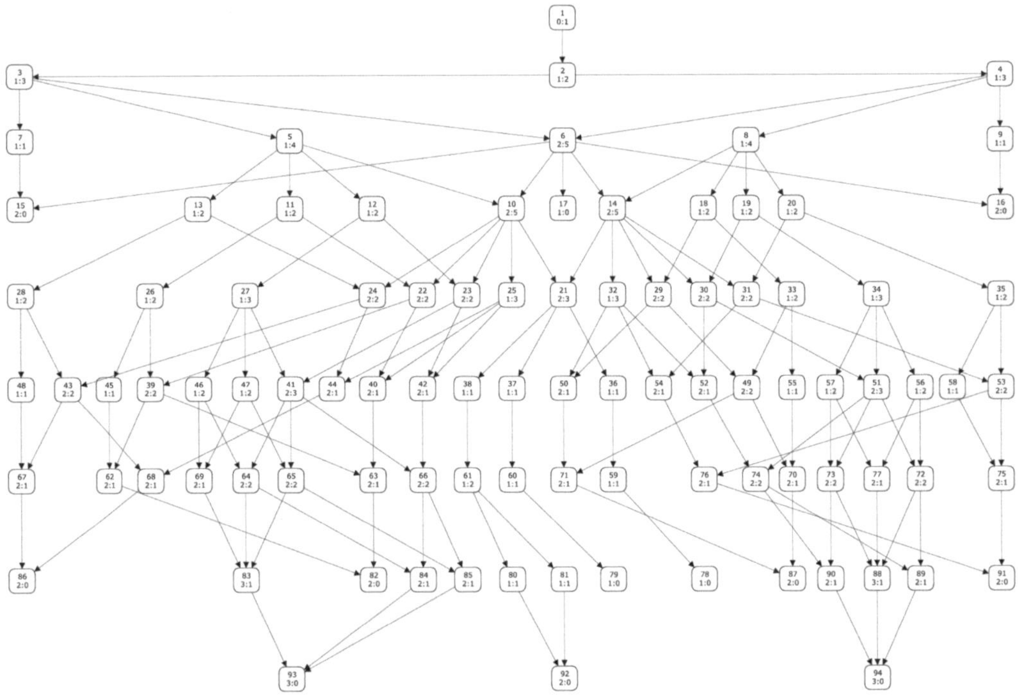

Fig. 24. Reachability tree

Analyzing the tree, the following is found:

- Nodes 13, 14, 15 y 32 lead to satisfactory terminations of the product, therefore, Q_m = {13, 14, 15,32}
- Nodes 17 and 31 do not lead to satisfactory terminations of the product, due to they enable R_2 with out HR_4 enable thus are forbidden states. Language $L = \{HR_2, R_2, HR_1, R_1\}$ is not permitted.
- The supervisor synthesis algorithm is applied, and the forbidden states and those leading to blockings are removed. The non-blocking property is verified with the base in the expression $\overline{L_m(G)} = L(G)$
- The possible configurations are established through the languages obtained from the initial state to the final states, following all trajectories. For instance, language $L = \{HR_1, R_1, HR_3, HR_2\}$ conduces to final state 32, thus 10 configuration is valid.
- Configurations incapable of achieving the mission are discarded, based in the capacity offers presented by the holons.
- The criteria of optimization are applied over the remaining configurations to select the definite configuration. This uses the operation cost information sent by the holon in the negotiation phase.
- The valid configurations for the example shown are: 1, 2, 3, 4, 10.

4.3 Holarchy formation

The holon resources that end up connected among themselves to enable cooperation, form a holarchy. The languages of the configurations enable establishing connections between holons and thus establish holarchies. For instance, from language $L = \{HR_1, R_1, HR_3\}$ the holarchy H_1 is obtained, formed by HR_1 and HR_3, in which these holons are connected by R_1. From language $L = \{HR_1, R_1, HR_3, HR_4, HR_2\}$ an HPU formed by holon HR_2 and holarchy $H = HR_1 + HR_3 + HR_4$ is obtained, connected through R_1.

5. Reconfiguracion

The holonic approach establishes the following disturbance response framework:

- If there is failure, the holon tries to adjust its control laws and its infrastructure to take care of the disturbance (autonomy attribute).
- If it is not capable, it turns to the holarchy to interiorly solve the situation through the cooperation of holons (cooperation attribute).
- And if the holarchy is not able to solve it, it turns to to other holarchies in the HPU.
- If the disturbance cannot be taken care of by the holarchies that form the HPU, a mission renegotiation is requested.

In the work presented, a PN of each holarchy is created, and the procedure presented for the determination of the HPU´s configurations is followed for reconfiguration.

Suppose, for the example presented, that the HPU operates with the configuration of Figure 25. The PN model of the holarchy is that of Figure 26. If it is presented a failure in HR_4, the PN marking is [111100101101011000000. . .] (following the net from left to right and from top to bottom) and the tree it is in figure 27. And the HPU gets the configuration shown in figure 28.

The allowed states are 4 and 13. These states determine all possible configuration is $HR_1 + HR_3$ or HR_1 and the holarchy can resolve the disturbance inside. The criteria of optimization are applied to redistribute the mission among the holons. The holarchy has been reconfigured according to the method proposed which uses PNs and the supervisory control theory.

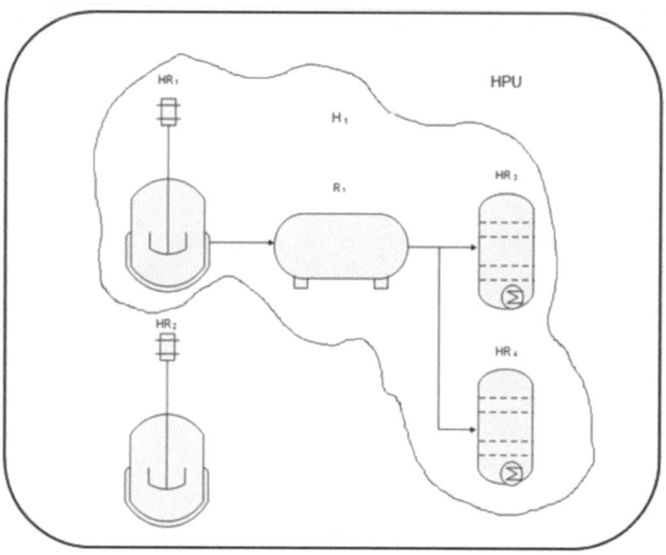

Fig. 25. Holarchy

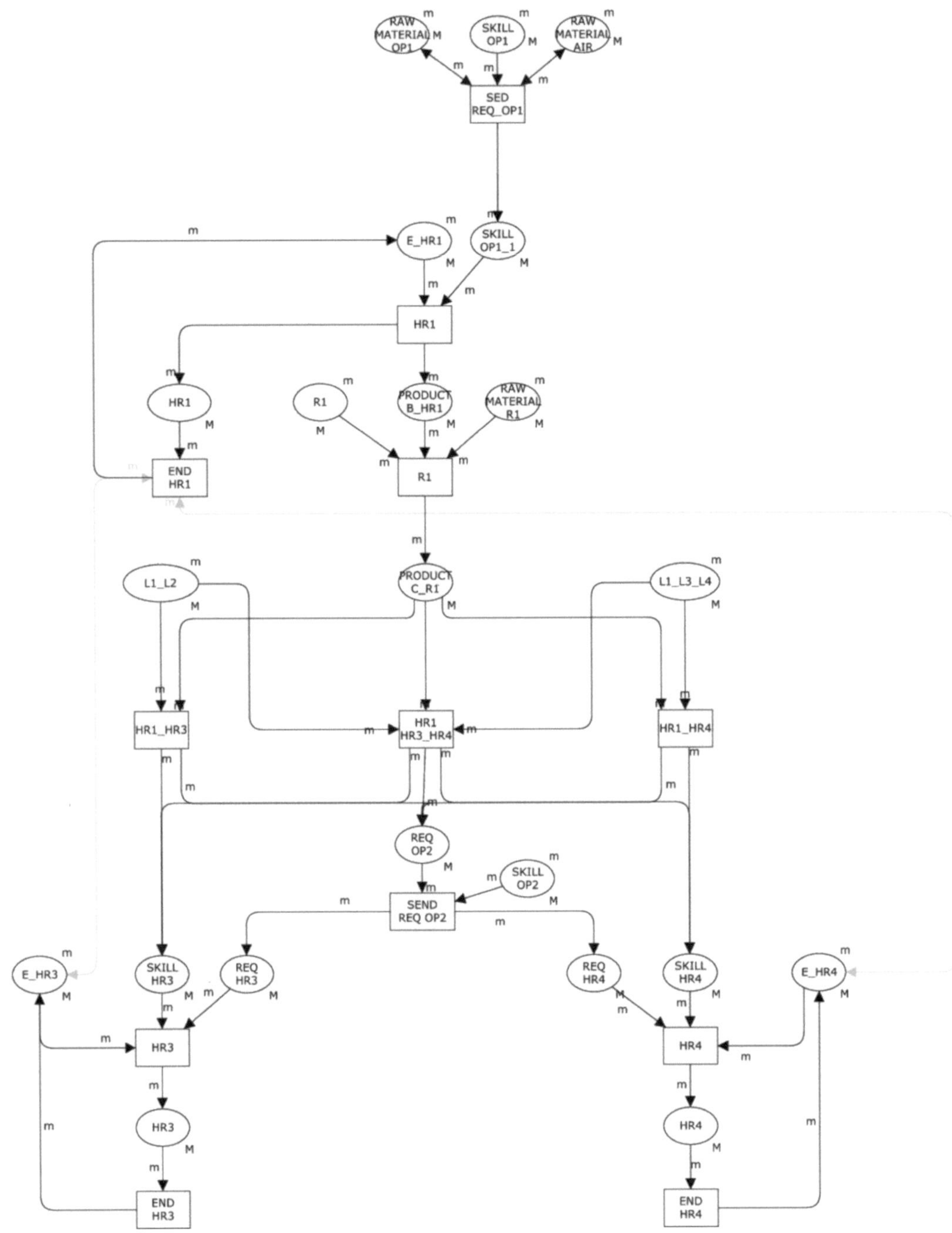

Fig. 26. Holarchy PN model

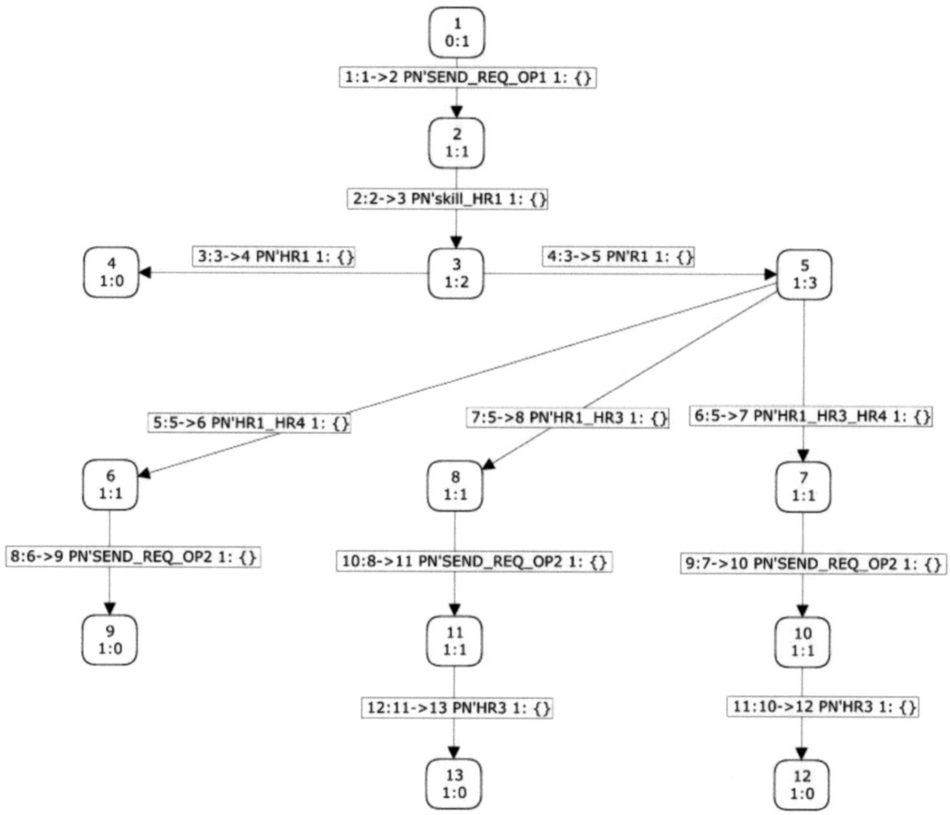

Fig. 27. New reachability tree

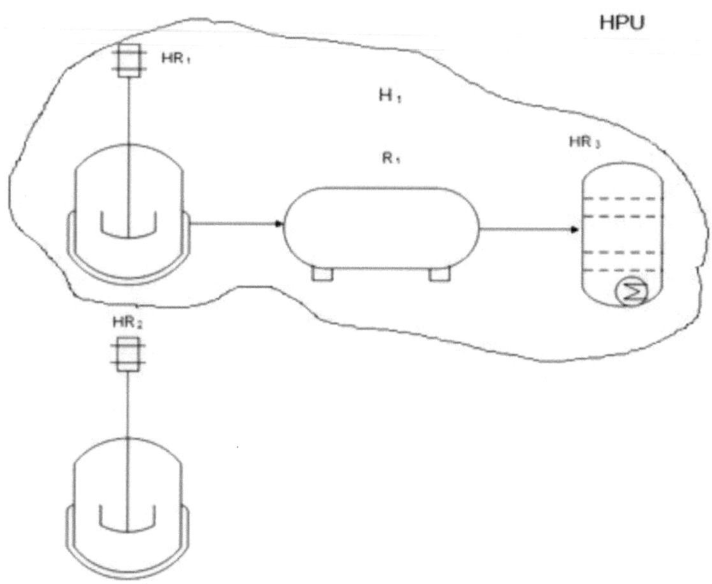

Fig. 28. New configuration

6. Conclusions and future papers

The work presented has shown the potential of the holonic paradigm by combining Petri Nets and the Supervisory Control Theory to solve configuration problems of continuous production processes in real time. The decrease in the problem´s complexity by applying the concept of holarchies is evident. This enables generating solutions with good temporary performances. Improving response times to face disturbances, an advantage of the holonic approach, is complied with in this manner.

In order to preserve the criteria of global optimization in the determination of the initial configuration, a composed model of the complete HPU is used. This model may not have a good performance in real time because it may be subject to explosion of the states. However, the determination of the initial configuration is part of the production scheduling function which can occur out of line. In this manner, another characteristic of the holonic approach is complied with: to conserve hierarchical structures that guarantee global optimums.

With regards to future papers, it is important to advance in the automatic generation of PNs from P-Graph models of the product, resource models and connections between them, and their automatic execution based on Petri Net engines.

The proposed methodology has been successfully proven in academic applications of production scheduling in thermal energy power plants.

7. References

Adam, E., Mandiau, R. & Kolski, C. (n.d.). Homascow: a holonic multi-agent system for cooperative work, *Database and Expert Systems Applications, 2000. Proceedings. 11th International Workshop on*, pp. 247–253.

Agre, J., MCFarlane, D., Elsley, G., Cheng, J. & Gunn, B. (1994). Holonic control of a water cooling system for a steel rod mill.

Akesson, K. (2002). *Methods and Tools in Supervisory Control Theory*, PhD thesis.

Balasubramanian, S., Brennan, R. W. & Norrie, D. H. (n.d.). Requirements for holonic manufacturing systems control, *Database and Expert Systems Applications, 2000. Proceedings. 11th International Workshop on*, pp. 214–218.

Bongaerts, L. (1998). Integration of scheduling and control in holonic manufacturing systems.

Brennan, R. W., Hall, K., Marik, V., Maturana, F. & Norrie, D. H. (2003). *A Real-Time Interface for Holonic Control Devices*, pp. 1088–1088.

Caramihai, S. (n.d.). An agent-based des supported modeling framework for enterprises.

Celaya, R., Desrochers, A. & Graves, R. (2009). Modeling and analysis of multi-agent systems using petri nets., *Journal of Computers.* 4: 981 - 996.

Chacón, E., Besembel, I., Narciso, F., Moltival & J y Colina, E. (2003). An integration architecture for the automation of a continuous production complex.

Chacón, E., Besembel, I., Rivero, D. & Cardillo, J. (2008). The holonic production unit: an approach for an architecture of embedded production process, *Advances in Robotics, Automation and Control* .

Chacón, E. & Colmenares,W. (2005). A way to implement supervisors for holonic production units.

Cheng, F.-T., Chang, C.-F. & Wu, S.-L. (2004). Development of holonic manufacturing execution systems, *Journal of Intelligent Manufacturing* 15(2): 253–267.

Chirn, J. & McFarlane, D. (n.d.). Evaluating holonic control systems: A case study.

Chokshi, N. & McFarlane, D. (2008a). A distributed architecture for reconfigurable control of continuous process operations, *Journal of Intelligent Manufacturing* 19(2): 215–232.

Chokshi, N. N. & McFarlane, D. C. (2008b). *A Distributed Coordination Approach to Reconfigurable Process Control*, Springer Series in Advanced Manufacturing, Springer, Hardcover.

Chokshi, N. N. & McFarlane, D. C. (n.d.). Rationales for holonic manufacturing systems in chemical process industries, *Database and Expert Systems Applications, 2001. Proceedings. 12th International Workshop on*, pp. 616–620.

Durán, J. (2006). Técnicas emergentes para la automatización integrada de procesos de producción integraciÓn en automatizaciÓn- reporte técnico 2.

El Kebbe, D. (2002). *Towards the MaSHReC Manufacturing System under real time constraints: a contribution to the application of real time system advances to production control*, PhD thesis.

Falkman, P., Lennartson, B. & Tittus, M. (2009). Specification of a batch plant using process algebra and petri nets, *Control Engineering Practice* 17(9): 1004–1015.

Fischer John, B. T. O. (n.d.). *Workbook for Designing Distributed Control Applications using Rockwell Automation's HOLOBLOC Prototyping Software.*

Fu-Shiung, H. (n.d.). Collaborative timed petri net for holonic process planning, *American Control Conference, 2003. Proceedings of the 2003*, Vol. 1, pp. 344–349 vol.1.

Ghaeli, M., Bahri, P. A., Lee, P. & Gu, T. (2005). Petri-net based formulation and algorithm for short-term scheduling of batch plants, *Computers & Chemical Engineering* 29(2): 249–259.

HMS (2004). Holonic manufacturing systems consortium. http://hms.ifw.uni-hannover.de.

Holonic Manufacturing Systems (2008). pp. 7–20.

Hsieh, F.-S. (2006). Analysis of contract net in multi-agent systems, *Automatica* 42(5): 733 740.

http://research.curtin.edu.au/ (2010). Chemical engineering example a. summary of proposed research program for doctor of philosophy, scheduling of batch and mixed batch/continuous process plants using petri-nets.

URL:http://research.curtin.edu.au/guides/hdrguidelines/docs/CandEx_ChemEng_A.pdf

Jensen, K. (2003). *Coloured Petri Nets : Basic Concepts, Analysis Methods and Practical Use. Volume 1 (Monographs in Theoretical Computer Science. An EATCS Series)*, Springer.

Koestler, A. (1968). The ghost in the machine.

Langer, G. (1999). Homucs - a methodology and architecture for holonic multi - cell control systems.

Leitao, P. (2004). *An Agile and Adaptive Holonic Architecture for Manufacturing Control Dissertation*, PhD thesis.

Leitao, P., Valckenaers, P. & Emmanuel, A. (2009). Self-adaptation for robustness and cooperation in holonic multi-agent systems.

Lennartson, B., Fabian, M. & Falkman, F. (n.d.). Control architecture for flexible production systems, *Automation Science and Engineering, 2005. IEEE International Conference on*, pp. 307–312.

Lennartson, B., Tittus, M. & Fabian, M. (n.d.). Modeling, specification and controller synthesis for discrete event systems, *Systems, Man, and Cybernetics, 1998. 1998 IEEE International Conference on*, Vol. 1, pp. 698–703 vol.1.

Lobo, C. (2003). Sistema multiagente para coordinar unidades de producción.

Maturana, F. P., Tichy, P., Slechta, P., Staron, R. J., Discenzo, F. M., Hall, K. & Marik, V. (n.d.). Cost-based dynamic reconfiguration system for intelligent agent negotiation, *Intelligent Agent Technology, 2003. IAT 2003. IEEE/WIC International Conference on*, pp. 629- 632.

McFarlane, D. (1995). Holonic manufacturing systems in continuous processing: concepts and control requirements, *In Proceedings of ASI' 95* p. 11.

Mcfarlane, D. C. & Bussman, S. (2000). Developments in holonic production planning and control, *Production Planning & Control* 11(6).

Music, G. & D., M. (1998). Petri net based supervisory control of flexible batch plants.

Peréz, L. (n.d.).

Pétin, J.-F., Gouyon, D. & Morel, G. (2007). Supervisory synthesis for product-driven automation and its application to a flexible assembly cell, *Control Engineering Practice* 15(5): 595–614.

Ramadge, P. J. G. & Wonham, W. M. (1989). The control of discrete event systems, *Proceedings of the IEEE* 77(1): 81–98.

Ramos, C. (n.d.). A holonic approach for task scheduling in manufacturing systems, *Robotics and Automation, 1996. Proceedings., 1996 IEEE International Conference on*, Vol. 3, pp. 2511–2516 vol.3.

Reveliotis, S. (1999). Real-time control of flexibly automated production systems, *AutoSimulations Symposium '99* .

Silva, M. (n.d.). Las redes de petri en la automática y la informática, *Technical report*.

Sousa, P. & Ramos, C. (1998). A dynamic scheduling holon for manufacturing orders, *Journal of Intelligent Manufacturing* 9(2): 107–112.

Suda, H. (1989). Future factory system formulated in japan, *Japanese Journal of Advanced Automation Technology* 1.

Tittus, M. & Akesson, K. (1999). Petri net models in batch control.

Tittus, M., Akesson & K (n.d.). Deadlock avoidance in batch processes.

Tittus, M. & Lennartson, B. (1997). Hierarchical supervisory control for batch processes, *Control Systems Technology, IEEE Transactions on* 7(5): 542–554.

Tuncel, G. & Bayhan, G. (2007). Applications of petri nets in production scheduling: a review, *The International Journal of Advanced Manufacturing Technology* 34(7): 762–773.

Wyns, J. (1999). Reference architecture for holonic manufacturing systems.

Zhou, M. (1995). Petri nets in flexible and agile automation.

6

Parameter Perturbation Analysis through Stochastic Petri Nets: Application to an Inventory System

Labadi Karim[1], Darcherif Moumen[1], Haoxun Chen[2]
[1]*EPMI (ECS EA 3649), Ecole d'Electricité, de Production et de Méthodes Industrielles Cergy-Pontoise,*
[2]*UTT (LOSI- FRE CNRS 2848), Université de Technologie de Troyes, Troyes, France*

1. Introduction

Sensitivity analysis is used to determine how "sensitive" a performance measure of a model is with respect to a change in the value of the parameters of the model. Parameter sensitivity analysis of a model is usually performed as a series of tests in which the model analyst sets different values for the parameters of the model to see how a change in the parameters causes a change in the dynamic behavior of the model. Broadly speaking, this analysis is to see what happens when the value of some crucial parameters of a model changes. If a small change in the value of a parameter leads to a big change in the performance of the model, the parameter needs a closer look. It is a useful tool for performance evaluation of a model as well as its model building. Hence, sensitivity analysis can help the modeler to understand the dynamics of a system.

Sensitivity analysis is often used to estimate the sensitivity of a performance measure of a system with respect to its decision variables (parameters) by evaluating the gradient (derivatives) of the performance measure at each given value of the parameters. With the gradient, the system performance measure can be optimized by using a gradient method. Moreover, sensitivity analysis can be used to identify key parameters of a system by discovering the parameters whose small change in value leads to a big change in the behavior of the system. In model building, sensitivity analysis can be used to validate a model with unkown parameters by studying the uncertainties of the model associated with the parameters.

In the past, sensitivity analysis was usually based on simulation. One of the major research fields in this area is perturbation analysis (PA). The approach firstly applied to an engineering problem was proposed by Ho, Eyler and Chien in 1979. With great efforts made by many researchers in more than one decade, fundamental results for PA have been obtained. Currently, formal sensitivity analysis approaches based on stochastic processes were proposed in the literature. Particularly, efficient algorithms were developed to compute the performance derivates of Markov processes with respect to infinitesimal changes of their parameters (infinitesimal generators) (Cao *et al.*, 1998, 1997). Besides the fundamental works in developing its theory and algorithms, perturbation analysis has also been successfully applied to a number of practical engineering problems (Brooks & Varaiya, 1994; Caramanis & Liberopouls, 1992; Haurie *et al.*, 1994; Xiao *et al.*, 1994; Yan & Zhou 1994). In this chapter, we deal with sensitivity analysis with respect to timing parameters based on stochastic Petri nets. Besides the great scientific and practical interest of the sensitivity analysis, this work is motivated by two reasons:

- Petri nets (Murata, 1989) are a powerful graphical and mathematical formalism which has been gaining popularity as a tool particularly suitable for modelling and analysis of discrete event systems. The literature on Petri nets is ample and their applications in practical manufacturing problems are numerous (Zhou and Kurapati, 1999; Zurawski and Zhou, 1994; Silva and Teruel, 1997). Several books were published in 1990s (Ajmone Marsan *et al.*, 1995; Haas, 2002; Lindeman, 1998; Zhou and DiCesare 1993).
- Although the literature on Petri nets is plentiful, very little work deals with sensitivity analysis or perturbation analysis of Petri net models. Few exceptions are: a perturbation analysis method based on stochastic Petri net models to estimate the derivatives of performance measures with respect to timing parameters can be found in (Xie 1998; Archetti et al., 1993). For Markov regenerative stochastic Petri nets, a mathematical formulation for sensitivity of the steady state probabilities is developed in (Mainkar and al. 1993). Furthermore, performance sensitivity formulas are given by exploring structural characteristics of Petri nets (Feng, Desrochers, 1993; Proth *et al.*, 1993).

In this chapter, we try to apply a perturbation analysis method based on stochastic Petri nets for parameter sensitivity analysis to the performance analysis of an inventory system. The remainder of the chapter is organized in two parts as follows:

- The first part of the chapter addresses the sensitivity analysis of stochastic discrete event systems described by Stochastic Petri nets (*SPN*) as a performance evaluation tool of the systems. By exploring some existing results on perturbation analysis of Markov processes (Cao *et al.*, 1997-1998; Dai, 1995-1996) and by a natural extension of them to the underlying stochastic processes of SPNs, a stochastic Petri net-based sensitivity analysis method with respect to timing parameters is presented. The approach is widely applicable because stochastic Petri nets (Ajmone Marsan *et al.*, 1995; Haas, 2002; Lindeman, 1998) have been proven to be one of the most fundamental models for stochastic discrete-event systems.
- The second part of the chapter is dedicated to a case study on an inventory system. Previously, the modeling and performances evaluation of the system were performed by using Batch stochastic Petri nets recently introduced in the literature (Labadi et al., 2007). In this part, the sensitivity analysis method developed in the first part of the chapter is used to estimate the sensitivity of performance measures with respect to the decision parameters of the inventory system.

2. Stochastic Petri nets models

Petri nets (*PN*), as a graphical and mathematical model, have been used for the study of qualitative properties of discrete event systems exhibiting concurrency and synchronization characteristics. A Petri net may be defined as a particular bipartite directed graph consisting of places, transitions, and arcs. Input arcs are ones connecting a place to a transition, whereas output arcs are ones connecting a transition to a place. A positive weight may be assigned to each arc. A place may contain tokens and the current state (the marking) of the modeled system is specified by the number of tokens in each place. Each transition usually models an

activity whose occurrence is represented by its firing. A transition can be fired only if it is enabled, which means that all preconditions for the corresponding activity are fulfilled (there are enough tokens available in the input places of the transition). When the transition is fired, tokens will be removed from its input places and added to its output places. The number of tokens removed/added is determined by the weight of the arc connecting the transition with the corresponding place. Graphically, places are represented by circles, transitions by bars or thin rectangles (filled or not filled), tokens by dots, respectively.
The use of PN-based techniques for the quantitative analysis of a system may require the introduction of temporal specifications in its basic untimed model. Time is then introduced in Petri nets by associating each transition with a firing delay (time). This delay specifies the duration during which the transition has to be enabled before it can actually be fired. In a stochastic Petri net, the time delays associated with certain transitions are random variables and the underlying marking process (state evolution process) of the net is a stochastic process. There are several variants of this model type, among them we have stochastic Petri net (*SPN*) models where each transition is associated with an exponentially distributed time delay. Stochastic Petri net models were proposed with the goal of developing a tool which integrates formal description, proof of correctness, and performance evaluation of systems. For what concerns the performance evaluation, many previous proposals aimed at establishing an equivalence between *SPN* and Markov models. Stochastic Petri net-based Markov modelling is thus a potentially very powerful and generic approach for performance evaluation of a variety of systems such as computer systems, communication networks and manufacturing systems.

2.1 The basic SPN model

The *SPN*s are obtained by associating each transition with an exponentially distributed firing time whose firing rate (average firing time) may be marking dependent.
A formal definition of SPN is thus given by:

$$SPN = (P, T, I, O, M_0, \Lambda) \tag{1}$$

where (P, T, I, O, M_0) is the marked untimed *PN* underlying the *SPN*, which as usual comprises:
$P = (p_1, p_2,..., p_n)$ is a finite set of places, where $n > 0$; $T = (t_1, t_2,..., t_m)$ is a finite set of exponentially distributed transitions, where $m > 0$, with $P \cup T \neq \varnothing$ and $P \cap T \neq \varnothing$; $I: P \times T \rightarrow N$ is an input function that defines the set of directed arcs from P to T where N is the set of natural numbers; $O: T \times P \rightarrow N$ is an output function that defines the set of directed arcs from T to P; M_0 is the initial marking of the net whose i^{th} component represents the number of tokens in the ith place and $\Lambda = (\lambda_1, \lambda_2,..., \lambda_n)$ is an array of firing rates associated with transitions. Each rate is defined as the inverse of the average firing time of the corresponding transition.

2.2 Stochastic behaviour analysis

According to (Molloy, 1982), the *SPN*s are isomorphic to continuous time Markov chains *(CTMC)* due to the memoryless property of the exponential distributions of the firings times of their transitions. The *SPN* markings correspond to the states of the corresponding Markov chain so that the *SPN* model allows the calculation of the steady state probabilities of its states. As in Markov analysis, ergodic (irreducible) property of *SPN* is of special interest. For

an ergodic *SPN*, the steady state probability of the model in any state always exists and is independent of the initial state. If the firing rates of all transitions do not depend upon time, a stationary (homogeneous) Markov chain is obtained. In particular, k bounded *SPN*s are isomorphic to finite Markov chains.
The reachability graph of an *SPN* is identical to that of the underlying untimed *PN*. The nodes of the graph represent all markings reachable from the initial marking. Each arc is labelled by its corresponding fired transition. The *CTMC* state space $S = \{S_0, S_1, ..., S_m\}$ corresponds to the set of all markings in the reachability graph $M^* = \{M_0, M_1, ..., M_m\}$. The transition rate from state S_i (M_i) to state S_j (M_j) is obtained as the sum of the firing rates of the transitions that are enabled in M_i and whose firing produces the marking M_j. The steady-state solution of the model is then obtained by solving a system of linear equations:

$$\begin{cases} \pi \times A = 0 \\ \sum_{i=0}^{m} \pi_i = 1 \end{cases} \tag{2}$$

where:

- $\pi = (\pi_0, \pi_1, ..., \pi_m)$ denotes the steady-state probability of each marking M_i (and of state S_i as well, since there is a one-to-one correspondence between markings and states).
- $A = [a_{ij}]_{(m+1)\times(m+1)}$ is the transition rate matrix of the *CTMC*. For $i = 0, 1, 2, \ldots m$, the ith row, i.e., the elements a_{ij}, $j = 0, 1, 2, \ldots, m$, are obtained as follows:
  - If $j \neq i$, a_{ij} is the sum of the firing rates of all the outgoing arcs from state M_i to M_j.
  - If $i = j$, a_{ij} represents the sum of the firing rates of all transitions enabled at M_i.

2.3 Performance evaluation

The analysis of an *SPN* model usually aims at the computation of more aggregate performance indices than the steady-state probabilities of individual markings. Several aggregate performance indices are easily obtained from the steady-state distribution of reachable markings.
The required performance estimates of a system modelled by an *SPN* can be computed using a unifying approach in which proper index functions (also called reward functions) are defined over the markings of the *SPN* and an average reward for each reward function is derived using the steady-state probability distribution of the *SPN*. Assuming that f represents one of such reward functions, its average reward can be computed using the following weighted sum:

$$P = \sum_{i=0}^{m} \pi_i . f_i = \pi \cdot f \tag{3}$$

where f_i is incurred per unit time at each reachable marking M_i of the underlying stochastic process of the *SPN*.

3. Parameter sensitivity analysis

3.1 Perturbation realization

Consider first the nominal behavior of a system modeled as an SPN. Let P_θ a performance function defined over the marking process of the net under a nominal parameter vector θ

which is a set of parameters of the system (here, it represents the firing rates associated with the transitions of the net). That is:

$$P_\theta = \sum_{i=1}^{m} \pi_i . f_i = \pi \cdot f \tag{4}$$

where π_i denotes the steady-state probability of each marking M_i and f_i is a measure of the performance function f incurred at the marking M_i of the stochastic marking process of the net. Consider now a perturbation δ on one or more parameters of the underlying Markov process that is equivalent to a perturbation in the transition rates matrix A. With the perturbation, the transition matrix A changes to:

$$A_\delta = A + \delta \cdot Q \tag{5}$$

where A_δ is the transition rate matrix of the perturbed behavior system, δ is a very small positive real number and $Q = [q_{ij}]$ is a matrix representing the direction of the perturbation.

- q_{ij} equals 0 indicates that the matrix entry A_{ij} is not perturbed.
- q_{ij} equals x different from 0 indicates that the matrix entry A_{ij} is perturbed by an amount $x\delta$.

The only condition on the structure of Q is that the matrix A_δ is also a transition matrix i.e. the sum of each row equals 0.

Under this formulation, A_δ is also a well-defined infinitesimal generator, and hence its steady state probabilities $\pi_\delta = (\pi_{\delta 0}, \pi_{\delta 1}, \ldots, \pi_{\delta m})$, of the perturbed marking process is also defined. That is:

$$\pi_\delta \times A_\delta = 0 \quad \text{and} \quad \sum_{i=0}^{m} \pi_{\delta i} = 1 \tag{6}$$

Then, the stationary performance measure of the perturbed Markov process (that is the Markov process with transition matrix A_δ) can be defined as:

$$P_\delta = \sum_{i=0}^{m} \pi_{\delta,i} . f_i = \pi_\delta \cdot f \tag{7}$$

3.2 Computation of sensitivity measures

Many solutions have been proposed in the literature to evaluate sensitivity measures corresponding to partial derivates.

1. Exact solutions rely on Frank's approach (Frank, 1978): the classical set of differential equations is extended to a bigger set of equations including the sensitivity factor equations. However, this approach is computationally burdensome and almost unusable or highly inefficient on realistic-size systems because the state space dimension is too great. To cope with this problem, some approximate solutions have been proposed (Ou et al., 2003) but applicable to a limited class of systems.
2. Many simulation methods have been also proposed to estimate derivative measure. See for example (Glynn 1990; Glassermann et al., 1992). Concerning Markov process modelling and stationary performance measure, perturbation realization is well adapted (Cao et al., 1997-1998; Dai, 1996). It allows:

- The evaluation of sensitivity of performance measures formulated under the marking process of a stochastic Petri net model:
  The sensitivity of a performance measure P of a system due to the introduced changes in the infinitesimal generator A, can be analyzed by computing the derivate of P_δ in the direction of Q (noted below by SPerf). It can be defined as:

$$\text{SPerf} = \frac{dP}{dQ} = \lim_{\delta \to 0} \frac{P - P_\delta}{\delta} \tag{8}$$

- The evaluation of sensitivity of steady-state probabilities of the marking process:
  The sensitivity of steady sate probabilities can also be defined as:

$$\text{SProb} = \frac{d\pi}{dQ} = \lim_{\delta \to 0} \frac{\pi - \pi_\delta}{\delta} \tag{9}$$

3.3 Calculation of the performance derivates

The particular structure of the Chapman-Kolmogorov equations and the linearity of the performance measure lead to the following expression of the measure derivatives (Cao et al., 1997-1998):

$$\text{SPerf} = \frac{dP}{dQ} = -\pi \cdot Q \cdot A^{\#} \cdot f \tag{10}$$

where:
$A^{\#}$ is defined as:

$$A^{\#} = (A + e\pi)^{-1} - e\pi \tag{11}$$

where:
- $e = (1, 1, \ldots)^T$ is a column vector of size $(m \times 1)$ with $e_{i,1} = 1$ for any i.
- $g = -A^{\#} \cdot f$ is called the performance potential vector.

Then, according to the equation (8), *SPerf* can be written as:

$$\text{SPerf} = \frac{dP}{dQ} = -\pi \cdot Q \cdot A^{\#} \cdot f = \pi \cdot Q \cdot g \tag{12}$$

Similarly, according to the equation (9), the steady state derivate, *SProb,* can be computed using the following formula:

$$\text{SProb} = \frac{d\pi}{dQ} = -\pi_\delta \cdot Q \cdot A^{\#} \tag{13}$$

4. Inventory system modelling and performance analysis

This part of the chapter is dedicated to a case study on an inventory system represented in Fig. 1. The presented approach in the previous section is then applied to estimate the sensitivity of performance measures with respect to some parameters of the inventory system.

4.1 Modelling of the inventory system

Consider the continuous review *(s, S)* inventory system shown in Fig. 1. In this application, it is assumed that the system has the following characteristics: the inventory replenishment time is subject to an exponential distribution; customer demand is Poisson and in batch; and the system has no backorder.

The modeling and performance evaluation of the system will be performed by using Batch stochastic Petri nets introduced in the literature as a powerful modelling tool for both analysis and simulation of logistic systems. The capability of the model to meet real needs is shown through applications dedicated to modelling and performance optimization of inventory control systems (see Labadi et al., 2007) and a real-life supply chain (see Chen et al., 2005; Amodeo et al., 2007).

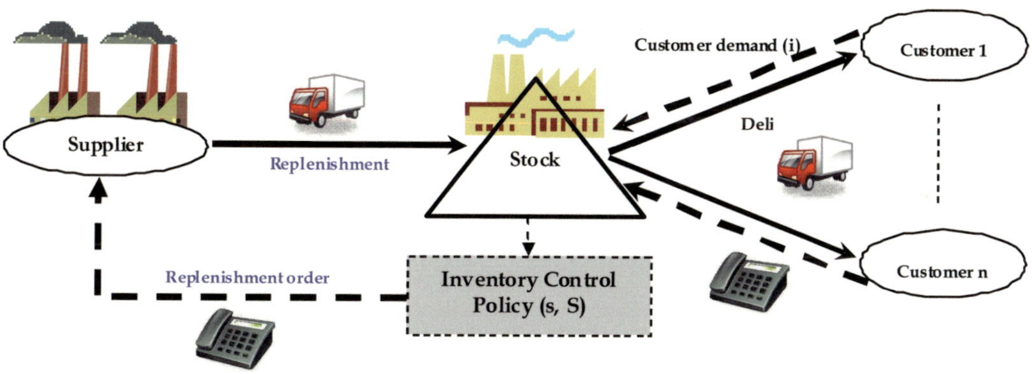

Fig. 1. A continuous (*s*, *S*) inventory system

We model the dynamics of the above mentioned supply chain by using a Batch Stochastic Petri net represented in Fig. 2. In the model, discrete place *p1* represents the on-hand inventory of the considered stock and place *p3* represents outstanding orders. Discrete place *p2* represents the on-hand inventory of the stock plus its outstanding orders (the orders that are placed by stock *p1* but not filled yet), that is, $M(p2) = M(p1) + M(p3)$. The operations of the system such as generation of replenishment orders (*t3*), inventory replenishment (*t2*), and order delivery (*t1*) are performed in a batch way because of the batch nature of customer orders (generated by the batch place *p4* and the batch transition *t1*) and the batch nature of the outstanding orders recorded in batch place *p3*. The fulfillment of a customer order will decrease on-hand inventory of the stock as well as its inventory level. This is described by the arcs from places *p1*, *p4* and *p2* to transition *t1*. Batch customer demand is assumed to be a Poisson process, which is specified by the batch transition t_1 whose firing time is subject to an exponential distribution. We assume that transition t_1 generates randomly with the same probability batch customer orders of two different sizes (1 or 2) available in batch place *p4* (i.e.; $\mu(p4) = \{1, 2\}$). The inventory control policy used in the system is a continuous review *(s, S)* policy specified by the immediate transition *t3*. It is assumed that the reorder point and the order-up-to-level of the policy are taken as $s = 4$ and $S = 6$ respectively, and the initial μ-marking of the net is $\mu_0 = (6, 6, \varnothing, \{1, 2\})$. Furthermore, the firing delays of batch transitions *t1* and *t2* (the demand rate and the inventory replenishment rate) are assumed to be exponentially distributed with rates $\lambda_{1[q]} = \lambda_1$ and $\lambda_{2[q]} = \lambda_2$ respectively for any feasible batch firing index q.

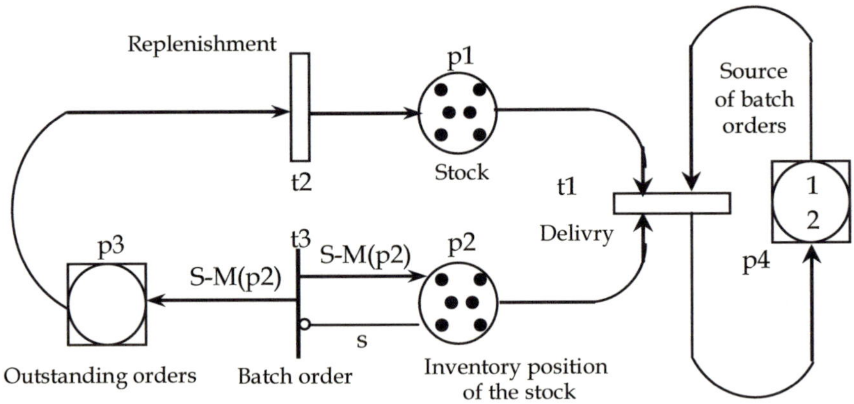

Fig. 2. Batch stochastic Petri net model of the supply chain with *(s, S)* inventory control policy

4.2 Dynamic behaviour analysis

The state space of the Petri net is represented by its μ-reachability graph shown in Fig. 3. In the graph, each directed edge is associated with a label representing the transition whose firing generates the successor μ-marking. Each batch transition is marked by its corresponding batch firing index *q*.

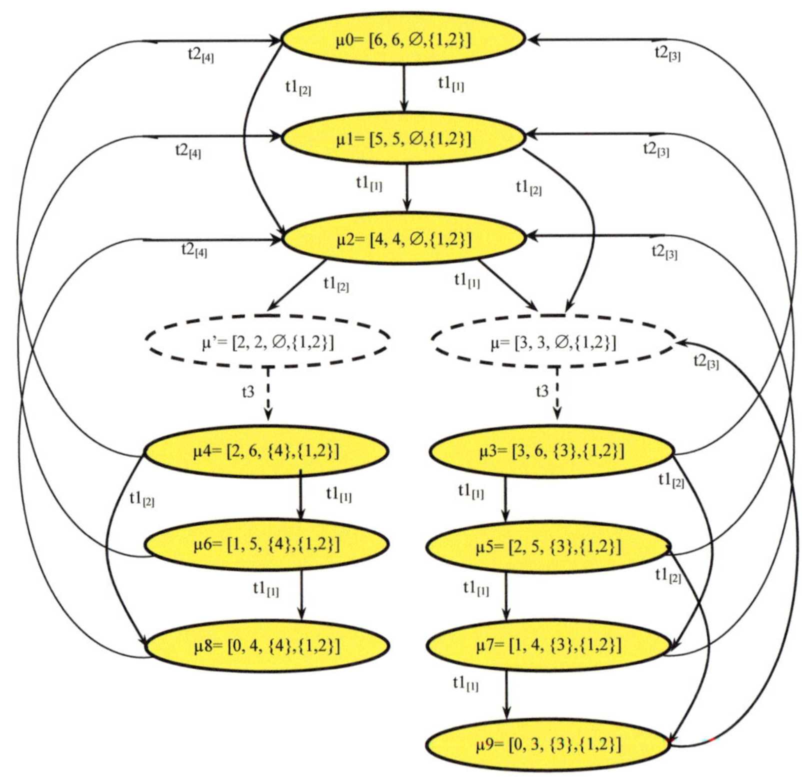

Fig. 3. The μ-reachability graph of the batch stochastic Petri net model shown in Fig. 2

The μ-markings obtained can be classified into *vanishing* and *tangible* μ-markings. A vanishing μ-marking is one in which at least one immediate transition is enabled, and a tangible μ-marking is one in which no immediate transition is enabled. In the μ-reachability graph, the vanishing μ-markings μ_i *(i = 0 to 9)* are represented by rectangles and two tangible μ-markings μ and μ' are represented by dotted rectangles. After eliminating the vanishing μ-markings by merging them with their successor tangible μ-markings and converting the reduced μ-reachability graph to its corresponding stochastic process, we get a continuous timed Markov chain *(CTMC)* represented in Fig. 4.
By solving the linear equations system (14) where A is the infinitesimal generator matrix (transition rate matrix) of the *CTMC*, the steady-state probabilities $\pi = (\pi_1, \pi_2, \ldots, \pi_9)$ can be explicitly obtained as functions of parameters $\lambda 1$ and $\lambda 2$ given in Table 1.

$$\begin{cases} \pi \times A = 0 \\ \sum_{i=0}^{9} \pi_i = 1 \end{cases} \tag{14}$$

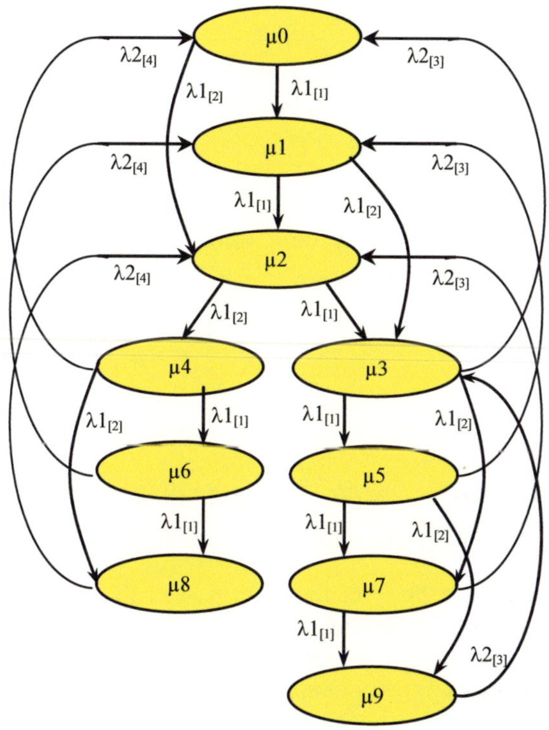

Fig. 4. The underlying Markov chain of the batch stochastic Petri net model shown in Fig. 2

4.3. Performance analysis of the system

With the steady state probabilities $\pi = (\pi_1, \pi_2, \ldots, \pi_9)$, we can easily compute several important performance measures of the supply chain such as the average inventory level, the stockout rate, the average inventory turnover, etc.

π_0	$2(\lambda_2)^2[45(\lambda_2)^2(\lambda_1)^2+25\lambda_2(\lambda_1)^3+32(\lambda_2)^3\lambda_1+8(\lambda_2)^4+4(\lambda_1)^4] \div$ $[351(\lambda_2)^4(\lambda_1)^2+180(\lambda_2)^5(\lambda_1)+342(\lambda_2)^3(\lambda_1)^3+184(\lambda_1)^4(\lambda_2)^2+58(\lambda_1)^5(\lambda_2)+8(\lambda_1)^6+36(\lambda_2)^6]$
π_1	$(\lambda_2)^2[69(\lambda_2)^2(\lambda_1)^2+46\lambda_2(\lambda_1)^3+40(\lambda_2)^3\lambda_1+8(\lambda_2)^4+8(\lambda_1)^4] \div$ $[351(\lambda_2)^4(\lambda_1)^2+180(\lambda_2)^5(\lambda_1)+342(\lambda_2)^3(\lambda_1)^3+184(\lambda_1)^4(\lambda_2)^2+58(\lambda_1)^5(\lambda_2)+8(\lambda_1)^6+36(\lambda_2)^6]$
π_2	$(4(\lambda_1+\lambda_2)^2(\lambda_2)^2).[9\lambda_1\lambda_2+7(\lambda_1)^2+3(\lambda_2)^2] \div$ $[351(\lambda_2)^4(\lambda_1)^2+180(\lambda_2)^5(\lambda_1)+342(\lambda_2)^3(\lambda_1)^3+184(\lambda_1)^4(\lambda_2)^2+58(\lambda_1)^5(\lambda_2)+8(\lambda_1)^6+36(\lambda_2)^6]$
π_3	$2\lambda_1\lambda_2[29(\lambda_2)^2(\lambda_1)^2+18\lambda_2(\lambda_1)^3+20(\lambda_2)^3\lambda_1+5(\lambda_2)^4+4(\lambda_1)^4] \div$ $[351(\lambda_2)^4(\lambda_1)^2+180(\lambda_2)^5(\lambda_1)+342(\lambda_2)^3(\lambda_1)^3+184(\lambda_1)^4(\lambda_2)^2+58(\lambda_1)^5(\lambda_2)+8(\lambda_1)^6+36(\lambda_2)^6]$
π_4	$(2(\lambda_1+\lambda_2)(\lambda_2)^2\lambda_1).[9\lambda_1\lambda_2+7(\lambda_1)^2+3(\lambda_2)^3] \div$ $[351(\lambda_2)^4(\lambda_1)^2+180(\lambda_2)^5(\lambda_1)+342(\lambda_2)^3(\lambda_1)^3+184(\lambda_1)^4(\lambda_2)^2+58(\lambda_1)^5(\lambda_2)+8(\lambda_1)^6+36(\lambda_2)^6]$
π_5	$\lambda_2(\lambda_1)^2[15(\lambda_2)^2\lambda_1+14\lambda_2(\lambda_1)^2+5(\lambda_2)^3+4(\lambda_1)^3] \div$ $[351(\lambda_2)^4(\lambda_1)^2+180(\lambda_2)^5(\lambda_1)+342(\lambda_2)^3(\lambda_1)^3+184(\lambda_1)^4(\lambda_2)^2+58(\lambda_1)^5(\lambda_2)+8(\lambda_1)^6+36(\lambda_2)^6]$
π_6	$(\lambda_2)^2(\lambda_1)^2.[9(\lambda_2\lambda_1+7(\lambda_1)^2+3(\lambda_2)^2] \div$ $[351(\lambda_2)^4(\lambda_1)^2+180(\lambda_2)^5(\lambda_1)+342(\lambda_2)^3(\lambda_1)^3+184(\lambda_1)^4(\lambda_2)^2+58(\lambda_1)^5(\lambda_2)+8(\lambda_1)^6+36(\lambda_2)^6]$
π_7	$0.5.(12(\lambda_1)^3+38\lambda_2(\lambda_1)^2+35(\lambda_2)^2\lambda_1+10(\lambda_2)^3)\ (\lambda_1)^2\lambda_2 \div$ $[351(\lambda_2)^4(\lambda_1)^2+180(\lambda_2)^5(\lambda_1)+342(\lambda_2)^3(\lambda_1)^3+184(\lambda_1)^4(\lambda_2)^2+58(\lambda_1)^5(\lambda_2)+8(\lambda_1)^6+36(\lambda_2)^6]$
π_8	$\lambda_2(\lambda_1)^2(9\lambda_2\lambda_1+7(\lambda_1)^2+3(\lambda_2)^2)(2\lambda_1+\lambda_1) \div$ $[351(\lambda_2)^4(\lambda_1)^2+180(\lambda_2)^5(\lambda_1)+342(\lambda_2)^3(\lambda_1)^3+184(\lambda_1)^4(\lambda_2)^2+58(\lambda_1)^5(\lambda_2)+8(\lambda_1)^6+36(\lambda_2)^6]$
π_9	$0.5(\lambda_1)^3[52\lambda_1(\lambda_1)^2+15(\lambda_2)^3+50(\lambda_2)^2\lambda_1+16(\lambda_1)^3] \div$ $[351(\lambda_2)^4(\lambda_1)^2+180(\lambda_2)^5(\lambda_1)+342(\lambda_2)^3(\lambda_1)^3+184(\lambda_1)^4(\lambda_2)^2+58(\lambda_1)^5(\lambda_2)+8(\lambda_1)^6+36(\lambda_2)^6]$

Table 1. μ-markings (states) probabilities

- *The average inventory level* of the system $S_{avg}(\lambda_1, \lambda_2)$ which corresponds to the mean number of tokens in discrete place p_1 can be calculated by applying the formula:

$$S_{avg}(\lambda 1, \lambda 2) = \overline{\mu(p1)} = \sum_{i=0}^{9} \pi_i \times \mu(p1) \tag{15}$$

$$S_{avg}(\lambda 1, \lambda 2) =$$

$$\frac{0.5\lambda_2 \times \left[368(\lambda_2)^5+1732(\lambda_1)(\lambda_2)^4+780(\lambda_1)^4(\lambda_2)+3038(\lambda_1)^2(\lambda_2)^3+2385(\lambda_1)^3(\lambda_2)^2+76(\lambda_1)^5\right]}{8(\lambda_1)^6+58(\lambda_1)^5(\lambda_2)+184(\lambda_1)^4(\lambda_2)^2+342(\lambda_2)^3(\lambda_1)^3+351(\lambda_1)^2(\lambda_2)^4+180(\lambda_2)^5(\lambda_1)+36(\lambda_2)^6}$$

- *The stockout rate* is the probability of the emptiness of the stock. In the μ-marking graph of the Petri net model in Fig. 3, the marking of the discrete place p_1 is equal to zero ($M(p_1) = 0$) in two μ-markings which are μ_8 and μ_9. Thus the stock-out rate of the inventory system $Prob_{S=0}(\lambda_1, \lambda_2)$ is given by the formula:

$$\text{Prob}_{S=0}(\lambda 1, \lambda 2) = 0 = \text{Prob}\left[\mu(p1) = 0\right] = \pi_8 + \pi_9 \tag{16}$$

$$\text{Prob}_{S=0}(\lambda 1, \lambda 2) =$$

$$\frac{0.5(\lambda_1)^2 \times \left[80(\lambda_1)^3(\lambda_2)+100(\lambda_1)^2(\lambda_2)^2+45(\lambda_1)(\lambda_2)^3+6(\lambda_2)^4+16(\lambda_1)^4\right]}{8(\lambda_1)^6+58(\lambda_1)^5(\lambda_2)+184(\lambda_1)^4(\lambda_2)^2+342(\lambda_2)^3(\lambda_1)^3+351(\lambda_1)^2(\lambda_2)^4+180(\lambda_2)^5(\lambda_1)+36(\lambda_2)^6}$$

- *The average replenishment frequency* of the stock, $FA_{avg}(\lambda 1,\lambda 2)$ corresponds to the average firing frequency of batch transition *t2*. Thus, it is the sum of the average firing frequencies $F(t2_{[3]})$ and $F(t2_{[4]})$ of the transitions $t2_{[3]}$ and $t2_{[4]}$ respectively. These transitions are generated by batch transition *t2* with two different batch firing indexes. $FA_{avg}(\lambda 1, \lambda 2)$ is thus given as follows:

$$FA_{avg}(\lambda 1,\lambda 2) = F(t2_{[3]}) + F\left(t2_{[4]}\right) = \sum_{i|\mu_i \in S(t2_{[3]})} \left(\lambda 2_{[3]} \times \pi_i\right) + \sum_{i|\mu_i \in S(t2_{[4]})} \left(\lambda 2_{[4]} \times \pi_i\right) \tag{17}$$

where $S(t2_{[3]}) = \{\mu_3, \mu_5, \mu_7, \mu_9\}$ is the set of the μ-markings in which batch transition *t2* is fired with index 3 (firing of $t2_{[3]}$) and $S(t2_{[4]}) = \{\mu_4, \mu_6, \mu_8\}$ is the set of the μ-markings in which batch transition *t2* is fired with index 4 (firing of $t2_{[4]}$).

Since $\lambda 2_{[3]} = \lambda 2_{[4]} = \lambda 2$, we obtain that:

$$\begin{aligned} FA_{avg}(\lambda 1,\lambda 2) = F(t2_{[3]}) + F(t2_{[4]}) &= \sum_{i|\mu_i \in S(t2_{[3]}) \cap S(t2_{[4]})} \pi_i \times \lambda 2 \\ &= (\pi_3 + \pi_4 + \pi_5 + \pi_6 + \pi_7 + \pi_8 + \pi_9) \times \lambda 2 \end{aligned} \tag{18}$$

$$FA_{avg}(\lambda 1,\lambda 2) = \frac{2(\lambda_1)\times\left[8(\lambda_2)^5+4(\lambda_1)^5+77(\lambda_2)^3(\lambda_1)^2+70(\lambda_2)^2(\lambda_1)^3+40(\lambda_2)^4(\lambda_1)+29(\lambda_2)(\lambda_1)^4\right]}{8(\lambda_1)^6+58(\lambda_1)^5(\lambda_2)+184(\lambda_1)^4(\lambda_2)^2+342(\lambda_2)^3(\lambda_1)^3+351(\lambda_1)^2(\lambda_2)^4+180(\lambda_2)^5(\lambda_1)+36(\lambda_2)^6}$$

The average inventory level, the stock-out rate, and the average replenishment frequency of the stock as functions of parameters *λ1* and *λ2* are depicted in Fig. 5, Fig. 6, and Fig. 7, respectively.

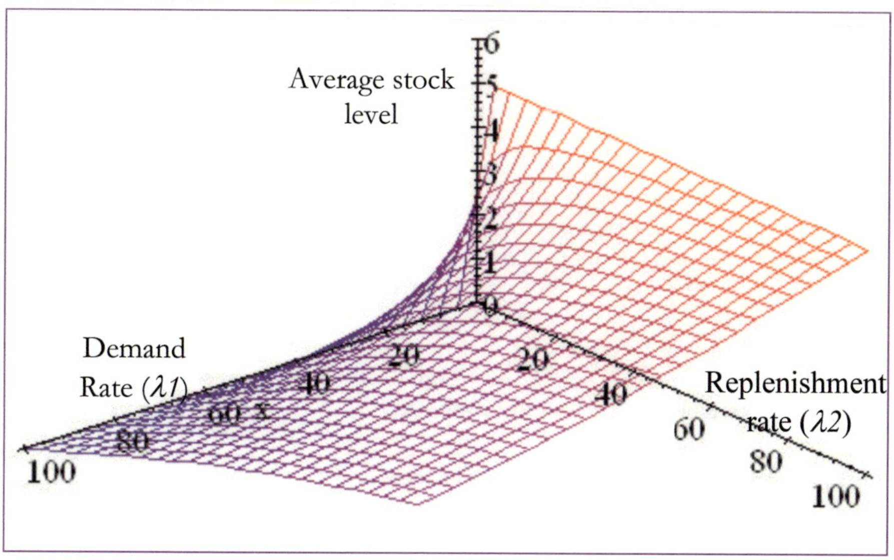

Fig. 5. Average inventory level of the stock

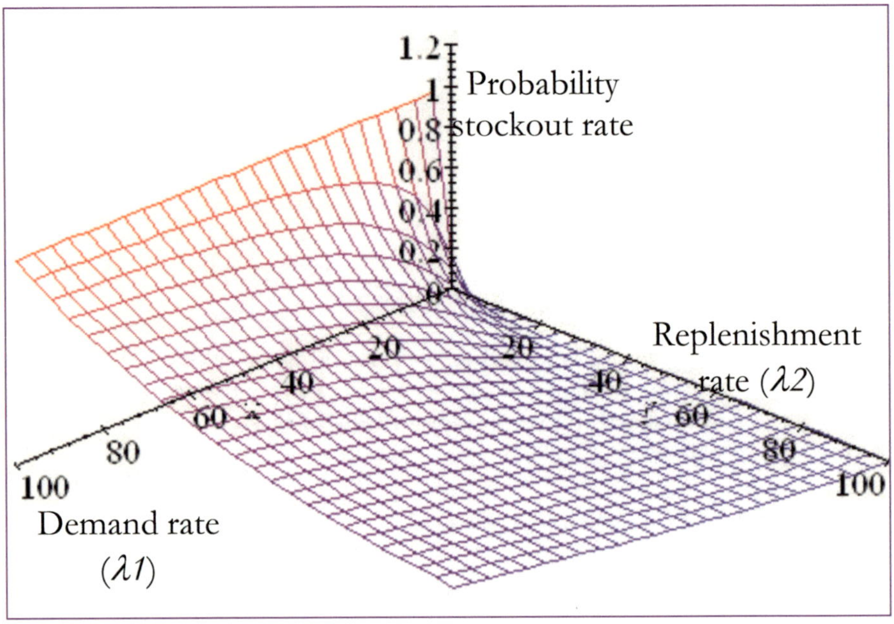

Fig. 6. Stock-out rate of the stock

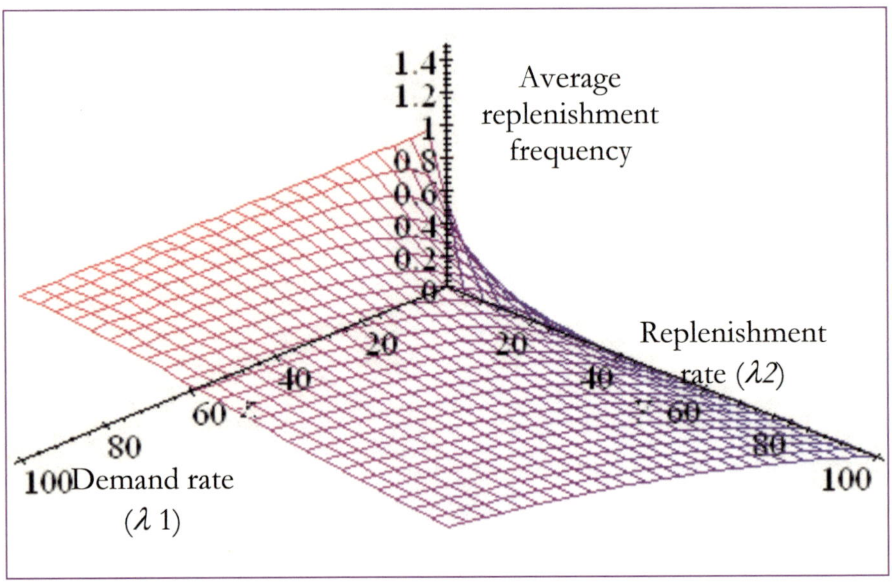

Fig. 7. Average frequency replenishment of the stock

4.4 Parameter sensitivity analysis of the system

This section is dedicated to sensitivity analysis of the inventory system. We consider the following parameters for it: $\lambda 1_{[1]} = \lambda 1_{[2]} = \lambda 1 = 0.5$ and $\lambda 2_{[3]} = \lambda 2_{[4]} = \lambda 2 = 0.5$. Its transition rate matrix is thus as follows:

$$A = \begin{pmatrix} -1 & 0.5 & 0.5 & 0 & 0 & 0 & 0 & 0 & 0 & 0 \\ 0 & -1 & 0.5 & 0.5 & 0 & 0 & 0 & 0 & 0 & 0 \\ 0 & 0 & -1 & 0.5 & 0.5 & 0 & 0 & 0 & 0 & 0 \\ 0.5 & 0 & 0 & -1.5 & 0 & 0.5 & 0 & 0.5 & 0 & 0 \\ 0.5 & 0 & 0 & 0 & -1.5 & 0 & 0.5 & 0 & 0.5 & 0 \\ 0 & 0.5 & 0 & 0 & 0 & -1.5 & 0 & 0.5 & 0 & 0.5 \\ 0 & 0.5 & 0 & 0 & 0 & 0 & -1 & 0 & 0.5 & 0 \\ 0 & 0 & 0.5 & 0 & 0 & 0 & 0 & -1 & 0 & 0.5 \\ 0 & 0 & 0.5 & 0 & 0 & 0 & 0 & 0 & -0.5 & 0 \\ 0 & 0 & 0 & 0.5 & 0 & 0 & 0 & 0 & 0 & -0.5 \end{pmatrix}$$

In this case, the steady state probabilities, denoted by π_i, $i = 0, \ldots, 9$, obtained by solving the corresponding equations system (14) is :

$$\pi = \begin{pmatrix} 0.1025 & 0.09075 & 0.1915 & 0.1411 & 0.0638 & 0.0471 & 0.0320 & 0.0942 & 0.0958 & 0.1411 \end{pmatrix}$$

4.4.1 Sensitivity analysis with respect to one parameter

- **Sensitivity analysis of the average inventory level of the stock with respect to the customer demand rate**

In the Petri net model, the stock is modeled by the discrete place *p1*. In other words, the inventory level of the stock, in each state, corresponds to *M(p1)*, the marking of the place *p1*. Thus, the corresponding performance function is:

$$f = \begin{pmatrix} 6 & 5 & 4 & 3 & 2 & 2 & 1 & 1 & 0 & 0 \end{pmatrix}$$

where $f(i)$, $i = 0, 1, \ldots, 9$, corresponds to the marking of the place *p1*, $M(p_1)$, (the inventory level) at the state M_i (see the marking graph of the Petri net model in Fig. 3).
Consider now the perturbation on a parameter $\lambda 1$ (customer demand rate associated with the transition *t1*) and its influence on the directional matrix Q given as follows:

$$Q = \begin{pmatrix} -2\delta & \delta & \delta & 0 & 0 & 0 & 0 & 0 & 0 & 0 \\ 0 & -2\delta & \delta & \delta & 0 & 0 & 0 & 0 & 0 & 0 \\ 0 & 0 & -2\delta & \delta & \delta & 0 & 0 & 0 & 0 & 0 \\ 0 & 0 & 0 & -2\delta & 0 & \delta & 0 & \delta & 0 & 0 \\ 0 & 0 & 0 & 0 & -2\delta & 0 & \delta & 0 & \delta & 0 \\ 0 & 0 & 0 & 0 & 0 & -2\delta & 0 & \delta & 0 & \delta \\ 0 & 0 & 0 & 0 & 0 & 0 & -\delta & 0 & \delta & 0 \\ 0 & 0 & 0 & 0 & 0 & 0 & 0 & -\delta & 0 & \delta \\ 0 & 0 & 0 & 0 & 0 & 0 & 0 & 0 & 0 & 0 \\ 0 & 0 & 0 & 0 & 0 & 0 & 0 & 0 & 0 & 0 \end{pmatrix}$$

where δ is a very small positive real number corresponding to an infinitesimal change of the parameter $\lambda 1$. The perturbation is illustrated in Fig. 8.

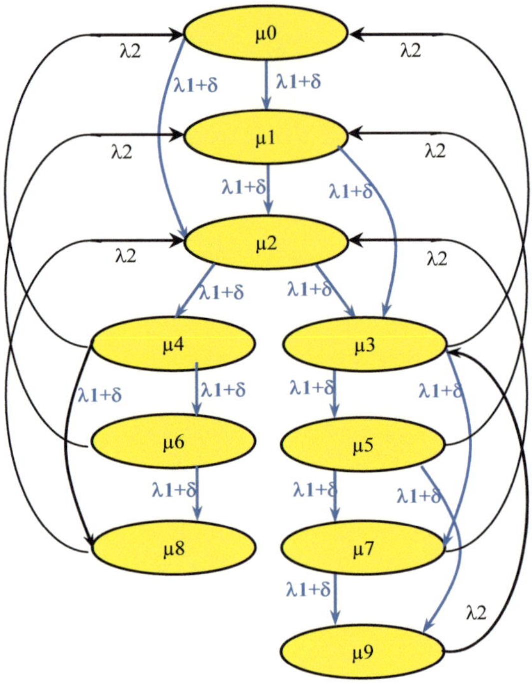

Fig. 8. Perturbation on customer demand rate (*λ1*)

By applying the equation (12), the derivate of the considered performance (average inventory level of the stock) with respect to the parameter *λ1* is given by the following linear function represented in Fig. 9.

$$SPerf = -3.2381.\delta$$

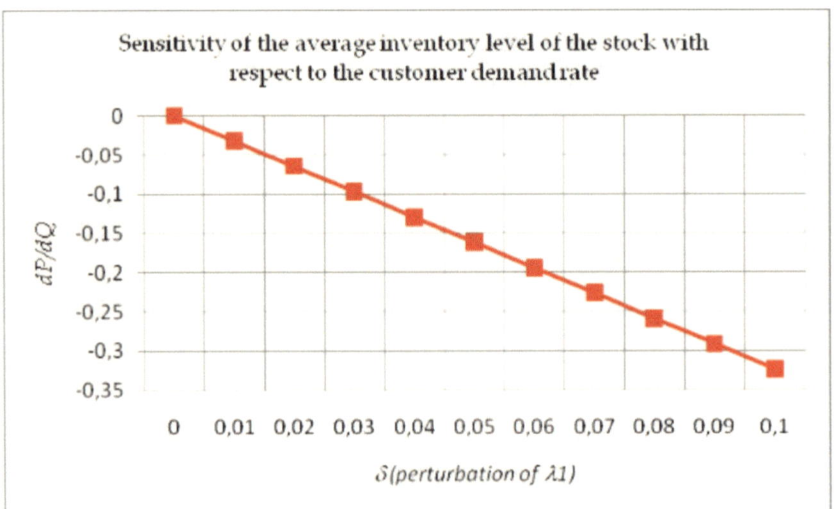

Fig. 9. Sensitivity of the average inventory level of the stock with respect to the customer demand rate (*λ1*)

Clearly, this derivate means that if the customer demand rate $\lambda 1$ of the inventory system is increased by an amount δ, then average inventory level of the stock will decrease by an amount 3,2381·δ.

- **Sensitivity analysis of the stockout rate with respect to the supplier replenishment rate**

The stockout rate is defined in the previous section as the probability of the emptiness of the stock. In the μ-marking graph of the Petri net model in Fig. 3, the marking of the discrete place p_1 is equal to zero ($M(p_1) = 0$) in two markings which are μ_8 and μ_9. Thus, the corresponding performance function is:

$$f = \begin{pmatrix} 0 & 0 & 0 & 0 & 0 & 0 & 0 & 0 & 1 & 1 \end{pmatrix}$$

where $f(i) = 1$ for only $i = 8$ and $i = 9$ corresponding to the two μ-markings μ_8 and μ_9 where the marking of the place $p1$ (the inventory level), $M(p_1)$ is equal to zero (see the μ-marking graph of the Petri net model in Fig. 3).

Consider now the perturbation on a parameter $\lambda 2$ (replenishment rate associated with the transition $t2$) and its influence on the directional matrix Q given as follows:

$$Q = \begin{pmatrix} 0 & 0 & 0 & 0 & 0 & 0 & 0 & 0 & 0 & 0 \\ 0 & 0 & 0 & 0 & 0 & 0 & 0 & 0 & 0 & 0 \\ 0 & 0 & 0 & 0 & 0 & 0 & 0 & 0 & 0 & 0 \\ \delta & 0 & 0 & -\delta & 0 & 0 & 0 & 0 & 0 & 0 \\ \delta & 0 & 0 & 0 & -\delta & 0 & 0 & 0 & 0 & 0 \\ 0 & \delta & 0 & 0 & 0 & -\delta & 0 & 0 & 0 & 0 \\ 0 & \delta & 0 & 0 & 0 & 0 & -\delta & 0 & 0 & 0 \\ 0 & 0 & \delta & 0 & 0 & 0 & 0 & -\delta & 0 & 0 \\ 0 & 0 & \delta & 0 & 0 & 0 & 0 & 0 & -\delta & 0 \\ 0 & 0 & 0 & \delta & 0 & 0 & 0 & 0 & 0 & -\delta \end{pmatrix}$$

By applying the equation (12), the derivate of the considered performance (stockout rate) with respect to the parameter $\lambda 2$ is given by the following linear function represented in Fig. 10.

$$SPerf = -5.5736.\delta$$

Clearly, this derivate means that if the supplier replenishment rate λ2 of the supply chain is increased by an amount δ, then the stockout out rate will decrease by an amount 5,5736·δ.

4.4.2 Sensitivity analysis with respect to a group of parameters

Here, the perturbations on a group of parameters are illustrated. The sensitivity level in these directions can be used to identify the relative importance of each parameter in the group. For instance in our system, the directional matrix Q corresponding to the perturbation of the parameters $\lambda 1$ (the customer demand rate) and $\lambda 2$ (the supplier replenishment rate) at the same time is:

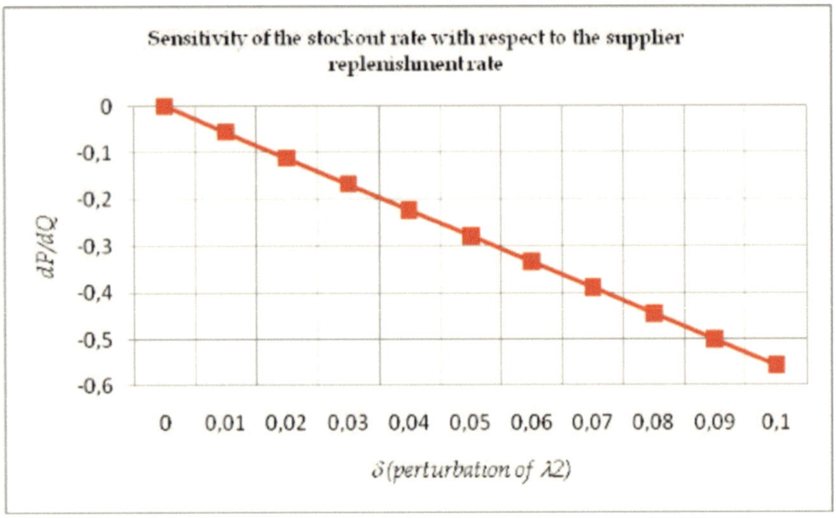

Fig. 10. Sensitivity of the stockout rate with respect to the supplier replenishment rate *(λ2)*

$$Q=\begin{pmatrix}
-2\delta_1 & \delta_1 & \delta_1 & 0 & 0 & 0 & 0 & 0 & 0 & 0\\
0 & -2\delta_1 & \delta_1 & \delta_1 & 0 & 0 & 0 & 0 & 0 & 0\\
0 & 0 & -2\delta_1 & \delta_1 & \delta_1 & 0 & 0 & 0 & 0 & 0\\
\delta_2 & 0 & 0 & -2\delta_1-\delta_2 & 0 & \delta_1 & 0 & \delta_1 & 0 & 0\\
\delta_2 & 0 & 0 & 0 & -2\delta_1-\delta_2 & 0 & \delta_1 & 0 & \delta_1 & 0\\
0 & \delta_2 & 0 & 0 & 0 & -2\delta_1-\delta_2 & 0 & \delta_1 & 0 & \delta_1\\
0 & \delta_2 & 0 & 0 & 0 & 0 & -\delta_1-\delta_2 & 0 & \delta_1 & 0\\
0 & 0 & \delta_2 & 0 & 0 & 0 & 0 & -\delta_1-\delta_2 & 0 & \delta_1\\
0 & 0 & \delta_2 & 0 & 0 & 0 & 0 & 0 & -\delta_2 & 0\\
0 & 0 & 0 & \delta_2 & 0 & 0 & 0 & 0 & 0 & -\delta_2
\end{pmatrix}$$

By using this directional matrix, and the function *f* expressed in the previous sub-section, the stockout rate derivate with respect to the two parameters *λ1* and *λ2* can be expressed as the following linear function:

$$SPerf = 5.57\ (\delta_1 - \delta_2)$$

Note that because of the linear structure of equation (12), if a perturbation matrix *Q* is a linear function of elementary perturbations matrixes Q_i, it is possible to evaluate the multidirectional sensitivity measures related to *Q* on the basis of the elementary perturbation measures related to the Q_i.
In our example, it is clear that:

$$Q_{(\lambda 1,\lambda 2)} = Q_{(\lambda 1)} + Q_{(\lambda 2)}$$

Then, we can write that:

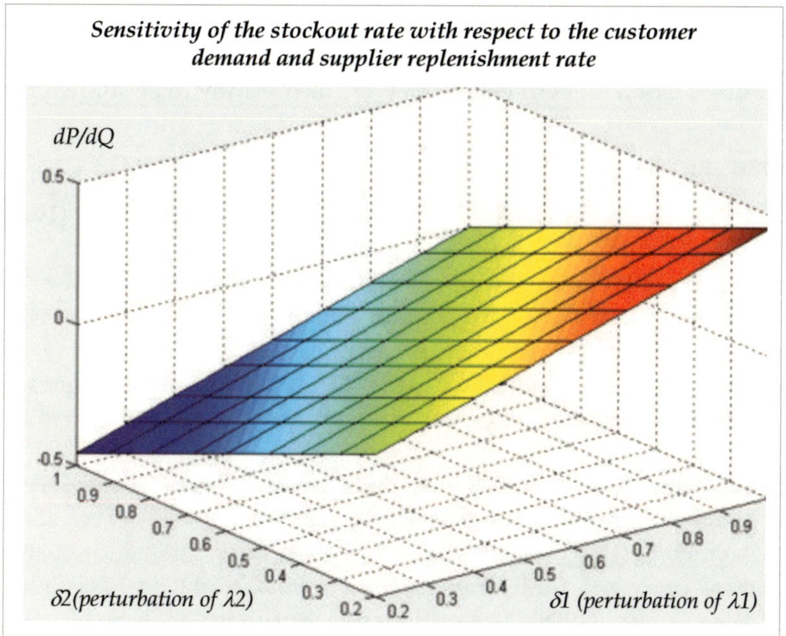

Fig. 11. Sensitivity of the stockout rate with respect to two parameters *λ1* (the customer demand rate) and *λ2* (the supplier replenishment rate).

$$\text{SPerf} = \frac{dP}{dQ_{(\lambda 1,\lambda 2)}} = -\pi \cdot Q_{(\lambda 1,\lambda 2)} \cdot A^{\#} \cdot f$$

$$= \frac{dP}{dQ_{(\lambda 1)}} + \frac{dP}{dQ_{(\lambda 2)}} = -\pi \cdot A^{\#} \cdot f \cdot \left(Q_{(\lambda 1)} + Q_{(\lambda 2)}\right)$$

Previously, we obtained that $SPerf = 5.57\,(\delta_1 - \delta_2) = 5.57\delta_1 - 5.57\delta_2$. In this function, we can identify two terms which are:

- The term ($-5.57\delta_2$) correspond to the sensitivity measure with respect to the parameter *λ2* computed in the previous sub-section.
- The term ($-5.57\delta_1$) correspond to the sensitivity measure with respect to the parameter *λ1*.

6. Conclusion

The theoretical results presented in this chapter are a natural extension of the recent development on sensitivity analysis of stochastic processes. The main idea is to obtain the derivates of a performance measure of a discrete event dynamic system based on its stochastic Petri model. In this work, the SPN model is studied. A Parameter Sensitivity analysis approach for the model is developed and an application to a supply chain is studied. We note that the proposed methodology is also applicable to GSPN (Generalized Stochastic Petri Nets) models since the marking process of a bounded GSPN is also a Markov process. The development of sensitivity analysis methods for non Markovian stochastic Petri nets and the application of perturbation realization to the sensitivity analysis of dynamic systems with unbounded stochastic processes are two important research issues. Simulation methods based on Petri nets models are also worthy to be studied further.

6. References

Ajmone Marsan M., Balbo G., Conte G., Donatelli, S., Franceschinis G., (1995) *"Modelling with generalized stochastic Petri Nets"*, John Wiley and Sons.

Amodeo L., Chen H., El Hadji A., "Multiobjective supply chain optimization: An industrial case study", *Evoworkshops 2007, Lecture Notes in Computer Science*, 4448, pp 732-741, 2007.

Archetti, E., Gaivoronski, A., Sciomachen, A., (1993), Sensitivity Analysis and Optimization of Stochastic Petri Nets, *Discrete Event Dynamic Systems: Theory and Applications 3, pp.5-37.*

Brooks, C. A. and Varaiya, P., (1994), "Using perturbation analysis to solve the capacity and flow assignment problem for general and ATM networks," *in Proc. IEEE Globcom.*

Cao. X. R et Chen. H. F, (1997), Potentials, Perturbation Realization and sensitivity analysis of Markov processes, *IEEE, Trans Automat Control, vol.42, pp. 1382-1393.*

Cao. X. R. et Wan. Y. W., (1998), "Algorithms for sensitivity analysis of markov systems through potentials and perturbation realization", *IEEE, Transactions on control systems technology, vol.6, n°4, pp.482-494.*

Caramanis, M., and Liberopoulos, G., (1992), Perturbation analysis for the design of flexible manufacturing system flow controllers," *Operations Res., vol.40, pp. 1107-1125.*

Chen H., Amodeo L., Chu F., Labadi K., « Performance Evaluation and Optimization of Supply Chains Modelled by Batch Deterministic and Stochastic Petri » *IEEE transactions on Automation Science and Engineering*, vol. 2, N° 2, pp. 132-144, April 2005.

Chiola, G., Franceschinis, G., Gaeta, R., and Ribaudo, M., (1995), GreatSPN1.7: Graphical Editor and Analyzer for Timed and Stochastic Petri Nets, *Performance Evaluation 24, Special Issues on Performance Modelling Tools.*

Ciardo, G., Muppala, J., and Trivedi, K.S., (1993), SPNP: stochastic Petri net package, *In proceedings International Workshop on Petri Nets and Performance Models- PNPM89, IEEE Computer Society, pp.142-151.*

Dai L.Y., and Ho, Y.C., (1995), "Structural infinitesimal perturbation analysis (SIPA) for derivative estimation of discrete event dynamic systems," *IEEE Trans. Automat. Contr., vol. 40, pp. 1154–1166.*

Dai, L. (1996) Sensitivity analysis of stationary performance measures for Markov chains, *Mathematical and Computer Modelling, vol. 23, n°11-12, pp. 143–160.*

David R. et Alla H., (1992) *"Du Grafcet aux réseaux de Petri"*, Editions Hermès, Paris.

Do Van, P., Barros, A., and Bérenguer, C. (2008) Reliability importance analysis of Markovian systems at steady state using perturbation analysis. *Reliability engineering & systems safety, vol. 93, n°1, pp.1605- 1615.*

Feng, C., Desrochers, A.A., (1993), Sensitivity analysis of a FMS by a Petri net-based perturbation method, *IEEE International Conference on Robotics and Automation, Proceedings, 1993, vol.3, pp. 564-569.*

Frank P., (1978), Introduction to system sensitivity. *New York: Academic Press.*

Glasserman P. (1992), Derivative estimates from simulation of continuous-time Markov chains, *Oper Res; 40(2), pp. 292–308.*

Glynn PW., (1990), Likelihood ratio gradient estimation for stochastic systems, *Commun ACM 1990; 33: pp. 75–84.*

Haas P. J., (2002), *"Stochastic Petri nets: modelling, stability, simulation"*, Springer-Verlag, New York.

Haurie, A., L'Ecuyer, P., and Van Delft, C., (1994) "Convergence of stochastic approximation coupled with perturbation analysis in a class of manufacturing flow control models," *Discrete Event Dynamic Syst.: Theory Appl., vol. 4, pp. 87–111.*

Ho, Y.C., Eyler, M.A., Chien, T.T, (1979), A gradient technique for general buffer storage design in a production line, *Int. J. of production Research, vol. 17 n°6, pp. 557-580.*

Labadi K., Chen H., Amodeo L., « Modelling and Performance Evaluation of Inventory Systems Using Batch Deterministic and Stochastic Petri Nets », IEEE Transactions on Systems, Man and Cybernetics, Part C: Applications and reviews, vol. 37, N° 6, November 2007.

Lindeman, C., (1995), DSPNexpress: a software package for the efficient solution of deterministic and stochastic Petri nets. *Performance Evaluation 22*, pp. 3-21.

Lindeman, C., (1998) *"Performance modelling with deterministic and stochastic Petri nets"*, John Wiley and Sons Edition.

Mainkar, V., Choi, H., Trivedi, K., (1993), Sensitivity Analysis of Markov Regenerative Stochastic Petri Nets, *Fifth International Workshop on Petri Nets and Performance Models (PNPM'93), Toulouse France, pp. 180-189.*

Molloy M.K., (1982), Performance analysis using Stochastic Petri Nets, *IEEE Transactions on Computers, C-31(9): pp. 913-917.*

Murata T., (1989), Petri nets: Properties, analysis, and applications, *in Proc. of the IEEE, vol.77, no.4, pp. 541-580.*

Ou Y., Bechta-Dugan, J., (1994), *Realization Probabilities: The Dynamics of Queueing Systems*, New York: Springer-Verlag.

Proth, J-M, Sauer, N., Wardi, Y., and Xie, X., (1993), Marking Optimization of Stochastic Timed Event Graphs using IPA, *Proceedings of the 32nd Conference on Decision Control, pp. 686-691.*

Silva M., Teruel E., (1997) "Petri nets for the design and operation of manufacturing systems". *European Journal of Control, 3(3): pp. 182-199.*

Wang Jiacun, (1998) *"Timed Petri Nets: Theory and Application"*, Kluwer Academic Publishers.

Xiao, N., Wu, F. F., and Lun, S.M., "Dynamic bandwidth allocation using infinitesimal perturbation analysis," *IEEE Infocom'94*, pp. 383–389.

Xie, X., (1998), Perturbation analysis of stochastic Petri nets, *IEEE Transactions on Automatic Control, vol.43, n°1, pp. 76-80.*

Yan H., and Zhou, X.Y., (1994), "Finding optimal number of Kanbans in a manufacturing system via perturbation analysis," *Lecture Notes in Control and Information Sciences*, vol. 199. New York: Springer-Verlag, pp. 572–578.

Zhou Mengchu and Kurapati Venkatesh., (1999), "Modeling, simulation, and control of flexible manufacturing systems: *A Petri net approach", vol 6 of Series in Intelligent Control and Intelligent Automation, World Scientific.*

Zhou MengChu, and DiCesare Frank., (1993), *"Petri net synthesis for discrete control of manufacturing systems"*, Kluwer Academic Publishers.

Zurawski R., and Zhou Mengchu., (1994), "Petri nets and industrial applications: A tutorial", *IEEE Transactions on Industrial Electronics,* vol. 41, no. 6, pp. 567-583.

7

Modelling Multimedia Synchronization using a Time Petri Net Based Approach

Abdelghani Ghomari[1] and Chabane Djeraba[2]
[1]Department of Computer Science, University of Es-Senia Oran
[2]University of sciences and Technologies of Lille 1
[1]Algeria
[2]France

1. Introduction

Multimedia refers to the presentation of collections of both static and dynamic data (i.e., data with natural time dependencies e.g., audio or video) in a specified order and time. Therefore, their mutual synchronization must assure a proper temporal order of presentation events. Multimedia synchronization can be defined as a mutual assignment of data items and time instants. These time instants may be known in advance (e.g., standard consumer data players) or they can be also results of some unknown function of time (event driven synchronization) or known with some limited accuracy (e.g., random network delays).

The modelling and the presentation of multimedia scenarios are challenges of multimedia applications. Multimedia scenarios are results of temporal composition and user interactions of multimedia objects in an application domain, and lot of works discussed this notion (Adjeroh & Lee, 1995; Perez-Luque & Little, 1996). Temporal compositions consist in presenting multimedia objects which requires synchronization among different media.

Most of specification models are based on Allen's relations (Allen, 1983). Allen defined seven basic relations between two temporal intervals. For example, a TV program starts at 9:00 pm, and finishes at 11:00 pm. The TV program can be considered as one of multimedia objects. In addition, "interval" is considered as a range from 9:00 pm to 11:00 pm, and "duration" as two hours. Allen's relations require this duration of the interval. Before designing the specification model, interval duration must be known. This means that multimedia database systems must determine duration of multimedia objects, because presentations are almost dependent of duration.

Our approach defines a tool that has two important inter-dependent features:

User temporal specification based on an appropriate temporal specification language, which is itself based on an extension of Allen's temporal relations (Allen, 1983). This extension models both existing temporal arrangement and dependency relations between multimedia objects, and this is an interesting point of our work.

Automatic generation of a time Petri net based on the previous temporal specification. The time Petri net is stored in an object called "scenario object". The user may request the simulation and the interpretation of the scenario object which leads to scenario

presentations with domain expert interactions. The Petri net permits a formal specification and a proof of scenarios. The simulation and the proofs are two advantages of the Petri net.
A first version of our approach (Ghomari & Djeraba, 2003) considers multimedia objects of known or unknown duration and interactive relations, but doesn't consider dependency temporal relations between multimedia objects and the management of multimedia scenario in a database system. This is the main differences between the first version of our approach and the second one that will be described in this chapter. This approach provides the following benefits (Ghomari & Djeraba, 2010):

1. The ability to deal with non-deterministic time intervals, e.g. objects with an unknown duration, objects whose reproduction can fail and objects that represent user interactions.
2. The possibility of automatic detection of inconsistent synchronization conditions such as "A *precedes* B, B *precedes* C, C *precedes* A".
3. A graphical notation to describe and simulate the presentation.
4. An editor which abstracts the internal Petri net representation and allows the user to think in familiar terms such as "*precedence*" or "*overlap*".
5. Automatic generation of a MP-RdPT net based on the previous temporal specification.
6. Automatic analysis of the multimedia scenarios properties, like: safeness, liveness, reversibility and consistency.

In this chapter, we highlight the following points: related works (Section 2), our scenario temporal specification (Section 3), the multimedia p-time Petri net (Section 4), object oriented database modelling of the multimedia specification (Section 5), and the architecture of the system prototype (Section 6).

2. Related work

Existing temporal models for multimedia may be decomposed into two classes: instant-based and interval-based (Hamblin, 1972; Blakowski & Steinmetz, 1996). In instant-based models, the elementary units are instants in a time space. Each event in the model has its associated time instants. The time instants arranged according to some relations such as *precede, simultaneous* or *after* form complex multimedia presentations. An example of the instant-based approach is timeline, in which media objects are placed on several time axes called tracks, one per each media type. All events such as the beginning or the end of a segment are totally ordered on the time line.
Several approaches support instant-based models such as Hy-Time (ISO, 1992). The model is well suited for temporal composition of media segments of known durations; however it falls short for unknown durations.
Interval-based models consider elementary media entities as time intervals ordered according to some relations. Existing models are mainly based on the relations defined by Allen for expressing the knowledge about time (Allen, 1983). However, using Allen's relations for multimedia composition faces several problems. First, the relations were designed to express existing relationships between intervals of fixed duration and not for specifying relationships that must be always satisfied even when interval durations are changed. Consider for example an existing relation *before* between intervals a and b (see Fig. 1). When we increase the duration of interval a, the relation changes from *before* to *during* passing through intermediate relations *meets, overlaps,* and *finishes*. This drawback makes the Allen relations not suitable for specifying composition of intervals with unknown duration.

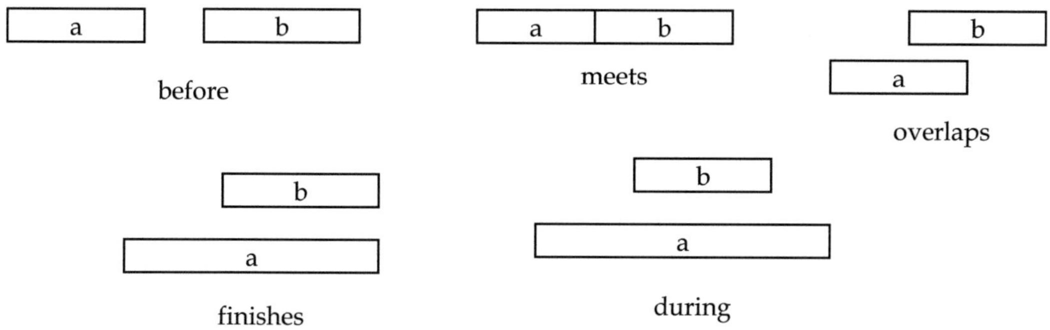

Fig. 1. Relations change when the interval duration is modified

Another problem with the Allen's relations is their descriptive character. They allow expression of an existing, a posteriori arrangement of intervals, but they do not express any causal or functional relation between intervals. For example, relation *meets* only states that the end of the first interval coincides with the end of the second one, but it does not say whether the first interval starts the second one, whether the second interval stops the first one or whether it is a pure coincidence (see Fig. 2). So, the Allen's relations can be useful for characterizing an existing, instantiated presentation (a presentation for which all start and termination instants of media segments are known).

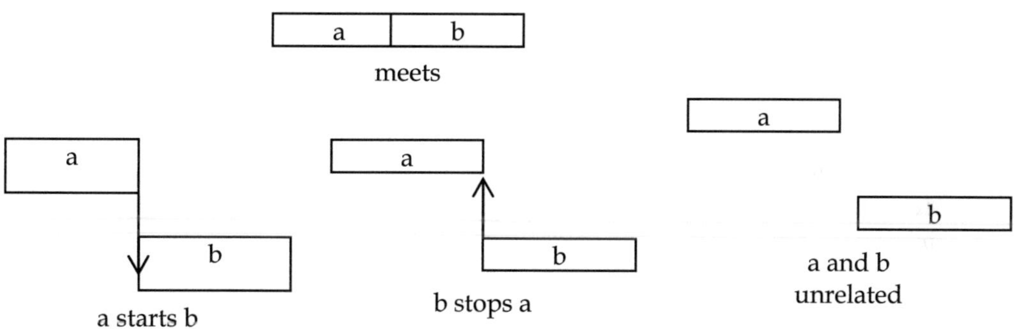

Fig. 2. Meets represents temporal coincidence not a functional relationship.

The third problem with the Allen's relations is related to inconsistent specifications that can be introduced in a multimedia presentation. Detecting inconsistent specification requires algorithms of complexity [$O(N^2)$], where N is the number of intervals (Allen, 1983).

Many approaches are based on time interval-based model. For example:

- King (King, 1994), proposes a different formalism based on a temporal logic. He/She shows how the Allen's relations can be expressed using temporal logic formulae. Although his formalism has solid mathematical bases, composition of multimedia presentations using declarative formulae is awkward. Logic formulae are difficult to use by any author unaware of formal methods. Moreover, to be useful, the formalism must be supported by a consistency checker and an interpreter to execute a given temporal specification.
- Courtiat and De Oliveira (Courtiat and Oliveira, 1996), presented a synchronization model for the formal description of multimedia documents that consider network

performances. This model automatically translates the user formalization into a real-time LOTOS formal specification and verifies a multimedia document aiming to identify potential temporal inconsistencies.

- Blakowski and Steinmetz (Blakowski & Steinmetz, 1996), recognized an event-based representation of a multimedia scenario as one of the four categories for modelling a multimedia presentation. Events are represented in the Hypermedia/Time-Based Structuring Language (HyTime) and Hypermedia Office Document Architecture (HyperODA). Events are defined in HyTime as presentations of media objects along with the playout specifications and finite coordinate system (FCS) coordinates. HyperODA events happen instantaneously and mainly correspond to start and end of media objects or timers. This approach suffers from poor semantics conveyed by the events and moreover it does not provide any scheme for composition and consumption architectures.

Another group of approaches consider the PN tool for multimedia synchronization. For example:

- Object Composition Petri Net Model (OCPN) (Little and Ghafoor, 1993). However, the OCPN approach does not inherently support modelling of interaction.
- Hierarchical Time Stream Petri Net (HTSPN) Model (Senac et al., 1995). However, in the HTSPN approach, it is unspecified what would happen to tokens representing streams left behind the synchronization. If those "dead tokens" were remained in the state, a semantic inconsistency between the model and the real system would be produced.
- Multimedia Organization Employing a Network Approach (MORENA) (Botafogo and Moss, 1995). However, since MORENA does not fully follow PN theory, it may not be easy to analyse the output model using the existing techniques developed in the Petri net field.
- High-Level Petri Net-Based Hypermedia System (Na Cheo and Furuta, 2001). However, the authoring environment used to specify multimedia scenarios with coloured timed Petri nets is not user-friendly, like in the user community.
- Dynamic Fuzzy Multimedia Petri Net (DFMN) (Chen and Huang, 2005). However, in the approach of Shterev (Shterev, 2005) using the DFMN model for modelling of interaction on multimedia streams and objects, none analysis or simulation tools of multimedia presentation are provided.

Special attention should be paid to the upcoming standard Synchronized Multimedia Integration Language (SMIL) (W3C, 2001). SMIL is a meta-language for authoring and presentation of multimedia documents. However, SMIL is a script language and does not support analysis to the same degree that Petri-net-based systems do.

An interesting survey on authoring models and approaches are presented in (Jourdan et al. 1997; Roisin & Sèdes, 2004; Boronat et al., 2008).

Our approach is a compromise between formal specification useful for checking inconsistency and high level language for user specification.

3. Our scenario temporal specification

We will present a model for temporal composition of multimedia objects. The model is based on time-interval and Weiss relations (Weiss et al., 1995). We consider the seven relations of Allen (Allen, 1983) (*equals, meets, before, finishes, starts, overlaps, during*) with the following features:

Firstly, the temporal relations are designed to specify relations between multimedia objects of both determined and undetermined duration. Secondly, the temporal relations describe both existing arrangement of multimedia objects, and dependency relations between multimedia objects. For example, x *meets* y means that the end of multimedia object x coincides with the start of multimedia object y, but it doesn't describe whether multimedia object x starts multimedia object y, or whether multimedia object y stops multimedia object x. Thirdly, the detection of inconsistent specification is not necessary.

3.1 Interval

Our elementary entities are time intervals. Time interval I is defined by the end points (I.begin ≤ I.end) as I = {t | I.begin≤ t ≤ I.end }. The duration of interval I is d = I.end - I.begin and can be constant (e.g. 5 seconds), dependent on the intrinsic playing time of the medium (e.g. playing time of a video segment) or unspecified (e.g. user interaction or live feed). In this paper each interval corresponds to the presentation of one object (e.g. an image or a music selection). In that sense, the beginning and the end of an interval are logical times which will really correspond to physical time during the effective presentation to the user.

3.2 Temporal relations

Several relationships have been defined on time intervals: *equals, before, meets, finishes, starts, during, overlaps,* (Allen, 1983). Usually, they are binary relationships but can be easily extended to n-ary ones (Little & Ghafoor, 1993). Sequential relationships combine intervals which share the same timeline (mutual exclusion), occurring one after the other with (before) or without delay (meet) between them. Parallel relationships relate intervals which have their own timeline. In our model these relations are used for composing and synchronizing multimedia objects in presentations.

Temporal aspects are also discussed in standards like HyTime (ISO, 1992) where the concept of finite coordinate system is used to define a set of axes of finite dimensions. The system designer defines both the number of axes and the units of dimension used along each of them. Hence, an x-y-time coordinate system can be used to model spatial as well as temporal aspects for database objects belonging to presentations.

A program of our temporal specification language is divided into four parts: declaration, assignation, temporal and interactive relations.

Declaration: the declaration part contains the declarations of multimedia objects and returns as a result: multimedia-object (min, opt, max): media-type.

Assignation: the assign part contains the assign functions between the objects declared in the first part and the data streams. For example, the data streams may be mpeg or jpeg when storing video or images objects respectively. For example: assign (video1, "file1.mpeg"); or assign (image1, "file2.jpeg").

When using several equal multimedia objects of the same media, we have to declare several multimedia objects with the same duration assigned to the same physical support. For example, if video3 and video4 share the same physical object with the same duration, we will have: video3 (min, opt, max): VIDEO; video4 (min, opt, max): VIDEO; assign (video3, "file3.mpeg"); assign (video4, "file3.mpeg").

When using several multimedia objects of the same media with different duration, we have to declare several multimedia objects with different duration assigned to the same physical support. For example, if video3 and video4 share the same physical object with different duration, we will have : video3 (min1, opt1, max1) : VIDEO; video4 (min2, opt2, max2) : VIDEO; assign(video3,"file3.mpeg");assign(video4,"file3.mpeg".

The temporal relations part contains a set of temporal relations, each one representing a binary Allen's relation between multimedia objects. These multimedia objects are either declared objects and assigned to physical supports, or objects resulting from temporal relations. A relation takes two multimedia objects as arguments and returns a multimedia object as a result: temporal-relation (multimedia object1, multimedia object2) -> multimedia object3. The resulting multimedia object may be used as an argument of another temporal relation. Example: *equal (start (meets (video1, video2), meets (text1, text2)), image1)*. The Fig. 3 summarizes the Backus-Naur Form (BNF) of the grammar of our temporal specification language.

```
<Scenario> ::= Scenario <ScenarioName> : Idf elements <Declaration_assignation> <Var1> Relations
<Interactive _temporal_relation> End.
<Declaration_assignation > ::= <Declaration > | <Declaration >; <Scenario>
<Declaration> ::= <Declaration> | <Assignation>
<Declaration> ::= idf (min, opt, max) : <Type> : Path ; <Post_decl>
<Post_decl> ::= <Declaration> | λ
<Assignation> ::= Assign (Idf, Path); <Post_assign>
<Post_assign> ::= <Assignation> | λ
<Var1> ::= Variables <Var2> | λ
<Var2> ::= <Mise> <Post_mise>
<Mise> ::= idf ::= <Temporal_interactive_Relation >
<Post_mise> ::= <Var2> |λ
<Type> ::=  Audio | Video | Image | Text | Button
< Interactive _temporal_relation > ::= (<Temporal _Relation >|<Interactive_Relation > ); <Post_ Interactive
_temporal_relation >
<Temporal_Relation> ::= <Relation> <Post_relation> |<NomScenario>
<Relation> ::= <Equal> | <meet> | <before> | <begin> | <during> | <finish> | <overlap>
<Post-relation> ::= <Temporal_Relation> | λ
<equals> ::= equals (<Relation>, <Relation>)
<meets> ::= meets (<Relation>, <Relation>)
<before> ::= before (<Relation>, <Relation>, <Delay>)
<starts> ::= starts (<Relation>, <Relation>, <Delay>)
<during> ::= during (<Relation>, <Relation>, <Delay>)
<finishes> ::= finishes (<Relation>, <Relation>, <Delay>)
<overlaps> ::= overlaps (<Relation>, <Relation>, <Delay>)
<Interactive_Relation> ::= <Relation_int> <Post_link> | <ScenarioName>
<relation_int> ::=par-min | par-max | par-master |
<post_link> ::= <relation_int> | λ
with :
Idf = [a-zA-Z]([a-zA-Z]\[0-9])*
Path = [a-zA-Z0-9]+\. [a-zA-Z0-9]+
min, opt, max, delai = [1-9][0-9]*
λ = empty expression
```

Fig. 3. BNF form of the grammar

3.2.1 Temporal interaction

Our approach synchronizes the scenario with the user (i.e an expert of the application domain). The interaction takes the form of temporal interaction (*start, stop, pause, reverse, forward*) and browsing interactions.

Temporal interactions concern user elementary operations such as *pause/resume, reverse* and *forward*. In pause/resume operations, the system records the current state of presentation modelled by a p-time Petri net, and when resume operation is executed, the system loads the amount of time that the presentation had paused, and starts the presentation again from where it stopped. The reverse operation is specified in terms of temporal skip given by the user. Example "go back 15 minutes".

When the reverse operation is requested, then the Petri net deals with objects associated with places currently being presented. If the reverse operation involves objects that are further behind a place P_i in the presentation graph, the presentation graph is traversed backward until the target object is reached. The forward operation is similar to the reverse operation.

3.2.2 Browsing interaction

In browsing interactions, the user branches out of the current presentations, so he/she effectively modifies the current presentation. Let us consider a multimedia database representing scenes from a visitor while visiting art objects in a gallery. The highlight on a spatial art object is possible through animation. When the database contains images of all possible art objects, visiting may include highlight and corresponding jumps out of the sequential nature of the sequence of images corresponding to art objects. To approach this problem, we use the hierarchical modelling capability of the Petri net representation. A place can be another Petri net. So, there is a global Petri net that is composed of sub-nets of smaller Petri nets corresponding to presentations.

Branching to different presentation graph is then equivalent to following a hypermedia relation, so the user can select a branch to any part of the global presentation graph, or follow the presentation schedule as previously defined in the current presentation graph. The entry point into a branch is represented as a hypermedia node with a link to the desired presentation. Thus for the node where there is a branch, the object represented by the Petri net place at that node is just a hypermedia button indicating a branch to different presentations.

At each branching point, our approach models a hypermedia node, in parallel to the object that the branch presentation is related to. Before the branch presentation is chosen, the hypermedia node appears as a hypermedia button, with an internal duration independent of the multimedia object duration of the button. So, if the branch is not selected by the user, the presentation represented by the sub-net will not be presented, and the Petri net associated with it will not be executed. We declare the branch node as follow:

branch-node (0,-,+∝) : HYPERMEDIA;

video1 (20,30,40): VIDEO;

4. The multimedia p-time Petri net (Mp-RdPT)

4.1 Differences with other approaches

Our Petri net may be considered as a variant of the temporal Petri net developed in several works (Little & Ghafoor, 1990), (Adjeroh & Lee, 1995), (Senac et al., 1995) with these interesting features:

First, the Petri net is generated automatically on the basis of the user's temporal specifications that help him to define temporal relations naturally and simply without any considerations of the Petri net details.

Secondly, the Petri net models relations that consider both existing temporal arrangement and causal temporal relations between multimedia objects.

Thirdly, during the generation of the Petri net on the basis of the temporal specification, it is not necessary to detect temporal inconsistencies like in the current approaches based on time interval.
Fourthly, after the generation of the Petri net, the system returns, when requested by the user, the simulation of the scenario that corresponds to the Petri net generated and may detect two kinds of errors: graph design errors (i.e. a multimedia object that is declared but never used) and allocation resource errors (i.e. allocation of the same resource to several multimedia objects, it is the classical problem of mutual exclusion on a critical resource).
Fifthly, in our approach, all scenarios can be expressed and executed by using our specification language, some authors, such as (Weiss et al. 1995), say that the resulting graph becomes complicated and difficult to manipulate and to modify. In our approach, the modification is very simple, because it does not concern the Petri net, but the temporal specification which is natural and simple to use.
We think that few approaches implement these features together. We can find some features of our Petri net in a powerful Hierarchical Time Stream Petri Net model HTSPN of (Senac et al., 1995).

4.2 Formal definition of Mp-RdPT

Petri nets (PN) (Peterson, 1977) are designed to model systems with interacting concurrent components. The basic PN structure is composed of four parts: a set of places P, a set of transitions T, an input or (backward) function B and an output or (forward) function F. The input and output functions relate transitions and places. A basic PN graph is graphically represented as a bipartite directed graph, in which the circular nodes are called places and the bar nodes are called transitions. A dot in a place represents a token, and a place containing one or more tokens is said to be marked.
Allen's relations have the problem that multimedia objects expressions are dependent of multimedia objects duration. The temporal relations are designed to specify relations between multimedia objects of determined duration. Therefore, they are not appropriate for undetermined duration. If creators produce a video digest from several multimedia objects, they need to modify the temporal relations between multimedia objects after their duration changes. In order to solve this problem, the system should represent relations between multimedia objects with unknown duration. We must study the model of temporal relations independently of duration changes. PN is one of graph representations and considers multimedia objects with known or unknown duration; also, the simulation of the scenario may detect errors, such as: specification errors, graph design errors, graph configuration errors, or allocation resources errors.
The PN tool has been chosen as a tool of synchronization and analysis because PN allows modelling the dynamic behavior of multimedia scenarios that can be characterized by the qualitative properties of PN corresponding. These properties are liveness, boundedness, reversibility and consistency. In the context of a temporal synchronization modelling, a class of enhanced PN model has been developed which assign a firing delay to each place and a type of synchronization to a transition (Ghomari & Djeraba, 2003; Ghomari & Djeraba, 2010). This model is called Multimedia p-Time Petri Nets (Mp-RdPT) and it is defined as follows:
A Mp-RdPT is a tuple (P, T, B, F, M_0, IS, SYN, MP, R), where:

- (P, T, B, F, M_0) defines a PN, where P is a non empty finite set of places, T is a non empty finite set of transitions, with $P \cap T = \emptyset$, B: $P \times T \rightarrow N$ is the backward function, similarly, $F : P \times T \rightarrow N$ is the forward function, $M_0 : P \rightarrow N$ is the initial marking. As usual, we denote by $\bullet t = \{p \in P \setminus B(p, t) \geq 1\}$ the set of ingoing places and $t\bullet = \{ p \in P \setminus F(p, t) \geq 1 \}$ the set of outgoing places of a transition t. Similarly, $\bullet p = \{ t \in T \setminus F(p, t) \geq 1 \}$ and $p\bullet = \{ t \in T \setminus B(p, t) \geq 1 \}$ are the sets of ingoing transitions and outgoing transitions of a place p.

The set of markings a Mp-RdPT can reach from its initial marking M_0 will be denoted as $S(M_0)$.

- $\forall p \in P$, $\forall M \in S(M_0)$, $M(p) \leq 1$ (Mp-RdPT is safe),
- IS: is the static interval function, IS: $P \rightarrow (Q+ \cup 0) \cup (Q+ \cup 0) \cup (Q+ \cup \infty)$,
  The IS function associates with each ingoing place a static validity time interval, where (a, n, b), associated with a place, represents respectively the earliest, the nominal and the latest firing times. The firing time of a place is a timing interval during which the newly created tokens are valid to fire a transition.
- SYN is the synchronization function that defines the firing rule associated to a transition.

- SYN: $T \rightarrow$ Rules, with Rules $=_{def}$ *{strong-or, weak-and, master}*, the set of synchronization rules. This synchronization semantics defines synchronization instants from a place statically or dynamically chosen.
  MP is the function which indicates the master place of each transition from which the rule of transition requires a master, defined by: MP : $T_{master} =_{def} \{t \setminus SYN(t) = master \}$,
  - The strong-or synchronization rule is driven by the earliest media. If either one of the two media objects finishes, the other one has to stop, and $[Min(a_i), Min(b_i)]$ is the sensibilisation interval.
  - The weak-and synchronization rule is driven by the latest media. All the media objects are presented completely and $[Max(a_i), Max(b_i)]$ is the sensibilisation interval.
  - The master synchronization rule is driven by the master media. If two multimedia objects are presented simultaneously, when the higher priority media finishes, the other has to stop.

The multimedia presentation continues after that, and $[a_m, b_m]$ is the sensibilisation interval, with P_m indicating the master place.

We define a_m, b_m by: let MP (t) = p_m and IS (p_m) = $[a_m, b_m]$.

- R: $P \rightarrow \{r_1, r_2 \ldots r_n\}$, a mapping from the set of places to a set of resources (e.g., audio/video card, processor, virtual memory, and others operating system resources).

4.3 Mp-RdPT generation

To create the temporal Petri net, each temporal relation is associated with a Petri net as illustrated by (Hamblin, 1972), and modelled in several approaches, such as in OCPN (Little and Ghafoor, 1990). This mapping is helpful for automatic creation of a time Petri net. In the Fig. 4, T_α, T_β, T_δ model respectively the duration of places P_α, P_β and P_δ.

4.4 Rules of translations

The created Mp-RdPT net is then translated to an equivalent t-time Petri net (Merlin and Farber, 1976) for analyzing by the tool Tina (Berthomieu et al., 2004). For this, we use three rules of translation (see Fig. 5) inspired from (Senac et al., 1995).

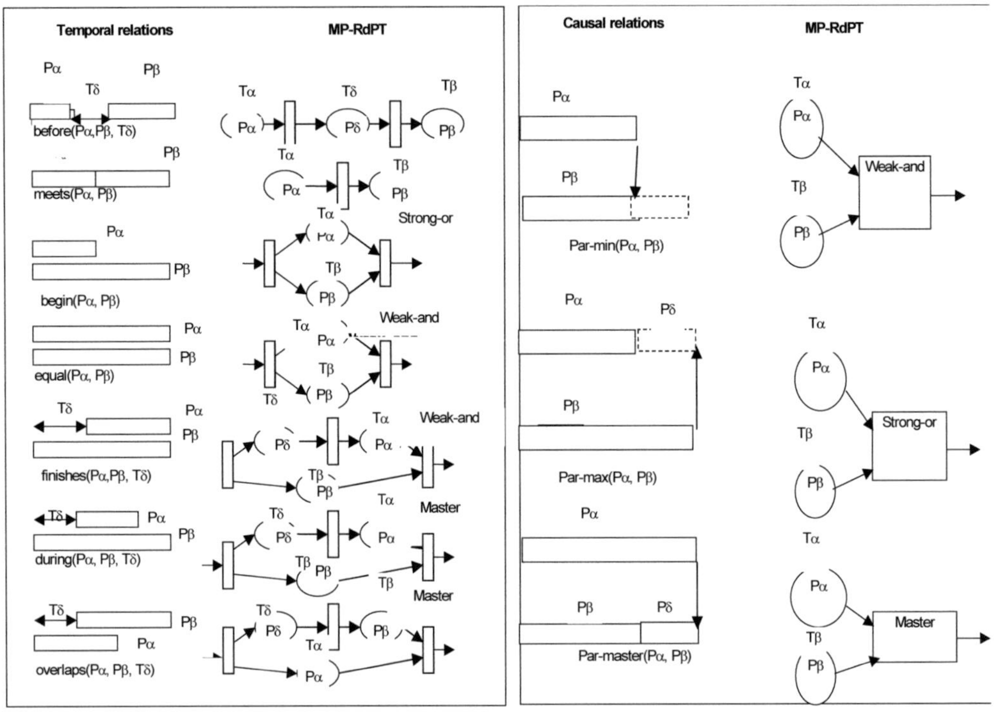

Fig. 4. Diagram of association

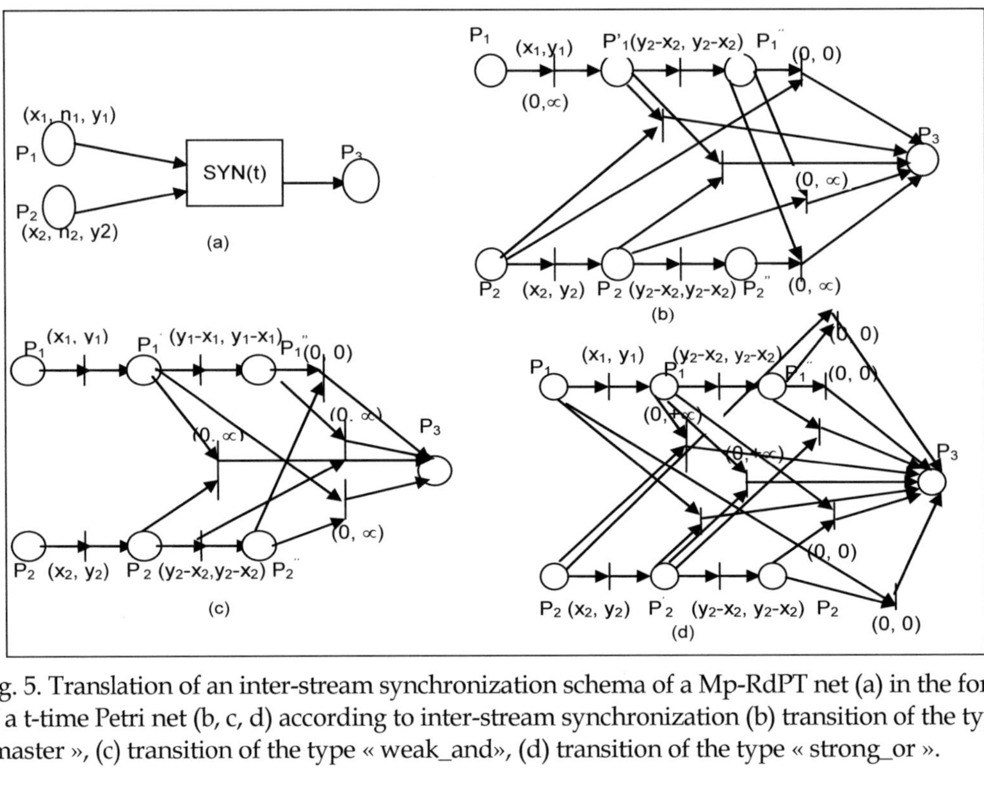

Fig. 5. Translation of an inter-stream synchronization schema of a Mp-RdPT net (a) in the form of a t-time Petri net (b, c, d) according to inter-stream synchronization (b) transition of the type «master », (c) transition of the type « weak_and», (d) transition of the type « strong_or ».

5. Analysis of multimedia scenarios using the tool Tina

Tina (Time Petri Net Analyser) (Berthomieu et al., 2004) is a software environment to edit and analyze Petri Net and t-time Petri Net (Merlin and Farber, 1976). In addition to the usual editing and analysis facilities of such environments (computation of marking reachability sets, coverability trees, semi-flows), Tina offers various abstract state spaces constructions that preserve specific classes of properties of the concrete state spaces of the nets. Classes of properties may be general properties (reachability properties, deadlock freeness, liveness), specific properties relying on the linear structure of the concrete space state properties relying on the linear concrete space state (linear time temporal logic properties).
After generating the t-time Petri net, the author investigates the scenario specification before it is delivered to the reader by using the analysis tool Tina. Currently, the following characteristics can be verified by the analysis tool: terminate state existence (i.e., if a state m exists in which non transitions are enabled), safeness (i.e., if every place has only one token), liveness (i.e., if blocking will never occur), reversibility (i.e., if the Petri net come back to its initial state whatever state it reaches), consistency (is a necessary condition for the reversibility that is a difficult property to establish.

6. Object oriented modelling

Our multimedia framework looks to the framework proposed in (Gibbs et al., 1993). It is composed of abstract classes serving to specify interfaces, and suggested procedures for using the classes. The abstract classes are specialized for different multimedia platforms. So, applications using the abstract classes may adapt to variations in platform functionality.
The classes of our framework belong to two distinct groups: media classes and scenario classes. Media classes correspond to audio, video, image, text, and other media types, their basic properties and operations, and scenario classes model temporal composition of media objects. In this paper, we will focus on scenario classes which are a main difference with the framework presented in (Gibbs et al., 1993).
Scenarios are divided into types corresponding to application domains. Each type is represented by a class. These are called scenario classes and form a hierarchy (see Fig. 6).
Nodes depict classes and edges depict superclass/subclass relationships. An edge points from the superclass to the subclass. Instances of scenario classes are called scenario objects. A scenario class models scenario object properties and operations.

7. Architecture of the system prototype

The system prototype is implemented on Compaq Intel Pentium 4 platform using the programming language C++ and Oracle DBMS, and run in a window environment. According to the architecture of the system prototype (depicted in Fig. 7) the following components can be described: (1) Authoring tool which use an editing language of temporal and causal relations; (2) parser which reads and analyses the specification file that contains the temporal specification language; (3) generator which generate the Mp-RdPT model; (4) Translator which translate the Mp-RdPT model to t-time PN; (5) Analysis tool Tina which analyses and verifies properties of the time PN. Manager which manages the multimedia scenarios, such as: the generation, the simulation and the interpretation of Mp-RdPT, object-relational oracle database which stores media objects as large binary objects (BLOBs) in mpeg, gif or jpeg files.

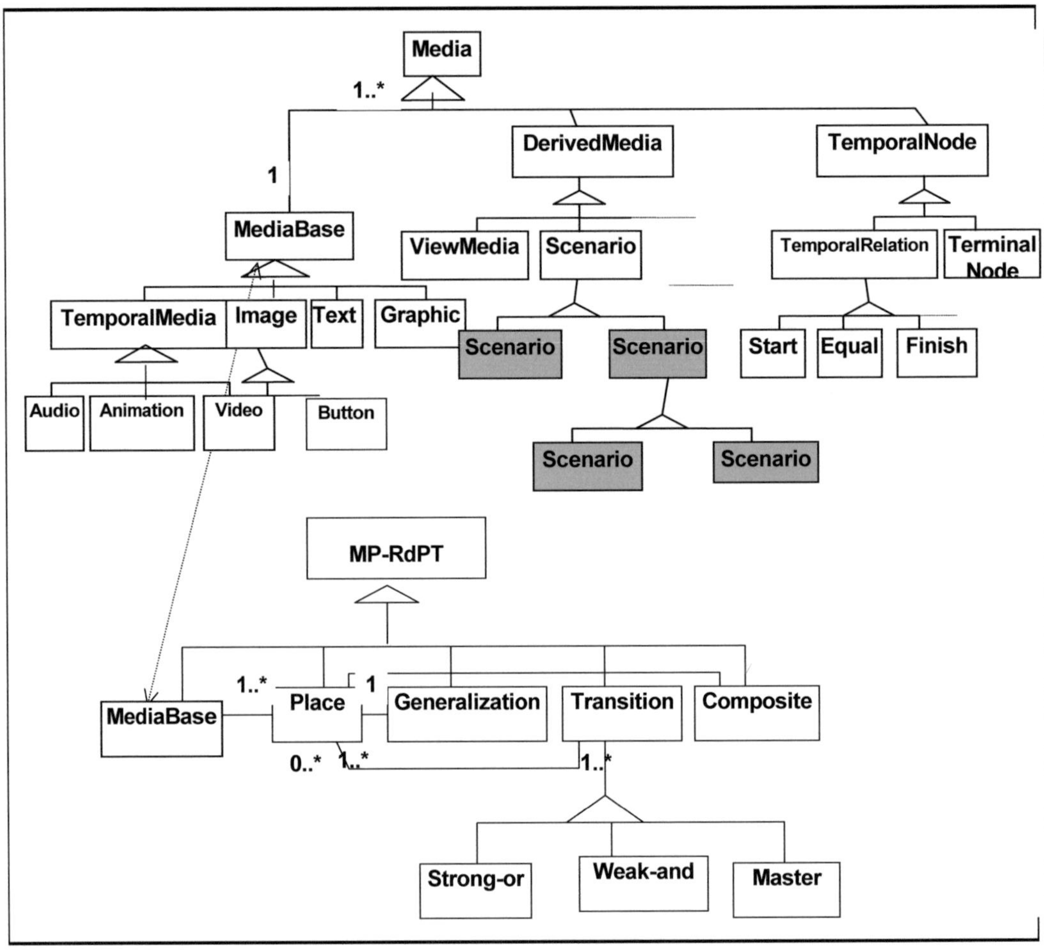

Fig. 6. A class diagram with UML formalism

8. Conclusion and future work

We have presented an approach for multimedia scenario generation in an object oriented database. Our language features consider: - object-oriented concepts for multimedia and scenario modelling; - temporal specification based on temporal and interactive relation; the temporal relations are based on both existing temporal arrangement and causal relations between multimedia objects; - powerful time Petri net automatic generation based on temporal specifications; - and finally user interactions based on composite time Petri net.

In the future, we will perform the algorithms that detect inconsistencies in the Mp-RdPT net generated, and we will provide a support for the programmer to develop distributed multimedia applications using the object-oriented model. It is important to provide communication of various types of data over the high speed ATM network and the synchronization of the multimedia objects at the target system. The target system is the location in which the final synchronization is executed respecting the network delay with insignificant modifications of the earlier synchronization.

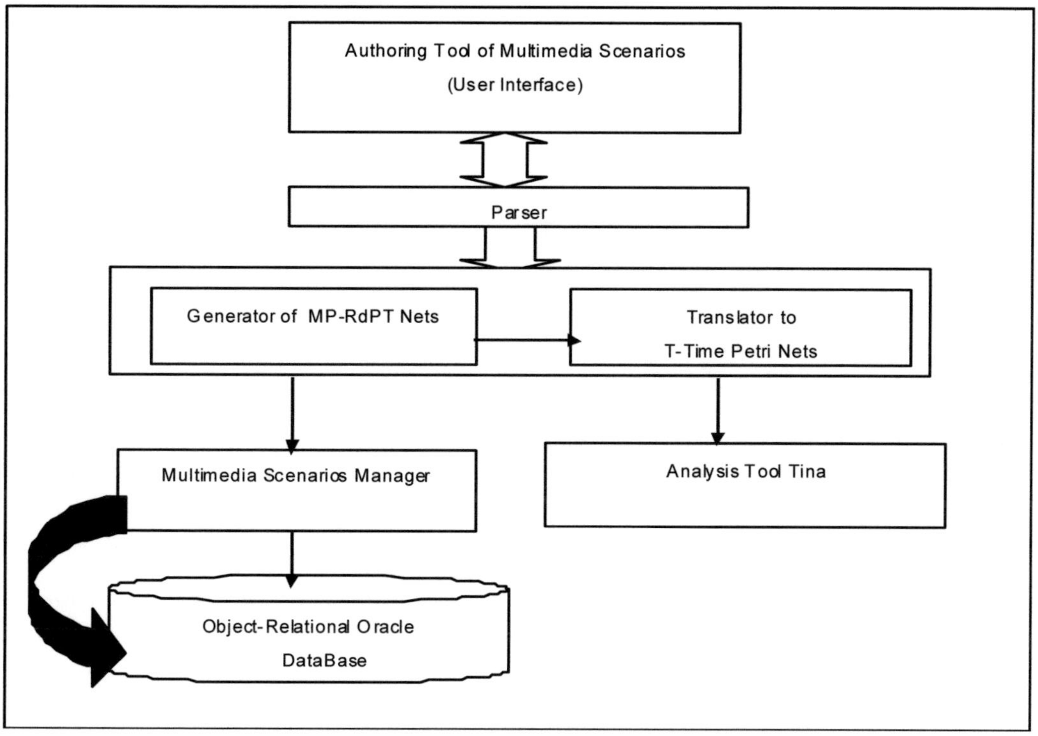

Fig. 7. System prototype architecture

9. References

Adjeroh, D.A & Lee, M.C. (1995). " Synchronization Mechanisms for Distributed Multimedia Presentation Systems, *Proceedings of IWMDMS,* (1995), August, Blue-Mountain Lake, Newark.

Allen, J.F. (1983). "Maintaining Knowledge about Temporal Intervals ". *Communications of the ACM,* 26(11):832-843.

Berthomieu, B.et al., (2004). "The tool TINA - Construction of Abstract State Spaces for Petri Nets and Time Petri Nets". *International Journal of Production Research.* Vol. 42(4) http://www.laas.fr/tina

Blakowski, G. & Steinmetz, R. (1996). " A Media Synchronization Survey : Reference Model, Specification, and Case Studies ", *IEEE journal on selected areas in communications,* Vol. 14(1).

Boronat, F et al. (2008). " Multimedia group and inter-stream synchronization techniques : A comparative study". *Journal of Information Systems.*

Botafogo, B & Moss, D. (1995). "The MORENA model for hypermedia authoring". *Proceedings of the international conference on multimedia computing and systems,* (1995), IEEE Computer Society Press, Los Alamitos, CA.

Chen J-N & Huang, Y-M. (2005). " Using dynamic fuzzy Petri nets for navigation learning. *Exploring Innovation in Education and Research,* Tainan, Taiwan.

Courtiat, J-P. & de Oliveira. R. C. (1996). "Proving Temporal Consistency in a New Multimedia Synchronization Model". *Proceedings of the ACM International Conference on Multimedia,* (1996), Boston, MA.

Gibbs, S. et al. (1993)." Audio/Video Databases : An Object-Oriented Approach ". *Proceedings of IEEE Ninth International Conference on Data Engineering,* (1993), Vienna, Austria.

Ghomari, A & Djeraba, C. (2003). "Towards a Timed-Petri Net Based Approach for the synchronization of a Multimedia Scenario". *Proceedings of the 5th International Conference on Enterprise Information Systems,* April, (2003), Angers, France.

Ghomari, A. & Djeraba, C. (2010). " An approach for synchronization and management of multimedia scenarios in an object-oriented database ". *Proceedings of the International Conference on Research Challenges in Information Science (RCIS),* Ed. IEEE, ISBN #978-1-4244-4840-1, May (2010), Nice, France.

Hamblin, C. L. " Instants and Intervals ". *Proceedings of the 1st Conference of the International Society for the Study of Time,* (1972), New York.

ISO, (1992) " International Standard. Information Technology Hypermedia/Time-Based Structuring Language (HyTime)". ISO/IEC IS 10744:1997.

Jourdan M. et al. (1997). " A Survey on Authoring Techniques for Temporal Scenarios of Multimedia Documents ", *In Handbook on multimedia computing,* CRC Press.

King, P.R. (1994). "Towards a temporal logic based formalism for expressing temporal constraints in multimedia documents, *Technical Report 942,* Orsay, France: LRI, Université de Paris-Sud.

Little, T.D.C. & Gafoor, A. (1990). "Synchronization and Storage Models for Multimedia Objects ", *IEEE Journal on Selected Areas in Communication,* vol.8(3).

Little, T.D.C. & Ghafoor, A. (1993). " Interval-Based Conceptual Models for Time-Dependant Multimedia Data ". *IEEE Transactions on Knowledge and Data Engineering,* 5(4).

Merlin, P.M. & Farber, D.J. (1976): "Recoverability of communication protocols: Implications of a theoretical study ". *IEEE Trans. Comm.* 24(9).

Na Cheo, J-C. & Furuta, R. (2001) " Dynamic documents: authoring, browsing, and analysis using a high-level Petri net-based hypermedia system. *Proceedings of the ACM Symposium on Document Engineering,* (2001), Atlanta, CA .

Peterson, J.L. "Petri Nets", *Computing Surveys,* 9(3), 225-252, 1977.

Perez-Luque, M.J. & Little. T.D.C. (1996): "A Temporal Reference Framework for Multimedia Synchronization", *IEEE Journal on Selected Areas in Communications* (Special Issue: Synchronization Issues in Multimedia Communication), Vol. 14(1).

Roisin, C & Sèdes, F. (2004). " Time and Documents, *Numeric Document,* 8(4), 23-39.

Shterev, J. "Modelling of Interaction on multimedia Stream and objects by application of Petri nets. *Proceedings of the International Conference on Computer Systems and Technologies,* (2005), Varna, Bulagria.

Senac, P. et al. (1995). "Hierarchical Time Stream Petri Net : Amodel for Hypermedia Systems". *Proceedings of Application and Theory of Petri Nets,* (1995), Giogio de Michelis, Michel Diaz (eds). Lecture Notes in Computer Science N° 935.

Weiss, R. et al. (1995). " Composition and Search with a Video Algebra ". *IEEE Multimedia,* 2(1).

W3C. (2001). "Working draft specification of SMIL, URL: http://www.w3.org/TR/SMIL 2.0

8

Hybrid Petri Nets and Metaheuristic Approach to Farm Work Scheduling

Senlin Guan[1], Morikazu Nakamura[1] and Takeshi Shikanai[2]
[1]*Faculty of Engineering,*
[2]*Faculty of Agriculture,*
University of the Ryukyus, 1 Senbaru Nishihara,
Okinawa
Japan

1. Introduction

Scheduling problems for general cases are characterized as NP hard, and the computation time required to obtain the optimal schedule will grow exponentially with the problem size. The scheduling problems that consider the limited or shared resources, alterable constraints or environmental changes become very complex in both formulation and solution. Since the solution for these problems has great serviceability and reliability against environmental changes, much research has been devoted in optimization strategy in the presence of a wide range of uncertainties (Li & Ierapetritou, 2008). Such research with application is applicable to not only the manufacturing in industry, but also production in agriculture. Modeling and scheduling in the agricultural domain may be more promising because of the requirement of new approaches to handling the uncertainties in the nature environment.

In agriculture, a system that aims to produce maximum amount of profit from available land by high inputs of capital, labour, or efficient usage of machinery, is defined as intensive farming (or intensive agriculture). Like common businesses, many intensive farming units are operating their businesses by the ways to improving profits in farming while reducing costs. In Japan, there are over 190,000 intensive farming units such as farmers' cooperatives/ agricultural corporations that aim at efficient and large-scale farm management (The Ministry of Agriculture, Forestry and Fisheries of Japan, 2006). These corporations lease and consolidate agricultural lands in vicinal regions, manage large-scale farmland with full mechanization, and carry out farm works entrusted by vicinal farmers. The farmlands managed by these corporations sometimes number over thousands and are scattered within a wide area. In order to gain substantial economic increase and further development, these corporations need to improve the daily work management, extend the contracts of leasing farmland, lease more farmlands, and carry out more extra works. As a consequence, they considerably require wise management decisions such as timeliness in all operations, equipment adjustments, crop rotations, land rent, taxes and so on. The best decision certainly conduces to the increase of yield, profitability, and work efficiency.

Solving the farm work scheduling problem requires appropriate approaches to modeling and optimization. There are plenty of mathematical models and approaches have addressed optimization for scheduling for different demands (Bassett et al., 1997; Balasubramanian & Grossmann, 2003; Janak & Floudas, 2006; Lin et al., 2004; Till et al., 2007; Wang, 2004; Santiago- Mozos et al., 2005; Suliman, 2000). In agriculture, the existing researches on scheduling in the cropping system involve such as the farming and planning systems for paddy rice production (Nanseki, 1998; Nanseki et al., 2003; Daikoku, 2005), a stochastic farm work scheduling algorithm based on short-range weather variation (Astika et al., 1999), several models simulating a single operation (Arjona et al., 2001; Higgins & Davies, 2005) and operating with one or more crops (Chen & McClendon, 1985; Tsai et al., 1987; Lal et al., 1991; Haffar & Khoury, 1992), and so on. However, none of these studies paid attention to the scheduling in the intensive farming system by using a more promising tool - Petri nets model. A Petri net is a very applicable to model distributed, concurrent, nondeterministic and/or stochastic events, and considerably accommodates nondeterministic events in the farming system such as machine breakdown and labor absence, or concurrent activities such as cooperative works.

In this study, we proposed a hybrid Petri nets and metaheuristic approach to the farm work scheduling in the cropping system. We used sugarcane farming as an example to demonstrate the approache to constructing an efficient farm work plan. The farm work scheduling comprises a model for modeling the farm works and a scheduling system for optimizing the farm work schedule. The model, which is a hybrid Petri nets first introduced into agricultural production (Guan et al., 2008), graphically formulates the farm work flow and simulates the overall status of the progress of farm work and the state of resources. The scheduling system performs the resource assignment and the computation for a long-term schedule (Guan et al., 2009). A part of contents and experiment data in this chapter are originally published in these two articles.

2. Modeling and formulating the farm work scheduling

In this section, we neglect the basic definition of discrete Petri net and continuous Petri net and briefly review the key concepts of hybrid Petri nets.

2.1 Hybrid Petri nets

As defined in Murata (1989), a Petri net is a graphical and mathematical modeling tool for describing and simulating the distributed systems. A hybrid Petri nets informally contains a discrete part and a continuous part (Fig. 2). The discrete part of hybrid Petri nets usually models the state of resource, and the continuous part simulates the process over time.

A hybrid Petri net system is defined as $\mathcal{N} = \langle P,T,Pre,Post,m_0, h\rangle$, where P is a set of places; T, a set of transitions; *Pre* (*Post*), the pre- (post-) incidence function representing the input (output) arcs; m_0, a function representing the initial number of tokens in each place; h, a hybrid function that indicates a discrete or continuous node. In a hybrid Petri net, all discrete input places must also be output places with arcs of the same weight, and vice-versa.

Figure 1 illustrates a hybrid Petri nets. The double circles, boxes and blue arcs are the continuous part of Petri nets. At time $t = 0$, continuous transition T_{11} starts firing because of the existence of a token in discrete place P_1. Discrete transition T_1 fires when the token in continuous place P_{11} decreases to 2100 at time $t = 3$, and the system is in the break state. After T_2 fires at $t = 3.25$, the system switches to the working state again. Likewise, a continuous transition can be flexibly broken and well controlled by handling with the tokens in the discrete places.

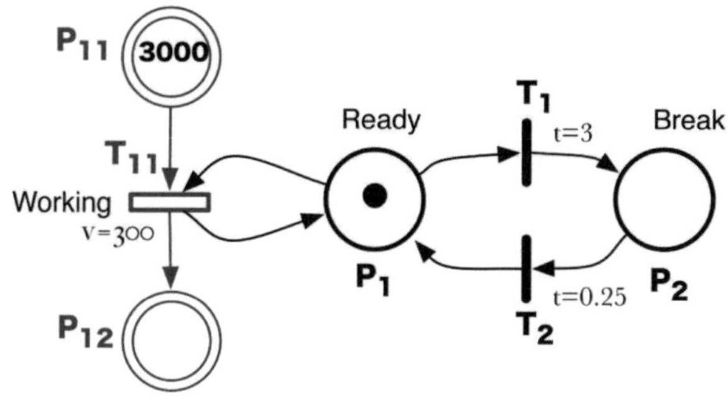

Fig. 1. A hybrid Petri nets system

In a hybrid Petri net that time is associated either with the places or with the transitions, the marking m at time t of hybrid Petri nets can be written as:

$$m(t) = m(0) + A \cdot \left(n(t) + \int_0^t v(\tau) \cdot d\tau \right) \tag{1}$$

where A is the incidence matrix, and $n(t)$ denotes the number of firings of the discrete transitions from the initial time to time t. $v(\tau)$ is the firing speed of the continuous transitions at an arbitrary time τ.

2.2 Hybrid Petri nets modeling for farm work flow

In order to model the variable farming process due to environmental changes, we applied the hybrid Petri net to model the discrete and continuous farming activities. For example, the major works for sugarcane production involve tilling, planting, irrigating, weeding, fertilizing and harvesting. Each work starts when satisfying the conditions such as timeliness of operation, availability of farmland, machinery, labor and so on. After completion of the work, the farmland shifts into the next state, and the resources such as the machinery and the labor are released and ready for the other works. In our proposed model, the farm work is defined as the transition; the condition, or state of a farmland or a resource as the place, and resources like labor or machinery as the tokens. The transitions corresponding to the farm work and the places corresponding to the farmland are the continuous part of the model; otherwise, the places are discrete. A farming process is a continuous transition which the working speed is determined by the capability of the labor, the efficiency of the machinery or a combination of both of them. Uncertainties such as machinery breakdown and breaks, and the state of resources, farmland and machine are considered as discrete objects. The work flow of producing sugarcane by certain resources and the simple model for modeling the work flow in one farmland are illustrated in Fig. 2.

In the figure, continuous places P_{ij} and transitions T_{ij} represent the status of the farmland and execution of the farm work, respectively. The discrete places correspond the status of the resources such as the tractor, rotary tiller, labor, and so on. P_{ij} is a timed continuous place associated with time window for timeliness of operation. The real number in places P_{ij} means the amount the farm work. Note that the resources are assigned to only two works of the tilling and harvesting in this figure. At the initial state, the existence of the token in P_{11} indicates that the farmland is ready for the work of tilling. Along with the execution of the subsequent work with the available resources of R_1,R_2,R_3, the value in P_{11} decreases while

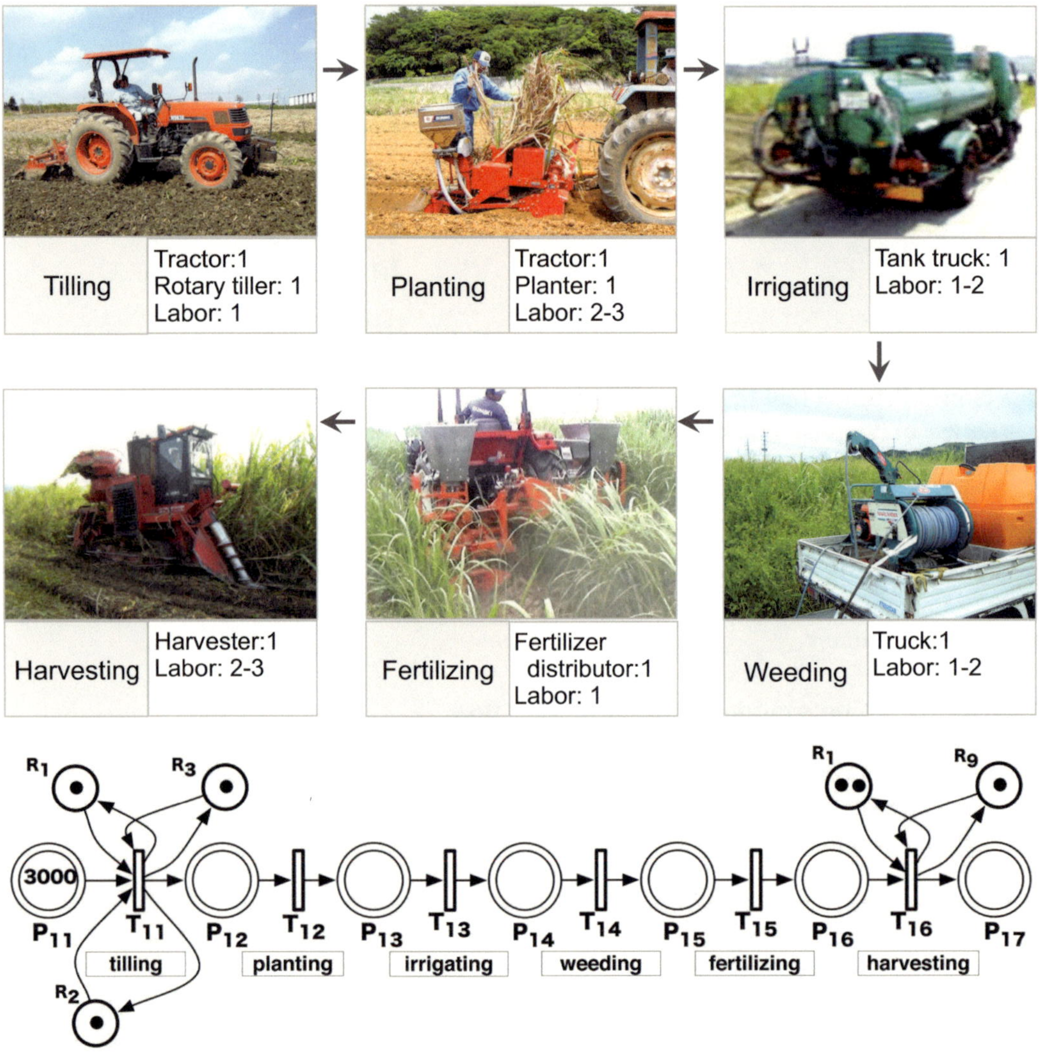

Fig. 2. Hybrid Petri nets modeling for farm work flow in sugarcane production

that in P_{12} increases. When the work of tilling is completed, the token in P_{11} and P_{12} reach 0 and 3,000, respectively, and the resources are released and ready for the works in the other farmlands. The model for modeling the farm works in multiple farmlands is based on this elementary model.

2.3 Formulating the farm work scheduling on hybrid Petri nets

A farm work schedule is to plan the farm works in the farmlands with the necessary resources over time. The farm works in a farmland range from the tilling to harvesting in a crop growth cycle. Since more than one of machinery and labor are available for any work, the cooperative work sometimes takes place for early completion of the work.

Figure 3 simulates the scheduled farm work on the hybrid Petri nets model. A continuous transition denotes the execution of task w_{ijk}. Not only cooperative work but also breaks are modeled in the figure. From the initial state, the first work in farmland F_1 is started cooperatively by resource R_1 and R_2. At the same time, the first work in F_2 is also started by only one resource R_3. The break time includes the normal break time and the time that may be consumed by uncertainties such as machinery breakdown, poor weather, and so on. For each resource R_k, the break and resumption for task w_{ijk} are modeled by the discrete part of Petri net connected to a continuous transition, which consists two discrete places and two timed discrete transitions.

The model acts as modeling the farm work process as well as simulating farm work schedule. Since the marking of hybrid Petri net implies the farming progress and the state of farmlands and resources, we can monitor the entire state of the system by the marking migration according to Equation (1).

Generating the hybrid Petri nets in Fig. 3 requires assigning resources to the discrete places and designating the firing sequence of the transitions in advance. We stipulate the rules for resource assignment and firing operation of hybrid Petri nets as follows:

1. The number of assigned resources for the cooperative work is limited from at least one to the total number of available resources for this work. In the dynamically generated hybrid Petri nets, the number of continuous transitions is equal to the number of assigned resources. If the resource assignment is determined, the hybrid Petri nets model including the continuous places, continuous transitions, and discrete places except the arcs from the continuous transition to the discrete place can be generated. The cooperative work may cause a deadlock that a resource is scheduled to an already completed work. For this case in the computing process, this resource will be rescheduled to the next task.
2. The firing operation of the hybrid Petri nets stops when all tasks are completed.
3. A resource cannot be assigned to two works at the same time.
4. The timed continuous places and transitions are enabled during the time window and over the waiting time, respectively.
5. The firing operation suffers from the *precedence constrained* relationship. For example, tasks w_{124} and w_{125} cannot be started if the token in P_{12} is less than 2880.
6. The moving time of the resource between farmlands is associated to the discrete transition.
7. Arbitrary breaks are possible during the farm work.

2.4 Formulating the farm work scheduling in mathematical method

In this subsection, we redefine the farm work scheduling problem in mathematical method and compare it with the one by hybrid Petri nets. The variables for the farm work scheduling and their descriptions are listed in Table 1. In the table, resource R_k is not an individual resource but rather a set of the minimum machinery and labor required for the work. m_{ij} represents the amount of scheduled work W_j in farmland F_i. W_j can be carried out only if $m_{ij} > 0$ and $I_{ij} = 1$. Waiting time O_{ij} and time window U_j are used to define an appropriate cultivation time. The execution time of task w_{ijk} is subject to the completion time of the pervious work, waiting time O_{ij} and the period of $[U_j(s), U_j(e)]$. The relations between these variables are shown in Fig. 4.

In Fig. 4, w_{bjk} may be performed in cooperation with other resources. Such cooperative work is defined as a process where multiple machineries perform the same work, and the entry time of a resource to perform cooperative farming work is arbitrary. The execution of work

W_j requires at least one resource, and the total number of assigned resources is less than or equal to the number of resources available to perform W_k ($\Sigma_k S_{jk}$). The number of assigned resources for the execution of work W_j, $\Sigma_k S'_{jk}$, , corresponds to the following condition:

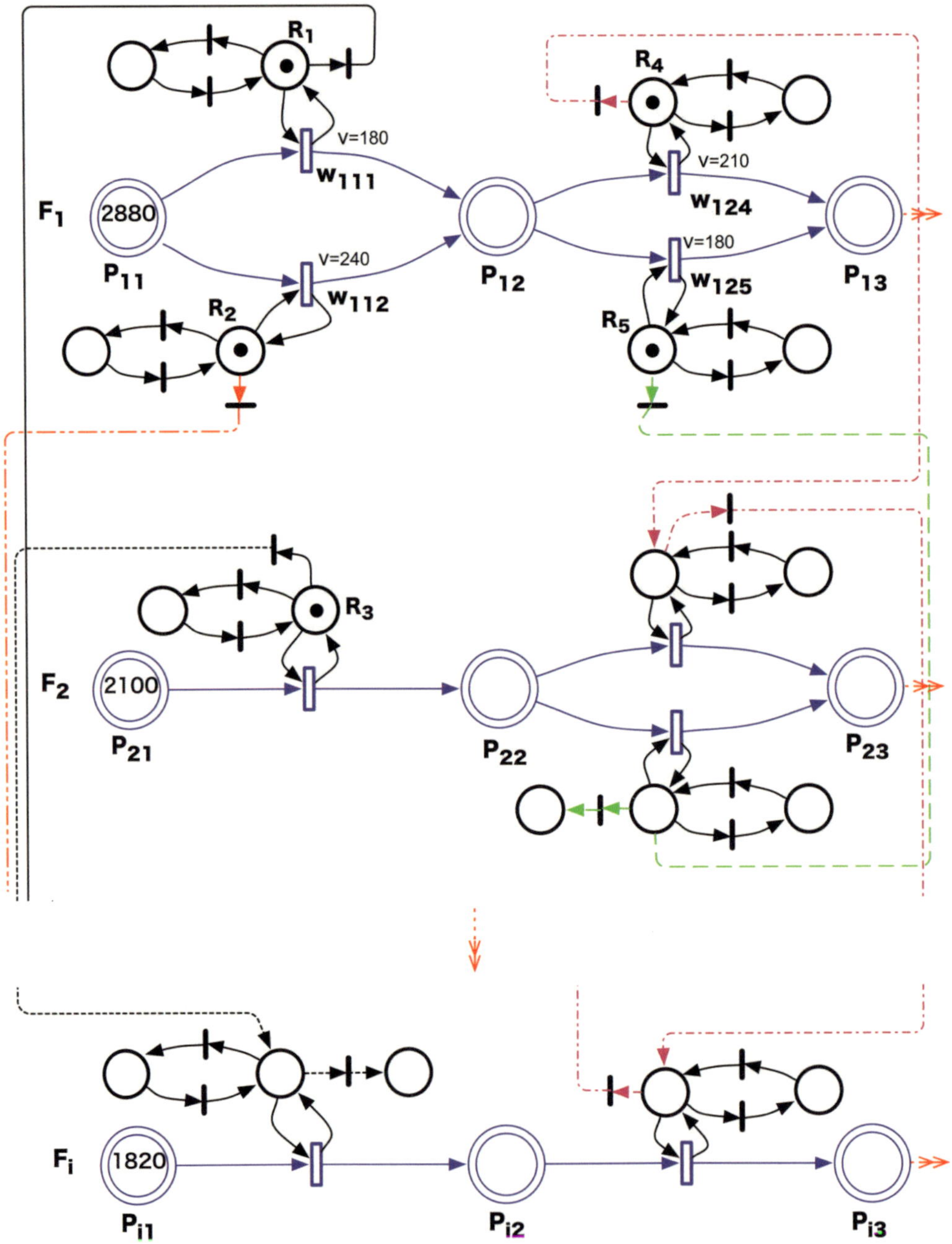

Fig. 3. Hybrid Petri nets model simulates the scheduled farm work

Notation	Definition
N_F	Total number of farmlands
N_W	Total number of works in a crop growth cycle
N_R	Total number of available resources for a work
F_i	Farmland i, $i \in \{1,\ldots, N_F\}$
W_j	Work j, $j \in \{1,\ldots, N_W\}$
R_k	Resource k, $k \in \{1,\ldots, N_R\}$
A_i	Area of F_i
I_{ij}	$I_{ij} \in \{0,1\}$, 1: W_j should be performed in F_i; otherwise, 0
m_{ij}	Amount of scheduled work W_j in F_i, $m_{ij} \in [0, A_i]$
S_{jk}	$S_{jk} \in \{0,1\}$, 1: R_k is available to perform W_j; otherwise, 0
S'_{jk}	$S'_{jk} \in \{0,1\}$, 1: R_k is scheduled to perform W_j; otherwise, 0
v_k	Average working speed of R_k
O_{ij}	Waiting time between end time of W_{j-1} and start time of W_j in F_i
U_j	Time window [start time $U_j(s)$, end time $U_j(e)$] for W_j
w_{ijk}	Task in F_j by R_k, for W_j
t_{ijk}	Working time [Start time $t_{ijk}(s)$, end time $t_{ijk}(e)$] of W_j in F_i by R_k
v'_k	Moving speed of R_k
D_{ab}	Distance between F_a and F_b, $a, b \in \{1,\ldots, N_F\}$

Table 1. Notations for farm work scheduling

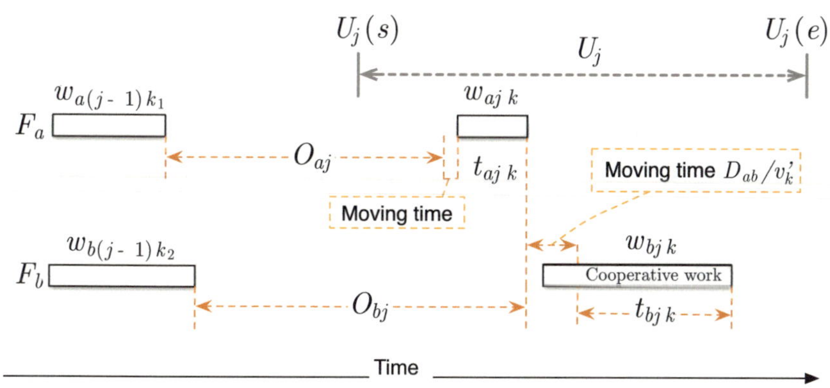

Fig. 4. Defined variables on time axis

$$1 \le \sum_k S'_{jk} \le \sum_k S_{jk} \tag{2}$$

The amount of scheduled work m_{ij} must be completed by certain resources R_k during t_{ijk} at working speed v_k. As a consequence, the following equation exists:

$$\begin{bmatrix} t_{ij1} & t_{ij2} & \cdots & t_{ijk} \end{bmatrix} \begin{bmatrix} v_1 \\ v_2 \\ \vdots \\ v_k \end{bmatrix} = m_{ij} \tag{3}$$

In order to avoid the superposition of work time by a same resource, we have the following equation:

$$\begin{aligned} \forall i,j,p,q,k, \quad & i \neq p, j \neq q, p \in \{1,...,N_F\}, q \in \{1,...,N_W\} \\ & t_{ijk}(e) < t_{pqk}(s) \cdots \text{if } t_{ijk}(s) < t_{pqk}(s) \end{aligned} \tag{4}$$

For the timeliness of the work, the start working time $t_{ijk}(s)$ and the end working time $t_{ijk}(e)$ are subject to the additional conditions stated in Equation (5).

$$\begin{aligned} \forall i,j,k,k', \quad & k' \in \{1,...,N_R\} \\ & t_{ijk}(s) \geq max(U_j(s), t_{i(j-1)k'}(e) + O_{ij}) \\ & t_{ijk}(e) \leq U_j(e) \end{aligned} \tag{5}$$

In a farmland, work W_j can only start after the completion of the former one W_{j-1}, which is defined in the form

$$\forall i,j,k,k', \quad t_{ijk}(s) > t_{i(j-1)k}(e) \tag{6}$$

Considering the moving time between farmlands, we have

$$\begin{aligned} \forall a,b,j,k, \quad & a \neq b \\ & t_{ajk}(s) \geq t_{bjk}(e) + D_{ab} / v'_k \cdots \text{if } t_{ajk}(e) < t_{bjk}(s) \end{aligned} \tag{7}$$

2.5 Comparison between the two formulation methods

Although the objectives of the farm work scheduling can take many forms such as minimizing the make-span, maximizing plant throughput, maximizing profit or minimizing production costs, we only consider minimizing the idle time between works for both formulation methods in this paper. For the formulation by mathematical definition, the objective function is written as

$$\min \left(\sum\nolimits_{a,b,j,k} [t_{bjk}(s) - t_{ajk}(e)]\right) \tag{8}$$

where task w_{bjk} is a latter task of w_{ajk} ($t_{bjk}(s) \geq t_{ajk}(e)$). It is apparent that the problem defined by Equations (2) - (8) corresponds to a mixed integer nonlinear programming (MINLP). In contrast with mathematical definition, the scheduling objective for the formulation by hybrid Petri nets is to find a firing sequence in that the idle time is minimum.

The firing rules or natural characteristics of Petri nets completely accommodate the constraints defined in the above equations. For example, Rule 1, 2, 3, 4, 5 and 6 accord with Equation (2), (3), (4), (5), (6) and (7), respectively. Rule 7 is reserved for the real-time scheduling and has not defined in mathematical method. The corresponding relation indicates that the formulation by the hybrid Petri nets substantially reduce the complexity of problem, which is also agued in Ghaeli et al. (2006); Sadrieh et al. (2007). Furthermore, the scheduling by the hybrid Petri nets is more representable and comprehensible for the farm work corporations than that in the form of mathematical equations.

3. Metaheuristic approach for optimization

Generating a farm work schedule on the hybrid Petri nets includes the two phases for assigning resources and arranging the work sequence. In the first phase, a scheme of resource assignment to each task is supposed and optimized by a simulated annealing (SA) algorithm; and in the second phase, the seeking for the best work sequence based on the resource assignment obtained in the first phase is executed by the procedure of a genetic algorithm (GA). The work sequence here is designated as a priority list in which works are arranged according to a specific priority. The second phase is in charge of inheriting the present best task sequence, dynamically creating Petri nets, simulating the activities on Petri nets, and evaluating the schedule. At the end of the GA procedure, the present best resource assignment scheme is obtained, and it will be inherited in the continuing first phase.

3.1 SA for optimizing resource assignment

The cooperative work during the farm work process has to be taken into account. The number of assignable resources is defined in Rule 1 or Equation (2). An independent variable x in the SA procedure is set to a resource assignment scheme. x', that is, another independent variable in the neighboring region of x, represents an alterable resource assignment scheme. The pseudo code of the SA in the first phase is described as:

```
begin
  initialize temperature Γ, neighboring space n;
  initialize resource assignment x, and minimum fitness min;
  evaluate fitness f_x (= gaPls(x)) in 2nd phase;
  while (not termination-condition) do
    for i = 1 to n
      generate another resource assignment x';
      evaluate fitness f_x' (= gaPls(x')) in 2nd phase;
      if (f_x' < f_x) then
        replace x with x';
      else
        if (random(0,1) < exp(f_x − f_x')/Γ) then
          replace x with x';
        end if
      end if
      if (f_x' < min) then
        update min with f_x', and memorize x';
      end if
    end for
    replace Γ with (Γ − Γ * α); //0 < α < 1
  end while
end
```

At the end of the first phase, a resource assignment is obtained. And then, the length of chromosomes in the GA in the next phase can be designated, and the places and transitions of the hybrid Petri nets can be constructed before the iteration computation by the GA.

3.2 GA for scheduling

Based on the assigned resources, the second metaheuristic GA seeks priority lists to generate the present optimal schedules. The priority list is encoded into a chromosome, in which the tasks (genes) are grouped by the same works W_j. Be similar to operations in traditional GAs, the one-point order crossover, one-bit reverse mutation, roulette selection and an elite selection are incorporated in the GA procedure. The crossover and mutation operations are restricted to those between the tasks in the same works W_j. The fitness function is to evaluate the sum of the moving time and the idle time between the tasks. This objective is achieved by firing the hybrid Petri nets until no continuous transition can fire. When the firing operation stops, the generated schedule will be memorized along with the priority list if it has the current best fitness. The pseudo code of the GA is briefly described in procedure gaPls(x), followed by the procedure of evaluating the fitness.

```
procedure gaPls(x)
begin
  initialize population c with the chromosomes inherited
            from the present best priority list;
  construct continuous part of hybrid Petri nets;
  evaluation(c);
  while not-termination-condition do
    selection;
    crossover;
    mutation;
    evaluation(c);
  end while
end
```

```
procedure evaluation(c)
begin
  for r = 1 to popSize
    construct the discrete part of the hybrid Petri nets;
    initial time interval δ; current time s = 0;
    while tasks-are-not-completed do
      if (firing-conditions-are-satisfied) then
        firing and update the amount of tokens in the corresponding places;
      end if
      update s with s + δ;
      update the sum of moving time and idle time;
    end while
    if (best-fitness-found) then
      update current best fitness, priority list, and schedule;
    end if
  end for
end
```

3.3 Deadlock removal

A deadlock in farm work scheduling is a situation where two or more competing works await the release of resources and neither obtains the necessary resources. In general, conflicts on resource use have to be examined for deadlock removal in a conventional optimization. For example, assigning a resource to a work in a conventional optimization have to check whether or not the resource is already being used for another work simultaneously; if no resource is available for the work, the computing will shift into a waiting state until some resource is released. Since the computation time in the GA iteration is the product of the size of the population, generation, and evaluation, a long evaluation time that is wasted in resolving the deadlock of resource use results in an inefficient search. Furthermore, some randomly generated individuals in the iterations may be infeasible solutions if the work is scheduled across the time window for cultivation.

In contrast, assigning resources in the first phase before the GA iterations may remarkably prevent deadlocks caused by resource conflict. The assigned resources are independent each other, and the inheriting operation in the second phase avoids resuming a search from an unknown origin; therefore, the searching efficiency is improved.

4. Computational results

We conducted a simulation experiment on the farm work scheduling, and the experiment data was mainly obtained from a sugarcane-producing agricultural corporation. The major farm works of cultivating spring-growth sugarcane in 76 farmlands, defined as W_j, involved from the work of the tilling to the harvesting within a predefined time window. The number of available resources required for these works W_1, W_2, ...W_6 was assumed to 2, 1, 1, 1, 1, and 3, respectively. The program was written in the C language, and a Mac Pro with Quad-Core Intel Xeon and 4GB RAM running Mac OS X 10.5 was used as the computing platform. The computation time relied on the parameters of the SA, GA, and time increment in the hybrid Petri nets. The terminate condition was set as $\Gamma < 0.1$ and total computation time ≤ 2 h when $n = 200$, $\alpha = 0.02$ in the SA; population size = 20 and the number of generations = 200 in the GA; and time increment = 10 min in the hybrid Petri nets.

4.1 Optimizing resource assignment and priority list

The impact on evolutionary solution by the particular emphasis on resource assignment was examined in the experiment. Figure 5 shows the contrastive effect on optimizing resource assignment and priority list by the different generation sizes of the GA. The curves are plotted with the current best solution over the computation time. Curve "gen-100" represents the evolution process for the high frequency of optimizing resource assignment but a short computation time for the GA iterations. Compared with curve "gen-100", curve "gen-1000" emphasizes optimizing the priority list in the GA but results in a reduction in the frequency for optimizing resource assignment in the SA at the same computation time. As shown in the figure, not only a fast evolution but also a good solution quality appears in curve "gen-100" in the evolution. This reveals that increasing the frequency of optimizing resource assignment is conductive to a fast evolution and convergence, and is more efficient than the optimization computation on the priority list.

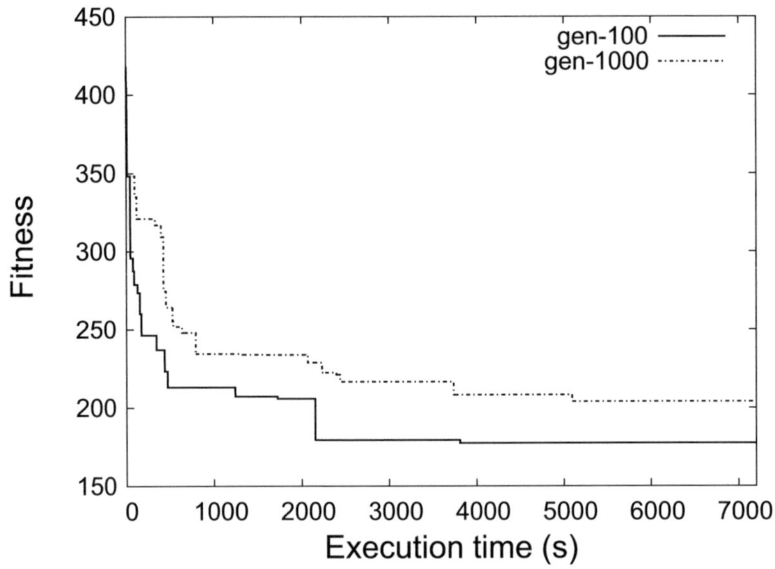

Fig. 5. Evolution based on optimizing resource assignment and priority list

4.2 Inheriting operation

Inheriting the present best work sequence starts with initializing the population for the second scheme of resource assignment. Before the inheriting operation, the procedure gaPls(x) is completed, and the present best work sequence for each resource is ascertained. In general, an inheriting operation can reserve and further improve the solution quality. Accordingly, the inheriting rate for the present best work sequence may impact the evolutionary computation. In order to clarify this, we have investigated the effect of inheriting operation at different inheriting rates and show the comparison of the obtained results in Fig. 6.

In the figure, curve "cpr-0%" indicates that the inheriting rate is zero, and the chromosomes in the initial population are entirely randomly generated. Similarly, curve "cpr-10%" implies that 10% of the chromosomes are inherited from the best priority list from the previous scheme of resource assignment, and the remaining chromosomes are randomly generated. Although several curves intersect at the beginning of the evolution, the best fitness is finally arranged in the descending order of the inheriting rate. The comparison result demonstrates that both the better solution and evolution speed is obtained by the higher inheriting rate. Conventionally, the inheriting operation for all chromosomes in the initial population may be disadvantageous because of a lack of variety in the chromosomes. Nevertheless, in our experiment, the inherited chromosomes continue to exhibit varieties because the resource assignment is renewed and the partial genes in the chromosomes are generated randomly after the inheriting operation.

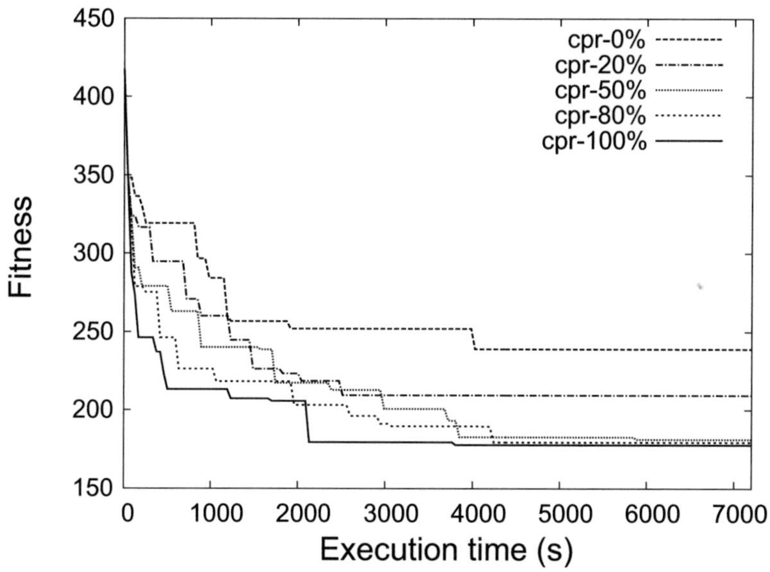

Fig. 6. Effect of inheriting the present best priority list

4.3 Scheduling result

The information on the schedule with the best fitness is listed in Table 2. Resources $R_1 \rightarrow R_2$, $R_7 \rightarrow R_9$ are available to perform W_1 and W_6 in cooperation, respectively. Such cooperative works are performed eight times. The idle time caused by waiting time O_{ij} is very short; and the average rate of utilization for each resource reaches 94.0%, which does not involve the moving time. The schedule length, which is the time period between the start of the first task and the completion of the last task, is applicable to the farm works in a growth cycle because a sugarcane-producing agricultural corporation usually requires time to carry out extra farm works. In order to reserve the time for these extra farm works and the risks such as rain and other uncertainties, we calculate the unscheduled time for each resource. This is very valuable to make an estimate of how much extra works the agricultural corporation can carry out.

Resource	R_1	R_2	R_3	R_4	R_5	R_6	R_7	R_8	R_9
Moving time (h)	14.7	19.7	15.8	25.8	24.7	26.5	14.2	15.8	10.0
Idle time (h)	1.0	0.3	0.0	0.0	0.0	1.8	0.0	0.0	0.0
Number of tasks	47	56	47	76	71	74	47	39	41
Work duration (h)	292.5	289.2	310.8	432.5	405.2	464.2	209.5	207	209.7
Rate of utilization	95.0	93.2	94.9	94.0	93.9	94.3	93.2	92.4	95.2
Unscheduled time	91.2	95.2	79.3	0.0	0.0	8.3	94.0	108.3	101.2
Times of performing work cooperatively					8				
Total area of farmland (hectare)					9.36				
Total amount of work (hectare)					48.9				
Schedule length (h)					2128.8				

Table 2. Information on generated schedule

5. Conclusions and future works

In this study, a hybrid Petri nets model was developed for modeling and formulating the farm work scheduling, and a metaheuristic approach for optimizing the schedule. A comparison on the formulating method between by hybrid Petri nets and mathematical definition was clarified according to their corresponding relations. In the experiment, the computational result revealed that a fast evolution and good solution quality were obtained by emphasizing the resource assignment optimization, and initializing the priority lists inherited from the present best task sequence in the previous resource assignment. Assigning resources first in the two-phase optimization for deadlocks removal considerably improved searching efficiency. Finally, the generated schedule had a high ratio of resource utilization, and it was applicable for devising a practical farm work plan in the agricultural corporation.

We put emphasis on the methodology of formulating and solving the farm work scheduling problem. The generated schedule was for the long-term schedule in a crop growth cycling, but not for the real-time schedule in which the schedule should be calculated in a short time. The proposed model has adequate compatibility and expansibility for modeling the discrete, continuous, concurrent, static, and dynamic events in farming processes. The stochastic event such as the data of weather can be also formulated on the Petri nets model by associating a time vector with a probability distribution to transitions. Although such environmental changes or breaks were ignored in the experiment, they will be considered in the real-time scheduling on a mobile device in our continuing work.

With respect to the computation time, the maximum time was required for the GA iterations and the simulation computation for the firing of the hybrid Petri nets. We are considering some approaches to reduction of computation time such as improved the crossover of the GA operations, parallel computing and an alterable strategy for simulating the firing operations of the hybrid Petri nets.

6. References

Arjona, E., Bueno, G. & Salazar, L. (2001). An activity simulation model for the analysis of the harvesting and transportation systems of a sugarcane plantation, *Computers and Electronics in Agriculture* 32: 247–264.

Astika, I. W., Sasao, A., Sakai, K. & Shibusawa, S. (1999). Stochastic farm work scheduling algorithm based on short range weather variation, *Journal of the Japanese Society of Agricultural Machinery* 61: (2)157–164, (3)83–94, (4)141–150.

Balasubramanian, J. & Grossmann, I. E. (2003). Scheduling optimization under uncertainty - an alternative approach, *Computers and Chemical Engineering* 27(4): 469 – 490.

Bassett, M. H., Pekny, J. F. & Reklaitis, G. V. (1997). Using detailed scheduling to obtain realistic operating policies for a batch processing facility, *Industrial Engineering and Chemical Research* 36: 1717–1726.

Chen, L. H. & McClendon, R. W. (1985). Soybean and wheat double cropping simulation model, *Transaction of the ASAE* 28(1): 65–69.

Daikoku, M. (2005). Development of computer-assisted system for planning work schedule of paddy and transplanting in distributed fields, *Japanese Journal of Farm Work Research* 40(4): 210–214. (In Japanese).

Ghaeli, M., Bahri, P. A. & Lee, P. L. (2006). Timed arc hybrid Petri nets based scheduling of mixed batch/continuous plants, *Proceedings of the 17th IMACS World Congress*.

Guan, S., Nakamura, M., Shikanai, T. & Okazaki, T. (2008). Hybrid petri nets modeling for farm work flow, *Computers and Electronics in Agriculture* 62(2): 149–158.

Guan, S., Nakamura, M., Shikanai, T. & Okazaki, T. (2009). Resource assignment and scheduling based on a two-phase metaheuristic for cropping system, *Computers and Electronics in Agriculture* 66(2): 181–190.

Haffar, I. & Khoury, R. (1992). A computer model for field machinery selection under multiple cropping, *Computers and Electronics in Agriculture* 7: 219–229.

Higgins, A. & Davies, I. (2005). A simulation model for capacity planning in sugarcane transport, *Computers and Electronics in Agriculture* 47: 85–102.

Janak, S. L. & Floudas, C. A. (2006). Production scheduling of a large-scale industrial batch plant. II. Reactive scheduling, *Industrial and Engineering Chemistry Research* 45(25): 8253–8269.

Lal, H., Peart, R. M., Jones, J. W. & Shoup, W. D. (1991). An object-oriented field operation simulator in PROLOG, *Transaction of the ASAE* 34(3): 1031–1039.

Li, Z. & Ierapetritou, G. (2008). Process scheduling under uncertainty: Review and challenges, *Computers and Chemical Engineering* 32: 715–727.

Lin, X., Janak, S. & Floudas, C. (2004). A new robust optimization approach for scheduling under uncertainty: I. Bounded uncertainty, *Computers and Chemical Engineering* 28: 1069–1085.

Murata, T. (1989). Petri nets: Properties, analysis and applications, *Proceedings of the IEEE* 77(4): 541–580.

Nanseki, T. (1998). Operations of FAPS97: A decision support system for evaluating agricultural technology and farm planning, *Miscellaneous Publication Tohoku National Agricultural Experiment Station* 21: 1–119. (In Japanese).

Nanseki, T., Matsushita, S. & Ikeda, M. (2003). A farming-systems database for farm planning, *Agricultural Information Research* 12: 133–152. (In Japanese).

Sadrieh, S., Ghaeli, M., Bahri, P. & Lee, P. (2007). An integrated Petri nets and GA based approach for scheduling of hybrid plants, *Computers in Industry* 58: 519–530.

Santiago-Mozos, R., Salcedo-Sanz, S., DePrado-Cumpli, M. & Bousono-Calzon, C. (2005). A two-phase heuristic evolutionary algorithm for personalizing course timetables: A case study in a Spanish university, *Computers and Operations Research* 32(7): 1761–1776.

Suliman, S. (2000). A two-phase heuristic approach to the permutation flow-shop scheduling problem, *International Journal of Production Economics* 64: 143–152.

The Ministry of Agriculture, Forestry and Fisheries of Japan (2006). Japan's post-war agricultural land reform and subsequent agricultural land system, *National Report for the International Conference on Agrarian Reform and Rural Development*.

Till, J., Sand, G., Urselmann, M. & Engell, S. (2007). A hybrid evolutionary algorithm for solving two-stage stochastic integer programs in chemical batch scheduling, *Computers and Chemical Engineering* 31: 630–647.

Tsai, Y. J., Jones, J. & Mishoe, J. (1987). Optimizing multiple cropping systems: A systems approach, *Transaction of the ASAE* 30(6): 1554–1561.

Wang, J. (2004). A fuzzy robust scheduling approach for product development projects, *European Journal of Operational Research* 152: 180–194.

9

Parallel Application Scheduling Model Based on Petri Net with Changeable Structure

Xiangang Zhao, Caiying Wei, Manyun Lin,
Xiaohu Feng and Wei Lan
National Satellite Meteorological Center
China

1. Introduction

In Parallel computing environments, each user can submit his job that is represented as a workflow composed of tasks that require multiple types of computational resources. How to develop a mechanism that ensures the success of these workflows is a challenging issue because the resources they use are dynamic and heterogeneous.

In order to schedule these workflows conveniently, a model is needed to describe them in a simple, intuitive way. Script-based method is a simple way to describe workflows. However, because those scripts often consist of so many elements with complex syntax that the users cannot understand them quickly. The graphic description for a workflow is an intuitive way, such as directed acyclic graph (DAG) and Petri Net. Compared to script-based descriptions, DAG is easier to use and more intuitional. However, DAG offers only a limited expressiveness [1], e.g. loops cannot be expressed directly. Moreover, as DAG only has a single node type, data flowing through the net cannot be modeled easily.

Petri net [2] is a modeling tool used for modeling discrete, dynamic, parallel and asynchronous system. Because of the function of simple graphical description and interpretation ability, Petri net is widely used for system modeling and performance analysis in recent years. Many researches have already introduced this method to model workflow [3-5].

In this paper, we model scheduling nets and job nets based on Petri Net techniques. To be convenient to analyze the performance of parallel jobs and to make net models compact and intuitional, we separate the scheduling net from the job net and model them respectively. A hierarchical colored Petri Net is proposed for the scheduling net that is designed into four levels according to the granularity of parallel applications. The hierarchical scheduling model makes each level scheduling only pay attention to its responsibility and it can reduce the structure complexity of the scheduling net at the same time. This paper also designs a extended Petri net with changeable structure for the job net model, which can change its structure dynamically according to the real-time state of running job. This model supports the mergence and division of subtasks and has ability to deal with the abnormity of subtasks. The models are validated with reachability tree techniques and their performances are analyzed with transition trees.

2. Related work

Jia Yu and Rajkumar Buyya et al[6-8] have done many researches on workflow in parallel environments. They propose a taxonomy that characterizes and classifies various approaches for building and executing workflows on Grids. They model workflow applications as a DAG and present many algorithms to address scheduling optimization problems in workflow applications based on QoS constraints. The emphases of their researches are the development of workflow management systems and scheduling algorithms.
BPEL4WS[9] builds on top of XML and web services specifications and provides a rich method for modeling web services based on the description of business process. However, its representation is script-based and it only composes workflows from web services.
Jin Hai et al[10] propose a workflow model based on colored Petri net for grid service composition, in which the image date transmission was taken as requirements for the service flow to improve the efficiency of settling service flow and reduce tasks' execution time. However, the model does not take the failure of task into consideration and does not support dynamic structures.
A general scheduling framework[11] modeled by Petri net is proposed, which locates on the layer of Grid scheduler and is used for independent tasks in computational Grid.
A three-level scheduling scheme[12] is proposed based on a high-level timed Petri net. The scheme divides Grid scheduling into three levels: Grid scheduler, Local Scheduler and Home Scheduler. It constructs different Petri net models for these levels. However, this scheme only focuses on independent tasks. In order to deal with the scheduling problem of task that consists of a set of communicating subtasks, an extended timed Petri net model[3] is proposed. Based on composition and reduction of Petri nets, the model can reduce the complexity of model and solve the state explosion problem in reachability analysis of Petri nets. But this model does not concern about the abnormity of running tasks and has no ability to change structure dynamically.

3. Definitions of extended Petri Nets

The jobs are dynamic and hierarchical in a parallel environment. According to these characteristics, we design two types of enhanced Petri Net, which are extended from the original Petri Net.
Definition 1 A Hierarchical Color Petri Net (HCPN) is designed into 9-tuple.

$$HCPN = \{P,T;F,D,C,I,O,K,M_0\}$$

1. P is a finite set of places.
2. T is a finite set of transitions and $T = \{T_s \cup T_c\}$, where T_s is a set of simple transitions, T_c is a set of complex transitions and $(P \cup T \neq \varnothing)\Lambda(P \cap T = \varnothing)$.
3. F is a finite set of arcs and $F \subseteq (P \times S) \cup ((S \times P))$.
4. D is a finite set of colors.
5. C is a finite set of color functions. $C: P \cup T \rightarrow \psi(D)$, where $\psi(D)$ is the power set of colors.
6. I and O are the input and output arc functions respectively.

$$\forall (p,t)\in (P\times T)\Rightarrow I(p,t)\in \left[C(p)_{MS}\rightarrow C(t)_{MS}\right]_L$$

$$\forall (t,p)\in (T\times P)\Rightarrow O(t,p)\in \left[C(t)_{MS}\rightarrow C(p)_{MS}\right]_L$$

When a transition needs to consume all tokens in a place, the input arc function is $I(p,t)=\gamma C(p)$.

7. K is a set of capacity functions. $K:P\rightarrow N\cup\omega$, $N=\{1,2,3,\cdots\}$ and ω denotes infinite.
8. $M_0:P\rightarrow D_{MS}$ is the initial token marking. $\forall p\in P: M_0(p)\in C(p)_{MS}$, where $C(p)_{MS}$ is the multiple set of the color tokens in p.

Definition 2

1. $^{\bullet}p=\{<t,p>|t\in T\}$, $p^{\bullet}=\{<p,t>|t\in T\}$,
   $^{\bullet}p^{\bullet}=\{^{\bullet}p\cup p^{\bullet}\}$.
2. $^{\otimes}p=\{t|<t,p>\in F\}$, $p^{\otimes}=\{t|<p,t>\in F\}$.
3. $^{\otimes}t=\{p|<p,t>\in F\}$, $t^{\otimes}=\{p|<t,p>\in F\}$.
4. $^{\otimes\otimes}t=\{t'\,|\,p\in {}^{\otimes}t\wedge <t',p>\in F\}$,
   $t^{\otimes\otimes}=\{t'\,|\,p\in t^{\otimes}\wedge <p,t'>\in F\}$.
5. In $HCPN$, the firing rules of transition is
   $\forall p\in {}^{\otimes}t: M(p)\geq O(p,t)\wedge \forall p\in t^{\otimes}$:
   $M(p)+I(p,t)\leq K(p)$.
6. There exist only one p_k and one p_l in $HCPN$, which satisfy the condition: $^{\otimes}p_k=\varnothing\wedge p_l^{\otimes}=\varnothing\wedge p_k\neq p_l$. p_k and p_l are called Beginning Place and End Place of $HCPN$ respectively.

Definition 3

Any complex transition in $HCPN$ can be extended to a subnet. The subnet of complex transition t_i is defined as:

$$S\_HCPN_i=\{P_i,T_i;F_i,D_i,C_i,I_i,O_i,K_i,M_0^i\}.$$

1. $P_i=\{p_{begin}^i,p_{end}^i,P_i'\}$ is a set of places. P_i' is the set of inner places in S_HCPN_i. p_{begin}^i and p_{end}^i are additional places used to denote the beginning and end places of S_HCPN_i.
   $^{\bullet}p_{begin}^i=\varnothing$, $(p_{end}^i)^{\bullet}=\varnothing$;
   $C(p_{begin}^i)=\{\cup_{k=1}^{m}C(p_k)\,|\,p_k\in {}^{\otimes}t_i\}$;
   $C(p_{end}^i)=\{\cup_{k=1}^{m}C(p_k)\,|\,p_k\in t_i^{\otimes}\}$.
2. $F_i=\{(p_{begin}^i)^{\bullet}\cup {}^{\bullet}p_{end}^i\cup F_i'\}$ is a set of arcs. F_i' is the set of inner arcs in S_HCPN_i.
3. T_i, D_i, C_i, I_i, O_i, K_i and M_0^i are the sets of transitions, colors, color functions, input arc functions, output arc functions, capacity functions and initial token marking respectively.

Definition 4

A Petri Net with changeable structure is designed to11-tuple.

$$CSCTPN_k = \left\{P_k, T_k; F_k, D_k, C_k, I_k, O_k, \Gamma_k, Q_k, M_0^k, M_0^{k-1}\right\}$$

4. P_k, T_k, F_k, D_k, C_k, I_k, and O_k are the sets of places, transitions, arcs, colors, color functions, input arc functions and output arc functions respectively after the structure of $CSCTPN$ is changed k times.
5. 2) Γ_k is a set of times after $CSCTPN$ have changed k times. Its element is defined as $< t_i, \tau_b, \tau_l, \tau_d >$, which denotes the earliest start time, the latest start time and duration time of transition t_i are τ_b, τ_l, and τ_d respectively. $\Gamma_b(t_i) = \tau_b$, $\Gamma_l(t_i) = \tau_l$, $\Gamma_d(t_i) = \tau_d$.
6. Q_k is a set of cost after $CSCTPN$ have changed k times. Its element is defined as $< t_i, q_r, q_m >$, which denotes that the maximal cost of transition t_i is q_m and the real cost is q_r. $Q_r(t_i) = q_r$, $Q_m(t_i) = q_m$, and $q_r \le q_m$
7. M_0^k is the initial token marking after $CSCTPN$ have changed k times and $M_0^{-1} = M_0^0$.

4. Parallel application scheduling model

In this section, we propose a four-level scheduling model firstly according to the characteristics of parallel jobs. Then, Parallel job net is designed based on Petri Net with changeable structure and the conversion rules of the job net are presented at the same time.

4.1 Four-level scheduling net

In a Parallel environment, users use resources by submitting their applications. A user application is called a parallel job that can implement some functions specifically. A parallel job is usually composed of many steps and each step has certain input and output sets. Each step is called a subjob that can be divided into two types: computing subjob and data transferring subjob. A computing subjob needs to transfer its inputs firstly and then perform computing operation, so a computing subjob can be divided into transferring tasks and computing tasks. Similarly, a data transferring subjob often has many data inputs and it can be divided into many transferring tasks. A data transferring task has only one input and one output. The input data of a computing task is already transferred to local computing node. Because a data resource may have many replicas that locate on different nodes, to speed up the transfer a data transferring task can be divided into many subtasks according to the number of replicas and the QoS requirements of the user. Each subtask transfers a part of data from different replicas. If a computing task can be processed in parallel we call it a parallel computing task, otherwise we call it an unparallel computing task. A parallel computing task can be divided into many subtasks that run on different computing node. According to job, subjob, task and subtask, the parallel allocation scheduling model is designed into four levels: job scheduling net, subjob scheduling net, task scheduling net and subtask scheduling net. Only subtasks use computing or data resources directly, so all resource allocations take place in subtask scheduling net.

4.1.1 Job scheduling net.

The job scheduling net mainly manages the states of jobs. Its function includes job selection and monitoring. There are four states of a job: waiting, running, completed and failed. When all subjobs of a job are completed, the job is completed. If any subjob failes, the state of the job is failed. When a job has running subjobs and has no failed subjobs, the state of the job is running. The job scheduling net is modeled based on *HCPN*, which is shown as Fig.4-1. The detailed definition is shown as follows:

$$HCPN = \{P,T;F,D,C,I,O,K,M_0\}$$

1. $P = \{p_i \mid 1 \le i \le 7\}$;
2. $T = \{t_i \mid 1 \le i \le 7\}$, t_1: select a job for running; t_2: start a job; t_3: select a job for monitoring; t_4: check the states of jobs, which is a complex transition; t_5: mark a job; t_6: return a completed job; t_7: return a failed job.
3. $D = \{d_i \mid 1 \le i \le 8\}$, d_1: jobs submitted by users; d_2: jobs waiting to be started; d_3: running jobs; d_4: jobs waiting for being checked; d_5: jobs validated to run normally; d_6: completed jobs; d_7 :failed jobs; d_8: returned jobs; d_9: tokens used for restricting the number of jobs that are running at the same time.
4. $C(p_1) = \{d_1\}$, $C(p_2) = \{d_2\}$, $C(p_3) = \{d_3\}$, $C(p_4) = \{d_4\}$, $C(p_5) = \{d_5, d_6, d_7\}$, $C(p_6) = \{d_9\}$, $C(p_7) = \{d_8\}$; $C(t_1) = \{d_1\}$, $C(t_2) = \{d_2, d_9\}$, $C(t_3) = \{d_3\}$, $C(t_4) = \{d_4\}$, $C(t_5) = \{d_5\}$, $C(t_6) = \{d_6\}$, $C(t_7) = \{d_7\}$.
5. $K(p_1) = K(p_2) = m$, $K(p_3) = n$, $K(p_4) = K(p_5) = 1$, $K(p_6) = n$, $K(p_7) = \omega$.
   $M_0 = \{k,0,0,0,0,n,0\}$, where $1 \le k \le m$.

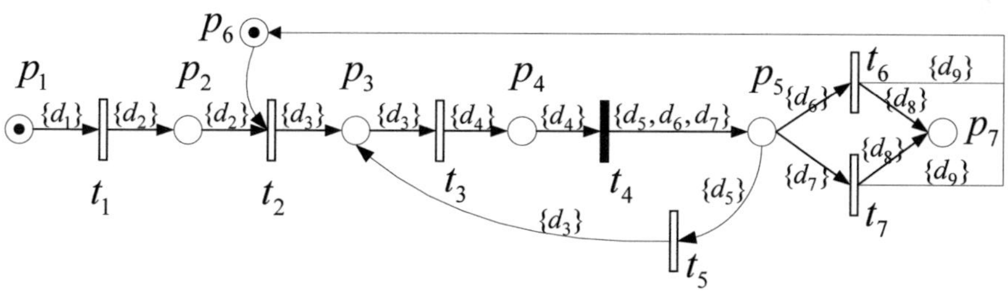

Fig. 4.1. Job Scheduling Net

4.1.2 Subjob scheduling net.

The subjob scheduling net is a subnet of the job scheduling net, which is extended from the complex transition t_4. The subjob scheduling net mainly manages the states of subjob and is used to analyze jobs, create subjobs, order the running sequence of subjobs and monitor the states of subjobs. The subjob scheduling net is shown as Fig.4-2, which is modeled based on *S_HCPN* and the detailed definition is shown as follows:

$$S\_HCPN_4 = \{P_4, T_4; F_4, D_4, C_4, I_4, O_4, K_4, M_0^4\}$$

1. $P_4 = \{p_{begin}^4, p_{end}^4, p_i^4 \mid 1 \le i \le 10\}$.
2. $T_4 = \{t_i^4 \mid 1 \le i \le 15\}$, t_1^4: check whether a job is initialized; t_2^4: analyze a job net; t_3^4: get the set of running subjobs; t_4^4: start subjobs; t_5^4: select a subjob for monitoring; t_6^4: monitor subjobs, which is a complex transition; t_7^4: creat a token for clearing out all subjobs; t_8^4: mark a normal subjob; t_9^4: mark a completed subjob; t_{10}^4: check whether all subjobs of the job have already been checked in this scheduling round; t_{11}^4: creat a token for selecting a subjob; t_{12}^4: mark a failed job; t_{13}^4: check whether all subjobs of the job have already accomplished. t_{14}^4: mark a completed job; t_{15}^4: mark a normal job.

3. $D_4 = \{C(p_{begin}^4) \cup C(p_{end}^4) \cup d^4\}$, where
$d^4 = \{d_i^4 \mid 1 \le i \le 15\}$, d_1^4: initialized jobs; d_2^4: uninitialized jobs; d_3^4: subjob nets; d_4^4:running subjobs; d_5^4: subjobs waiting to be checked; d_6^4: subjobs running normally; d_7^4: completed subjobs; d_8^4: failed subjobs; d_9^4: marked subjobs; d_{10}^4: jobs whose subjobs have been checked completely in this scheduling round; d_{11}^4: jobs whose subjobs have been checked incompletely in this scheduling round; d_{12}^4: tokens for selecting a subjob; d_{13}^4: tokens for clearing out all subjobs; d_{14}^4: jobs whose subjobs have accomplished completely; d_{15}^4: jobs whose subjobs have accomplished incompletely.
4. $C(p_{begin}^4) = \{d_4\}$, $C(p_{end}^4) = \{d_5, d_6, d_7\}$,
$C(p_1^4) = \{d_1^4, d_2^4\}$, $C(p_2^4) = \{d_3^4\}$, $C(p_3^4) = \{d_4^4\}$, $C(p_4^4) = \{d_5^4\}$, $C(p_5^4) = \{d_6^4, d_7^4, d_8^4\}$, $C(p_6^4) = \{d_9^4\}$, $C(p_7^4) = \{d_{10}^4, d_{11}^4\}$, $C(p_8^4) = \{d_{12}^4\}$, $C(p_9^4) = \{d_{13}^4\}$, $C(p_{10}^4) = \{d_{14}^4, d_{15}^4\}$; $C(t_1^4) = \{d_4\}$, $C(t_2^4) = \{d_2^4\}$, $C(t_3^4) = \{d_1^4\}$, $C(t_4^4) = \{d_3^4\}$, $C(t_5^4) = \{d_4^4, d_{12}^4\}$, $C(t_6^4) = \{d_5^4\}$, $C(t_7^4) = \{d_8^4\}$, $C(t_8^4) = \{d_6^4\}$, $C(t_9^4) = \{d_7^4\}$, $C(t_{10}^4) = \{d_9^4\}$, $C(t_{11}^4) = \{d_{11}^4\}$, $C(t_{12}^4) = \{d_4^4, d_{13}^4\}$ $C(t_{13}^4) = \{d_{10}^4\}$, $C(t_{14}^4) = \{d_{14}^4\}$, $C(t_{15}^4) = \{d_{15}^4\}$.
5. $K(p_3^4) = n$ and others are 1.
6. $M_0^4 = \{1,0,0,0,0,0,0,0,0,0,0,0\}$.

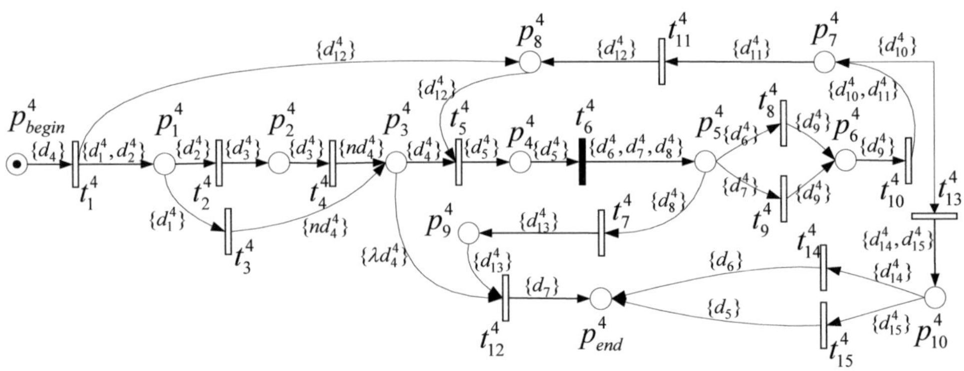

Fig. 4.2. Subjob Scheduling Net

4.1.3 Task scheduling net.

The task scheduling net is a subnet of the subjob scheduling net, which is extended from the complex transition t_6^4. The task scheduling net mainly manages the states of tasks and is used to analyze subjobs, create tasks, order the running sequence of task and monitor the states of tasks. A task scheduling net is shown as Fig. 4-3, which is modeled based on *S_HCPN* and the detailed definition is shown as follows:

$$S\_HCPN_{4,6} = \left\{P_{4,6}, T_{4,6}; F_{4,6}, D_{4,6}, C_{4,6}, I_{4,6}, O_{4,6}, K_{4,6}, M_0^{4,6}\right\}$$

1. $P_{4,6} = \{p_{begin}^{4,6}, p_{end}^{4,6}, p_i^{4,6} \mid 1 \le i \le 10\}$.

2. $T_{4,6}=\{t_i^{4,6}\mid 1\le i\le 15\}$, $T_4=\{t_i^{4}\mid 1\le i\le 15\}$, $t_1^{4,6}$: check whether a subjob is initialized; $t_2^{4,6}$: transform a subjob scheduling net into a job scheduling net; $t_3^{4,6}$: get the set of running tasks; $t_4^{4,6}$: start tasks; $t_5^{4,6}$: select a task for monitoring; $t_6^{4,6}$: monitor tasks, which is a complex transition; $t_7^{4,6}$: create a token for clearing out all tasks; $t_8^{4,6}$: mark a normal task; $t_9^{4,6}$: mark a completed task; $t_{10}^{4,6}$: check whether all tasks of the subjob have already been checked in this scheduling round; $t_{11}^{4,6}$: create a token for selecting a task; $t_{12}^{4,6}$: mark a failed task; $t_{13}^{4,6}$: check whether all tasks of the subjob have already accomplished. $t_{14}^{4,6}$: mark a completed subjob; $t_{15}^{4,6}$: mark a normal subjob.
3. $D_{4,6}=\{C(p_{begin}^{4,6})\cup C(p_{end}^{4,6})\cup d^{4,6}\}$, where

   $d^{4,6}=\{d_i^{4,6}\mid 1\le i\le 15\}$, $d_1^{4,6}$: initialized subjobs; $d_2^{4,6}$:uninitialized subjobs; $d_3^{4,6}$: task net; $d_4^{4,6}$: running tasks; $d_5^{4,6}$: tasks waiting to be checked; $d_6^{4,6}$: tasks running normally; $d_7^{4,6}$: completed tasks; $d_8^{4,6}$: failed tasks; $d_9^{4,6}$: marked tasks; $d_{10}^{4,6}$: subjobs whose tasks have been checked completely in this scheduling round; $d_{11}^{4,6}$: subjobs whose tasks have been checked incompletely in this scheduling round; $d_{12}^{4,6}$: tokens for selecting a task; $d_{13}^{4,6}$: tokens for clearing out all tasks; $d_{14}^{4,6}$: subjobs whose tasks have accomplished completely; $d_{15}^{4,6}$: subjobs whose tasks have accomplished incompletely.
4. $C(p_{begin}^{4,6})=\{d_5^4\}$, $C(p_{end}^{4,6})=\{d_6^4,d_7^4,d_8^4\}$, $C(p_1^{4,6})=\{d_1^{4,6},d_2^{4,6}\}$, $C(p_2^{4,6})=\{d_3^{4,6}\}$,

   $C(p_3^{4,6})=\{d_4^{4,6}\}$, $C(p_4^{4,6})=\{d_5^{4,6}\}$, $C(p_5^{4,6})=\{d_6^{4,6},d_7^{4,6},d_8^{4,6}\}$, $C(p_6^{4,6})=\{d_9^{4,6}\}$,

   $C(p_7^{4,6})=\{d_{10}^{4,6},d_{11}^{4,6}\}$, $C(p_8^{4,6})=\{d_{12}^{4,6}\}$, $C(p_9^{4,6})=\{d_{13}^{4,6}\}$, $C(p_{10}^{4,6})=\{d_{14}^{4,6},d_{15}^{4,6}\}$;

   $C(t_1^{4,6})=\{d_5^4\}$, $C(t_2^{4,6})=\{d_2^{4,6}\}$, $C(t_3^{4,6})=\{d_1^{4,6}\}$, $C(t_4^{4,6})=\{d_3^{4,6}\}$, $C(t_5^{4,6})=\{d_4^{4,6},d_{12}^{4,6}\}$,

   $C(t_6^{4,6})=\{d_5^{4,6}\}$, $C(t_7^{4,6})=\{d_8^{4,6}\}$, $C(t_8^{4,6})=\{d_6^{4,6}\}$, $C(t_9^{4,6})=\{d_7^{4,6}\}$, $C(t_{10}^{4,6})=\{d_9^{4,6}\}$,

   $C(t_{11}^{4,6})=\{d_{11}^{4,6}\}$, $C(t_{12}^{4,6})=\{d_4^{4,6},d_{13}^{4,6}\}$, $C(t_{13}^{4,6})=\{d_{10}^{4,6}\}$, $C(t_{14}^{4,6})=\{d_{14}^{4,6}\}$, $C(t_{15}^{4,6})=\{d_{15}^{4,6}\}$.
5. $K(p_3^{4,6})=n$ and others are 1.
6. $M_0^{4,6}=\{1,0,0,0,0,0,0,0,0,0,0,0\}$.

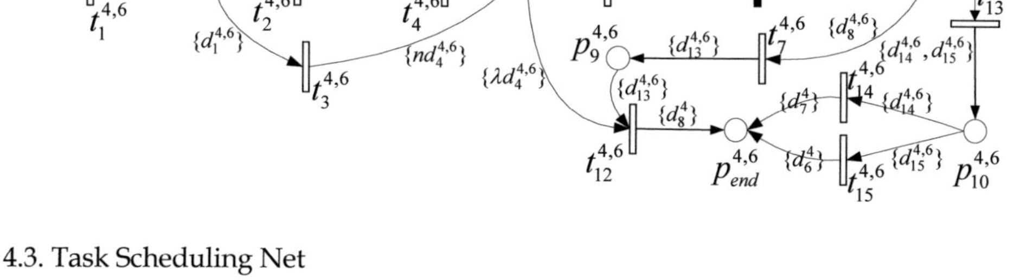

Fig. 4.3. Task Scheduling Net

4.1.4 Subtask scheduling net.

The subtask scheduling net is a subnet of the task scheduling net, which is extended from the complex transition $t_6^{4,6}$. The subtask scheduling net mainly manages the states of subtasks and is used to analyze tasks, create subtasks, allocate and reallocate resources, order the running sequence of subtask and monitor the states of subtasks. The subtask scheduling net is shows as Fig.4-4, which is modeled based on *S_HCPN* and the detailed definition is shown as follows:

$$S\_HCPN_{4,6,6} = \left\{P_{4,6,6}, T_{4,6,6}; F_{4,6,6}, D_{4,6,6}, C_{4,6,6}, I_{4,6,6}, O_{4,6,6}, K_{4,6,6}, M_0^{4,6,6}\right\}$$

1. $P_{4,6,6} = \{p_{begin}^{4,6,6}, p_{end}^{4,6,6}, p_i^{4,6,6} \mid 1 \le i \le 14\}$.
2. $T_{4,4,6} = \{t_i^{4,4,6} \mid 1 \le i \le 21\}$, $t_1^{4,4,6}$: check whether a task is initialized; $t_2^{4,4,6}$: get the set of running subtasks; $t_3^{4,4,6}$: search resources; $t_4^{4,4,6}$: select resources; $t_5^{4,4,6}$: create subtasks; $t_6^{4,4,6}$: start subtasks; $t_7^{4,4,6}$: select a subtask for monitoring; $t_8^{4,4,6}$: check a subtask; $t_9^{4,4,6}$: mark a completed subtask; $t_{10}^{4,4,6}$: mark a normal subtask; $t_{11}^{4,4,6}$: check whether all subtasks of the task have already been checked in this scheduling round; $t_{12}^{4,4,6}$: create a token for selecting a subtask; $t_{13}^{4,4,6}$: reallocate a subtask; $t_{14}^{4,4,6}$: start subtasks after reallocation; $t_{15}^{4,4,6}$: mark subtasks running normally after reallocation; $t_{16}^{4,4,6}$: create a token for clearing out all subtasks; $t_{17}^{4,4,6}$: mark a failed subtask; $t_{18}^{4,4,6}$: check whether all subtasks of the task have already accomplished. $t_{19}^{4,4,6}$: mark a normal task; $t_{20}^{4,4,6}$: mark a completed task; $t_{21}^{4,4,6}$: mark a failed task.
3. $D_{4,4,6} = \{C(p_{begin}^{4,4,6}) \cup C(p_{end}^{4,4,6}) \cup d^{4,4,6}\}$, where

   $d^{4,4,6} = \{d_i^{4,4,6} \mid 1 \le i \le 15\}$, $d_1^{4,6,6}$: uninitialized tasks; $d_2^{4,6,6}$: initialized tasks; $d_3^{4,6,6}$: running subtasks; $d_4^{4,6,6}$: resource list; $d_5^{4,6,6}$: selected resources; $d_6^{4,6,6}$: subtasks that have no inadequate resources; $d_7^{4,6,6}$: subtask net; $d_8^{4,6,6}$: tokens for selecting a subtask; $d_9^{4,6,6}$: subtasks waiting for monitoring; $d_{10}^{4,6,6}$: subtasks running normally; $d_{11}^{4,6,6}$: completed subtasks; $d_{12}^{4,6,6}$: subtasks running abnormally; $d_{13}^{4,6,6}$: marked subtasks; $d_{14}^{4,6,6}$: tasks whose subtasks have not been checked completely in this scheduling round; $d_{15}^{4,6,6}$: tasks whose subtasks have been checked completely in this scheduling round; $d_{16}^{4,6,6}$: tasks whose subtasks have already been accomplished; $d_{17}^{4,6,6}$: tasks whose subtasks have not been accomplished completely; $d_{18}^{4,6,6}$: subtasks reallocated successfully; $d_{19}^{4,6,6}$: subtasks reallocated unsuccessfully; $d_{20}^{4,6,6}$: subtasks running normally after reallocation; $d_{21}^{4,6,6}$: tokens for clearing out all subtasks.
4. $C(p_{begin}^{4,6,6}) = \{d_5^{4,6}\}$, $C(p_{end}^{4,6,6}) = \{d_6^{4,6}, d_7^{4,6}, d_8^{4,6}\}$, $C(p_1^{4,6,6}) = \{d_1^{4,6,6}, d_2^{4,6,6}\}$, $C(p_2^{4,6,6}) = \{d_3^{4,6,6}\}$, $C(p_3^{4,6,6}) = \{d_4^{4,6,6}\}$, $C(p_4^{4,6,6}) = \{d_5^{4,6,6}, d_6^{4,6,6}\}$, $C(p_5^{4,6,6}) = \{d_7^{4,6,6}\}$, $C(p_6^{4,6,6}) = \{d_9^{4,6,6}\}$, $C(p_7^{4,6,6}) = \{d_{10}^{4,6,6}, d_{11}^{4,6,6}, d_{12}^{4,6,6}\}$, $C(p_8^{4,6,6}) = \{d_{13}^{4,6,6}\}$, $C(p_9^{4,6,6}) = \{d_{14}^{4,6,6}, d_{15}^{4,6,6}\}$, $C(p_{10}^{4,6,6}) = \{d_8^{4,6,6}\}$, $C(p_{11}^{4,6,6}) = \{d_{18}^{4,6,6}, d_{19}^{4,6,6}\}$, $C(p_{12}^{4,6,6}) = \{d_{21}^{4,6,6}\}$, $C(p_{13}^{4,6,6}) = \{d_{20}^{4,6,6}\}$, $C(p_{14}^{4,6,6}) = \{d_{16}^{4,6,6}, d_{17}^{4,6,6}\}$;

   $C(t_1^{4,6,6}) = \{d_5^{4,6}\}$, $C(t_2^{4,6,6}) = \{d_2^{4,6,6}\}$, $C(t_3^{4,6,6}) = \{d_1^{4,6,6}\}$, $C(t_4^{4,6,6}) = \{d_4^{4,6,6}\}$, $C(t_5^{4,6,6}) = \{d_5^{4,6,6}\}$, $C(t_6^{4,6,6}) = \{d_7^{4,6,6}\}$, $C(t_7^{4,6,6}) = \{d_3^{4,6,6}, d_8^{4,6,6}\}$, $C(t_8^{4,6,6}) = \{d_9^{4,6,6}\}$,

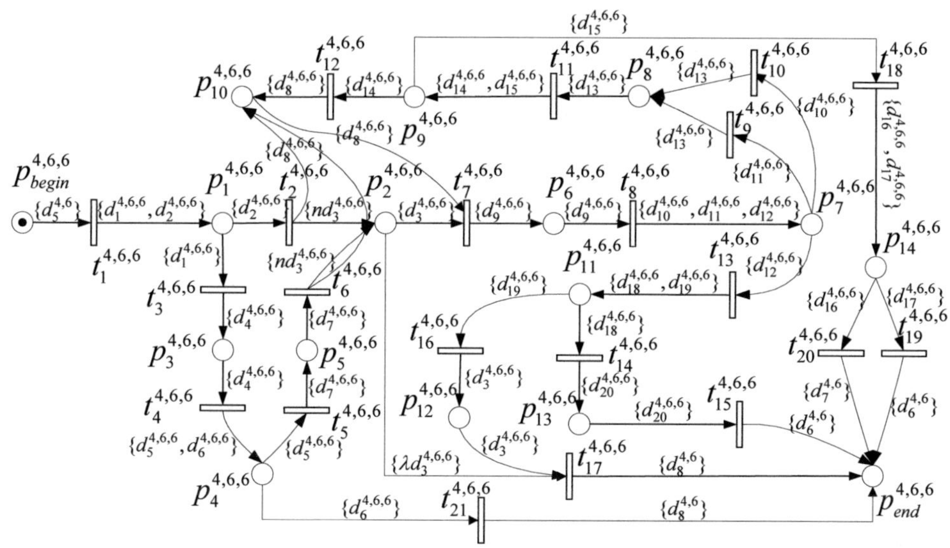

Fig. 4.4. Subtask Scheduling Net

$C(t_9^{4,6,6}) = \{d_{11}^{4,6,6}\}$, $C(t_{10}^{4,6,6}) = \{d_{10}^{4,6,6}\}$, $C(t_{11}^{4,6,6}) = \{d_{13}^{4,6,6}\}$, $C(t_{12}^{4,6,6}) = \{d_{14}^{4,6,6}\}$,
$C(t_{13}^{4,6,6}) = \{d_{12}^{4,6,6}\}$, $C(t_{14}^{4,6,6}) = \{d_{18}^{4,6,6}\}$, $C(t_{15}^{4,6,6}) = \{d_{20}^{4,6,6}\}$, $C(t_{16}^{4,6,6}) = \{d_{19}^{4,6,6}\}$,
$C(t_{17}^{4,6,6}) = \{\lambda d_3^{4,6,6}, d_{21}^{4,6,6}\}$, $C(t_{18}^{4,6,6}) = \{d_{15}^{4,6,6}\}$, $C(t_{19}^{4,6,6}) = \{d_{17}^{4,6,6}\}$, $C(t_{20}^{4,6,6}) = \{d_{16}^{4,6,6}\}$,
$C(t_{21}^{4,6,6}) = \{d_6^{4,6,6}\}$.

5. $K(p_2^{4,6,6}) = n$ and others are 1.
6. $M_0^{4,6,6} = \{1,0,0,0,0,0,0,0,0,0,0,0\}$.

4.2 Job Net

The job net describes the flow of parallel application submitted by users, which is a kind of workflow net and defines the relation of each step strictly. The job net is modeled based on $CSCTPN$ and its detailed definition is shows as follows:

$$CSCTPN_k = \left\{P_k, T_k; F_k, D_k, C_k, I_k, O_k, \Gamma_k, Q_k, M_0^k, M_0^{k-1}\right\}$$

$CSCTPN_0$ is the initial structure of the job net. In this level, we only concern about the time limit, cost, input and output of a job, which are defined as follows:

1. $P_0 = \{p_{in}, p_{out}\}$, they are places of input and output respectively;
2. $T_0 = \{t_0^1\}$, there is only a transition that denotes the whole process of the job;
3. $D_0 = \{d_{in}, d_{out}\}$, they are the input and output of the job;
4. $\Gamma_0 = \{< t_0^1, \tau_b, \tau_l, \tau_d >\}$, it denotes the time limit of t_0^1;
5. $Q_0 = \{< t_0^1, q_r, q_m >\}$, it denotes the cost limit of t_0^1.

There are four types of data in the job net: remote data, local data, outer data and inner data. For a job, outer data has already existed in the parallel environment and it is not produced by the job. The data produced temporarily by the jobs is called inner data.

In the job net, a user needs to indicate the maximum cost and the deadline of his job. In addition, the user needs to estimate the cost and durable time of each subjob according to his experiences, which are shown in the description file of the job. This is helpful to assign the cost and time characteristics of subjobs. Otherwise, the assignment methods of these values are the same with tasks and subtasks. For tasks and subtasks, we need to assign their cost and time characteristics dynamically within their limits according to the allocation results. The cost is proportional to the transferring traffic and the computing load [13,14] in our assignation strategy. Compared with cost assignation, time assignation is more complex than cost assignation. We refer to a method[15] to assign the times of tasks and subtasks within fixed-time constraints.

4.2.1 Subjob net.

A job consists of many subjobs that have own inputs, outputs and operations. The subjob net is $CSCTPN_1$ that is built by analyzing the description file of a job.

$$CSCTPN_1 = \left\{P_1, T_1; F_1, D_1, C_1, I_1, O_1, \Gamma_1, Q_1, M_0^1, M_0^0\right\}$$

1. P_1 : a set of places for inputs and outputs of subjobs.
2. $T_1 = J_t \cup J_c$, where J_t is a set of transferring subjobs and J_c is a set of computing subjobs.
3. $D_1 = \{d_i \mid 1 \le i \le 4\}$, where d_1 : remote data from outside; d_2 : local data from outside; d_3 : remote data from inside; d_4 : local data from inside.
4. Γ_1 : a time set of subjobs, $\forall t_1^i \in T_1(\Gamma_l(t_1^i) + \Gamma_d(t_1^i) \le \Gamma_l(t_0^1) + \Gamma_d(t_0^1))$.
5. Q_1 :a cost set of subjobs, $\sum_{i=1}^{m} Q_m(t_1^i) = Q_m(t_0^1)$, where m is the number of transitions in T_1.

4.2.2 Task net.

The task net is $CSCTPN_2$ that is built by decomposing the subjob net. $CSCTPN_2$ is defined as follows.

$$CSCTPN_2 = \left\{P_2, T_2; F_2, D_2, C_2, I_2, O_2, \Gamma_2, Q_2, M_0^2, M_0^1\right\}$$

1. P_2 : a set of places for inputs and outputs of tasks.
2. $T_2 = T_t \cup T_{npc} \cup T_{dpc} \cup T_{dnpc}$, where T_t : a set of data transferring tasks; T_{npc} : a set of computing tasks that can not run in parallel; T_{dpc} : a set of computing tasks whose data inputs can be divided; T_{ndpc} : a set of computing tasks whose data input can not be divided.
3. $D_2 = \{d_i \mid 1 \le i \le 4\}$, where d_1 : remote data from outside; d_2 : local data from outside; d_3 : remote data from inside; d_4 : local data from inside.
4. Γ_2 : a time set of tasks, $\forall t_2^i \in T_2(\Gamma_l(t_2^i) + \Gamma_d(t_2^i) \le \Gamma_l(t_0^1) + \Gamma_d(t_0^1))$.
5. Q_2 : a cost set of tasks, $\sum_{i=1}^{m} Q_m(t_2^i) = Q_m(t_0^1)$, where m is the number of transitions in T_2.

According to the input and output, a subjob can be divided into several tasks. Based on the types of subjobs, the division rules are defined as follows.

1. data transferring subjob

A data transferring subjob often has many data inputs and they may need to be transferred at the same time. In order to be convenient to deal with them, a data transferring subjob needs to be divided into many tasks and each task has only one data input. The division result is shown as Fig.4-5. The process satifies these conditions:

$$\sum_{r=1}^{s+k} Q_m(t_2^{i,r}) = Q_m(t_1^i),$$

$$\exists h(1 \le h \le (s+k) \wedge \Gamma_b(t_2^{i,h}) \le \Gamma_l(t_1^i))$$

$$\forall h(1 \le h \le (s+k) \to \Gamma_b(t_2^{i,h}) \ge \Gamma_b(t_1^i))$$

$$\max(\Gamma_l(t_2^{i,1}) + \Gamma_d(t_2^{i,1}), \cdots, \Gamma_l(t_2^{i,s+k}) + \Gamma_d(t_2^{i,s+k})) \\ \le \Gamma_l(t_1^i) + \Gamma_d(t_1^i))$$

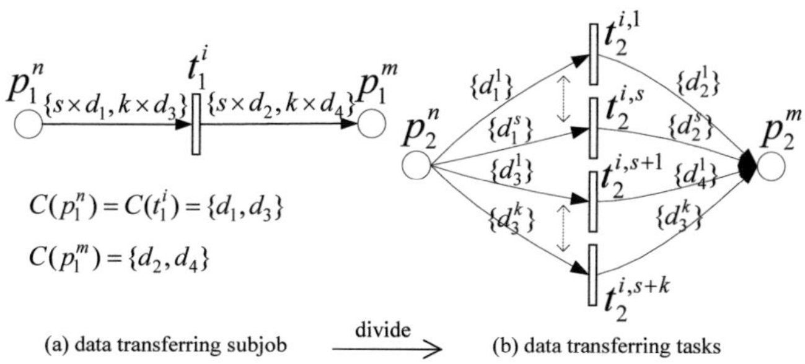

Fig. 4.5. Division result of data transferring subjob

2. computing subjob

Generally, a computing subjob has remote data inputs and these data need to be transferred to local node firstly. The division result for a computing subjob is show as Fig.4-6 and it satisfies these conditions:

$$\sum_{r=1}^{s+k} Q_m(t_2^{i,r}) + Q_m(t_2^i) = Q_m(t_1^i)$$

$$\exists h(1 \le h \le (s+k) \wedge \Gamma_b(t_2^{i,h}) \le \Gamma_l(t_1^i))$$

$$\forall h(1 \le h \le (s+k) \to \Gamma_b(t_2^{i,h}) \ge \Gamma_b(t_1^i))$$

$$\Gamma_b(t_2^i) \le \max(\Gamma_l(t_2^{i,1}) + \Gamma_d(t_2^{i,1}), \cdots, \Gamma_l(t_2^{i,s+k}) + \Gamma_d(t_2^{i,s+k})) \le \Gamma_l(t_2^i)$$

$$\Gamma_l(t_2^i) + \Gamma_d(t_2^i) \le \Gamma_l(t_1^i) + \Gamma_d(t_1^i)$$

4.2.3 Subtask net.

Subtask net is $CSCTPN_i$ ($i \ge 3$)that is built by decomposing task net, which is defined as follows.

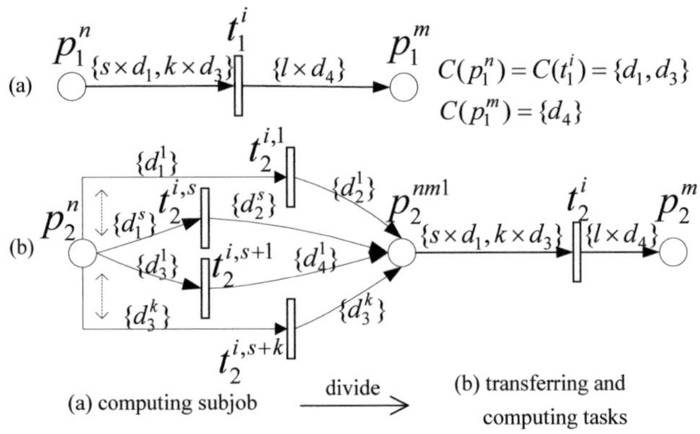

Fig. 4.6. Division result of computing subjob

$$CSCTPN_i = \left\{P_i, T_i; F_i, D_i, C_i, I_i, O_i, \Gamma_i, Q_i, M_0^i, M_0^{i-1}\right\}$$

1. P_i : a set of places for inputs and outputs of subtasks.
2. $T_i = J_t \cup J_c$, where J_t : a set of transferring subtasks; J_c : a set of computing subtasks.
3. $D_i = \{d_i \mid 1 \le i \le 5\}$, where d_1 : remote data from outside; d_2 : local data from outside; d_3 : remote data from inside; d_4 : local data from inside; d_5 : computing resources.
4. Γ_i : a time set of subtasks, $\forall t_2^i \in T_i(\Gamma_l(t_2^i) + \Gamma_d(t_2^i) \le \Gamma_l(t_0^1) + \Gamma_d(t_0^1))$.
5. Q_i : a cost set of subtasks, $\sum_{i=1}^{m} Q_m(t_2^i) = Q_m(t_0^1)$, where m is the number of transitions in T_i .

According to the number of data replicas or computing resources, a task can be divided into many subtasks. Based on the types of tasks, the division rules are defined as follows.

1. tasks transferring outer data

Outer data may have many replicas in a parallel environment, so a task transferring outer data can transfer parts of data from different replicas firstly in order to reduce the total transferring time. Then, these parts of data are merged into one by a merging subtask. Though a merging subtask is a computing subtask here, we do not allocate computing resource for it specially and it runs on the node that the data lies on. The detailed division is shown as Fig.4-7. t_2^i is a task transferring outer data. $t_3^{i,r} (1 \le r \le k)$ denotes the transferring subtasks running in parallel. t_3^i is the merging subtask. $R_k(d_1^j)$ denotes the task uses k replicas of d_1^j , and $R_k(d_1^j) = \{R_k^i(d_1^j) \mid 0 \le i \le k\}$. $E_k(b_m^j)$ denotes data b_m^j is divided into k pieces and $E_k(b_m^j) = \{E_k^i(b_m^j) \mid 0 \le i \le k\}$. The division satisfies these conditions:

$$\sum_{r=1}^{k} Q_r(t_3^{i,r}) + Q_r(t_3^i) \le Q_m(t_2^i)$$

$$\exists h(1 \le h \le k \wedge \Gamma_b(t_3^{i,h}) \le \Gamma_l(t_2^i))$$

$$\forall h(1 \le h \le k \rightarrow \Gamma_b(t_3^{i,h}) \ge \Gamma_b(t_2^i))$$

$$\Gamma_b(t_3^i) \le \max(\Gamma_l(t_3^{i,1}) + \Gamma_d(t_3^{i,1}), \cdots, \Gamma_l(t_3^{i,k}) + \Gamma_d(t_3^{i,k})) \le \Gamma_l(t_3^i) \quad \Gamma_l(t_3^i) + \Gamma_d(t_3^i) \le \Gamma_l(t_2^i) + \Gamma_d(t_2^i)$$

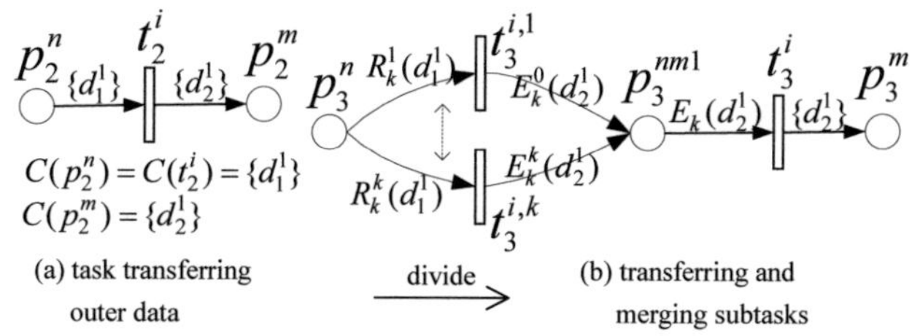

Fig. 4.7. Division result of task transferring outer data

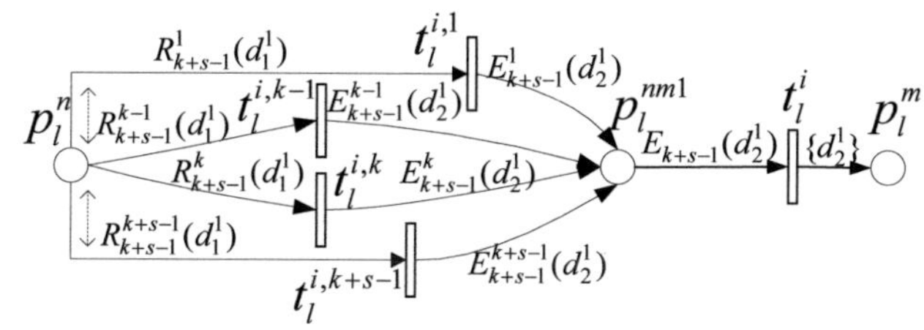

Fig. 4.8. Structure change of subtask net when subtasks transferring outer data become abnormal

When a subtask becomes abnormal because the data resources it uses are out of service or their performances decrease, this subtask needs to be reallocated in order to ensure it can be accomplished on time. The reallocation can lead to the structure change of the subtask net. The detail is shown as Fig.4-8. The number of subtasks that the abnormal subtask is divided into is s. The division accords with these conditions:

$$\sum_{r=1}^{k+s-1} Q_r(t_l^{i,r}) + Q_r(t_l^i) \le Q_m(t_2^i)$$

$$\exists h(1 \le h \le (k+s-1) \wedge \Gamma_b(t_l^{i,h}) \le \Gamma_l(t_2^i))$$

$$\forall h(1 \le h \le (k+s-1) \rightarrow \Gamma_b(t_l^{i,h}) \ge \Gamma_b(t_2^i))$$

$$\Gamma_l(t_3^i) \le \max(\Gamma_l(t_l^{i,1}) + \Gamma_d(t_l^{i,1}), \cdots, \Gamma_l(t_l^{i,k}) + \Gamma_d(t_l^{i,k})) \le \Gamma_l(t_3^i) \qquad \Gamma_l(t_3^i) + \Gamma_d(t_3^i) \le \Gamma_l(t_2^i) + \Gamma_d(t_2^i)$$

2. tasks transferring inner data

Inner data is produced by computing subtasks and it has no replicas. Therefore, a task transferring inner data has only one subtask. When its resource is out of service, the task fails because there are no other resources to use. Its division result is shown as Fig.4-9.

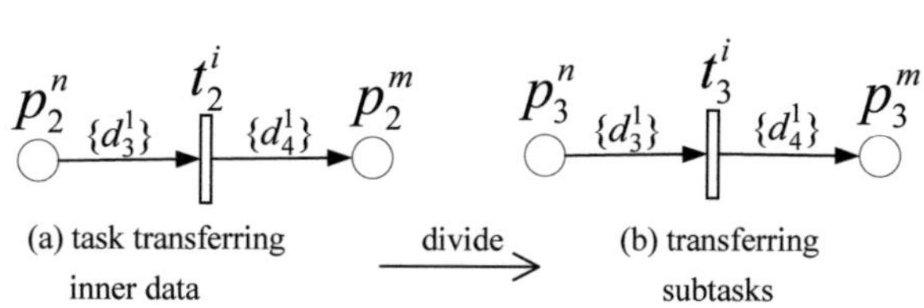

Fig. 4.9. Division result of task transferring inner data

3. parallel computing tasks

There are two kinds of parallel computing tasks: tasks whose data inputs can be divided and tasks whose data inputs can not be divided. According to the number of computing resources and QoS requirements, the former can be divided into many subtasks that only compute parts of the input data. Because these subtasks run on different nodes, the input data needs to be transferred into local node firstly. The detailed process is shown as Fig.4-10. t_2^i is a parallel computing task. $t_3^{i,r,h}(1 \le r \le s, 1 \le h \le k)$ are the transferring subtasks running in parallel. $t_3^{i,r}(1 \le r \le s)$ are the computing subtasks running in parallel. t_3^i is a merging subtask. The division accords with these conditions:

$$\sum_{r=1}^{s} Q_r(t_3^{i,r}) + \sum_{r=1}^{s}\sum_{h=1}^{k} Q_r(t_3^{i,r,h}) + Q_r(t_3^i) \le Q_m(t_2^i)$$

$$\exists h,u(1 \le h \le s \wedge 1 \le u \le k \wedge \Gamma_b(t_3^{i,h,u}) \le \Gamma_l(t_2^i))$$

$$\forall h,u(1 \le h \le s \wedge 1 \le u \le k \rightarrow \Gamma_b(t_3^{i,h,u}) \ge \Gamma_b(t_2^i))$$

$$\Gamma_b(t_3^i) \le \max(\Gamma_l(t_3^{i,1}) + \Gamma_d(t_3^{i,1}), \cdots, \Gamma_l(t_3^{i,s}) + \Gamma_d(t_3^{i,s})) \le \Gamma_l(t_3^i)$$

$$\Gamma_l(t_3^i) + \Gamma_d(t_3^i) \le \Gamma_l(t_2^i) + \Gamma_d(t_2^i)$$

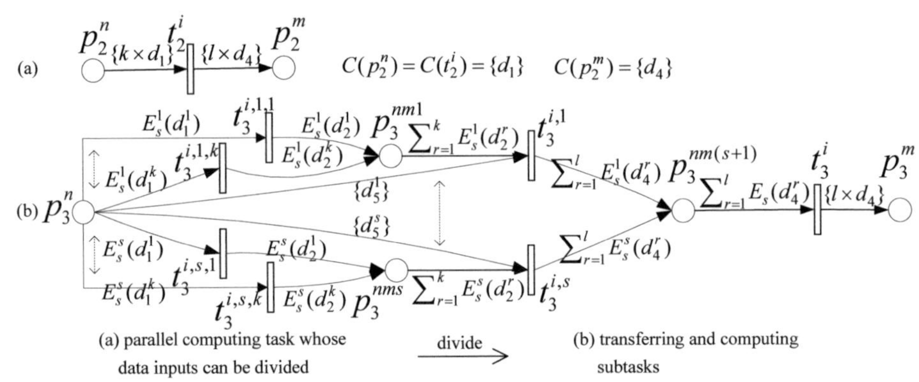

Fig. 4.10. Division result of parallel computing task whose data inputs can be divided

When one subtask of a parallel computing task becomes abnormal because the computing resource it uses is out of service or its performance decreases, this subtask needs to be reallocated in order to ensure it can be accomplished on time. The reallocation can lead to the structure change of the subtask net. The detail is shown as Fig.4-11. s is the number of subtasks that the abnormal subtask is divided into according to the number of computing resources and QoS requirements. The division accords with these conditions:

$$\sum_{r=1}^{v+s-1}\sum_{h=1}^{k} Q_r(t_z^{i,r,h}) + \sum_{r=1}^{s+v-1} Q_r(t_z^{i,r}) + Q_r(t_z^i) \le Q_m(t_2^i)$$

$$\exists h,u(1 \le h \le (s+v-1) \wedge 1 \le u \le k \wedge \Gamma_b(t_z^{i,h,u}) \le \Gamma_l(t_2^i))$$

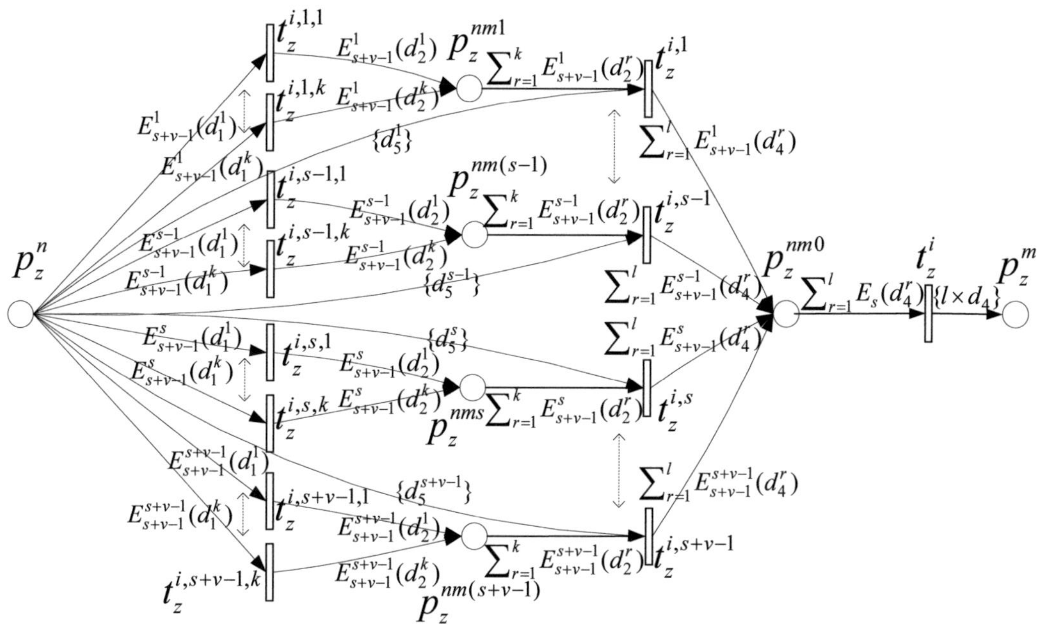

Fig. 4.11. Structure change of the subtask net when parallel computing subtasks become abnormal

$$\exists h,u(1 \le h \le (s+v-1) \wedge 1 \le u \le k \wedge \Gamma_b(t_z^{i,h,u}) \ge \Gamma_b(t_2^i))$$

$$\forall h(1 \le h \le (s+v-1) \rightarrow \Gamma_b(t_z^{i,h}) \le \max(\Gamma_l(t_z^{i,h,1}) + \Gamma_d(t_z^{i,h,1}),\cdots,\Gamma_l(t_z^{i,h,k}) + \Gamma_d(t_z^{i,h,k})) \le \Gamma_l(t_z^{i,h}))$$

$$\Gamma_b(t_z^i) \le \max(\Gamma_l(t_z^{i,1}) + \Gamma_d(t_z^{i,1}),\cdots,\Gamma_l(t_z^{i,s}) + \Gamma_d(t_z^{i,s})) \le \Gamma_l(t_z^i)$$

$$\Gamma_l(t_z^i) + \Gamma_d(t_z^i) \le \Gamma_l(t_2^i) + \Gamma_d(t_2^i)$$

The division of a parallel computing task whose data inputs can not be divided is similar to a task whose data inputs can be divided. The difference between them is that the input data of transferring subtask is the data or parts of it.

4. computing tasks that cannot run in parallel

A computing task that can not run in parallel only has a subtask and Fig.4-12 shows the division result.

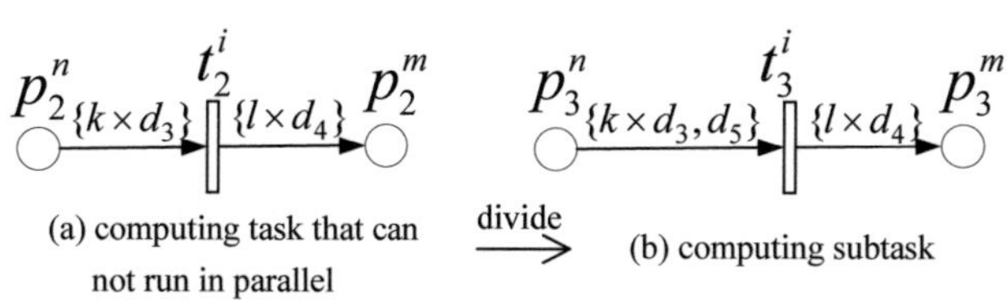

Fig. 4.12. Division result of computing task that can not run in parallel

Within an unparallel computing task, when a subtask becomes abnormal because the computing resource it uses is out of service or its performance decreases, this subtask needs to be reallocated in order to ensure it can be accomplished on time. For unparallel computing tasks, the reallocation can not lead to the structure change of the subtask net, but it can result in the states change. The detail is shown as Fig.4-13. Because the computing node is replaced, the data needs to be transferred to a new computing node. t_z^i is the new computing subtask and $t_z^{i,r}(1 \le r \le k)$ denotes transferring subtasks. The change accords with these conditions:

$$\sum_{r=1}^{k} Q_r(t_z^{i,r}) + Q_r(t_z^i) \le Q_m(t_2^i)$$

$$\exists h(1 \le h \le k \wedge \Gamma_b(t_3^{i,h}) \le \Gamma_l(t_2^i))$$

$$\forall h(1 \le h \le k \rightarrow \Gamma_b(t_3^{i,h}) \ge \Gamma_b(t_2^i))$$

$$\Gamma_b(t_z^i) \le \max(\Gamma_l(t_z^{i,1}) + \Gamma_d(t_z^{i,1}), \cdots, \Gamma_l(t_z^{i,k}) + \Gamma_d(t_z^{i,k})) \le \Gamma_l(t_z^i)$$

$$\Gamma_l(t_z^i) + \Gamma_d(t_z^i) \le \Gamma_l(t_2^i) + \Gamma_d(t_2^i)$$

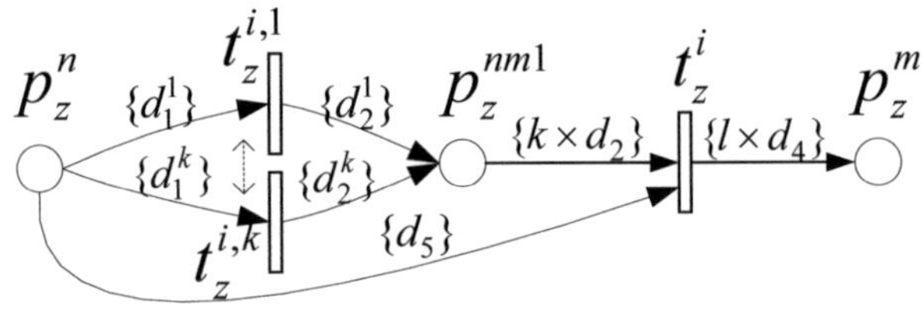

Fig. 4.13. Structure change of subtask net when computing subtasks that can not run in parallel become abnormal

5. Analysis and optimization

In this section, we adjust the structure of subtask net firstly in order to optimize the process of subtasks. Then, we analyze the validity of the scheduling net and the job net. Finally, we analyze the performance of the job net.

5.1 Structure optimization

In order to keep the consistency of the model and make the process of structure change clear and intuitive, we divide parallel computing tasks in standard way. However, this way results in redundant data transfer within a subjob and this part of subtask net need to be optimized further.

Suppose the number of remote data inputs in a computing subjob t_1^i is k. t_1^i has remote data inputs $\{d_1^r \mid 1 \le r \le k\}$ and a computing task t_2^i whose subtasks are $t_3^{i,r}(1 \le r \le s)$. h_a^b is the number of replicas of number b data that number a subtask uses. Within a subjob, the optimization result is shown as Fig.5-1. Compared with the former, the total number of reduced transitions is k, the saved money is $\sum_{r=1}^{k} Q_r(t_2^{i,r})$ and the reduced time is $\max(\Gamma_d(t_2^{i,1}),\cdots,\Gamma_d(t_2^{i,k}))$.

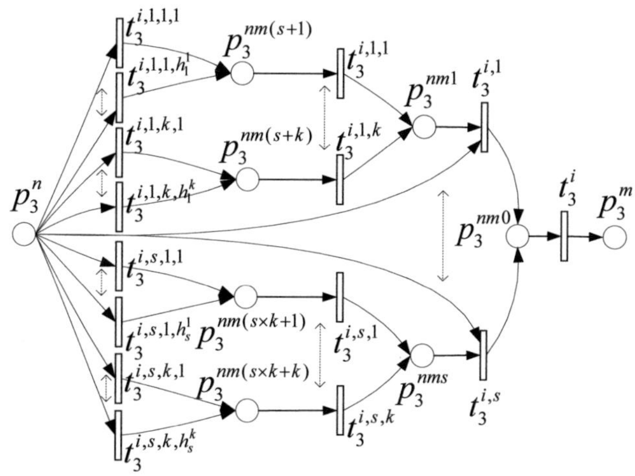

Fig. 5.1. Structure optimization of parallel computing subtasks

5.2 Validity analysis

Validity analysis is necessary for a model based on Petri Net to ensure the success of model in practice. For the scheduling net, we analyze its structure to verify its correctness. For the job net, besides structure analysis we also need to analyze its time reachability to validate that the time limits of transitions are reasonable.

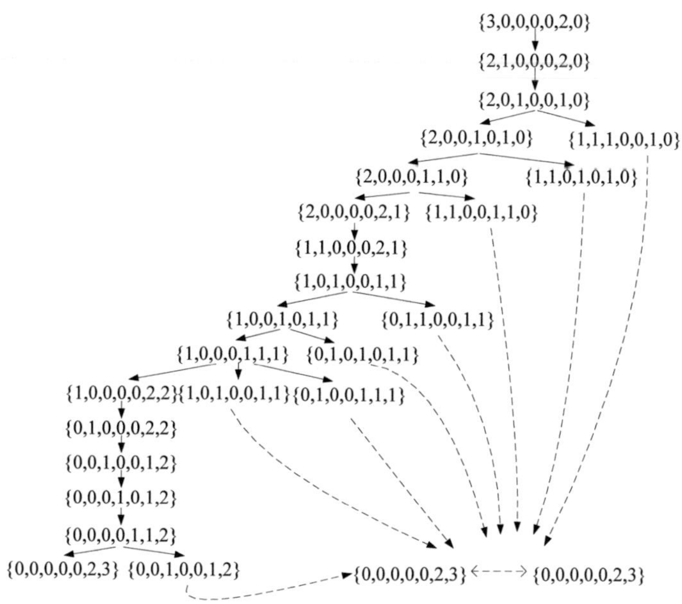

Fig. 5.2. A sample of reachability trees

The top level of scheduling net is a job scheduling net, which consists of circular structures and cannot stop without outside force. The end place and other places in the job scheduling net can have tokens at the same time. The maximal number of jobs that the job scheduling net can schedule simultaneously is $K(p_3)$ and these jobs are classified by the net according to their states.

The three lower levels of the scheduling net are workflow nets, which are driven by the job scheduling net and only schedule one subjob, one task or one subtask at the same time. The job net is also a workflow net and its validity [16] is described as follows:

1. For each state M reachable from state i, there exists a firing sequence leading from state M to state o.
2. State o is the only state reachable from state i with at least one token in place o.
3. There are no dead transitions in net.

The main work in structure analysis is reachability analysis. We can build reachability trees [17, 18] for the scheduling net and the job net to validate their reachability and three conditions above. There are too many reachability trees, so we only list a sample of them here. Fig.5-2 shows a sample of reachability tree built according to a job scheduling net, which has 3 jobs in the beginning and the maximal number of running jobs that scheduler can deal with simultaneity is 2. Therefore, $M_0=\{3,0,0,0,0,2,0\}$ and the end state is $\{0,0,0,0,0,2,3\}$. For a job scheduling net with $M_0=\{m,0,0,0,0,n,0\}$, its reachability tree is similar to Fig.4-15. The root of this tree is $\{m,0,0,0,0,n,0\}$ and all leaves are $\{0,0,0,0,0,n,m\}$. The number of tokens in the tree satisfies these conditions:

$$|C(p_1)_{ms}|+|C(p_2)_{ms}|+|C(p_3)_{ms}|+|C(p_4)_{ms}|+|C(p_5)_{ms}|+|C(p_7)_{ms}|=m$$

$$|C(p_6)_{ms}|+|C(p_3)_{ms}|+|C(p_4)_{ms}|+|C(p_5)_{ms}|=n$$

$$0\le|C(p_2)_{ms}|,\ |C(p_4)_{ms}|,|C(p_5)_{ms}|\le 1$$

$$|C(p_3)_{ms}|,\ |C(p_6)_{ms}|\le n$$

Time reachability is that the time requirements of transitions are satisfied within time limitations. After analyzing the validity of structure, we can validate the time reachability easily. In the job net, if $\forall t\in T(\forall t'\in {}^{\otimes\otimes}t\to\Gamma_l(t')+\Gamma_d(t')\le\Gamma_l(t)+\Gamma_d(t))$, the time reachability of the net is satisfied. Otherwise, the time reachability is not satisfied.

Validity analysis is necessary for a model based on Petri Net to ensure the success of model in practice. For the scheduling net, we analyze its structure to verify its correctness. For the job net, besides structure analysis we also need to analyze its time reachability to validate that the time limits of transitions are reasonable.

The top level of scheduling net is a job scheduling net, which consists of circular structures and cannot stop without outside force. The end place and other places in the job scheduling net can have tokens at the same time. The maximal number of jobs that the job scheduling net can schedule simultaneously is $K(p_3)$ and these jobs are classified by the net according to their states.

The three lower levels of the scheduling net are workflow nets, which are driven by the job scheduling net and only schedule one subjob, one task or one subtask at the same time. The job net is also a workflow net and its validity [16] is described as follows:

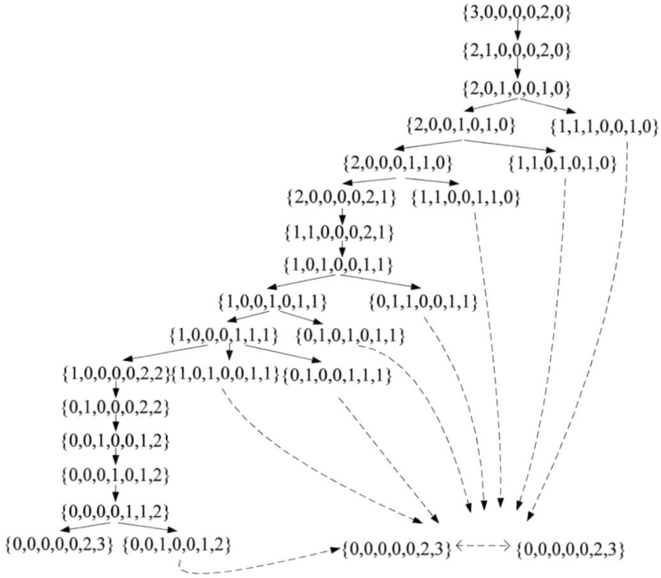

Fig. 5.3. A sample of reachability trees

1. For each state M reachable from state i, there exists a firing sequence leading from state M to state o.
2. State o is the only state reachable from state i with at least one token in place o.
3. There are no dead transitions in net.

The main work in structure analysis is reachability analysis. We can build reachability trees [17, 18] for the scheduling net and the job net to validate their reachability and three conditions above. There are too many reachability trees, so we only list a sample of them here. Fig.4-15 shows a sample of reachability tree built according to a job scheduling net, which has 3 jobs in the beginning and the maximal number of running jobs that scheduler can deal with simultaneity is 2. Therefore, M_0={3,0,0,0,0,2,0} and the end state is {0,0,0,0,0,2,3}. For a job scheduling net with M_0={m,0,0,0,0,n,0} , its reachability tree is similar to Fig.5-3. The root of this tree is {m,0,0,0,0,n,0} and all leaves are {0,0,0,0,0,n,m}. The number of tokens in the tree satisfies these conditions:

$$|C(p_1)_{ms}|+|C(p_2)_{ms}|+|C(p_3)_{ms}|+|C(p_4)_{ms}|+|C(p_5)_{ms}|+|C(p_7)_{ms}|=m$$

$$|C(p_6)_{ms}|+|C(p_3)_{ms}|+|C(p_4)_{ms}|+|C(p_5)_{ms}|=n$$

$$0\le|C(p_2)_{ms}|,\ |C(p_4)_{ms}|,|C(p_5)_{ms}|\le 1$$

$$|C(p_3)_{ms}|,\ |C(p_6)_{ms}|\le n$$

Time reachability is that the time requirements of transitions are satisfied within time limitations. After analyzing the validity of structure, we can validate the time reachability easily. In the job net, if $\forall t\in T(\forall t'\in {}^{\otimes\otimes}t\rightarrow \Gamma_l(t')+\Gamma_d(t')\le\Gamma_l(t)+\Gamma_d(t))$, the time reachability of the net is satisfied. Otherwise, the time reachability is not satisfied.

5.3 Validity analysis

Performance analysis mainly analyzes the time and cost characteristics of a job net. The total cost of a job net is the cost sum of all transitions in the net: $\sum Q_r(t)$. If $\sum Q_r(t) = Q_r(t_0^1) \le Q_m(t_0^1)$, the cost allocation succeeds, otherwise the cost allocation fails and the job net can not run correctly.

In order to be convenient to analyze time characteristics of a job net, we propose a transition tree algorithm that translates the transitions in a job net into a transition tree. The conversion rules are shown as follows:

1. The root of a transition tree is t_{root} whose time limits and cost are 0;
2. p_{begin} is the beginning place in the job net and all transitions in $p_{begin}^{\otimes}$ are the leaves of t_{root}.
3. For each leaf t, find $t^{\otimes\otimes}$ and all transitions in $t^{\otimes\otimes}$ are the leaves of t;
4. repeat step 3 until each leaf t satisfies the condition: $t^{\otimes\otimes} = \varnothing$.
5. The tree with root t_{root} is the corresponding transition tree of the job net.

According to the transition tree, it is convenient to analyze the time characteristics of the job net and optimize the allocation process for subtasks.

The maximum number of serial transitions is $D_T - 1$, where D_T is the depth of the transition tree.

To reduce the waiting time of transitions, for each transition $t({}^{\otimes\otimes}t = \{t_i \mid 1 \le i \le k\})$ in a job net, let $\Gamma_l(t) = \Gamma_b(t) = \max(\Gamma_l(t_1) + \Gamma_d(t_1), \cdots, \Gamma_l(t_k) + \Gamma_d(t_k))$.

Suppose there are s leaves $\{t'_r \mid 1 \le r \le s\}$ in a transition tree and each leaf has a path from it to root : $p(t'_i) = \{t_i^r \mid 1 \le r \le l_i\}$,where l_i is the number of transitions in $p(t'_i)$. Each path has a total time of transitions: $\Gamma(t'_i) = \sum_{r=1}^{l_i} \Gamma_d(t_i^r)$, the total durable time of the net is $\Gamma(t'_r)$, $\Gamma(t'_r) = \max(\Gamma(t'_1), \cdots, \Gamma(t'_k))$. The corresponding path of t'_r is the key path and l_r is the number of transitions on the key path.

The key path decides the total durable time of a job net and it is important for subtask allocation optimization. For each subtask, we should choose those resources with high performance. All computing subtask on the key path can run on the same node and this can reduce the data transferring time.

6. Conclusions and future work

This paper proposes two different models for the scheduling net and the job net based on the idea that the scheduling net is separated from the job net. This method makes models compact and intuitional. In addition, the separation benefits the analysis of the job net and the scheduling net respectively. According to the granularity of parallel applications, the scheduling net is designed to four levels, which is convenient to deploy distributed schedulers in parallel environment and is beneficial to the management of different parallel application granularities. Based on Petri Net with changeable structure, the job net model can change its structure dynamically according to the allocation results or states of jobs. Therefore, the model supports dynamic mergence and division of subtasks and can deal with the abnormity of subtasks. We validate the scheduling net and the job net using

reachability tree technologies. In addition, a transition tree algorithm is designed for analyzing the performances of the job net and optimizing the allocations of subtasks according to the key path in the job net.
In the future, we will optimize these models further and put emphasis upon researching algorithms used for optimizing resource allocations.

7. References

[1] M. Alt, S. Gorlatch, A. Hoheisel, H. W. Pohl, "Using High-Level Petri Nets for Hierarchical Grid Workflows," presented at Second IEEE International Conference on e-Science and Grid Computing, Amsterdam, The Netherlands 2006, pp. 13-13.
[2] M. Silva,L. Recalde, "Petri nets and integrality relaxations: A view of continuous Petri net models," *IEEE Transactions on Systems, Man and Cybernetics, Part C: Applications and Reviews*, vol. 32, pp. 314-327, 2002 (4).
[3] H. Yaojun,L. Xuemei, "Modeling and Performance Analysis of Grid Task Scheduling Based on Composition and Reduction of Petri Nets," 2006, pp. 331-334.
[4] S. Distefano, A. Puliafito, M. Scarpa, "GridSPN: a grid-based non Markovian Petri nets tool," presented at IEEE International Workshops on Enabling Technologies: Infrastructure for Collaborative Enterprise, 2005, pp. 331-336.
[5] X. Jiefeng, W. Zhaohui, C. Huajun, "Distributed Petri Net for Knowledge Base Grid reasoning," presented at IEEE International Conference on Systems, Man and Cybernetics, Hangzhou, China, 2003, pp. 593-597 vol.1.
[6] J. Yu, R. Buyya, C. K. Tham, "QoS-based Scheduling of Workflow Applications on Service Grids," presented at Proceedings of the 1st IEEE International Conference on e-Science and Grid Computing Melbourne, Australia, 2005.
[7] J. Yu,R. Buyya, "A Taxonomy of Scientific Workflow Systems for Grid Computing," *Special Issue on Scientific Workflows, SIGMOD Record*, vol. 34, pp. 44-49, 2005 (3).
[8] J. Yu,R. Buyya, "A Budget Constrained Scheduling of Workflow Applications on Utility Grids using Genetic Algorithms," presented at Workshop on Workflows in Support of Large-Scale Science, Proceedings of the 15th IEEE International Symposium on High Performance Distributed Computing Paris, France, 2006.
[9] BPEL4WS, "http://www.ebpml.org/bpel4ws.htm,"
[10] J. Hai,W. Shuzhen, "Grid workflow model based on colored Petri net," *J . Huazhong Univ. of Sci. & Tech. (Nature Science Edition)*, vol. 34, pp. 39-41, 2006 (7).
[11] Z. Hu, R. Hu, W. Gui, J. Chen, "General scheduling framework in computational Grid based on Petri net " *Journal of Central South University of Technology*, vol. 12, pp. 232-237, 2005
[12] H. Yaojun, J. Changjun, L. Xuemei, "Resource scheduling model for grid computing based on sharing synthesis of Petri net," 2005, pp. 367-372 Vol. 1.
[13] M. Dobber, R. van der Mei, G. Koole, "Effective Prediction of Job Processing Times in a Large-Scale Grid Environment," presented at 15th IEEE International Symposium on High Performance Distributed Computing, 2006, pp. 359-360.
[14] Z. Yuanyuan, S. Wei, Y. Inoguchi, "Predicting Running Time of Grid Tasks based on CPU Load Predictions," presented at 7th IEEE/ACM International Conference on Grid Computing, Barcelona, Spain, 2006, pp. 286-292.

[15] C. Jinjun,Y. Yun, "Assigning Local Fixed-time Constraints in Grid Workflow Systems," presented at Fifth International Conference on Grid and Cooperative Computing Workshops. WSGE '06. , Changsha, China, 2006, pp. 227-234.
[16] Z. Liang, "Research on Workflow Patterns based on Petri nets," presented at 2006 IEEE Conference on Robotics, Automation and Mechatronics, Bangkok, 2006, pp. 1-6.
[17] J. Mu Der,P. Mao Yu, "Augmented reachability trees for 1-place-unbounded generalized Petri nets," *IEEE Transactions on Systems, Man and Cybernetics, Part A*, vol. 29, pp. 173-183, 1999 (2).
[18] Y. Ru, W. Wu, C. N. Hadjicostis, "Comments on "A Modified Reachability Tree Approach to Analysis of Unbounded Petri Nets"," *IEEE Transactions on Systems, Man and Cybernetics, Part B*, vol. 36, pp. 1210-1210, 2006 (5).

10

Petri Nets Hierarchical Modelling Framework of Active Products' Community

Ahmed Zouinkhi[1,2], Eddy Bajic[1],
Eric Rondeau[1] and Mohamed Naceur Abdelkrim[2]
[1]Research Center for Automatic Control - CRAN - CNRS UMR 7039, Henri Poincaré University, Nancy, BP 239, 54506 Vandoeuvre-les-Nancy,
[2]Unit of research MACS (Modelling, Analysis and Control of Systems) National school of engineers of Gabes, Street Omar Ibn Elkhattab,Zrig–Gabes 6029,
[1]France
[2]Tunisia

1. Introduction

Nowadays in industrial process area it is necessary to manage in real time all informations related to the interactions between resources, products, processes and operators along the process zone. Amongst the main constraints and objectives in industrial processes is the security issue. Especially, in industrial environment workers have to deal with unavoidable threats from products, resources and machines that are parts of work risks. Currently, many security systems depend on safety measurements that are token by interacting devices eventually exposing people lives to unpredictable situation as an example in storage and transport activities of hazardous chemical substances.

Our research approach to study such fully distributed and discrete industrial environment is based on communicating object's concept which represents a physical product equipped with perception, communication, actuation and decision making capabilities. Products and resources when upgraded so to communicate with objects then become active products that are communicating with each others. So to cope with such a complete active products' community we propose to define a Petri nets hierarchical modelling framework in order to analyse and to solve cooperation and communication functionalities of active products.

The communicating object's approach has attracted the interest of several research projects as COBIS project (Collaborative Business Items) (CoBIs, 2008) that has developed a new approach to business processes involving physical entities such as goods and tools in enterprise. The intention is to embed business logic in the physical entities. Also, the computing department at Lancaster University (Strohbach et al., 2005) conceived cooperative products with perception, analysis and communication capacities that operate by information sharing principle.

Also, (Quanz et al., 2008) is considering the problem of Object Safety: how objects endowed with processing, communicating, and sensing capabilities can determine their safety. He assigned an agent to each object capable of looking out for its own self interests, while concurrently collaborating with its neighbours and learning / reinforcing its beliefs from them. Each product is represented by "an object safety agent", it deals with information from environmental sensors, in a known situation. When the agent detects a threat, it seeks confirmation from its neighbours.

Mainly focused on a security purpose but although extensible to other process management issue, our work involves transforming products with dangerous nature into communicating entities assuming the surveillance of its environment while collecting information from its surrounding. The aim of this work is to propose a Petri nets hierarchical modelling framework with internal cooperation model of active products by using the High Level Petri Nets (HLPN) formalism. Conceptual modelling was validated by the simulation software CPN-Tools from Aarhus University (Ratzer et al., 2003).

Our paper is organized as follows: after the introduction, the second part presents the concept of the active product for the security management. The third part presents the communication between active products. Modeling by Petri nets will be illustrated on section 4. Finally the last part will expose the Petri Nets modelling of a cooperation of active products. Future research developments will be discussed in the conclusion.

2. Active product

The concept of active product consists in endowing a product with the capacities of communicating, informing, acquiring, deciding and reacting to the stimulus and disruptions of its environment in order to allow the product to adjust, to influence, to cooperate, and to transform the behavior of its environment. The product is thus an intelligent and proactive actor in its ambient environment with which it interacts by means of wireless communication and its embarked sensors which allow the data entry of its environment (Zouinkhi et al., 2009).

This concept is shown in our application by integrating a sensor platform in every chemical container with a hazardous substance, therefore, upgrading it with interaction capacities in the middle of its action environment. If two active products are in the same proximity, they communicate through messages sent by radio frequency waves (See figure 1). So, an active product can communicate with the manager and the operator in the same way.

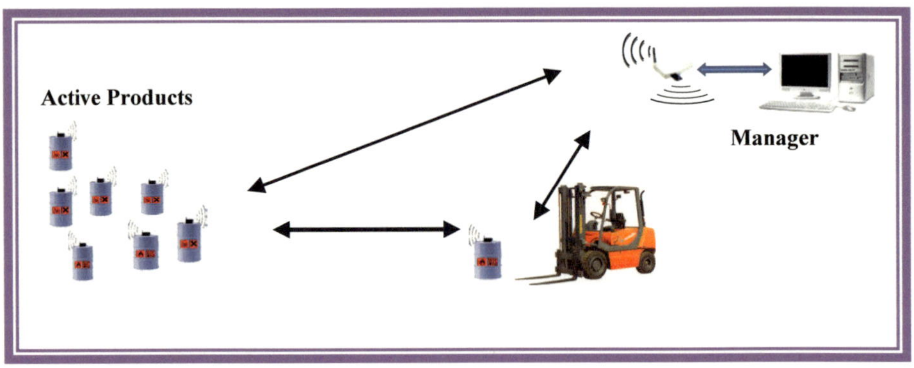

Fig. 1. Active Security management system

To insure a good security monitoring, three safety levels were established from Good to Dangerous (B: Good, M: Average and D: Dangerous). Determining security levels results after applying security rules (logical and analytical) we have designed which are divided into three categories: (Zouinkhi et al., 2009)

- **Static Rules**: engage the product alone in its environment, this product measures some values defining its safety level (such as temperature, humidity, shock, luminosity ... these can be used e.g. for fire detection) in order to keep itself in a stable sane state, these values should not exceed certain min or/and max limits.

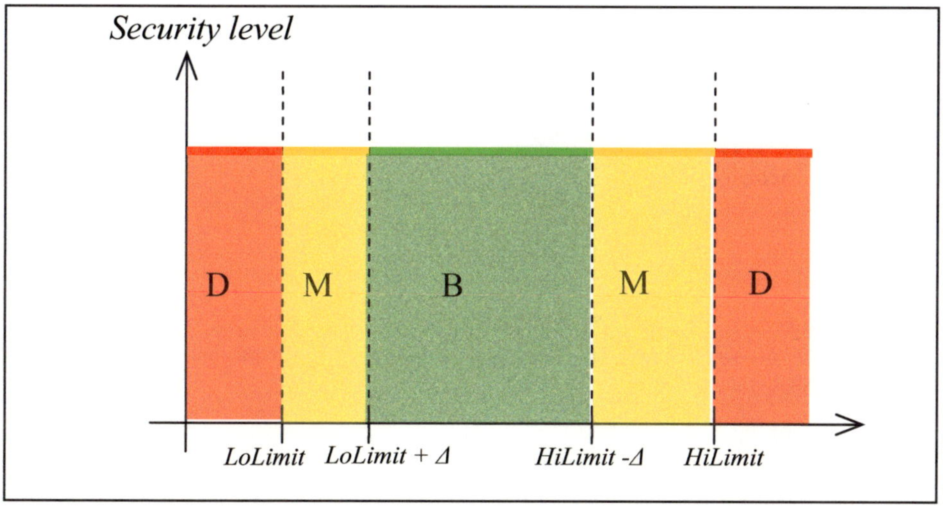

Fig. 2. Static rules

- **Dynamic rules:** these are rules related to the product by itself considering its state evolution through time. For example some product could not be affected if they reach a certain temperature threshold but the fact of reaching it several times in a period of time can bring the product in an alarming state.

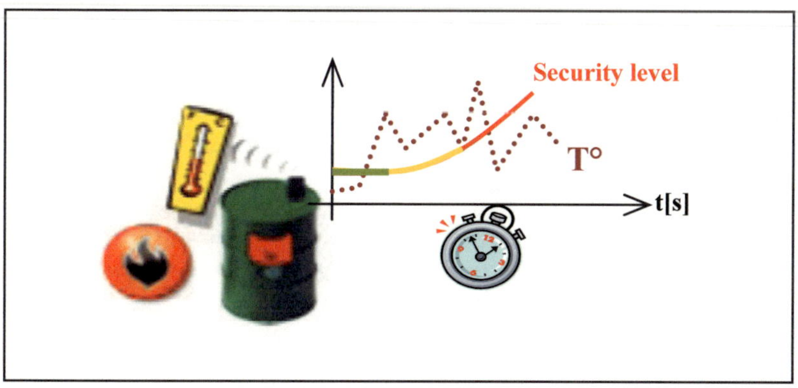

Fig. 3. Dynamic rules

- **Community rules:** depending on compatibility constraints with other products. Incompatibility is established from the security symbols and also from risk and safety phrases according to the European directives 67/548/EEC concerning chemical interaction. Also manipulation of product may require an operator with a specific fitness and aptitude; consequently, a product needs a well determined operator quality.

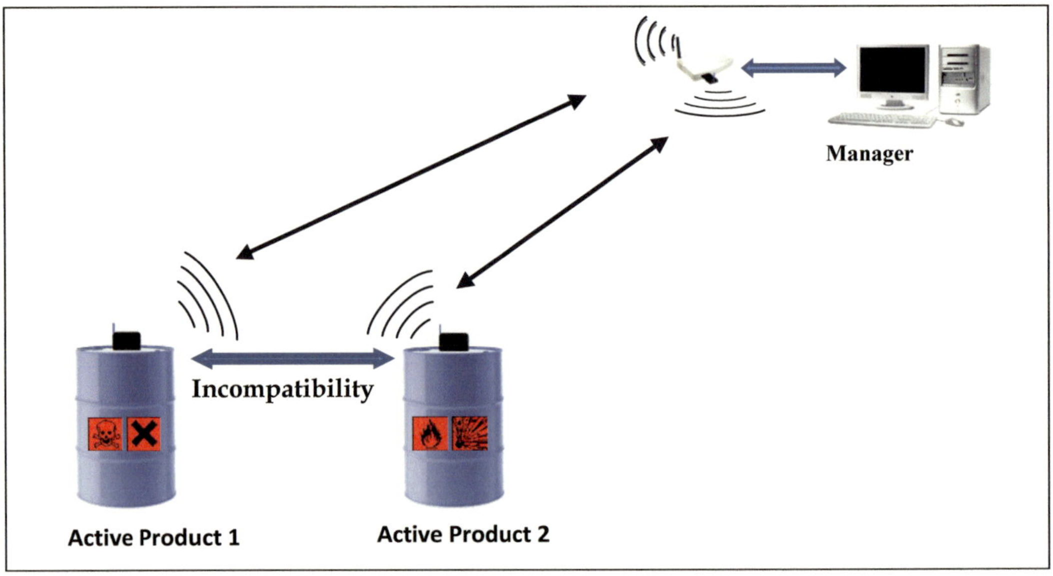

Fig. 4. Community rules

Our works promote a cooperation mechanism that integrates two approaches later centralized administration and decentralized cooperation between active products by the exchange of messages. Active products work together and exchange real-time information about the environment and the security level by a product that can manage asset's safety and security of its environment.

3. Communication between active products

Communication between products works by using several types of messages which are sent by a broadcasting mode and are classified according to their role that are intended to perform.

Product's announcement in the products' community has a great importance for the overall security management. For this, we propose two types of messages:

CTR (Control Timestamp Request): message which declares to the manager the arrival of a new product.

AckCTR: the acknowledgement message from the manager.

After the registration of the product which needs a setup configuration to allow it to interact within the community. This configuration concerns the type of product regarding its hazardous classification (safety symbols) and its static, dynamic and community related rules as well. When a product was not configured, a it announces its status with three types of messages.

NCF0: Product has no hazardous classification and no security rules configuration.

NCF1: Product has only hazardous classification configuration.

NCF2: Product has only security rules configuration.

Then the system manager answers by an appropriate product configuration command message respectively:

CMD1: Configuration of the product classification.

CMD3: Configuration of the security rules.

Once the product is correctly configured; it becomes completely capable of surveying its neighbourhood: it is now an effective Active Product.
Any environment modification or event that break individual or mutual security rules must be detected by products diagnosed and has to generate external actions allowing to recover the normal safety level by actions or directed information of the ambient environment. These interactions are made by means of the following messages:
GRE: Greeting Message carrying specific product information (name, safety symbols) and has a further role contributing to the calculation process of the distance separating two active products.
RSI: a message sent after the reception of a GRE message, indicates the APs Inter-distance value calculated with the power loss of received signal.
INA: this message carries the ambient sensors values embedded in the active product.
CFG: a message emitted by active product after an manager request, contains the specific configuration in the active product.
SER: a broadcast message containing the active product security rules values.
ALE: an alert message to report to the manager about a threat or a defective security state and can be sent as a rapp_D message if the state of active product is dangerous or rapp_M if the state is average.
The manager participates on the communication part by specific command messages.
CMD2: Manager requires the configuration of the active product through this message.
CMD4: Manager asks for Security rules Configurations.
CMD5: Manager asks for specific ambient information of active products.

4. Modeling by Petri Nets

The Petri nets are used for a long time as modeling tools of discrete events systems.
Petri Nets (PN) and particularly, Colored Petri Nets (CPN) (Jensen et al., 1997), are a powerful and a recognized modelling tool, endowed with a big expressiveness and allowing to represent the two aspects of system: static thanks to the PN structure and dynamic thanks to the token distribution evolution (Bouali and al., 2009).
Petri net (Murata, 1989) is an effective tool for modeling manufacturing systems. The advantages of applying Petri nets formalism are summarized as follows. First of all, the graphical nature of Petri nets can visualize sequences of firing via token passing over the net. Second, Petri nets have well-established formal mechanisms for modelling and analysis of manufacturing systems (Rudas et al., 1997) (Hsieh, 2004) (Zurawski, 2005). Third, the mathematical foundation of Petri nets can analyze structural and dynamic behaviours of a system. These advantages make Petri nets a suitable modelling and analysis tool.
(Song et al., 2008) define the Petri net as a tool modelling events that require a special synchronization as wireless sensor network. The system modelled is a safety system (evacuation) used in the mines of a coke which locates the positron of miners in an accident. The modelsation is devided into two phases: modeling of a particle (service and communication) and generalizing model to a large scale (performance evaluation and interaction between particles).
(Fu-Shiung, 2009) presents a concept of verification and resolution problem due to the mechanism of cooperation and interaction of Multiagent systems. These systems are often modeled by Petri nets and the approach consists in controling the vivacity of network, a character illustrating the efficiency of the interaction between particles.

(Khoukhi et al., 2010) notes that the classic Petri nets is unable to model uncertain systems what motivated the researchers to combine between the Petri nets and fuzzy logic to reach a Fuzzy Petri nets used in various application such as robotics and real-time control systems.
We choose High Level Petri Nets (HLPN) formalism to model the cooperation between active products. This model uses a generic and modular approach which requires the use of colouring and hierarchy.
Others authors used this formalism to model the Ethernet switch (Marsal, 2006). (Brahimi and al., 2008) are used HLPN formalism to propose an integrated modelling environment to represent globally the Networked Control Systems behaviour.
Hierarchical Coloured Petri Nets are used for modelling communication because Petri Nets are a formal method enabling to express parallelism, synchronisation, interaction, resource sharing, temporal (and stochastic) properties, and to achieve qualitative analysis (checking of the logic of the non temporal and/or temporal mechanisms) and quantitative analysis (performance evaluation and/or reliability). Then this formalism offers a framework well adapted and progressive for the representation and the analysis of the communication systems (Brahimi and al., 2008).

5. Model of cooperation between active products

The cooperation model has several components (P1, P2,...Pi, Manager) that communicate among themselves, within a wireless network. Each element is represented by a transition (hierarchical) which shows the services and the appropriate patches listed in detail in what follows.
As the figure 5, each element has two Capacities: "Net Input msg" and "Net Output msg" which are respectively output buffers of each product and the input.
These buffers have role in order to temporarily store messages received from network before being treated and those issued by products in the network.
The objective of our work is to represent the behaviour of the active product and the stream of messages through a wireless network in order to achieve cooperation interaction between products; we opted for colored Petri Nets models designed, validated with CPN-Tools software. CPN-Tools allow creating hierarchical models in order to simplify complex ones and divide it into other sub-models. What is meant here that in the hierarchical Petri net model certain transitions represent another Petri net sub-model.

5.1 Active products level

Figure 6 represents an internal model of an active product P1, in this structure the transitions hold a description of a functioning part of the product. The place "net Input msg P1" corresponds to the wireless communication network and collects messages emitted and received from all active products; let us note that the messages are sent in broadcasting mode. This characteristic is carried out by a transition which puts tokens in all the places corresponding to the various products. Messages intended for a specific active product will fire its own "net output msg P1" place. Circulating messages will be represented by colored tokens.
Each active product represents some internal and external tasks of which some conform the centralized approach however the others follow the approach of omnipresence, each transition in this network has a hierarchical structure described explicitly later.

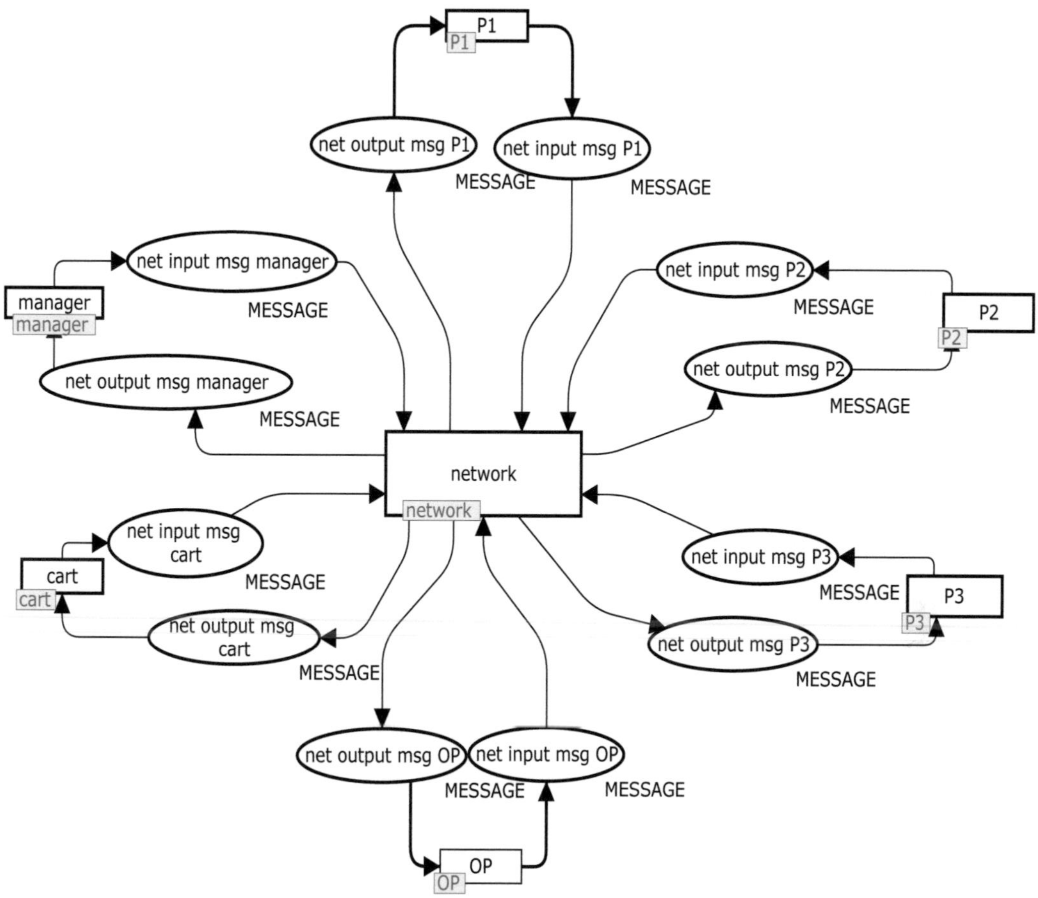

Fig. 5. Global cooperation model

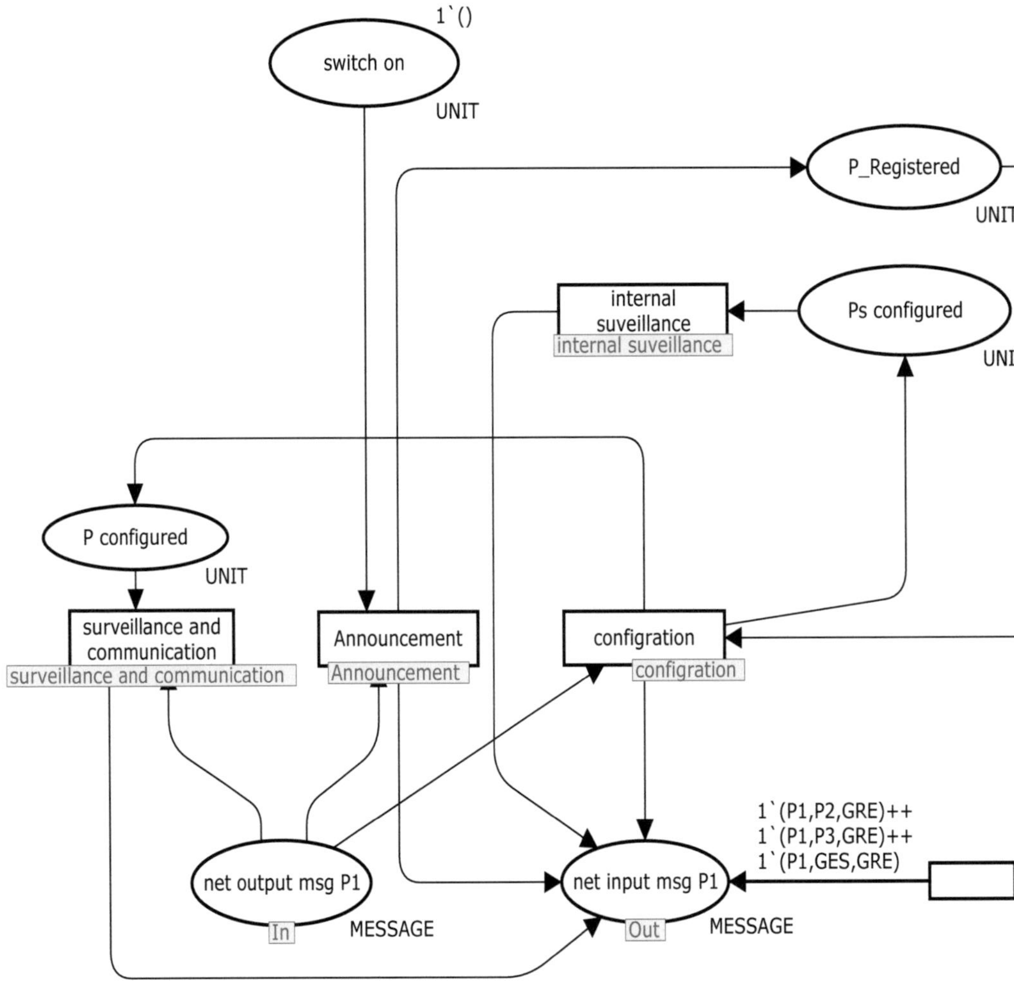

Fig. 6. Active product model

5.2 Product's dependence tasks

Two tasks represented of hierarchical transition: announcement (Figure 7) and configuration (Figure 8), illustrate the centralized approach where each product must refer to the manager initially to announce themselves (to enter in the network and to have an ID) and also to configure themselves (to ask the manager for the safety rules).

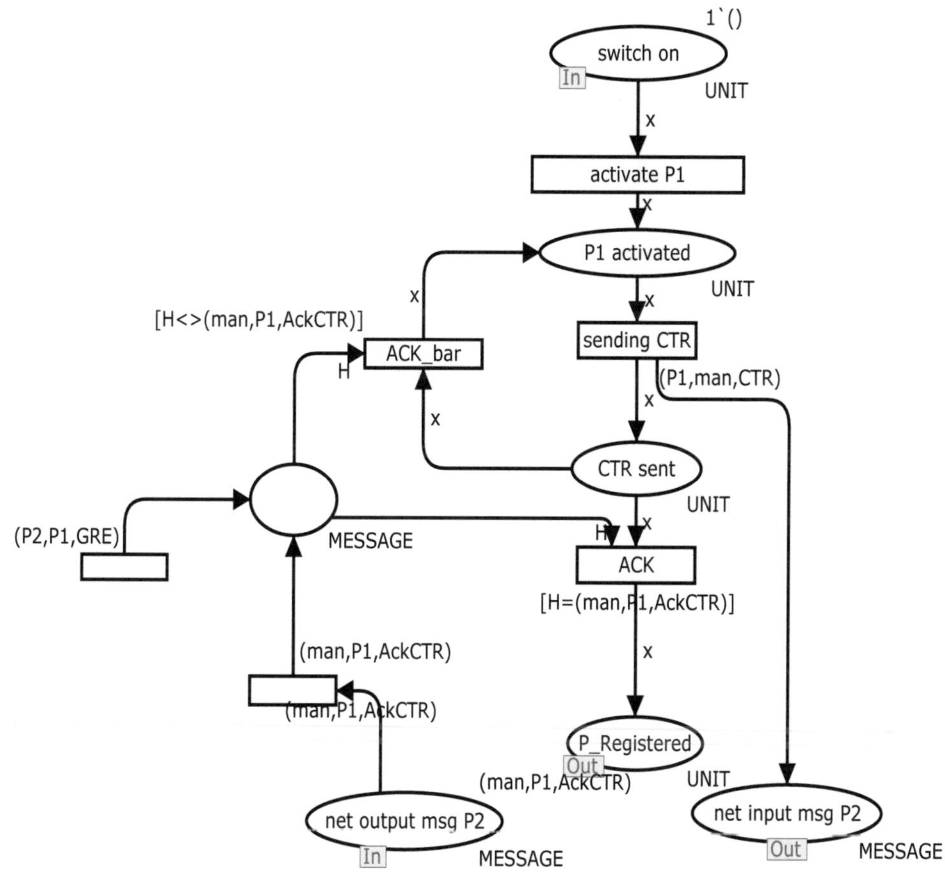

Fig. 7. Announcement model

Announcement is used to introduce a foreign product into the community of the other intelligent products. The need to launch out in this community requires announcement towards the manager so that this last detects it and adds it in its database which contains the products already existing.

The configuration's role is to provide to the intelligent product the necessary configurations enabling him to cooperate in the interaction with the community (the neighborhoods), each product must check that it has its safety rules (its ambient critical variable) as symbol of safety (which are the products that presents a threat to him).

And as shows in the figure ones announced the active product has to be configured by checking if it has a safety rules and safety symbols, in dead we have to notice 4 probable case: c_s (rules + symbols), c_ns (rules + messing symbols), nc_s (messing rules + symbols) and nc_ns (messing rule + massing symbols) so in each case the active product has to react in order to get messing feature from manager by sending a request for that. So we notice that we have a classification stage (c_s, c_ns, nc_s, nc_ns) to pick out in each case we are, ones classified and depending on the messing feature one token is going to be sent to the manager.

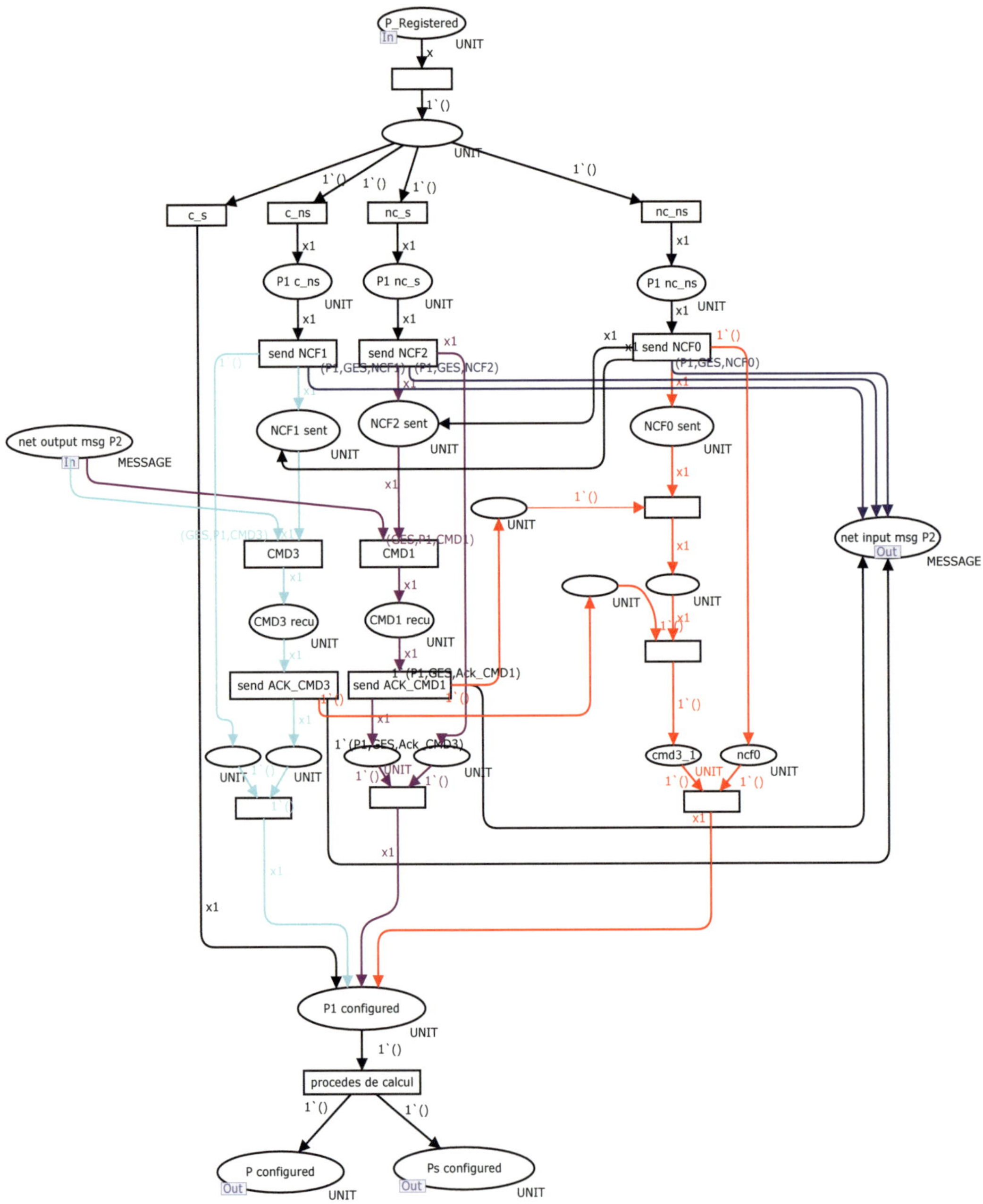

Fig. 8. Configuration model

5.3 Product's autonomic tasks

The two other hierarchical transitions represented in figure 6: surveillance and communication and internal surveillance, follow the distributed approach where each product is equipped with a decision capacity (autonomy) which illustrates the concept of reactivity.

The surveillance and communication model represented in figure 9, also illustrates the distributed intelligence by the concept of sociability.

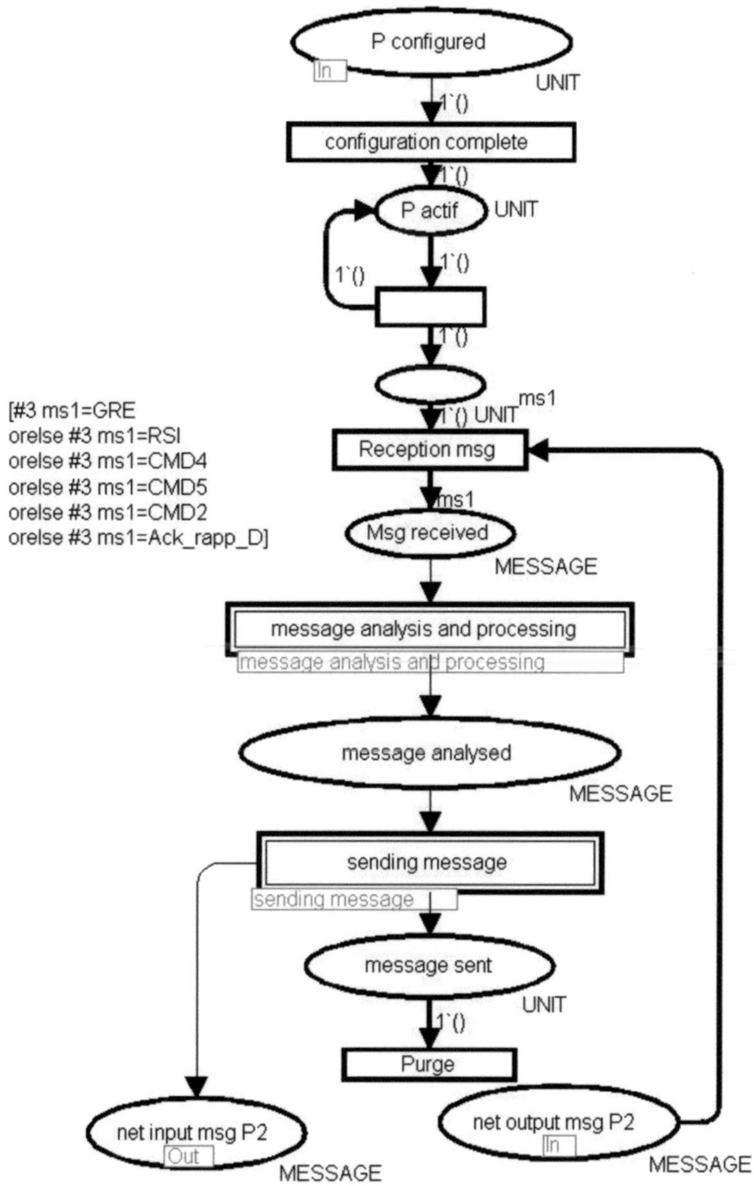

Fig. 9. Surveillance and communication model

In this model the accepted messages are CMD2, CMD4 and CMD5: received from manager (proactive concept) and RSSI messages: received from other products neighbourhood (sociability concept). RSSI Messages illustrate the collaboration between products: each time a product receives a GRE message and due to a module RSSI (Received Signal Strength Indicator) that product will estimate the distance that separates it from the sender product. This distance is compared to two values: L_inf and L_sup (received during the configuration). These messages are illustrated in figure 10. After the reception of these messages, a knowledge base serves for treating the different messages.

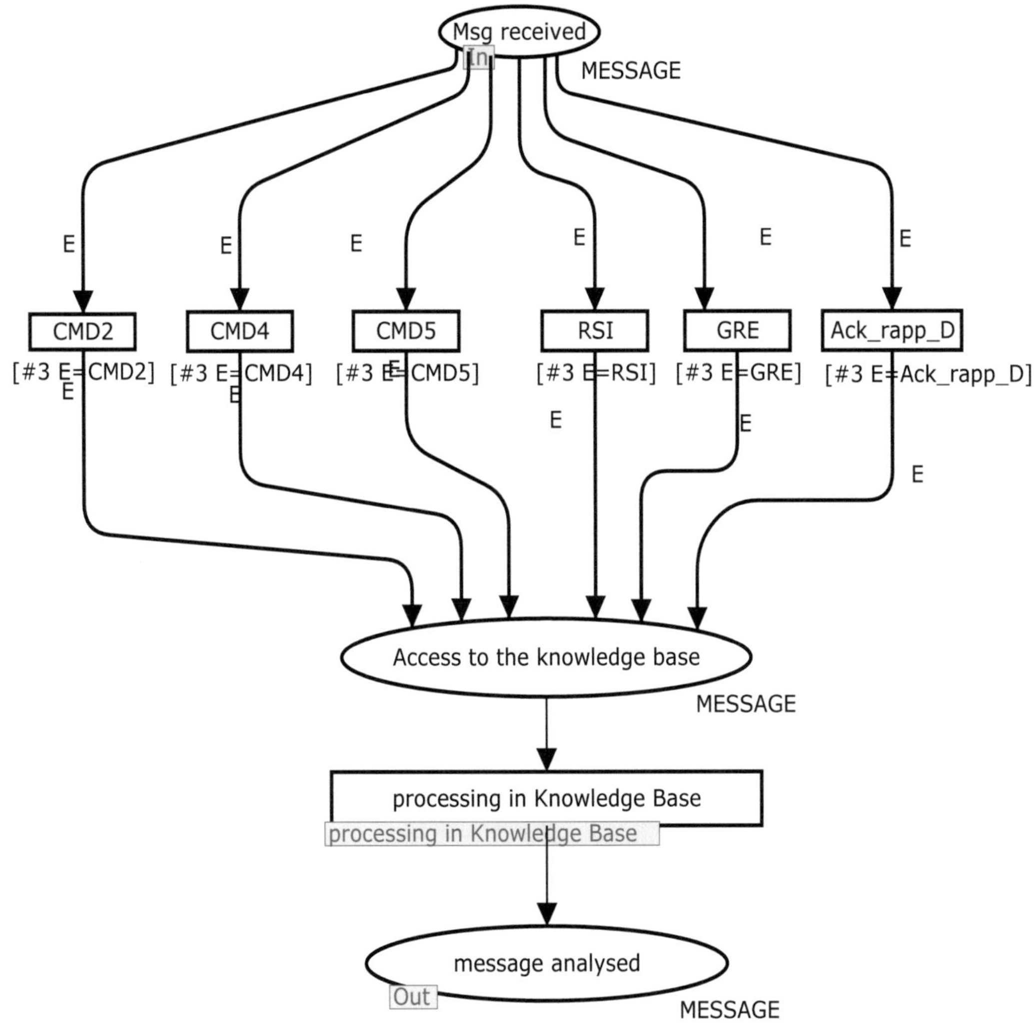

Fig. 10. Analysis and message processing model

The processing in knowledge base transition of the figure 10 represent a sub model that is represented by figure 11.

After the determination of the distance between incompatible products, three cases can be distinguished:

- If distance > L_supp: indicates that we have a comfort distance between the two products.
- If L_inf < distance < L_sup: indicates that the product is in bad condition which resulted in the sending of a message rapp_M (bad report).
- If D < L_inf: illustrates a state of danger because the distance between the two products are a critical distance where one has a risk of a dangerous chemical reaction, therefore a message rapp_D will be sent to the manager.

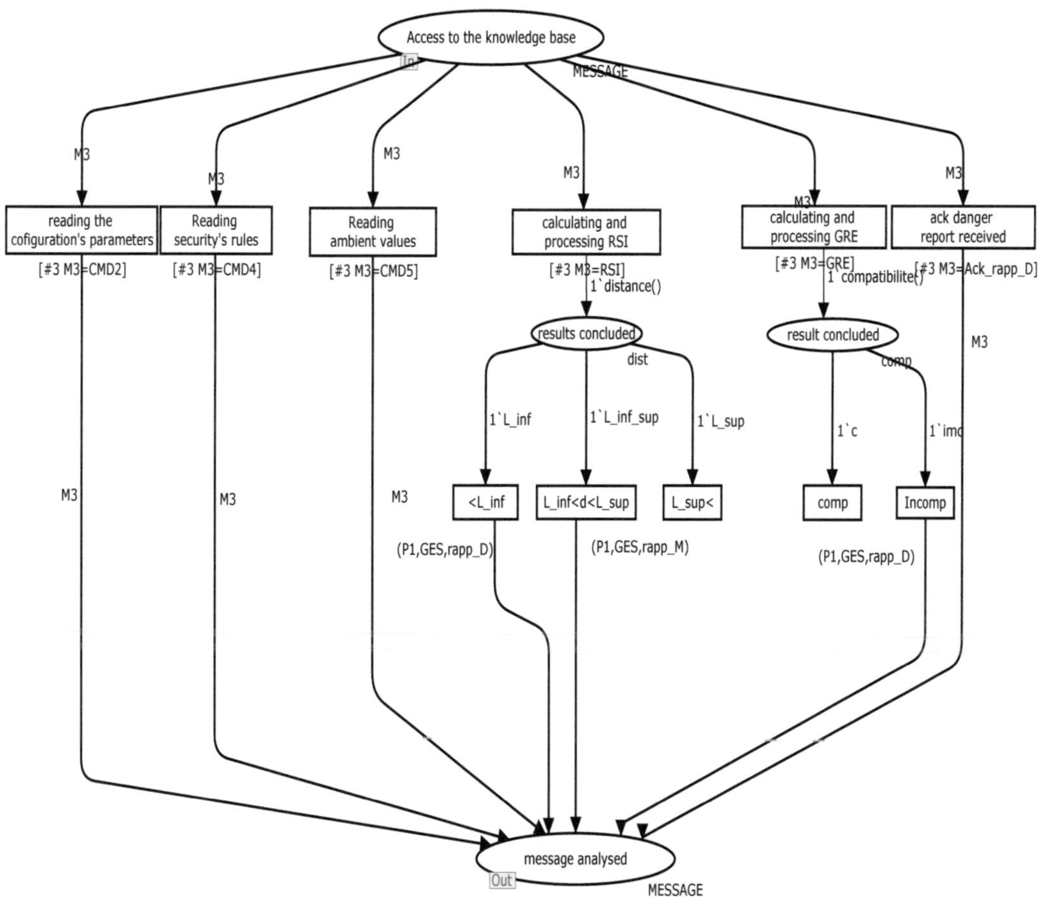

Fig. 11. Processing in knowledge base model

The sub model of sending message transition represented in figure 9 as follow; After analyzing the different messages received, the product reacts by sending a corresponding message;

- If the product receives a CMD2 message, it sends a CFG message.
- If the product receives a CMD4 message, it sends a SER message.
- If the product receives a CMD5 message, it sends an INA message.

If the product is in a danger state, a report will be sent to the manager and an alarm is activated until it receives an acknowledgment of the manager.

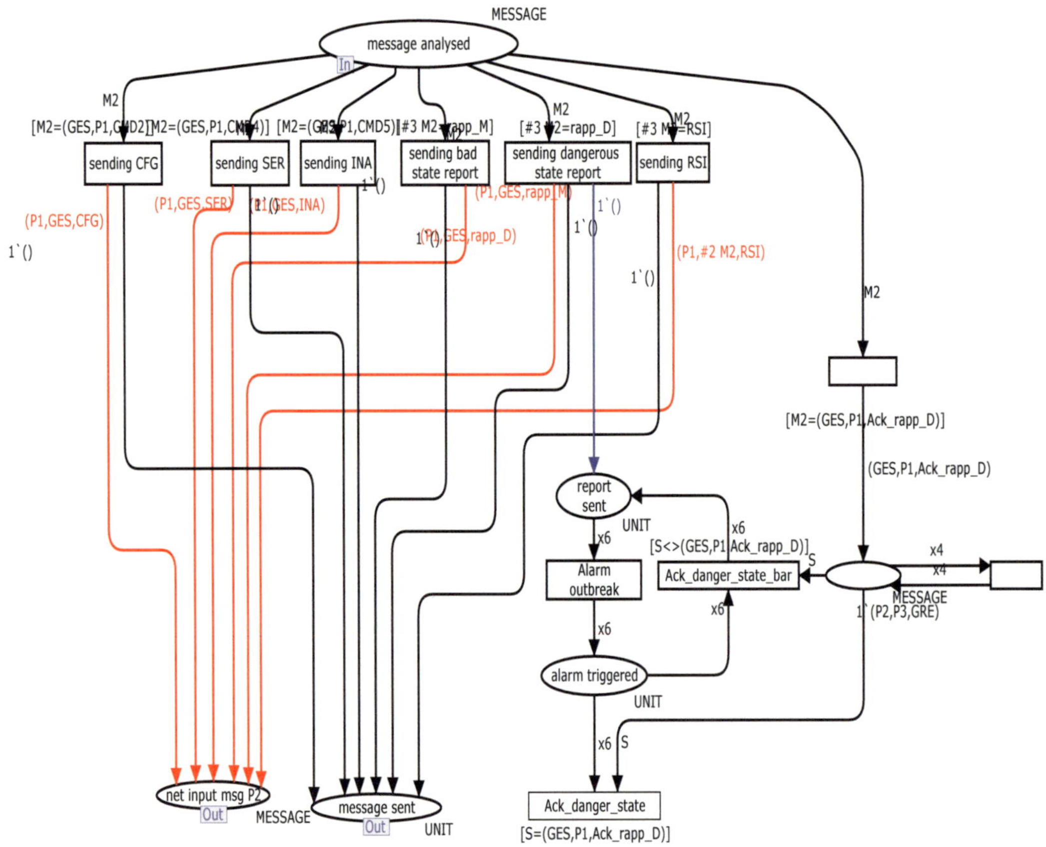

Fig. 12. Sending message in Surveillance and communication model

For the internal surveillance model represented in figure 13, each time, the product collects information from the sensors (temperature, light and moisture) and evaluates (for each variables) the safety level, so that, if a dangerous level is reached, the product sends a rapp_D message (dangerous report) to the manager to inform him that one of its sensor's variables reached a critical level (Zouinkhi et al., 2009).

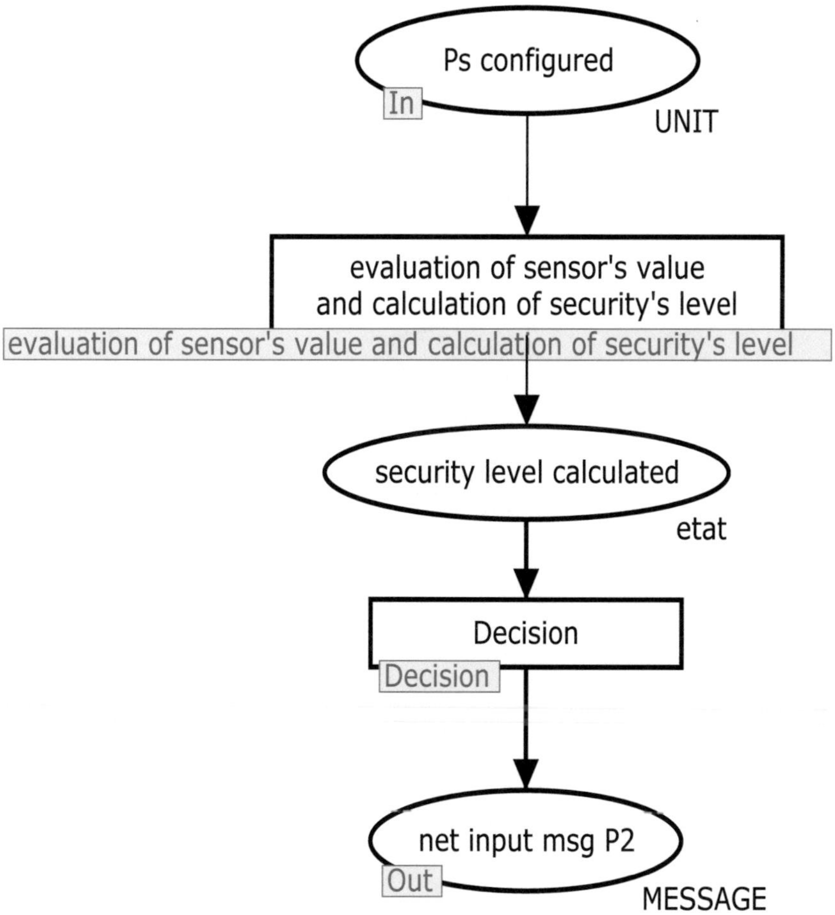

Fig. 13. Internal surveillance model

The decision transition can be represented by figure 14. After determining the security level, a state of the product is evaluated.

- If the state is average (bad), a GRE message is sent in broadcast in which the security level is indicated.
- If the state is dangerous, a rapp_M message is sent to the manager.

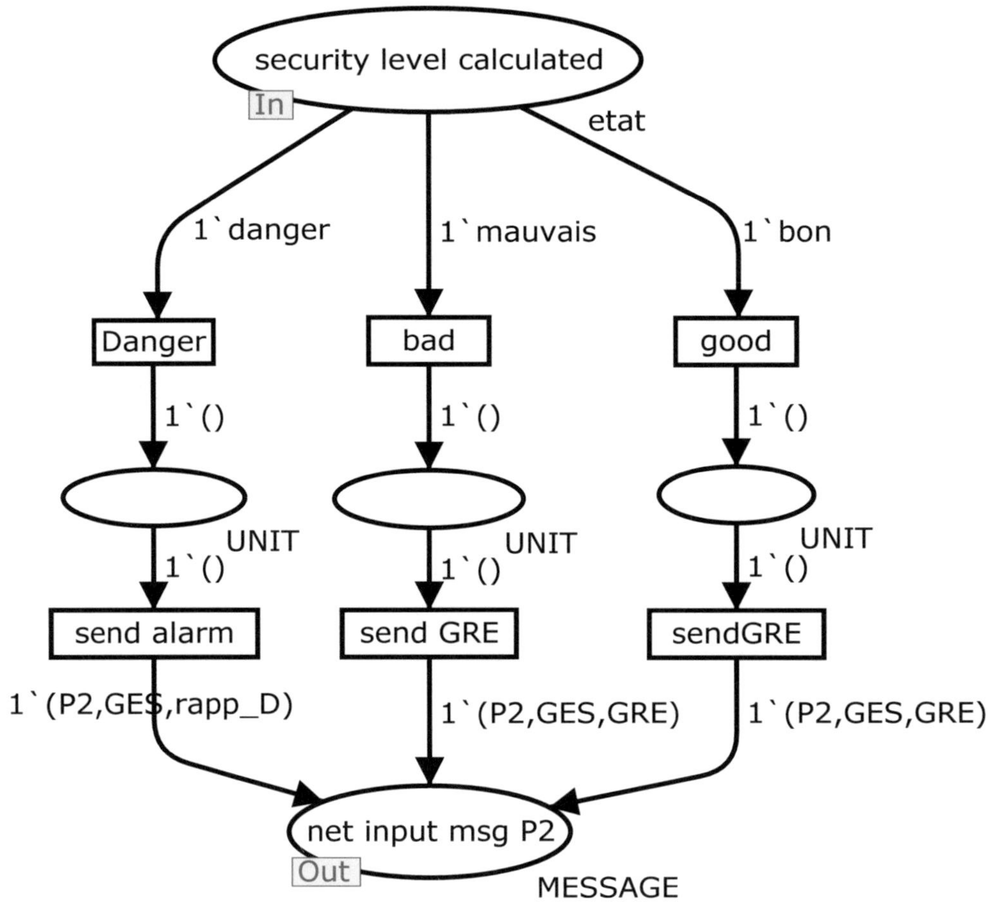

Fig. 14. Decision level in internal surveillance model

5.4 Manager model

The manager's model (Figure 15) can be subdivided in two parts according to the concept characterizing the product: reactif or pro-actif.

The manager's reactivity (Strobach et Al., 2005): when a token containing a message arrives to the entry's buffer of manager, this message passes by a stage of classification as the figure indicates it according to the nature of message (INA, CFG, LIKING, NCF0, NCF1, Ack_CMD1, NCF2, Ack_CMD3, CTR, RAPP_D, RAPP_M, NCFOP, CMP). According to each message received the manager must react either by updating his database or by sending messages to provide informations to the other products (safety rules, acknowledgment of the received reports…).

Pro-activity of manager (KASHIT et al., 2009): As figure 15 indicates it, the manager anticipates sometimes by asking randomly for the variable's information of product's environment by sending (CMD5, CMD4 and CMD2) to a hazardous chosen products.

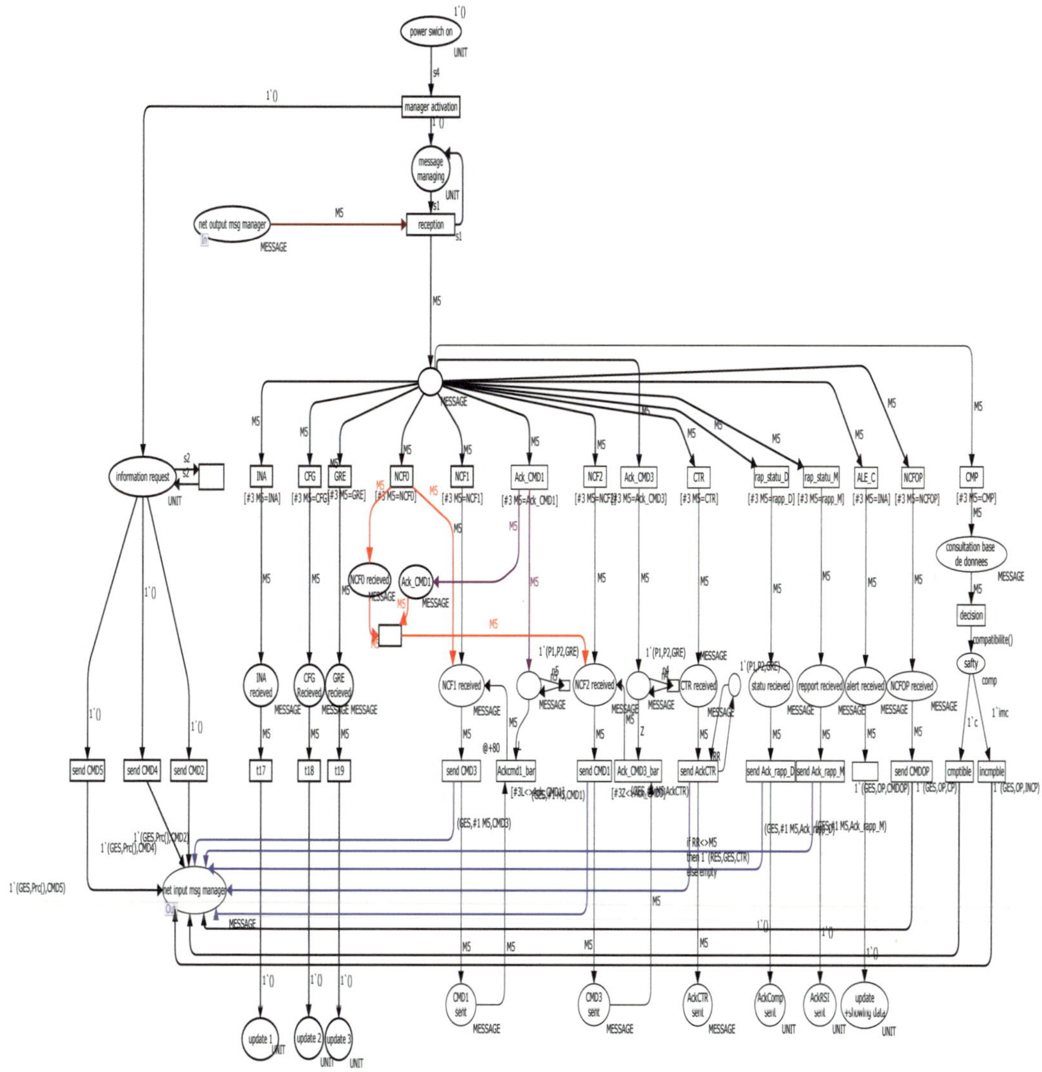

Fig. 15. Manager model

5.5 Network level

In this part, we will present the network's model where the sensor's products interact; firstly, we are going to model the hierarchical transition network which is represented by the figure 5 as a perfect network (without any disturbance) to evaluate the impact of progressive increasing of product's number existing in this network, and thereafter, we will create a disturbance in this network to check the robustness of allover the system.

5.5.1 Perfect network

The figure 16 indicates the lower level of the Network: the higher places Net input indicate the output's buffers of the product where the messages are stored before being emitted in the network; these messages pass by a classification's stage which classify them according to their transmitting products before being stored in the place "message sent through network". The network being perfect (without any disturbance), then all the messages will pass directly through the transition network (which is not simple transition) towards the buffers from exit of the network messages received thus, all the messages will be to reclassify again according to their destination before being emitted towards the entry's buffers of the products.

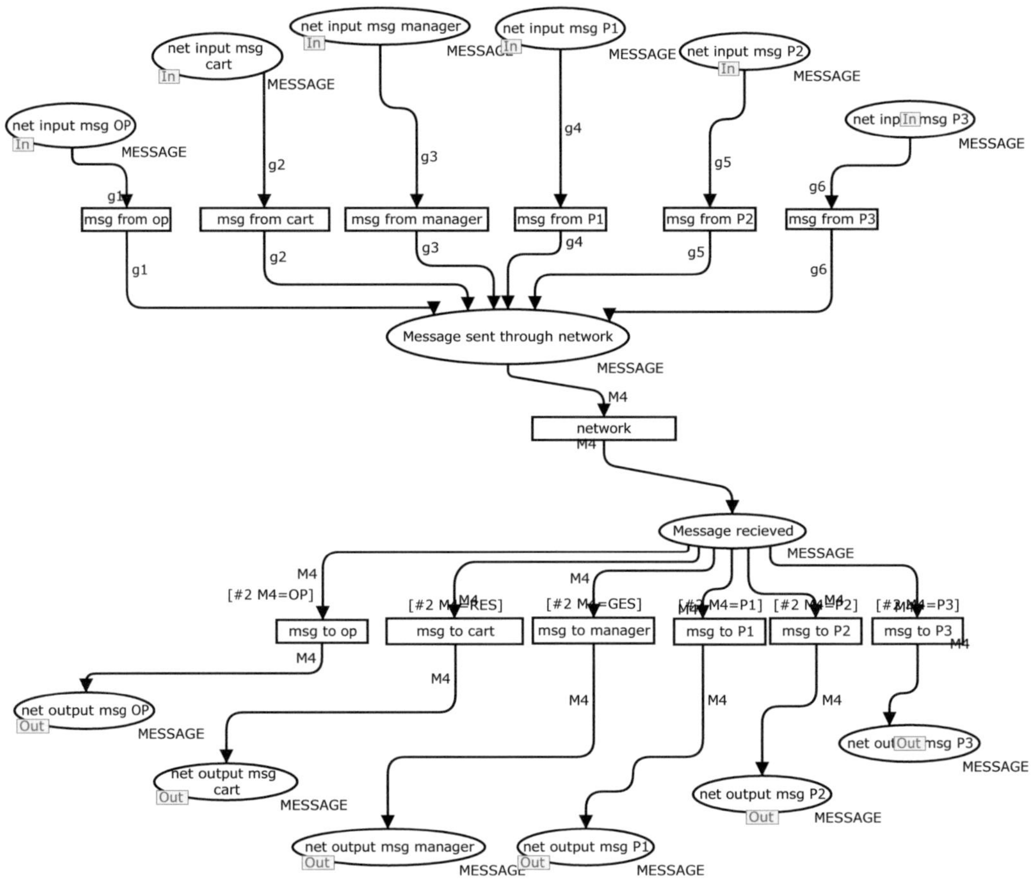

Fig. 16. Perfect Network model

5.5.2 Disturbed network

The network model presented on the figure 17 defines a disturbed network where there is a risk of loss of message. As figure indicates, each token (message), which is presented in the place (" message sent through network") of figure 16 must cross the transition where it will be to assign to another place, in this moment this token will be lost or passed, after this passage, this token enters a buffer of entry and afterwards enters a buffer of exit to be finally in the place " message received". This disturbance in network was presented by (Bitam et al., 2006) where they modeled a line of transmission with disturbance.

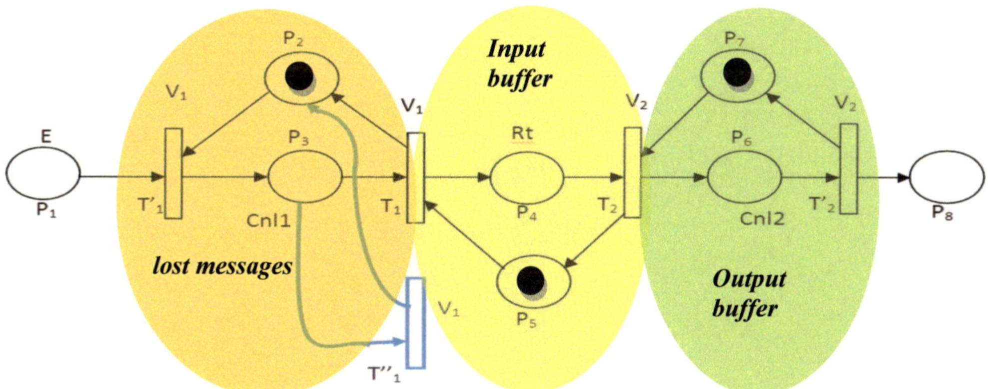

Fig. 17. Disturbed network model

This modeling of loss in a line of communication indicated in figure 17: when a message (token) is in place P_1 and another is in place P_2, the transition T'_1 may fire (is passable), So this message will go to the place P_3, at this moment there are two directions crossing T''_1 (this message will be lost) or passing of T_1 (the message will be issued) and after it passes to input buffer then that to output buffer (after crossing T_2). This phenomenon is explained as follows: at times the processing speed of an active product is much slower than receiving. So some messages will not get the chance to be treated by the active product of the limitation of the input place E.

The hierarchical model with different level is represented by figure 18. In this figure are shown different levels namely; Network level, product level, internal functions of an active product and message functions of an active product.

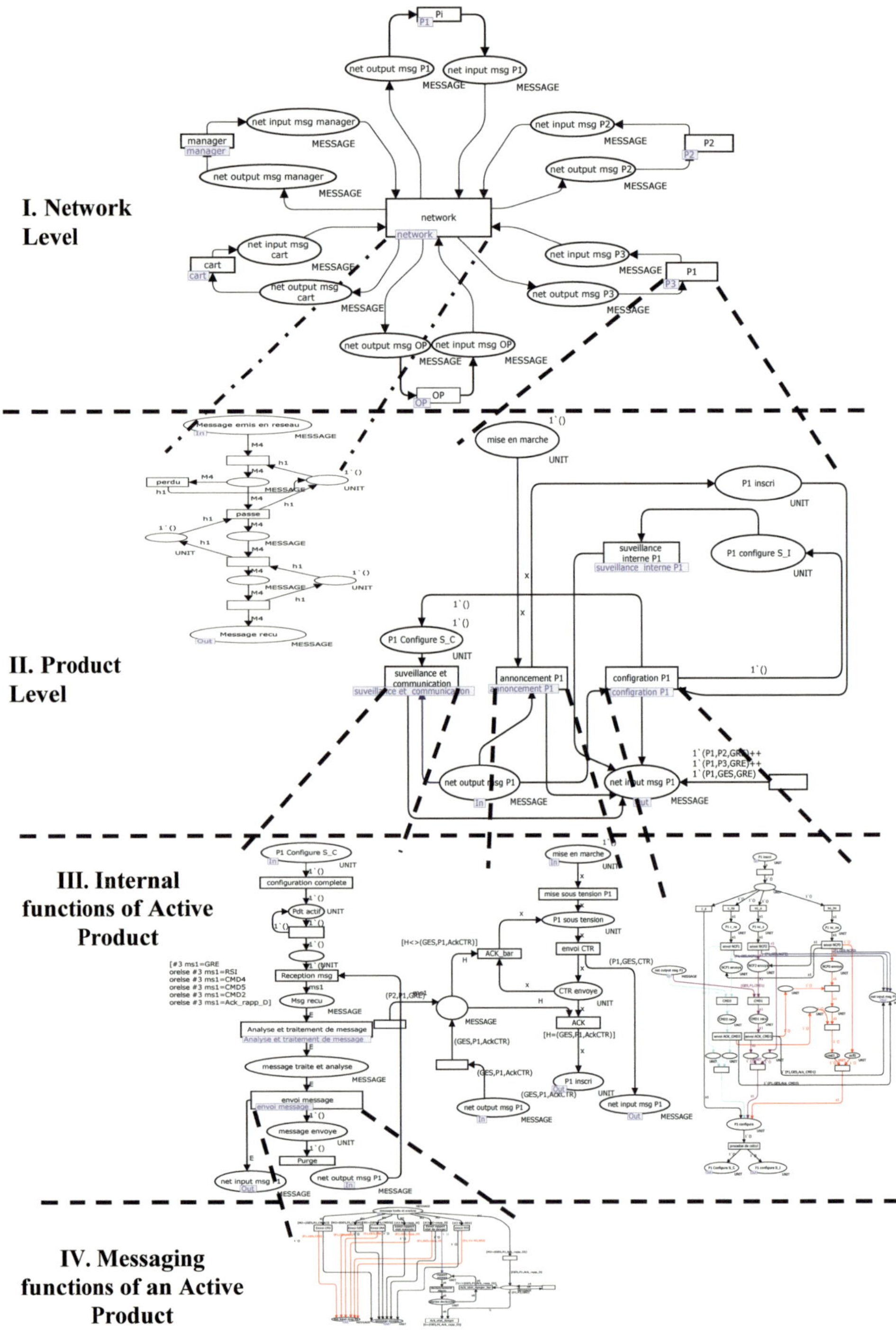

Fig. 18. Hierarchical models framework of an active product's community

6. Conclusion

In this work, we define the concept of an active security management in a distributed system, with Hierarchical Petri nets modelling of active product's behaviour. The target application is dedicated to security management of hazardous products but the concept is extensible to other application areas.

We proposed an active product's behaviour model represented by hierarchical coloured Petri nets. This hierarchy includes sub-models where each one allows displaying the evolution of every state of the active product (registration, configuration, surveillance and communication and internal surveillance). With Petri Nets, we have verified the consistency and non-blocking states of our model. Cooperation between active products is provided by exchange of messages in order to manage and control dynamically in real-time the global active security level. The proposed Active Product model will help in future steps of our work to study by large simulation the influence of the communication network on the system functioning (bounded time, messages loss, ...).

The proposed approach is very promising for the study and analysis of distributed system using the communicating object's approach or active product concept.

7. References

Bouali, M.; Barger, P. & Schon, W. (2009). Colored Petri Net inversion for Backward Reachability Analysis, In: Second IFAC Workshop on Depandable Control of Descrete Systems, Bari, Italy.

Brahimi, B. ; Rondeau, E. & Aubrun, C. (2008). Integrated Approach based on High Level Petri Nets for Evaluating Networked Control Systems, In: 16th Mediterranean Conference on Control an Automation, MED'08, Ajaccio, France.

CoBIs (2008). Collaborative business items. European Community FP6 STREP Project, IST 004270, Technical report.

Fu-Shiung, H. (2009). Developing cooperation mechanism for multi-agent systems with Petri nets. Engineering Applications of Artificial Intelligence vol. 22 (2009) pp. 616–627.

Hsieh, F.S.(2004). Fault tolerant deadlock avoidance algorithm for assembly processes, IEEE Transaction on System, Man and Cybernetics, Part A 34 (1), 65–79

Jensen, K. (992 à 1997). Colored petri nets - basic concepts, analysis methods and practical use. Basic Concepts, EATCS Monographs on Theoretical Computer Scienc. Springer-Verlag, Vol. 1 à 3, 1992 - 1997.

Kashif S.; Norsheila F.; Sharifah H.; Sharifah K. & Rozeha R. (2009). Autonomously Intelligent WSN Routing Protocol based on Ant Colony Optimization. In: Proceedings of 7th International Conference on Robotics, Vision, Signal Processing, & Power Applications (RoViSP 2009). Awana Porto Malai, Langkawi, Kedah, Malaysia.

Khoukhi, L. & Cherkaoui, S. (2010). Intelligent QoS management for multimedia services support in wireless mobile ad hoc networks. Journal of Computer Networks, Elsevier Edition.

Marsal, G. (2006). Evaluation of time performances of Ethernet-based Automation system by simulation of High Level Petri Nets, PhD dissertation de l'Ecole Normale Supérieure de Cachan et de l'Université de Kaiserslautern, Décembre 2006.

Murata, T. (1989). Petri nets: properties, analysis and applications, Proceedings of the IEEE 77 (4), 541–580.

Quanz, B. & Tsatsoulis, C. (2008). Determining Object Safety using a Multiagent Collaborative System, Workshop at Second IEEE International Conference on Self-Adaptive and Self-Organizing Systems, Venice, Italy, October 20-24.

Ratzer, A.V.; Wells, L.; Larsen, H.M.; Laursen, M.; Qvortrup, J.F.; Stissing, M.S.; Westergaard, M.; Christensen, S. & Jensen, K. (2003). Cpn-tools for editing, simulating, and analysing coloured petri net. LNC, 2679, pages 450– 462.

Rudas, I.J. & Horvath, L. (1997). Modeling of manufacturing processes using a Petri net representation, Engineering Applications of Artificial Intelligence 10(3), 243–255.

Song, C., Qi-Wei, G., Qian-Ming, S. & Qian, Z. (2008). Modeling and performance analysis of wireless sensor network systems using Petri nets. The 23rd International Technical Conference on Circuits/Systems, Computers and Communications (ITC-CSCC 2008), July 6-9, 2008, Kaikyo Messe Shimonoseki, Shimonoseki City, Yamaguchi-Pref., Japan, pp 1689-1692

Strohbach, M.; Kortuem, G. & Gellersen, H. (2005). Cooperative artefacts-a framework for embedding knowledge in realworld objects. International Workshop on Smart Object Systems, UbiComp, pages 91–99, Tokyo, Japan.

Zouinkhi, A.; Bajic, E.; ZIDI, R.; Ben Gayed, M.; RONDEAU, E. & Abdelkrim, M.N. (2009). Petri Net Modeling of active products cooperation for active security management. Sixth IEEE International Multi-Conférence on System, Signals & Devices (SSD'09), Tunisia.

Zurawski, R. (2005). Petri net models, functional abstractions, and reduction techniques: applications to the design of automated manufacturing systems. IEEE Transactions on Industrial Electronics 52 (2), 595–609.

11

Assessment Method of Business Process Model of EKD

Sílvia Inês Dallavalle de Pádua[1] and Ricardo Yassushi Inamasu[2]
[1]*University of São Paulo- College of Economics, Business and Accounting at Ribeirão Preto – FEARP-USP- Brazil*
[2]*Embrapa - Brazilian Agricultural Research Corporation Brazil*

1. Introduction

The business processes are the fundamental building blocks for a successful organization. The information technology (IT), when directed to the management and improvement of business processes, has helped the organization to complete its enterprise vision and improve its competitive position. The needs of the business should be provided by information technology looking forward to achieve business goals as competition, competitiveness and strategies. Systems that do not meet the needs of the organization may impede the development of the business.

The organizational modeling, in this context, facilitates the comprehension of business environment and it is recognized as a valuable activity for the development information system in accordance to Nurcan and Barrios (2003) and Persson (2000). The process of organizational modeling should bring answers to these questions: why, what, who, which, when, where and how. For so many, there are several modeling techniques in the literature with a significant range of notations.

The approach that will be used in this work is the EKD - Enterprise Knowledge Development - a methodology that provides a systematic and controlled way to analyze, understand, develop and document an organization and its components, using the Organizational Modeling (Rolland et at, (2000), Bubenko et al. (1998) and Nurcan (1998)). The EKD also contributes to make a decision in modern organizations that are highly dependent on information technology (Nurcan and Barrios (2003) and Nurcan and Rolland (2003)). According to Bubenko et al. (1998), the types of submodels of EKD method are: Goals Model, Business rules model, Concepts Model, Business Process Model, Actors and Resources Model and Requirements and Technicians Components Model. This methodology is explained in detail by: Pádua et al (2004a), Dallavalle and Cazarini (2001), and Pádua (2001). The main problem of the approach of Organizational Modeling, including the EKD, is the lack of a more complex technical analysis. It has been discussed by several authors the problem of informal structure of organizational techniques and business processes models.

Among them, some can be mentioned: Dongen et al (2007); Lenz et al. (2005); Mevius and Oberw (2005); Padua et al. (2004b); Koubarakis and Plexousakis (2002); Junginger et al.

The paper was published in: Gest. Prod. vol.15 no.3 São Carlos Sept./Dec. 2008 in portuguese language

(2001); Jonkers et al. (2003); Dehnert (2003), Padua (2004); Padua et al. (2003), Padua et al. (2002) and Aalst (1999).

According to Padua (2004), the syntax and the semantics of the EKD business processes model are not well defined formally and rigorously. As a result, the EKD business processes model may be ambiguous and of difficult analysis mainly in more complex systems, not being possible to check the consistency and completeness of the model. The absence of formal semantics also makes difficult the use of more efficient techniques analysis. In this work, these problems were studied under an approach based on Petri nets. The formalism of Petri nets makes it a powerful technique of modeling for representation of processes, allowing display of: competition, parallelism, synchronization, non-determinism and mutual exclusion. The main concepts of Petri nets are discussed by Padua et.al. (2002)

Many works have valued the formal structure of Petri nets for business processes representation, among them some can be mentioned: Verbeek et al. (2007), Guan et. al. (2006), Zhang and Shuzen (2006), Ou-Yang and Lin (2007), Aalst and Hee (2002), Padua (2004), Padua et al (2003), Padua et al (2004), Padua et al. (2002) and Aalst (1999). Therefore, this work presents a method of assessment of the Business Processes Model of the EKD. In order to the method could be created, it was necessary to develop the formalization of the business processes model of the EKD and the mapping of the business processes model on Petri nets.

The method of evaluation was applied in the process model of the human resources strategic plan developed in the project ESPRIT ELEKTRA ("Electrical Enterprise Transforming Knowledge for Applications") (BUBENKO et al 1998). The model mapped on Petri nets was simulated on the tool "Petri Net Tools" developed and implemented at the Simulation and Discrete Control Systems Laboratory at University of São Paulo in São Carlos (Soares, 2001). The editor had six modules. Four modules were in operation: Petri network L/T (local/transition), MFG (Mark Flow Graph), SFC (Sequential Flow Chart) and stochastic PN.

The editor allows the following types of analysis: reachability tree; incidence matrix; limitation; vivacity; verification of the final state, transitions and invariant places.

In the studies of Aalst and Hee (2002), Verbeek et al. (2002), Salimifard and Wright (2001) Aalst (1999), Aalst and Hofstede (2000), Voorhoeve (2000) and Mold and Valk (2000) the business processes are directly modeled on Petri nets.

In this study, the construction of the business processes model followed the EKD organizational modeling method and not directly onto Petri nets. The procedure of mapping the business processes model onto Petri nets was developed based on Petri nets place/transition. The power of analysis of the properties of the model would be reduced in case the mapping was based on extended and high-level nets. Methods to assess Petri colored net are computationally expensive and feasible only for simple models (Jensen, 1997).

The work is structured in nine sections, including this introduction. On section two important concepts related to nets of Petri in the context of business processes model will be introduced. In section three, a presentation of the formal model of business processes is made. Sections four and five will present the model of business processes on Petri nets map and assessment method of the EKD business processes model. The section six shows the application method. The ending considerations are outlined on section seven.

2. Petri Net and business process model

According to Hofstede and Aalst (2000), some mistakes are easily identified on the models of Petri nets like deadlock, when it is not possible performing any task; livelock, when a case is in infinite loop, being possible performing tasks, but no progress is possible and deadtask, when a task can never be run on any situation.

Some studies investigate the use of subclasses of Petri nets to increase the decision-making power without reducing the power of modeling of Petri networks. In these subclasses some structural restrictions are made on Petri nets. The subclass of Petri nets denominated free-choice enables the modeling of the parallelism conflict and the synchronization. When a place is an input of several transitions, this place is the only input of these transitions. Thus, all transitions will be qualified or no one will be, making possible the choice of the event freely. Formally, the definition of free-choice is: Be a Petri net = (P, T, I, O, K). I is the set of inputs to the transitions and O is the set of the outputs of the transitions. K is the capacity of places. This network is classified as a network of free-choice if, and only if, $I(t_j) = \{p_i\}$ ou $O(p_i) = \{t_j\}$, $\forall\, t_j \in T$ and $p_i \in I\,(t_j)$.

The main problem of the approach of Organizational modeling, including the EKD, is the lack of objective technical analysis. In this case, Petri nets have an excellent potential to solve this problem, since they have graphics representation, they are easy to learn, they work as a language of communication among experts from several areas, allowing the description of static and dynamic aspects of the system to be represented, and still have the Mathematical formalism that allows the use of methods of analysis. The several applications of Petri nets on Engineering are presented in Padua et al. (2003). Since Zisman (1977) used Petri nets to model workflow for the first time, many authors have published studies that also looked for the integration of the two subjects. Among them, some can be mentioned: Chrzastowski-Wachtel et al. (2003), Rinderle et al. (2003), Dehnert (2003), Grigorova (2003) and Verbeck et al. (2002), Aalst and Hee (2002) and Padua et al. (2004), explain that there are several reasons to use Petri nets for business processes modeling: formal semantics, graphic nature, expressiveness, properties, analysis and the advantage of not being dependent on the supplier.

The criterion of verifying correctness defined to workflow-nets is called soundness. Sound is synonymous of correct according to Aalst and Hee (2002). Aalst (1997) developed a technique that verifies that the procedure meets the following requirements (of soundness): no task should exist that does not contribute to the processing of cases; for any case, the procedure eventually will end and at the moment that the procedure ends for specific cases, all references to this case should be removed.

2.1 Formalizing the business processes model

To perform the mapping of the Business Processes Model onto Petri Nets, based on Aalst (1999), a formal definition of the Model of Business Processes of the EKD (BPM-EKD) was created.

In this way, it was possible to describe the requirements that a Business Processes Model should meet in order to do the mapping be development. Seeking for formal definition of the Model of Business Processes, it was created a set of connectors to the Business Processes Model of EKD. The set of connectors is represented by C and it is composed by C_{AND}, C_{OR}, C_J, C_S, C_{IP} and C_{PI}. The connectors C_{OR} and C_{AND} were created to identify exclusive choice and parallelism in order that the cases of parallelism and choice won't be modeled exactly in the same way, creating ambiguities and difficulties of comprehension. The connectors C_J and C_S define the connectors type join and split. To describe the nature of the flow of processes and their interactions, there is a set of terms, used in Workflow Management Coalition (1996) and in Aalst and Hee (2002), which are presented as follows:

- AND-Split: point where, from a single line of flow, two or more lines start and are performed in parallel.
- AND-Join: point where two or more activities, running in parallel, converge on a single line of common flow.
- OR-Split: point where a single line of flow makes a decision among a number of options.
- OR-Join: point at which an activity that has a number of alternatives, directs itself to a single option

According to these settings AND-Split, AND-Join, OR-Split and OR-Join the construction of Figure 1 are not allowed on formal BPM-EKD.

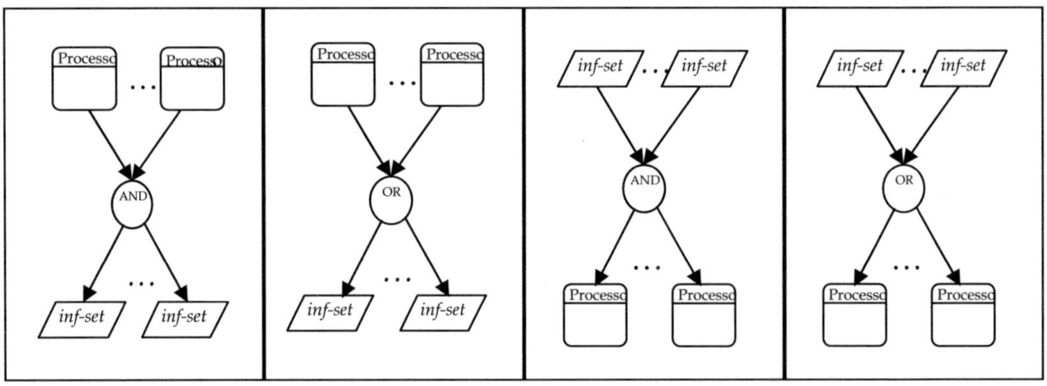

Fig. 1. Constructions that are not allowed in a formal BPM-EKD

The connectors C_{IP} and C_{PI} show that a connector C is a path from one inf-set to one process or a path from a process to an inf-set.

The initial and final states are not specified on Business Processes Model of EKD, it was necessary to create such states in order that the formalization could be effectively accomplished. This situation will be explained during the course of this chapter.

Definition 1. A BPM-EKD is a quintuple (I, P, C, Q, A):

- I is a finite set of inf-set (set of information).
- P is a finite set of processes,
- C is a finite set of logical connectors,
- $Q \in C \rightarrow \{AND, OR\}$ é is a function that maps each connector within an specific type of connector.
- $A \subseteq (I \times P) \cup (P \times I) \cup (I \times C) \cup (C \times I) \cup (P \times C) \cup (C \times P)$ is a set of arcs.

A BPM-EKD is composed of three types of elements: inf-set -set of information (I), processes (P) and connectors (C). The type of each connector is given by the function Q: Q(c) is the type (AND or OR) of a connector $c \in C$. The connection A specifies a set of arcs connecting processes, set of information (inf-set) and connectors. The definition 1 shows that it is not allowed to have an arc connecting two processes or two inf-sets or two connectors.

Definition 2. A directed path p from a node n_1 to a node n_k,is a sequence $<n_1, n_2, ...n_K>$ sequence, such as $<n_i, n_{i+1}> \in A$ for $1 \leq i \leq k - 1$. p is elementary if, and only if, for any of the nodes ni and nj in p, $i \neq j \rightarrow n_i \neq n_j$.

The definition of directed path will be used to limit the number of construction of routes that can be used. This definition allows the definition of C_{IP} (set of connectors from one inf-set to one process) and C_{PI} (set of connectors from one process to one inf-set). C_{IP} and C_{PI} divide the set of connectors C. Based on the Q function, the C is portioned in C_{AND} and C_{OR}. The set C_J and C_S is used to classify (rank) the connectors in connectors join or split.

Definition 3. Considering BPM-EKD = (I, P, C, Q, A) a:

- $N = I \cup P \cup C$ is a set of nodes of BPM-EKD
- $C_{AND} = \{c \in C \mid Q(c) = AND\}$;
- $C_{OR} = \{c \in C \mid Q(c) = OR\}$;
- Para $n \in N$: $\bullet n = \{m \mid (m,n) \in A\}$ is the set of input nodes, and $n\bullet = \{m \mid (n,m) \in A\}$ is the set of output nodes
- $C_J = \{c \in C \mid \ |\bullet c| \geq 2\}$ is the set of join connectors
- $Cs = \{c \in C \mid \ |c\bullet| \geq 2\}$ is the set of join connectors
- $C_{IP} \subseteq C$ such that $c \in C_{IP}$, if and only if there is a path $p = <n_1, n_2, n_3>$, tal que $n_1 \in I$, $n_2 \in C$, $n_3 \in P$; and
- $C_{PI} \subseteq C$ such that $c \in C_{PI}$ if and only if there is a path p $p = <n_1, n_2, n_3>$, tal que $n_1 \in P$, $n_2 \in C$, $n_3 \in I$.

Definition 3 enables to specify the additional requirements an **BPM-EKD** chain should satisfy.

Definition 4. A Business Process Model of EKD meets the following requirements:

- The sets I, P and C are pairwise disjoint, i.e, $I \cap P = \varnothing$, $I \cap C = \varnothing$, and $P \cap C = \varnothing$;
- For each $i \in I$: $|\bullet i| \leq 1$ and $|i\bullet| \leq 1$;
- There is at least one inf set $i \in I$, such that $|\bullet i| = 0$ (inf-set start);
- There is at least one inf-set $i \in I$, such that $|i\bullet| = 0$ (inf-set end);
- For each $p \in P$: $|\bullet p| = 1$ and $|p\bullet| = 1$;
- For each $c \in C$: $|\bullet c| \geq 1$ and $|c\bullet| \geq 1$;
- The graph induced by BPM-EKD C is weakly connected, if for every two nodes $n1, n2 \in N$, $(n1, n2) \in (A \cup A^{-1})^*$;
- C_J and Cs partition de C, i.e., $C_J \cap Cs = \varnothing$ and $C_J \cup Cs = C$; e
- C_{IP} and C_{PI} partition de C, *i.e.*, $C_{IP} \cap C_{PI} = \varnothing$ and $C_{IP} \cup C_{PI} = C$.

In the line of Aalst (1999), the first requirement states that each component has a unique identifier (name). The connector names are omitted in the diagram of an BPM-EKD. The other requirements correspond to restrictions on the relation A. Inf Sets cannot have multiple input arcs and there is at least one start inf set and one final inf set. Each function has exactly one input arc and one output arc. For every two nodes n1 and n2 there is a path from n1 to n2 (ignoring the direction of the arcs). A connector c is either a join connector $((|c\bullet| = 1$ and $|\bullet c| \geq 2)$ jc or a split connector $(|\bullet c| = 1$ and $|c\bullet| \geq 2)$. The last requirement states that a connector c is either on a path from an inf set to a process or on a path from a process to an inf set. The BPM-EKD is syntactically correct, if all the requirements stated in Definition 4 are satisfied.

3.2 The business processes model on Petri Nets mapping

In this section, the Business Processes Model on Petri nets mapping procedure will be presented. The mapping procedure was developed based on Petri nets place / transition. The definitions (1) and (4) presented only report the syntax of the Business Processes Model of EKD and not the semantics.

The places represent inf-sets or are necessary constructions to model the behavior of connector of BPM-EKD. The transitions represent processes or are representing the behavior of the connector. Each connector $c \in C$ corresponds to places, transitions and / or arcs.
The connector can correspond to a number of arcs of Petri net or to a small network of places and transitions. The connector OR corresponds to a behavior of a place. The AND connector corresponds to a transition behavior. On definition 5 the element Place of Petri nets will be represented by L to avoid confusion with the P of BPM-EKD process. The definition 5, presented as follows, shows how the mapping of the connectors of BPM-EKD is developed in this study.
On the BPM-EKD context the arcs always have equal weight as 1 because places correspond to conditions. On a Petri net, which corresponds to one correct (sound) BPM-EKD, a place will never contain multiple brands. The net is secure. The states with multiple brands in one place are results of projects errors and to identify these errors it is necessary to consider non-secure nets.
Definition 5. Let BPM-EKD = (I,P,C,Q,A). $N(EKD)=(L^{PN}, T^{PN}, F^{PN})$ is the Petri net generated by EPC BPM-EKD:

$$L^{PN} = I \cup \left(\bigcup_{c \in C} L_c^{PN} \right)$$

The set of places (L^{PN}) is formed by the union of all inf-sets with places that were included to represent connectors ($\bigcup_{c \in C} L_c^{PN}$).

$$T^{PN} = P \cup \left(\bigcup_{c \in C} T_c^{PN} \right)$$

The set of transitions (T^{PN}) is formed by the union of all Processes with transitions that were included to represent connectors ($\bigcup_{c \in C} T_c^{PN}$).

$$F^{PN} = (A \cap ((I \times P) \cup (P \times I))) \cup \left(\bigcup_{c \in C} F_c^{PN} \right)$$

The set of arcs of the net (F^{PN}) is formed by arcs of model that range from I to P and from P to I and the union of arcs included to represent connectors ($\bigcup_{c \in C} F_c^{PN}$).

Following, the definitions of L_c^{PN}, T_c^{PN} and F_c^{PN} will be presented according to the mapping rules related to the type of connectors of BPM-EKD. Right after each definition, examples that represent the utilized (applied) rules for mapping the connectors of EKD-MPN on Petri nets are presented.

Rule 1

$$c \in C_{IP} \cap C_J \cap C_{AND}$$

When the connector c belongs to C_{IP} (path from inf-set to process) intersection of C_J (join) intersection of Cand, the definitions of L_c^{PN}, T_c^{PN} and F_c^{PN} are the following:

1. $L_c^{PN} = \varnothing$
2. $T_c^{PN} = \varnothing$

3. $F_c^{PN} = \{(x, y) \mid x \in \bullet c \text{ e } y \in c\bullet\}$

The equation I states that it is not necessary to add places to represent this connector. The equation II states that it is necessary to add transitions to represent this connector. The equation III states that the arcs that go from the set of the connector input to the set of the connector output.

In this case, it is noticed that the connector AND-join corresponds to two or more arcs on Petri nets if, and only if, the output is a process. On Figure 2 an example of mapping of the connector $c \in C_{IP} \cap C_J \cap C_{AND}$ is presented.

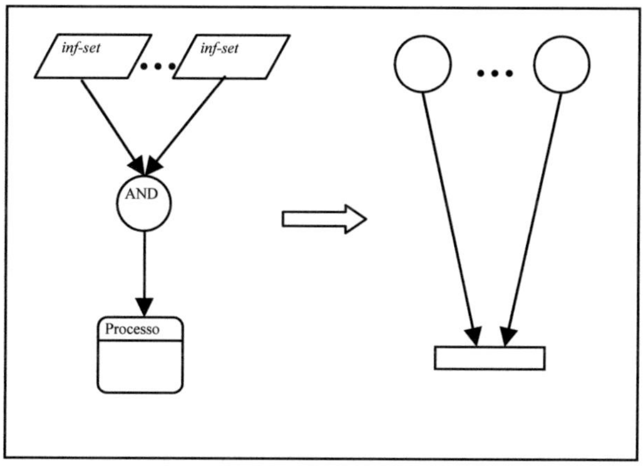

Fig. 2. Example of $\mathbf{C_{AND}}$ Mapping among two or more inf-sets for one process.

Rule 2

$$c \in C_{PI} \cap C_J \cap C_{AND}$$

When the connector c belongs to C_{PI} (path from process to inf-set) intersection of C_J (join) intersection of C_{AND}, the definitions of L_c^{PN}, T_c^{PN} e F_c^{PN} are the following:

1. $L_c^{PN} = \{ l_x^c \mid x \in \bullet c\}$
2. $T_c^{PN} = \{t^c\}$
3. $F_c^{PN} = \{(x, l_x^c) \mid x \in \bullet c\} \cup \{(l_x^c, t^c) \mid x \in \bullet c\} \cup \{(t^c, x) \mid x \in c\bullet\}$

On equation I it is stated that to represent this connector it is necessary to add one place for each process of the connector input. On equation II it is indicated that to represent this connector it is necessary to add a transition. On equation III it is stated that to represent the connector it is necessary to add arcs that connect the transitions to the places of the connector inputs, among the places and the corresponding transitions to the connector and between the transition and the place of the connector output.

In this case, the connector AND-join behaves as a transition. It is added one place for each process of the connector input. On figure 3 one example of the connector mapping $c \in C_{PI} \cap C_J \cap C_{AND}$ is presented.

Rule 3

$$c \in C_{IP} \cap C_J \cap C_{OR}$$

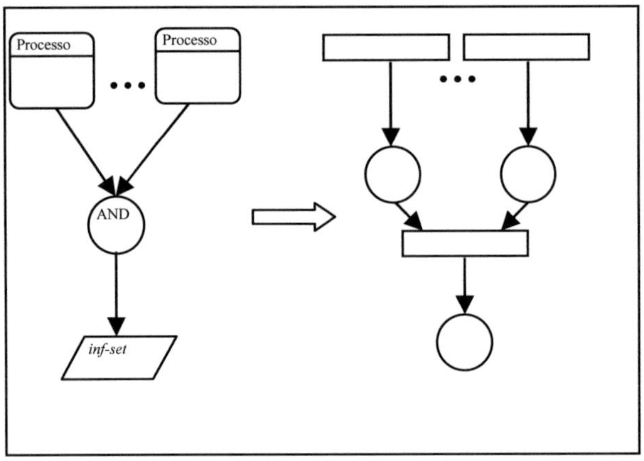

Fig. 3. Example of C_{AND} Mapping among two or more processes for one inf-set.

When the connector c belongs to C_{IP} (path from inf-set to process) intersection of C_J (join) intersection of C_{OR}, the definitions of L_c^{PN}, T_c^{PN} and F_c^{PN} are the following:

1. $L_c^{PN} = \{l^c\}$
2. $T_c^{PN} = \{ t_x^c \mid x \in \bullet c\}$
3. $F_c^{PN} = \{(x, t_x^c) \mid x \in \bullet c\} \cup \{(t_x^c, l^c) \mid x \in \bullet c\} \cup \{(l^c, x) \mid x \in c\bullet\}$

On equation I it is stated that to represent the connector it is necessary to add one place. On equation II it is established that to represent this connector it is necessary to add one transition for each inf-set of the connector input. On equation III it is stated that to represent this connector it is necessary to add a set of arcs from the places to the transitions of the connector input, among the transitions and the place that corresponds to the connector and between the place and the transition of the connector output.
The connector OR-join has the behavior of a place when the connector is C_{IP}. On Figure 4 an example of mapping of the connector $c \in C_{IP} \cap C_J \cap C_{OR}$. is presented.

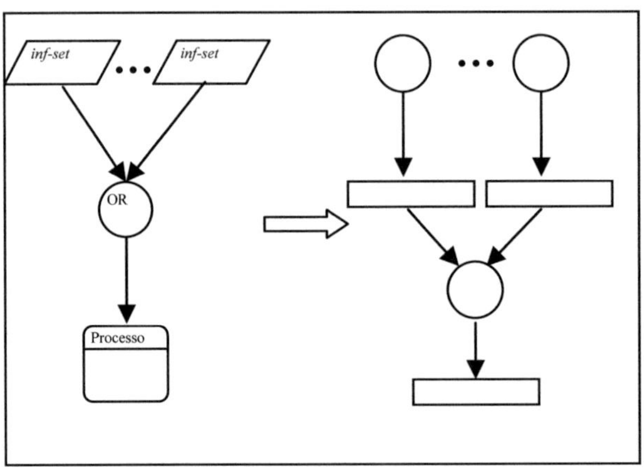

Fig. 4. Example C_{OR} Mapping among two or more inf-sets for one process.

Rule 4

$$c \in C_{PI} \cap C_J \cap C_{OR}$$

When the connector c belongs to C_{PI} (path from process to inf-set) intersection of C_J (join) intersection of C_{OR},, the definitions of L_c^{PN}, T_c^{PN} and F_c^{PN} and Fc PN are the following:

1. $L_c^{PN} = \varnothing$
2. $T_c^{PN} = \varnothing$
3. $F_c^{PN} = \{(x, y) \mid x \in \bullet c \text{ e } y \in c\bullet\}$

On equation I it is presented that it is not necessary to add places to represent this connector. On equation II it is stated that it is not necessary to add transitions to represent this connector. On equation III it is presented that the arcs set is between the input set and the output set.

The connector OR-join corresponds to two or more arcs on Petri nets if, and only if, the connector is C_{PI}. On Figure 5 an example of mapping of the connector $c \in C_{PI} \cap C_J \cap C_{OR}$ is presented

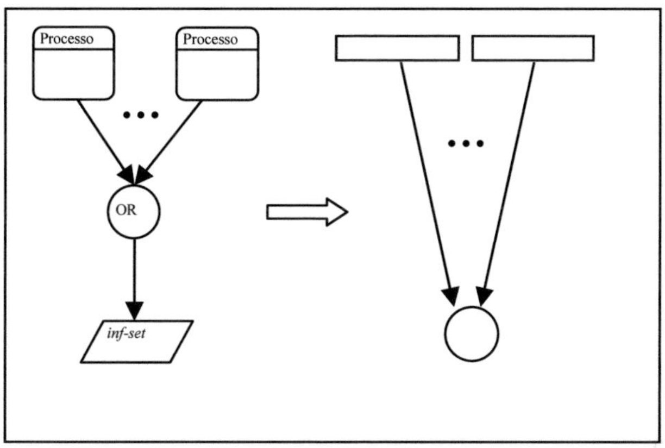

Fig. 5. Example of C_{OR} Mapping among two or more process for an inf-set.

Rule 5

$$c \in C_{IP} \cap C_s \cap C_{AND}$$

When the connector c belongs to C_{IP} (path from inf-set to process) intersection of C_S (join) intersection of C_{AND}, the definitions of L_c^{PN}, T_c^{PN} and F_c^{PN} are the following:

1. $L_c^{PN} = \{ l_x^c \mid x \in c\bullet\}$
2. $T_c^{PN} = \{t^c\}$
3. $F_c^{PN} = \{(x, t^c) \mid x \in \bullet c\} \cup \{(t^c, l_x^c) \mid x \in c\bullet\} \cup \{(l_x^c, x) \mid x \in c\bullet\}$

On equation I it is presented that it is necessary to add one place for each connector output. On equation II it is stated that to represent this connector it is necessary to add one transition. On equation III it is presented that the arcs set needed to represent this connector must be between the place and one corresponding transition to the connector, among one transition and the places of the connector output and among the places of the connector output and the transition.

Thus, the connector AND-split of type C_{IP} behaves as a transition followed by a number of places equal to a number of processes. On figure 6 one example of mapping of the connector $c \in C_{IP} \cap C_s \cap C_{AND}$ is presented.

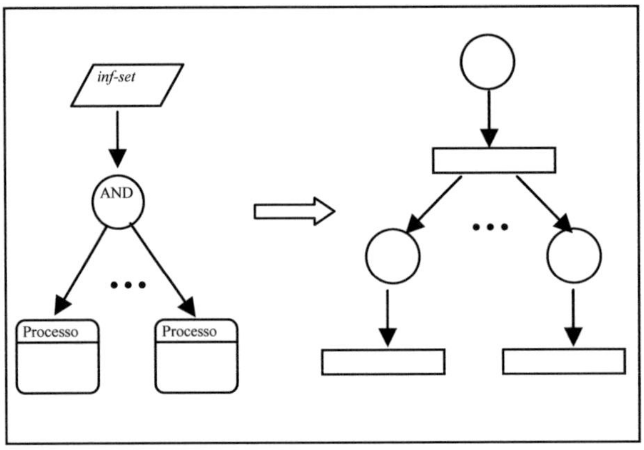

Fig. 6. Example of C_{AND} mapping a *inf-set* for to or more process.

Rule 6

$$c \in C_{PI} \cap C_s \cap C_{AND}$$

When the connector c belongs to C_{IP} (path from process to inf-set) intersection of C_S (join) intersection of C_{AND}, the definitions of L_c^{PN}, T_c^{PN} e F_c^{PN} are the following:

1. $L_c^{PN} = \emptyset$
2. $T_c^{PN} = \emptyset$
3. $F_c^{PN} = \{(x, y) \mid x \in \bullet c \text{ e } y \in c \bullet\}$

On equation I it is presented that it is not necessary to add places to represent this connector. On equation II it is stated that it is not necessary to add transitions to represent this connector. On equation III it is presented that the arcs set is between the input set and the output set.

The connector AND-split corresponds to a number of arcs on Petri nets if, and only if, the output is two or more inf-sets. On Figure 7 an example of the connector mapping $c \in C_{PI} \cap C_S \cap C_{AND}$ is presented.

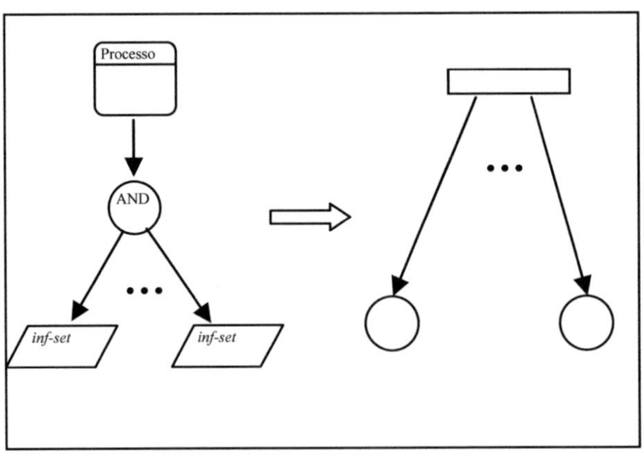

Fig. 7. Example of C_{AND} Mapping based one process to two or more inf-sets.

Rule 7

$$c \in C_{IP \cap C_s \cap C_{OR}}$$

When the connector c belongs to CIP (path from inf-set to process) intersection of C_S (join) intersection of C_{OR}, the definitions of L_c^{PN}, T_c^{PN} and F_c^{PN} are the following:

1. $L_c^{PN} = \varnothing$
2. $T_c^{PN} = \varnothing$
3. $F_c^{PN} = \{(x, y) \mid x \in \bullet c \text{ e } y \in c\bullet\}$

On equation I it is presented that it is not necessary to add places to represent this connector. On equation II it is stated that it is not necessary to add transitions to represent this connector. On equation III it is presented that the arcs set is between the input set and the output set.

The connector OR-split corresponds to a number of arcs on Petri nets if, and only if, the output is two or more processes On Figure 9 an example of the connector mapping $c \in C_{IP \cap C_s \cap C_{OR}}$. is presented.

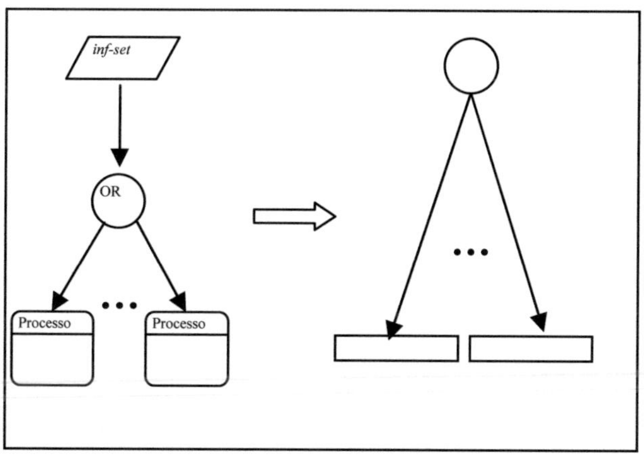

Fig. 8. Example of C_{OR} Mapping from one inf-set to two or more processes

Rule 8

$$c \in C_{PI \cap C_s \cap C_{OR}}$$

When the connector c belongs to C_{PI} (path from process to inf-set) intersection of C_S (join) intersection of C_{OR}, the definitions of L_c^{PN}, T_c^{PN} e F_c^{PN} are the following:

1. $L_c^{PN} = \{l^c\}$
2. $T_c^{PN} = \{ t_x^c \mid x \in c\bullet\}$
3. $F_c^{PN} = \{(x, l^c) \mid x \in \bullet c\} \cup \{(l^c, t_x^c) \mid x \in c\bullet\} \cup \{(t_x^c, x) \mid x \in c\bullet\}$

On equation I it is stated that to represent this connector it is necessary to add one place. On equation II it is presented that it is necessary to add a transition for each inf-set of the connector output. On equation III it is stated that the set of arcs should be between the initial transition and the correspondent place to the connector, among the place and the transitions of the connector output and among the transitions of the connector output and the places. The only way to exist a place with more than one output arc is the mapping of the connector OR-split from a process to two or more inf-sets. The rules of mapping ensure that the number of transitions is equal to the number of places. The net is free choice. On figure 9 one example of mapping of the connector $c \in C_{PI} \cap C_S \cap C_{OR}$ is presented.

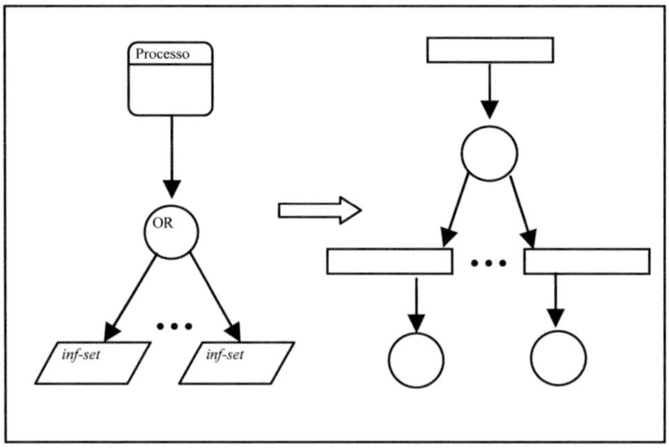

Fig. 9. Example of C_{OR} Mapping from one process to two or more inf-sets

The BPM-EKD (I, P, C, Q, A) is a Business process model of EKD and PN = N (BPM-EKD) the Petri net generated by BPM-EKD. PN is free choice.

Definition 6 . A BPM-EKD is a regular only if:

- BPM-EKD has two *inf-sets* special: i_{start} and i_{final}. *inf-set* i_{start} is a node sourcee: $\bullet i_{start} = \varnothing$. *inf-set* i_{final} is end node: $i_{final} \bullet = \varnothing$.
- Every node $n \in N$ is on a path from $i_{início}$ to i_{final}.

In the same line of Aalst (1999), the identification of inf-set start and e_inf-set final allows for a clear definition of the initial state and the final state. The BPM-EKD with multiple start inf-sets (i.e.inf-sets without any input arcs) or multiple final inf-sets (i.e. inf-sets without any output arcs) can easily be extended with an initialization and/or a termination part such that the first requirement is satisfied.

The second requirement demands that every inf-set is in the scope bordered by inf-set start and inf-set inicial. If the original BPM-EKD is extended with an initialization and/or a termination part such that the first requirement is satisfied, then the second requirement is quite natural. If the second requirement is not satisfied, then the BPM-EKD is:

1. composed of completely disjointed parts,
2. it has parts which are never activated or
3. parts of the event-driven process chain form a trap.

How does BPM-EKD describes the process instance, the two requirements are reasonable. The life cycle should have a clear start inf-set, an end inf-set, and all the steps should be on a path between these two events. As in Aalst (1999), in remainder of this chapter, the BPM-EKD will be assumed to be regular.

One BPM-EKD describes a procedure with an initial state and a final state. The procedure should be designed in such a way that always it ends properly. Moreover, it should be possible to run any process following the proper route of BPM-EKD.

Definition 7. A regular BPM-EKD is *"sound"* if, and only if:

1. For each M marking reachable from the initial state (for example, the state, where the $i_{initial}$ inf-set is the only inf-set that exists), there is a sequence of shots taking from the M marking to the final marking (for example, where the i_{final} inf-set is the only inf-set that exists).
2. The only existing mark at the end of the process is in the final state i_{final}.
3. There are no dead processes, for example, for each process p there is a *shot* sequence, which runs p.

The conformity, according to the ones of Petri nets, is the minimum requirement, so that any BPM-EKD should meet. A BPM-EKD *sound* is free of potential deadlocks and livelocks. If assuming fairness, then the first two requirements imply that eventually the final mark will be achieved (it is noticed that this is a result of the combination of ownership of soundness and free choice. The property free choice implies that for each transition t1 e t2, $\bullet t1 \cap \bullet t2 \neq \emptyset$ that implies that $\bullet t = \bullet t2$.

The complex BPM-EKD found in practice, the verification of property soundness is not simple. Fortunately, techniques and tools based on Petri nets can be used to analyze this property. The inspection of the tree coverage of Petri net that corresponds to BPM-EKD is sufficient to verify *soundness*. For complex BPM-EKD, the tree coverage can become very big. This phenomenon is known as the "explosion problem of state." One BPM-EKD with 80 processes can easily have more than 200,000 markings. Although the computers currently have trouble to analyze trees coverage of that size, there are many advanced techniques that explore the structure of Petri nets, in this case generated by one BPM-EKD. These techniques allow efficient procedures decision. Before presenting such procedure, primarily it is necessary to list some properties present in any Petri net generated by one BPM-EKD sound. The BPM-EKD = (I, P, C, Q, A) is sound and PN = N (BPM-EKD) the Petri net generated by the BPM-EKD. Consider PN be as PN with an additional t transition connecting i_{final} to $i_{initial}$ and let M to be the initial marking with a mark in $i_{initial}$ (Aalst, 1999).

- $\overline{PN}$ is strongly connected;
- $\overline{PN}$ is susceptible of coverage;
- ($\overline{PN}$, M) is live and
- ($\overline{PN}$, M) is limited.

A Petri net is strongly connected if, and only if, for each pair of nodes (places and transitions) x and y, there is a path from x until y (Aalst, 1999). PN is strongly connected because all nodes are on the path from the $i_{initial}$ to the i_{final} and i_{final} is connected in $i_{initial}$ through additional t. PN is WF-net according to Aalst (1997). Therefore, soundness coincides with vivacity and limitation. (PN, M) is free choice, alive and limited and, according to Aalst and Hee (2002), implies that PN is susceptible of coverage and (PN, M) is secure. Building the results presented in Aalst (1997), the property of soundness can be verified in polynomial time. One BPM-EKD corresponds to a WF-net free choice. One WF-net is sound if, and only if, the extended net is alive and limited. Vivacity and limitation can be verified in time polynomial. For that reason soundness can be verified in polynomial time.

In this way, it is possible to extend tools with efficient decision procedures to verify the soundness property of one BPM-EKD. For guiding the user to look for defects and fix them in a project of one BPM-EKD it is also possible to supply additional diagnoses based on the structure of BPM-EKD/Petri nets.

3.3 Assessment method of Business Processes Model of EKD

The assessment method of Business Processes Model of EKD consists of:

1. developing the organizational model EKD using the guidelines presented in Bubenko et al. (1998).

2. Developing Business Processes Model according to the formalization the BPM-EKD presented in this work. Check if the model meets the following requirements:

2.1. All processes must have input and output conditions. When a case doesn't have any input condition, it will not be clear when it may be performed. When a process doesn't have any output conditions, it does not contribute for the success of the process and can be omitted.

2.2. There must be at least one final *inf-set* and one initial *inf-set.*

2.3. The input of the process should be equal to 1.

2.4. The output of the process should be equal to 1.

2.5. The output of an inf-set should be equal or less than 1. In case it is less than 1, it is a final inf-set.

2.6. The input of inf-set should be equal or less than 1. In case it is less than 1, it is an initial inf-set.

2.7. The entry of the connector should be larger than or equal to 1.

2.8. The output of the connector should be larger or equal to 1.

2.9. Every connector should be OR or AND type.

2.10. Every connector should be Split or Join type.

2.11. Every connector should be PI or IP type.

2.12. A split-type connector should have the input equal to 1.

2.13. A split-type connector should have the output equal to 2 or larger than 2.

2.14. A join-type connector should have the input larger than 2 or equal to 2.

2.15. A join-type connector should have the output equal to 1.

2.16. It is not allowed to connect process to process.

2.17. It is not allowed to connect *inf-set* to *inf-set.*

2.18. It is not allowed to use the connector linking process(es) to process(es) and *inf-set (s)* to *inf-set (s).*

2.19. It is not allowed the connection of connector (s) with connector(s).

2.20. All the *inf-sets* that were not generated by the process should be enabled.

3. Model mapping on Petri nets. The *inf-sets* are represented by places and the processes are represented by transitions. For the connectors mapping it is necessary to follow the rules presented as follows:

3.1. The set of places is formed by the union of all *inf-sets* with places that were included to represent the connectors.

3.2. The set of transitions is formed by the union of all Processes with transitions that were included to represent connectors.

3.3. The set of net arcs is formed by model arcs that range from I (inf-set) to P (process) and from P to I and the union of the arcs included to represent connectors.

3.4. Rule 1 states that when the connector c belongs to C_{IP} (path from inf-set to process) intersection of C_J (join) intersection of C_{AND}, the connector ($c \in C_{IP} \cap C_J \cap C_{AND}$) corresponds to two or more arcs on Petri nets.

3.5. Rule 2 states that when the connector c belongs to C_{PI} (path from process to inf-set) intersection of C_J (join) intersection of C_{AND}, the connector ($c \in C_{PI} \cap C_J \cap C_{AND}$) behaves as one transition. A place for each connector input process is added.

3.6. Rule 3 states that when the connector c belongs to C_{IP} (path from inf-set to process) intersection of C_J (join) intersection of C_{OR}, the connector ($c \in C_{IP} \cap C_J \cap C_{OR}$) behaves as one place.
3.7. Rule 4 states that when the connector c belongs to C_{PI} (path from process to inf-set) intersection of C_J (join) intersection of C_{OR},, the connector ($c \in C_{PI} \cap C_J \cap C_{OR}$) corresponds to two or more arcs onto Petri nets.
3.8. Rule 5 states that when the connector c belongs to C_{IP} (path from inf-set to process) intersection of C_S (split) intersection of C_{AND}, the connector ($c \in C_{IP} \cap C_S \cap C_{AND}$) behaves as one transition followed by a number of places equal to the number of processes.
3.9. Rule 6 states that when the connector c belongs to C_{PI} (path from process to inf-set) intersection of C_S (Split) intersection of C_{AND}, the connector ($c \in C_{PI} \cap C_S \cap C_{AND}$) corresponds to a number of arcs onto Petri nets.
3.10. Rule 7 states that when the connector c belongs to C_{IP} (path from inf-set to process) intersection of C_S (Split) intersection of C_{OR}, the connector ($c \in C_{IP} \cap C_S \cap C_{OR}$) corresponds to a number of arcs onto Petri nets.
3.11. Rule 8 states that when the connector c belongs to C_{PI} (path from process to inf-set) intersection of C_S (Split) intersection of C_{OR}, the connector ($c \in C_{PI} \cap C_S \cap C_{OR}$) corresponds to one place followed by a number of transitions equal to the number of processes of the output of the connector.
4. Building the tree of reachability Through the tree of reachability is possible to verify several errors that may occur in the definition of process, even without specific knowledge of the business process. In lack of editing tool of Petri nets it is possible to verify the soundness property through the inspection of the reachability tree that corresponds to the BPM-EKD.
5. After making the mapping on Petri nets, assessing the model using an editing tool on Petri networks. In this work, Petri Net Tools have been used. The following items should be considered:
5.1. The verification of possible deadlock, *as to say* whenever it is not possible to run any task.
5.2. The elimination of cases that are in infinite loop (livelock).
5.3. The verification of possible tasks that can not be executed (deadtask).
5.4. The elimination of conflicts.
5.5. The verification of possible paths.
5.6. Checking the existence of marks in other places after the end condition order was completed. Once the mark appears at the end place, all other marks *must* have disappeared.
6. To present the report of the problems founded.

4. The application method.

The model that will be presented was developed on project ESPRIT ELEKTRA (Electrical Enterprise Knowledge for Transforming Applications) (ELEKTRA, 2000). The ELEKTRA project focuses mainly on application of EKD method for the management problems of changes within organizations from Greece and Sweden, generating a set of generic practices in order to apply them to other companies.
The Vattenfall case *was* chosen on ELEKTRA project. The project was based on a careful analysis not only of current practice and process but also of problems, of needs, of opportunities and realized future goals.

The model is from the strategic planning process of human resources. The planning process is conducted on a strategic level. It involves formulation of policies and goals for human resources planning for Vattenfall treating the metrics on achieving the formulated goals. The model describes how the human resources planning should be integrated with the business strategic planning. Initially, based on business planning goals, it is formulated a group of goals and indicators within the domain of competence, then the goals and indicators are reported to the business area into the documents: pre-conditions for business planning / budget guidelines. Paralleled or not, the policies, guidelines and instructions are formulated from the term of private and political goals. Afterwards, communications of these policies are effectuated.

The following procedures are: running activities within the substitute (proxy) domain on competency; returning trimestrially the goals and indicators with the help of System of Group Review; presenting a summary of achieved goals and indicators; comparing achieved goals and tendencies with the proposed goals according to the private policies and business planning and review goals. On Figure 11 the modified described model to be mapped on Petri nets is presented. The inputs of process 1 have been modified for not meeting the requirement method that states that the process can only have one input. Although the method states that one initial and final inf-set should be placed, it was not possible to place a final inf-set because the end of the procedure was not clear. The connectors were added.

On Figure 12 the same model mapped on Petri nets is presented according to the method presented in this work. The connectors of the model of the process of human resources strategic planning and their corresponding rules mapping are presented on Table 1. The elements of Petri Nets corresponding to the elements of BPM-EKD are presented on Table 2.

Test result

On Figure 13 the model simulated on Petri Net Tools is presented. A tree of reachability presented on figure 14 shows that the Pr6 transition will be shot unless there is a mark at IS8 place. As there is not such a mark before the shot of Pr7 transition there will be a deadlock. Moreover, there is not a clear end condition. The model is not sound.

5. Final considerations

It was emphasized that the main problem of Organizational modeling approaches, including the EKD, is the absence of techniques for objective analysis. The techniques of analysis with mathematical rigor are not usual for business area professionals. It was confirmed that the Petri nets solve this problem, once they have graphic representation, are easy to learn, function as language of communication among experts from several areas, allow the description of static and dynamic aspects of the system to be represented, and still have the mathematical formalism that allows the use of important methods of analysis.

The business processes, regularly, have a simple structure before being introduced in systems of advanced information, such as system of workflow. This simplicity is due mainly to the fact that a document can only be in one place at the same moment. The document serves as a set of marks that ensure the performance sequential tasks. Currently, after several years of development of systems in a sequential way, it is possible to model processes in a completely different order, once the information and data can be shared. Several people can work at the same time in the same case. For this reason it is not always possible to perform the tasks sequentially. Through the utilization of parallel business processes it is possible to achieve enormous reductions on the performance time. The business environment is opportune to perform the tasks in parallel according to the necessity. However, the utilization of sequential, parallel, selective and iterative routes in the same process makes the assessment of the defined processes difficult.

In this way, the research showed that the Business Processes Model should be developed with great care, because, in addition to problems resulting from errors in the project being difficult to detect, the costs of correcting the errors are high. The ambiguities and conflicts should be eliminated of the models.

It was possible to confirm that ambiguities and confusion cannot be prevented on informal Business Processes model. To solve this problem, a Business Processes Model with a formal semantic was developed. To develop this semantic a connector set for Business Processes Model of EKD was created. The connectors set represented by C and composed by C_{AND}, C_{OR}, C_J, C_S, C_{IP} and C_{PI}. The connectors C_{OR} and C_{AND} are important to identify (exclusive) choice and parallelism for the cases of parallelism and choice won't be exactly modeled in the same way, avoiding ambiguities and comprehension difficulties. The connectors C_J and C_S define connectors join and split type. The connectors C_{IP} and C_{PI} show that a connector c is a path from an inf-set to a process or a path from a process to an inf-set.

The initial and final states were included to enable that the formalization be effectively accomplished. These states are not specified in the Business Processes Model of original EKD.

In this work a procedure of formal mapping of Business Processes Model on Petri nets was developed. The procedure of mapping was developed based on Petri nets place transition. Through a business process model mapped on Petri nets in accordance with this procedure, it was possible to verify some requirements that ensure if the process was correctly modeled and other requirements that allow the process analysis.

Thus, the Assessment Method of Business Processes Model of EKD was created from the procedure of formal mapping of the Business Processes Model on Petri nets. The method consists on a sequence of steps that ranges from the development of organizational model to the construction of reachability tree and simulation of model in tool.

The application of the method allows verifying the presence of deadlock, in which the process can never be accomplished. Moreover, there is no clear end condition, so the model is not sound.

Based on these problems, it can be stated that the care on the modeling process is fundamental in order that the model represents faithfully the way the process is performed and that these problems are minimized when the model is developed in accordance with the method developed in this work.

The great convenience, as previously stated, in using Petri nets in business processes model is the possibility of a thorough tracking and non-ambiguous on each step of the operation.

Moreover, this work shows that Petri nets enable a formal mathematical representation and provide mechanisms of analysis that make possible the verification of the model correction and the checking of their properties.

The fact that some constructions are not allowed can be considered a disadvantage of the BPM-EKD formalization. But, during the process of modeling these constructions should be carefully analyzed, being important the discernment of the team or person who is modeling in order that the model be developed in accordance with the created settings in this work.

It is important to emphasize that the application of assessment method in many Business Processes Models can be impractical without a tool computer that supports all steps of the method.

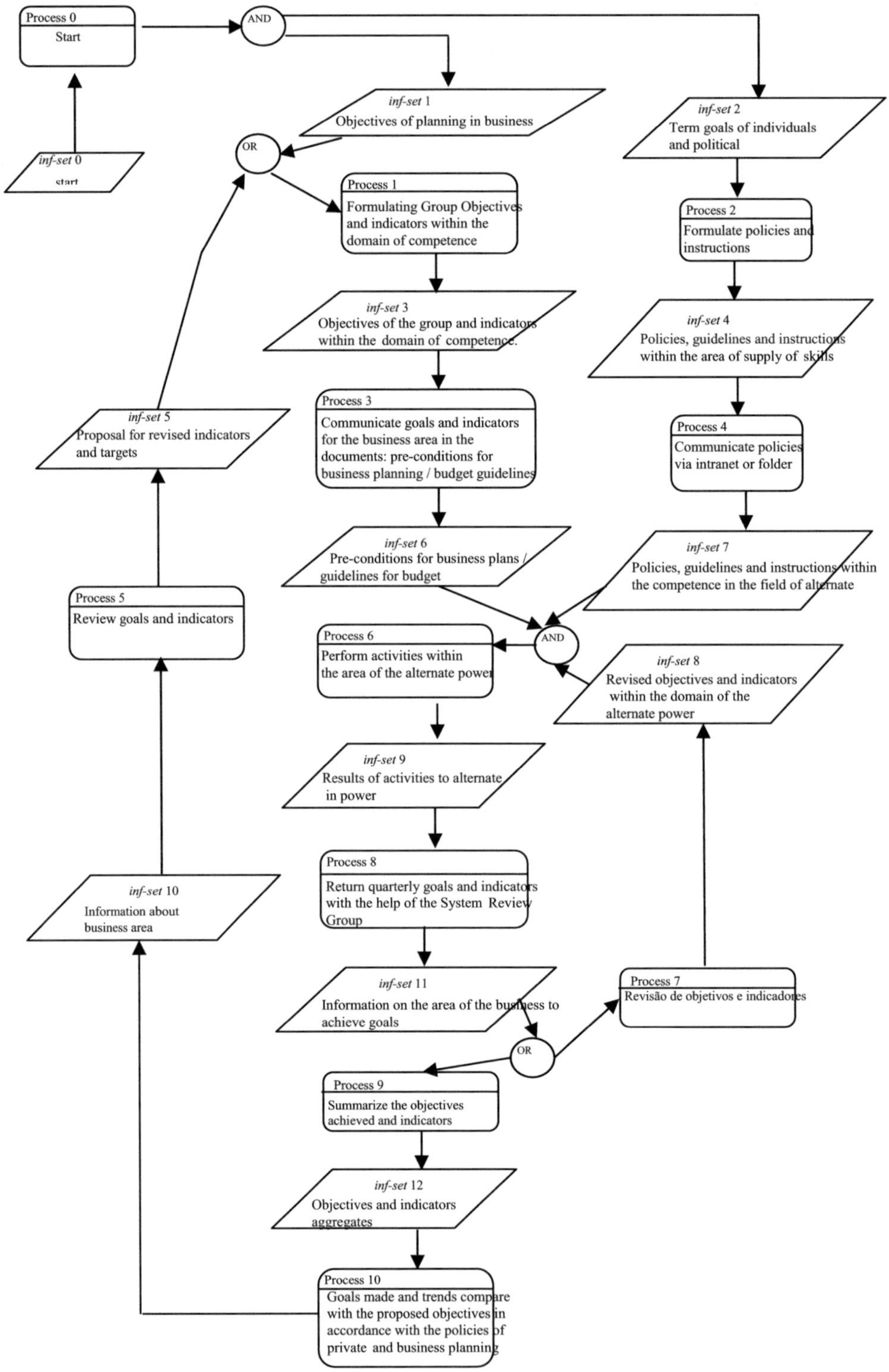

Fig. 10. Model Procedure for strategic planning of human resources changed.

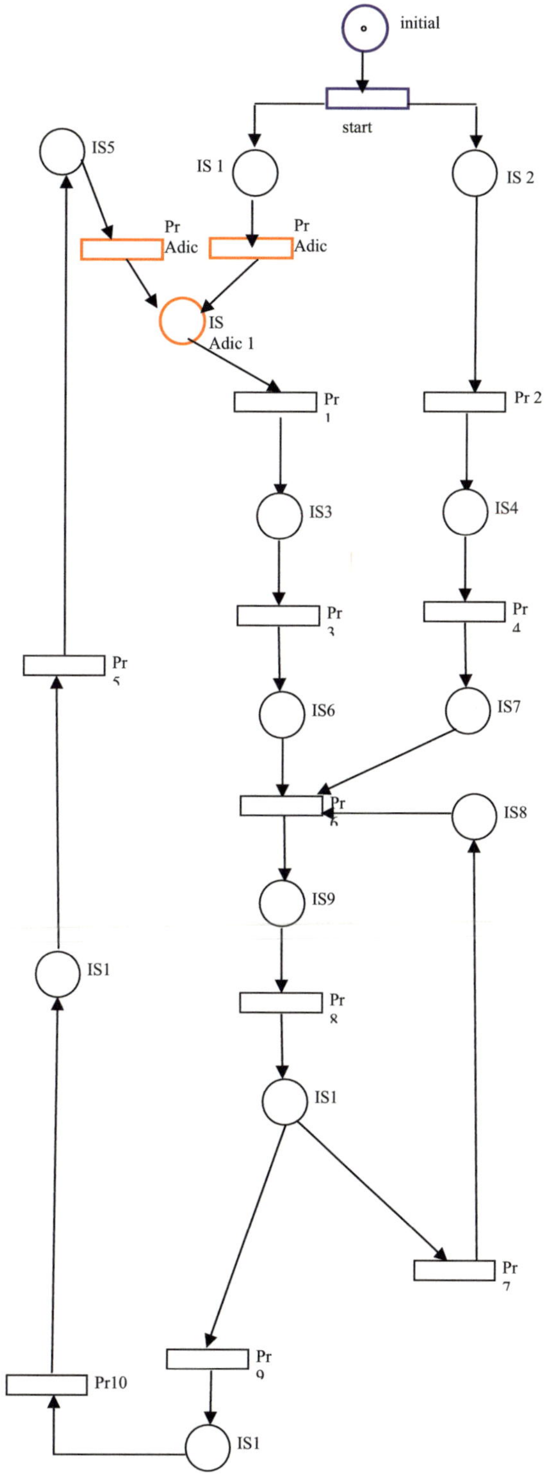

Fig. 11. Strategic planning model mapped to the Petri nets.

Conector	Rule corresponding
C_{PI} C_S C_{AND}	Rule 6
C_{IP} C_J C_{OR}	Rule 3
C_{IP} C_J C_{AND}	Rule 1
C_{IP} C_S C_{OR}	Rule 7

Table 1. Connectors used in the model of strategic human resource planning and mapping corresponding Rule.

PN	**BPM-EKD**	
Place	***inf-set***	**Description**
Is1	1	Objectives of planning in business
Is2	2	Term goals of individuals and political
Is3	3	Objectives of the group and indicators within the domain of competence.
Is4	4	Policies, guidelines and instructions within the area of supply of skills
Is5	5	Proposal for revised indicators and targets
Is6	6	Pre-conditions for business plans / guidelines for budget
Is7	7	Policies, guidelines and instructions within the competence in the field of alternate
Is8	8	Revised objectives and indicators within the domain of the alternate power
Is9	9	Results of activities to alternate in power
Is10	10	Information on area business
Is11	11	Information on the area of the business to achieve goals
Is12	12	Objectives and indicators aggregates
Tr	**Pr**	**Description**
Pr1	1	Formulating Group Objectives and indicators within the domain of competence
Pr2	2	Formulate policies
Pr3	3	Communicate goals and indicators for the business area in the documents: pre-conditions for business planning / budget guidelines
Pr4	4	Communicate policies via intranet or folder
Pr5	5	Review goals and indicators
Pr6	6	Perform activities within the area of the alternate power
Pr7	7	Review of objectives and indicators
Pr8	8	Return quarterly goals and indicators with the help of the System Review Group
Pr9	9	Overview of goals achieved and indicators
Pr10	10	Goals made and trends compare with the proposed objectives in accordance with the policies of private and business planning

Table 2. Elements of Petri networks corresponding to the elements of BPM-EKD of Strategic Planning

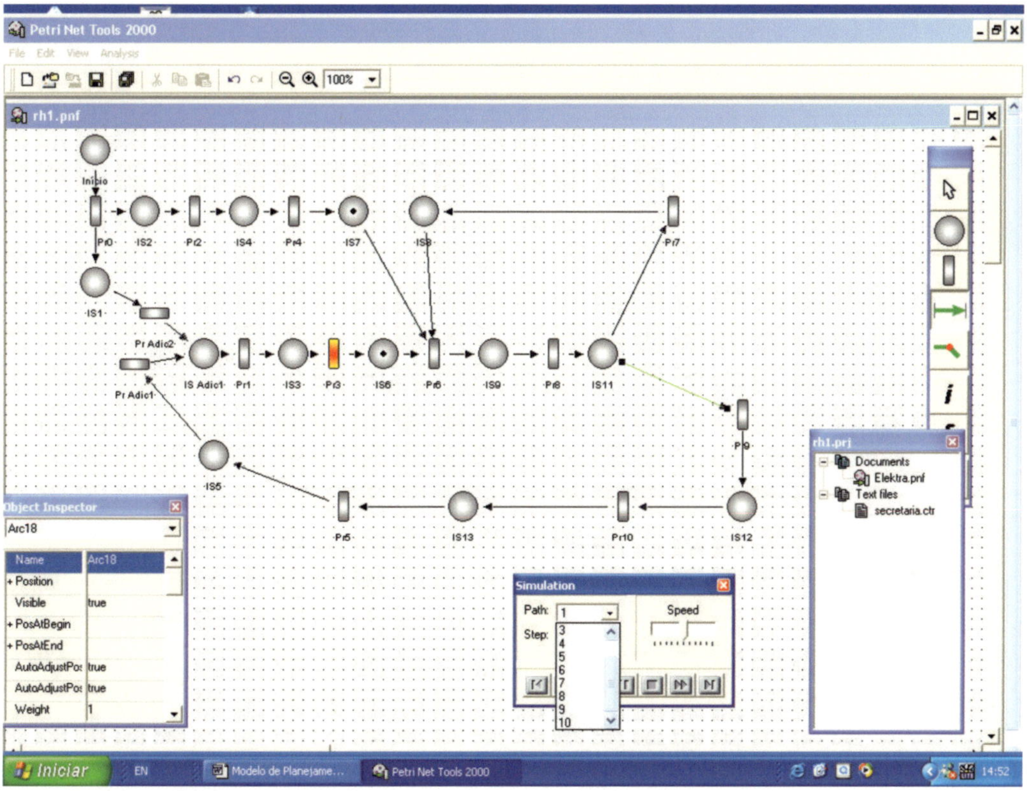

Fig. 12. Simulation Model of the Strategic Planning Tool in Petri Net Tools.

6. Acknowledgments

The authors of this paper are especially grateful to Prof. Dr. Adenilso da Silva Simão and the CAPES.

7. References

AALST, W.M.P.V.D. Formalization and verification of event-driven process chains. Information and Software Technology, London, v.41, n.10, p.639-650, July, 1999.

______. Verification of workflow nets. In: AZEMA, P.; BALBO, G. (Eds.). Application and theory of petri nets. Berlin: Springer-Verlag, 1997. (Lectures Notes in Computer Science).

AALST, W. M. P. V. D; HOFSTEDE, A. H. M. T. Verification of workflow task structures a petri-net-based approach. Information Systems, Oxford, v.25, n.1, p.43-69, 2000.

AALST, W.V.D.; HEE, V.K. Workflow management: models, methods and systems. Cambridge: MIT Press, 2002.

BUBENKO JR., J. A.; STIRNA, J.; BRASH, D. EKD user guide, Dpt of computer and systems sciences. Stockholm: Royal Institute of Technology, 1998.

CHRZASTOWSKI-WACHTEL, P. et al. A top-down petri net-based approach for dynamic workflow modeling. In: INTERNATIONAL CONFERENCE BPM, 2003, Eindhoven. Proceeding...Berlin: Springer, 2003. p. 336-353.

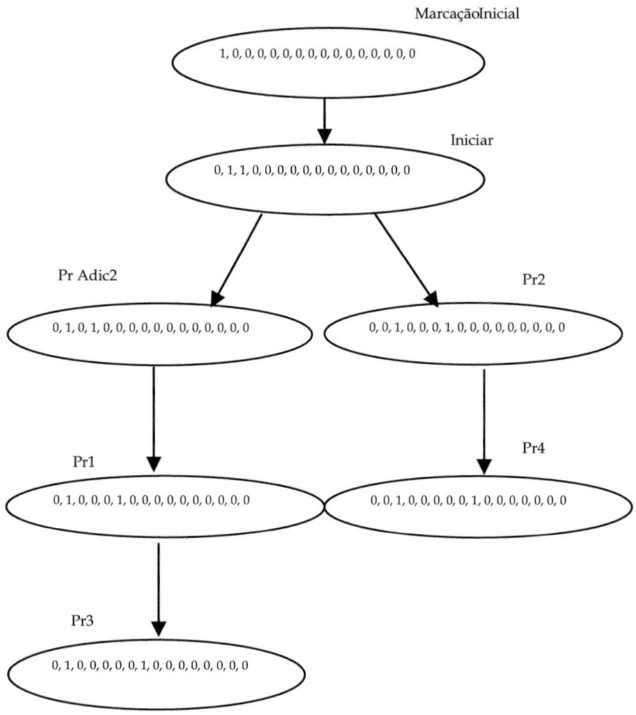

Fig. 13. Tree under the Model of Strategic Planning of Petri nets in mapped.

DALLAVALLE, S. I.; CAZARINI, E. W. Modelagem organizacional desenvolvimento do conhecimento organizacional, facilitador de desenvolvimento de sistemas de informação. In: Encontro Nacional de Engenharia de Produção, 11., 2001, Salvador. Anais... Salvador, 2001. CD-ROM.

DEHNERT, J. Four steps towards sound business process models. In: EHRIG., H. et al. (Eds.). Petri net technology for communication-based systems- advances in petri nets. Berlin: Springer, 2003. p. 66-82. (Lecture Notes in Computer Science, 2472).

DONGEN, V. B. F. et al. Verification of the SAP reference models using EPC reduction, state-space analysis, and invariants. Computers in Industry, Amsterdam, v. 58, n. 6, p. 578-601, 2007.

ELEKTRA. ELECTRICAL enterprise knowledge for transforming applications. The ELEKTRA project programme. Disponível em: <www.singular .gr/elektra.ekd.htm>. Acesso em: 27 Nov. 2000.

GRIGOROVA, K. Process modelling using petri nets. In: INTERNATIONAL CONFERENCE ON COMPUTER SYSTEMS AND TECHNOLOGIES: E-Learning, 4., 2003, Rousse. Disponível em: <http://doi.acm.org/10.1145/973620.973636>. Acesso em: 14 June. 2004.

GUAN, F. et al. Grid-flow: a grid-enabled scientific workflow system with a Petri-net-based interface. Concurrency and Computation: Practice and Experience, Chichester, v.18, n.10, p. 1115 - 1140, 2006.

INAMASU, R. Y. Modelo de FMS: uma plataforma para simulação e planejamento. 134p. Tese de Doutorado - Escola de Engenharia de São Carlos, Universidade de São Paulo, São Carlos, 1995

JACOBSON, I.; BOOCH, G.; RUMBAUGH, J. The unified software development process. Reading: Addison-Wesley, 1999.

JENSEN, K. A Brief Introduction to Coloured Petri Nets. In: Brinksma, E.: Lecture Notes in Computer Science, Vol. 1217: Tools and Algorithms for the Construction and Analysis of Systems. Proceedings of the TACAS'97 Workshop, Enschede, The Netherlands 1997, p. 201-208. Springer-Verlag, 1997.

JONKERS, H. et al. Towards a language for coherent enterprise architecture descriptions. In: IEEE INTERNATIONAL ENTERPRISE DISTRIBUTED OBJECT COMPUTING CONFERENCE, 7., 2003, Brisbane. Proceedings... Los Alamintos: IEEE Computer Society, 2003.

JUNGINGER, S. et al. Building complex workflow applications: how to overcome the limitations for the waterfall model. In: FISCHER, L. (Ed.). Workflow management coalition: the workflow handbook 2001. Disponível em:<http://www.boc-eu.com/english/papers/Complex_Workflow_Appl.pdf>. Acesso em: 16 apr. 2001.

KOUBARAKIS, M.; PLEXOUSAKIS, D. A formal framework for business process modelling and design. Information Systems, Oxford, v.27, n.5, p. 299-319, jul. 2002

KRUCHTEN, P. The rational unified process. 2nd ed. Harlow: Addison-Wesley, 2000.

LENZ, K.; MEVIUS, M.; OBERWEIS, A. Process-Oriented business performance management with petri nets. In: CHEUNG, W.; HSU, J. (Eds.). Proceeding of the 2nd IEEE conference on e-technology, e-commerce and e-service. Hong-Kong, 2005. p. 89-92.

MEVIUS, M.; OBERWEIS, A. A Petri-Net based approach to performance management of collaborative business processes. In: International Workshop on Database and Expert Systems Applications (DEXA'05), 16., 2005. Proceeding... Karlsruhe: University of Karlsruhepp, 2005. 987-991.

MOLD, D.; VALK, R. Object oriented petri net in business process modeling. In: AALST, V. D. W.; DESEL, J.; OBERWEIS, A. Business process management: models, techniques, and empirical studies. Berlin: Springer, 2000. p. 254-273. (Lectures Notes in Computer Sciences, 1806).

MURATA, T. (1989). Petri net: properties, analysis and applications. Proceedings of the IEEE, v.77, n.4, p.541-579.

NURCAN, A.; ROLLAND, C. A multi-method for defining the organizational change. Journal of Information and Software Technology, London, v. 45, n. 2, p.61-82, feb. 2003

NURCAN, S. Analysis and design of co-operative work process a framework. Information and Software Technology, London, v. 40, n. 3, p.143-156, jun. 1998.

NURCAN, S.; BARRIOS, J. Enterprise knowledge and information system modelling in na evolving enviroment. In: INTERNATIONAL WORKSHOP ON ENGINEERING METHODS TO SUPORT INFORMATION SYSTEMS EVOLUTION IN CONJUNCTION WITH, 2003, Geneva. Proceedings... Geneva: Switzerland, 2003 disponível em <http://cui.unige.ch/db-research/EMSISE03/Rp07.pdf>. acesso em 11 apr. 2008.

OU-YANG, C.; LIN Y. D. BPMN-based business process model feasibility analysis: a petri net approach. International Journal of Production Research, London, v. 45, n. 12, 2007.

PÁDUA, S. I. D. Investigação do processo de desenvolvimento de software a partir da modelagem organizacional, enfatizando regras do negócio. 145 p. Dissertação (Mestrado) - Escola de Engenharia de São Carlos, Universidade de São Paulo, São Carlos, 2001.

PÁDUA, S. I. D. Método de avaliação do modelo de processos de negócios. 252 p. Tese (Doutorado) - Escola de Engenharia de São Carlos, Universidade de São Paulo, São Carlos, 2004.

PÁDUA, S. I. D.; CAZARINI, E.W..; INAMASU, R. Y. Modelagem organizacional: captura dos requisitos organizacionais no desenvolvimento de sistemas de informação. Revista Gestão e Produção, São Carlos, v.11, n.2, p.1-20, maio-ago. 2004a.

PÁDUA, S. I. D.; SILVA, A. R. Y.; INAMASU, R. Y.; PORTO, A. J. V. Aplicações e potencial das redes de Petri na Engenharia de Produção. In: Simpósio de Engenharia de Produção, 10., 2003. Disponível em: http://www.bauru.unesp.br/acontece/simpep.html. Acesso em: 30 nov. 2003.

PÁDUA, S. I. D.; SILVA, A. R. Y.; INAMASU, R. Y.; PORTO, A. J. V. O potencial das redes de Petri em modelagem e análise de processos de negócios. Revista Gestão e Produção, São Carlos, v.11, n.1, p.1-11, abr. 2004b.

PÁDUA, S. I. D.; SILVA, A. R. Y.; INAMASU, R. Y.; PORTO, A. J. V. Redes de petri aplicadas aos sistemas de gerenciamento de Workflow. In: Encontro Nacional de Engenharia de Produção, 12., 2002, Curitiba. Anais... Curitiba, 2002. CD-ROM.

PERSSON, A. The utility of participative enterprise modelling in IS development: challenges and research issues. In: INTERNATIONAL WORKSHOP ON THE REQUIREMENTS ENGINEERING PROCESS, 2., 2000, Greenwich. Proceedings... Berlin: Springer, 2000. p. 978-982.

PETERSON, J.L. *Petri nets: theory and modelling of systems*. Englewood Cliffs: Prentice-Hall, 1981.

RINDERLE, S.; REICHERT, M.; DADAM, P. Evaluation of correctness criteria for dynamic workflow changes. In: INTERNATIONAL CONFERENCE BPM 2003, 2003, Eindhoven. Proceedings... Berlin: Springer, 2003. p.41-57. (Lecture Notes in Computer Science, 2678).

ROLLAND, C.; NURCAN, S.; GROSZ, G. A Decision making pattern for guiding the enterprise knowledge development process. Journal of Information and Software Technology, London, v.42, n. 5, p.313-331, apr. 2000.

SALIMIFARD, S.; WRIGHT M. Petri net based modelling of workflow systems: an overview. European Journal of Operational Research, Amsterdam, v.134, n.3, p.664-676, nov.2001.

SOARES, J.B. Editor de modelos de sistemas de eventos discretos, baseado em redes de Petri interpretadas. 2001. Dissertação (Mestrado) - Escola de Engenharia de São Carlos, Universidade de São Paulo, São Carlos, 2001.

VERBBEK H. M. W.; AALST, W. M. P.; HOFSTEDE, A. H. M. Verifying workflows with cancellation regions and OR-joins: an approach based on relaxed soundness and invariants. The Computer Journal Advance, Oxford, v. 50, n. 3, p. 294-314, 2007.

VERBEEK, H. M. W.; BASTEN, T.; AALST, W. M. P. Diagnosing workflow using woflan. Eindhoven: Eindhoven University of Technology, 2002. (BETA Working Paper Series, WP 48).

VOORHOEVE, M. Compositional modeling and verification of workflow process. In: AALST,V. D. W.; DESEL, J.; OBERWEIS, A. Business process management: models, techniques, and empirical studies. Berlin: Springer, 2000. p. 184-200. (Lectures Notes in Computer Sciences, 1806).

WORKFLOW management coliation: reference model. Hampshire, 1996. (Document Number WFMC-TC00-1003).

ZHANG, L.; SHUZHEN, Y. Research on workflow patterns based on Petri nets. In: IEEE CONFERENCE ON CYBERNETICS & INTELLIGENT SYSTEMS (CIS) ROBOTICS, AUTOMATION AND MECHATRONICS (RAM), 2006, Bangkok. Proceeding... Bangkok: IEEE Computer Society, 2006. p. 1-6.

ZISMAN, M. D. Representation, specification and automation of office procedures. Thesis (PhD) - University of Pennsylvania, Wharton School of Business, Pennsylvania, 1977.